D0014544

MEDIA, CULTURE, AND THE RELIGIOUS RIGHT

MEDIA, CULTURE, AND THE RELIGIOUS RIGHT

Linda Kintz and Julia Lesage, editors

UNIVERSITY OF MINNESOTA PRESS
Minneapolis
London

Chapter 3, "North American Protestant Fundamentalism," by Nancy T. Ammerman, was originally published in *Fundamentalisms Observed,* edited by Martin E. Marty and R. Scott Appleby (1994), copyright University of Chicago Press; reprinted by permission of the author and the University of Chicago Press. Chapter 11, "Conservative Media Activism: The Free Congress Foundation and National Empowerment Television," by Anna Williams, was originally published as "Citizen Weyrich: NET's Conservative Media Empire," in *Afterimage* 23, nos. 7/8; reprinted by permission of the author and *Afterimage*. Chapter 14, "Faultlines: Homophobic Innovation in *Gay Rights/Special Rights,*" by Ioannis Mookas, was originally published in *Afterimage* 23, nos. 7/8; reprinted by permission of the author and *Afterimage*.

Published by the University of Minnesota Press
111 Third Avenue South, Suite 290
Minneapolis, MN 55401-2520
http://www.upress.umn.edu

Library of Congress Cataloging-in-Publication Data
Media, culture, and the religious right / Linda Kintz and Julia Lesage, editors.
p. cm.
Includes bibliographical references (p.).
ISBN 0-8166-3084-4 (hardcover. : alk: paper). — ISBN 0-8166-3085-2 (pbk. : alk. paper)
1. Evangelicalism—United States. 2. Christianity and culture—United States. 3. Media—Religious aspects—Christianity. 4. Conservatism—Religious aspects—Christianity. I. Kintz, Linda. 1945– . II. Lesage, Julia.
BR1642.U5M43 1998
261'.0973—dc21 97–46351

Printed in the United States of America on acid-free paper

10 09 08 07 06 05 04 03 02 01 00 99 98 10 9 8 7 6 5 4 3 2 1

For our families.

Contents

Preface

Imagine an active mom who takes her children to a Montessori day care center, exercises to a Richard Simmons videotape, does volunteer work with a hospice, listens to *Morning Edition* on National Public Radio, and aspires to run a little home business once the children are in school. Such a person is often one of our fellow college teachers or one of our students. However, we can rephrase that exercise slightly: Imagine an active mom who takes her preschool children to a church-run Baptist day care center, works out to a "blessercize" video bought in a Christian bookstore, does volunteer work stuffing envelopes and preparing mailings for a conservative Republican candidate, listens to a Christian radio station and especially enjoys Rush Limbaugh, and aspires to run a little home business once the children are in school. In this case, many of our colleagues and students would find this woman "different" from their own families and friends and would assume she was someone with whom they have little in common. The world of university professors—in which the coeditors and many of the writers represented in this anthology live—often does not acknowledge the worldview of the religious right as textured, "livable," and, for those who live within it, "natural" and "reasonable." In writing this book, we have assumed that rejecting another lifestyle as distasteful is a common occurrence but that it does not suffice in terms of understanding another worldview and that worldview's functioning in U.S. culture and politics today.

As colleagues at the University of Oregon, we have several intellectual interests in common. Linda Kintz specializes in the study of religious right ideology, with special attention to the key role that motherhood plays within that symbolic system. Julia Lesage writes extensively on film and television, and especially on independent, "alternative" film and video, in which area she is also a producer of documentary video. As we discussed this project, we realized that we had certain foundational ideas in common: a concern to understand rather than to demonize a large segment of society, a concern at the same time for left and feminist social action, and a common intellectual approach. We find that approach well summarized in French sociologist Pierre Bourdieu's analysis, especially in his work *Distinction: A Social Critique of the Judgement of Taste*.[1] Of particular use to us in conceptualizing our book is Bourdieu's concept of the "habitus." By the habitus, Bourdieu means people's largely unconscious schemes of thought, perception, and action, easily observed in the way they "choose" objects of consumption or cultural practices. Lifestyle choices characterize different groups and segments of social classes because of the economic and social conditions that the habitus internalizes. According to Bourdieu, people are conditioned by their social and material conditions of existence (which can be objectively studied) to a habitus (171). The habitus generates unconscious patterns of classifying practices and objects as well as conscious ways of perceiving these classifications (which is "distinction," or "taste"). Out of these patterns comes a group's lifestyle, which is a system of classif*ied* objects and classif*ying* practices: "Dispositions are adjusted not only to a class condition, presenting itself as a set of possibilities and impossibilities, but also a relationally defined position . . . [and] are therefore always related, objectively at least, to the dispositions associated with other positions" (246).

When Bourdieu refers to taste, or more generally to the whole range of distinctions that people make, he means both classifying systems and lifestyle choices, which always express participation in a social group, or as Bourdieu calls it, a "class fraction." People's various, but interchangeable, choices and distinctions express their group's relative position in what Bourdieu calls the "field of power." Such "distinctions" assert that alternate lifestyle choices or other ways of symbolically classifying the world, especially at the opposite pole, are "not me." Indeed, other symbolic systems and other modes of taste are often regarded with disdain, since each person's own mode of distinction, shared by the primary groups to which he or she belongs, is taken for granted or felt to be natural. Seemingly incommensurable choices—such as preferences in music, area of residence, furnishings, television programs, and electoral candidates—are, in fact, systematic. Thus, the media viewing habits, the assertion that strictly defined gender roles or free-market autonomy or the United States Constitution are divinely inspired, Republican Party participation, and a taste for talk radio are very disparate traits. Nevertheless, these traits unite many members of the religious right. Like other social groups, the religious right elaborates its own classifying distinctions to assert, often with its unique style of moralizing, what it stands for and what it opposes. As Bourdieu puts it, such classifying patterns "unite all those who are the products of similar conditions while distinguishing them from all others" (56). In addition, he sees the persistent taste for moralizing as especially characteristic of the lower middle class.

Many social areas shaping people's lives reinforce each other; in this case, conservative religious people gain and express mutually supporting ways of looking at the world from their active church participation, the electoral organizing of conservative religious voters into the Republican Party, anti-abortion activism, a shared sense of being a cultural outsider and shared moral beliefs, and an ethic of individualism. Participation in these areas of social life or shared moral belief also implies opposition to other cultural phenomena or institutions, especially to mainstream news, Hollywood cinema and much of broadcast television, immigration, the educational establishment, New Age philosophy, and homosexuality. In this collection, essays by Linda Kintz, Eithne Johnson, Nancy Ammerman, and Jeff Land focus sharply on a set of interlocking beliefs and attitudes that members of the contemporary religious right often share. Such attitudes appear in political platforms (condemnations of welfare and teenage pregnancy, with racist implications), family advice videos (endorsing spanking), fundamentalist theology (the millennium and the reign of the just), and talk radio (indictment of pointy-headed intellectuals and "feminazis"). Kintz, in "Clarity, Mothers, and the Mass-Mediated National Soul: A Defense of Ambiguity," provides a theoretical discussion of the foundations of religious conservative ideology and the affect it elicits. The domestic domain is where intimacy and affect are nurtured, and they are prerequisites for belief in any form, left or right. Belief comes after the fact of emotional formation, which is why the religious right places such an emphasis on the family and codified gender roles. In "Culture and the Religious Right," Kintz draws on John Fulton's study of Antonio Gramsci, who showed the relation between political agency and religious belief, which, by providing attachments and emotions, generates a capacity for commitment and the energy to act.

In *Distinction,* Bourdieu does not just focus on the psychological conditioning revealed in the habitus; he also asserts the reality of institutions, state functions, and the economy, which he sees as organized in "fields," such as the field of cultural production, the field of power, the economic field, the field of religion. He uses the term "field" to emphasize that these areas are made up of both objective structures and the social space of relationships, which most people internalize or misrecognize in their daily lives. Furthermore, each field has its own semi-autonomous mode of organization, linked finally to the fields of the economy and power.

From this perspective, this book on media, culture, and the religious right uses a double-pronged approach. First, it analyzes the institutional structures developed or, more likely, used in a new way by the religious right, and second, it traces the ideology, affect, and lifestyle choices behind the use of those structures, that is, the desires and mind-set of the people being addressed, be they conservative political activists, fundamentalists and evangelicals, or those disenchanted with social welfare legislation. The authors in this anthology all approach the issues surrounding culture and the media using this twofold approach, tracing interlocking institutional developments and also corresponding attitudes, either those of religious and conservative cultural leaders or those of the people who choose to use these cultural forms.

A number of important institutional structures have been created or adapted by conservative religious people, especially evangelical Christians, for the sake of spreading the gospel and Christian values, but recently these institutions have developed strong ties to political structures and political process. Historically a cultural outsider, conservative Protestantism, both evangelical and fundamentalist, has created a large structure of parallel institutions to foment a specifically Christian culture in the United States. Nancy T. Ammerman, in "North American Protestant Fundamentalism," describes the growth of fundamentalist publishing, revivals, religious colleges, and parachurch institutions. Evangelicals have used the media and paid for airtime for many years. Their ways of appealing to patriotism and making the religious message entertaining are nothing new—for example, a revivalist from our grandparents' generation, Billy Sunday, built his audience by an appeal to jingoistic U.S. patriotism. In addition, Razelle Frankl, author of the groundbreaking study *Televangelism,* here traces major TV evangelist Pat Robertson's development into a producer of mainstream television with the Family Channel. In "Transformation of Televangelism: Repackaging Christian Family Values," she traces the institutional restructuring of televangelism after the Bakker/Swaggart scandals; and through extensive interviews with Family Channel executives, she illustrates one major televangelist's shift from a more explicitly religious "field," that of religious broadcasting, to the larger institutional field, "broadcast television." In "The Emergence of Christian Video and the Cultivation of Videovangelism," Eithne Johnson describes some of the other parallel institutions of the Christian right, namely, Christian bookstores, videotape evangelism, materials made for Christian home schooling, and family advice books and tapes, which are often then shown in Christian churches. She focuses on the media empire of one "megacommunicator," James C. Dobson, who has been appointed to many federal commissions and who also has a tie to a political lobbying group, Gary Bauer's Family Research Council.

More popular media institutions are described by Jeff Land in "Sitting in Limbaugh: Bombast in Broadcasting" and by Meryem Ersoz in "Gimme

That Old-Time Religion in a Postmodern Age: Semiotics of Christian Radio." Radio, Ersoz states, in general is undertheorized in media studies, especially in terms of its aesthetics and affective power. She provides an important new contribution to radio theory, and she uses as a case study the programming of the Christian station KRKS in the Denver/Boulder area. KRKS, which broadcasts one of the strongest signals on the FM dial, has as its signature "The Rock," combining a reference to Jesus and popular music in one term. Its success comes from self-consciously adopting the "adult contemporary" format of many popular stations, offering a variety of program styles while consistently conveying a "traditional values" message. In contrast, Limbaugh has built his reputation through his unique personality and bombastic rhetoric. Based on consummately middle-brow "distinctions," to use Bourdieu's term, Limbaugh expresses dumbfounded outrage at big government, the very poor, and the cultural elite. His show, although not religious in focus, has a great appeal to both secular and religious conservatives and to many Republican legislators, who stay in regular contact with him since he can mobilize thousands in support of a current issue at a moment's notice. Limbaugh's rapid-fire "attitudinizing" encapsulates much of the habitus, or shared dispositions, of many people on the religious right. The show's appeal comes from the fact that Limbaugh's fans, who call themselves "Dittoheads" because of their agreement with his views, relish participating in a community of listeners who are adamantly confirmed in repudiating everything they "are not."

One of the major focal points of this book is the entry of the religious right into mainstream electoral politics and its historical relation and ties to secular political conservatism. In "Conservative Media Activism: The Free Congress Foundation and National Empowerment Television," Anna Williams gives a brief history of political conservatism on the national level over the last twenty years. She offers as a case study the political career of Paul Weyrich, who has founded a conservative satellite television station, National Empowerment Television (NET), with a studio wherein Republican members of Congress and sympathetic talk show hosts can tape broadcasts for national distribution. Weyrich has a long history in Washington, D.C. He is cofounder of the Heritage Foundation, which has generous corporate backing. He is also the founder of the Free Congress Foundation, whose directives shape NET programming. From its beginning, the Free Congress Foundation has aimed to mobilize conservative Christians, especially at the local level, to change the political makeup of Congress, and to develop a political philosophy and public discourse of "cultural conservatism." Weyrich has long worked with groups seeking to organize conservative voters on the local level, a task he has shared organizationally with Jerry Falwell's Moral Majority, Pat Robertson, and Ralph Reed and the Christian Coalition.

The electoral organizing of the Christian Coalition is analyzed by Julia Lesage in "Christian Coalition Leadership Training," in which she describes a series of the Coalition's leadership training tapes. The tapes teach sophisticated political organizing tactics, detail the electoral political process, and identify the stages at which public policy can be influenced, especially in state and national legislatures. Furthermore, Lesage indicates what some of the potential effects for coalition activists might be; especially powerful is the sense of agency they can gain as they become actively involved in the social and political life of the community. This is an agency traditionally denied to conservative Christians but an agency that the tapes legitimize, indeed mandate, for them. Furthermore, in terms of economic trajectory, such activism could make the coalition's core members more upwardly mobile or more secure professionally, a process that scholars studying labor union bureaucracies call "embourgeoisement." Such an embourgeoisement and embeddedness in traditional electoral politics has consequences for the whole field of the religious right, a topic addressed by Steven Gardiner in "Through the Looking Glass and What the Christian Right Found There" in reference to the far right and to single-issue advocacy groups.

Advocacy media or alternative media exists on both the left and the right. Right-wing advocacy organizations and the media outlets they use are described by Chip Berlet in "Who Is Mediating the Storm? Right-Wing Alternative Information Networks." Berlet distinguishes between the secular conservative right, the theocratic right, and the hard right. He gives a particularly fascinating view of the way supremacist groups and their conspiracy theories find a ready outlet on the Internet. Furthermore, in terms of organizing against the Christian right, Berlet's notes indicate a wide range of "watchdog" organizations who monitor and counter the strategies of the right. Berlet discusses as an example of right organizing through media outlets its "marketing" of homophobia; Laurie Schulze and Frances Guilfoyle take up this topic in "'Facts Don't Hate; They Just Are,'" where they discuss the organizing tactics for and against Colorado's antihomosexual Amendment 2. Berlet, Schulze and Guilfoyle, Mookas, and Lesage in her chapter on Christian Coalition organizing all discuss the right's self-conscious strategy of "framing" or "reframing" the issues. In the political field, electoral organizing strategies consciously articulate many of the classifying systems or dispositions favored by the religious or conservative habitus, especially in denouncing the opposing side. In "Faultlines: Homophobic Innovation in *Gay Rights/Special Rights*," Ioannis Mookas analyzes the framing of the issues in the antihomosexual film *Gay Rights/Special Rights*. Mookas traces the ways in which the right's framing of issues around gay rights also involves a framing of the issues around civil rights in general: The civil rights struggle is considered to be over, having been waged by African Americans in the 1960s. Gays are seen as trying to "hitch their wagon" to rights won by people of color. And in a discourse of scarcity and deservedness, "special" rights for gays implies that there are not enough rights to go around in these economically hard times. In this kind of homophobic discourse, the connotations of "rights" and gender are overtly manipulated, based on information gained through market research into voters' attitudes. Other times, the framing of political issues reflects an unconscious or barely conscious profession of commonly held attitudes. As Julia Lesage points out in her introductory chapter, "Christian Media," such a tie to the religious right habitus is demonstrated by Justice Antonin Scalia in his dissenting opinion in the United States Supreme Court decision overturning Colorado's Amendment 2. There Scalia clearly articulates a notion of an undeserving homosexual "elite," and his statement un-self-consciously echoes the conspiracy theories of the supremacist right.

Ironically, as the religious right occupies the fields of religion and electoral politics, it faces major contradictions that conservative religious activists often encounter between these two areas of social practice. These contradictions, as worked out in present day electoral organizing, are articulated by Steven Gardiner in "Through the Looking Glass and What the Christian Right Found There," a case study of the Oregon Citizens Alliance (OCA), a successful activist group that has persistently organized against homosexual rights, especially by getting initiatives on the ballot in Oregon about homosexuality and then waging fierce electoral campaigns around these initiatives. The OCA, with its single-issue focus, has strained its relation with the Christian Coalition, which originally funded it. Furthermore, OCA members often sympathize with the ideology of the white supremacist right, particularly its conspiracy theories about the government; and such alliances, even when unofficial, make public identification with the OCA a political liability to Republican candidates seeking state or national office.

Pierre Bourdieu writes that the struggles around "classifying things and practices" are absolutely crucial in what he calls "the field of power." How people and groups represent the world and their relative position in it to themselves and to others—and what position they want to relegate other groups to—is the stuff of politics. Currently the religious right seeks to define both the stakes of the game (for example, free-market economy, denial of subsistence support for the very poor, state "subsidies" for the rich, especially in the form of reduced taxation, impositions of rigidly codified gender and family definitions, recoding of civil rights as a matter of individual merit and not group rights) and the legitimate means of struggle (for example, defunding public education, building more prisons, providing an entire support network for the Contras during the Reagan era). Coming full circle in terms of the book's organization, Linda Kintz, in her introductory chapter "Culture and the Religious Right," presents a theoretical argument of how the political and economic fields are well served by the habitus of the religious right. She emphasizes "the importance of symbolic meanings and culture in solidifying the power of political and financial interests, especially in the mass-mediated culture of an information society." Drawing on the work of Noam Chomsky, Kintz traces in detail the seemingly disparate, but symbolically united, ideological buttresses for North American–style market democracy, which ironically leaves "relatively invisible [the] presence of the most determinate structure of contemporary U.S. politics, the corporation in the age of an internationalized economy."

To conclude, the different habitus of various subcultures often make different groups distasteful to each other, unnatural, unreasonable, satisfyingly "not me." However, from conservative think tanks to groups like the Christian Coalition, the religious right has systematically studied the attitudes and lifestyle choices of the "liberals" or "secular humanists," as they often refer to us, and has turned that knowledge to effective political use. We hope that the information in this book will correspondingly do the same and so lead to better argumentation and more sophisticated rhetoric in encountering the often mean-spirited and authoritarian public policy proposals of the religious right. However, we also hope to make understandable another way of life and the cultural and political institutions that surround the religious right. We respect that group's desire for public agency and a meaningful participation in the public sphere, a desire that we also share. Democracy lies in the continued open encounter and understanding between us, contentious as it may be.

Notes

1. Pierre Bourdieu, *Distinction: A Social Critique of the Judgement of Taste,* trans. Richard Nice (Cambridge: Harvard University Press, 1984).

PART I
OVERVIEW OF CONTEMPORARY ISSUES

1

Culture and the Religious Right

Linda Kintz

What is in fact happening in the world has something to do with markets, but also with raw concentrated power and class war of the kind that was obvious to Adam Smith, but unmentionable in polite society today.

—*Noam Chomsky*

Gramsci . . . seems to believe that religion in general always ends up losing sight of the social character of human actions by individualizing all moral responsibility and by pretending an equality between human individuals which religion has never actually achieved.

—*John Fulton*

Though many secular observers have been taken by surprise by the religious right in the past decade, it is the visibility of conservative Christians that is new, not their activity and organization. This new visibility has been aided by an extraordinarily sophisticated network of electronic resources. As a result, the influence of the religious right might be described in paradoxical terms as a reaction against postmodernity that draws on postmodernity's best resources, a reaction that in many ways repeats the resistance to modernity that existed at the turn of the last century. Understanding the religious right, situating it within U.S. culture and politics, and describing its ability to combine religious absolutism with contemporary media sophistication requires studying it from a number of different directions. For if we have learned anything from postmodern theory and cultural studies, it is the importance of symbolic meanings and culture in solidifying the power of political and financial interests, especially in the mass-mediated culture of an information society. Symbolic meanings and cultural activities help deter-mine what is to count both as empirical fact and as historical evidence. In this volume, the concept of culture will be a key term that brings together a range of chapters from various disciplines.

The religious right's influence has most often been described in terms of its concern about culture and values, questions addressed from a number of different directions in this collection, part of an attempt to understand how it is that people come to believe deeply and passionately in what was called ideology in an earlier theoretical framework. Within postmodernity, however, the emotional resonances and passions of a mass-mediated culture require a range of analyses to update the concept of ideology in more nuanced ways. Those analyses constantly return to the relatively invisible presence of the most determinate structure of contemporary U.S. politics, the corporation in the age of an internationalized economy. It is the construction of this invisibility that may be the most important feature of contemporary U.S. politics.

As Noam Chomsky argues, U.S. politics after the Cold War shifted from a focus on containment, a politics that reacted to a global threat to market democracies, to what Anthony Lake calls "enlargement," a politics that seeks to enlarge the reach of those market democracies: "Throughout the Cold War, we contained a global threat to market democracies: Now we should seek to enlarge their reach."[1] However, the definitions of "market," "democracy," and "America" are precisely what is at issue here, for in contemporary post–Cold War politics, such "universal" values as liberty, equality, democracy, private property, and markets have become, in fact, narrow and partial concepts that refer to the liberty, equality, democracy, private property, and markets of very select groups, made up of those whom Chomsky, drawing on Adam Smith's term for those groups, refers to as the principal architects of policy.

The idea that democracy equals free-market activity is now considered to be a truth so obvious that it no longer requires argument or evidence because it has been so firmly located in a particular, culturally constructed concept of human nature. Yet the advocacy of market democracy belies the fact that the Reagan administration's efforts to spread democracy were failures. Chomsky quotes Thomas Carothers, a member of the Reagan State Department: "[Washington] inevitably sought only limited, top-down forms of democratic change that did not risk upsetting the traditional structures of powers with which the United States has long been allied." The United States sought instead "to maintain the basic order... of quite undemocratic societies" and to avoid "populist-based change" that might upset "established economic and political orders" and open "a leftist direction." Democracy was sponsored only if it came out our way.

This export of North American–style market democracy has had devastating effects on workers in the United States. The real enemy of the principal architects of policy, given their location in the internationalized economy, is the domestic population, illustrated not only by the explosive growth in security services and the construction of prisons but by attacks on workers' rights and benefits. Though corporate profits have risen dramatically, real wages have declined as work hours have increased, and the high labor costs of ten years ago, which included wages and benefits, have been reversed through free-trade agreements in which cheap labor, few benefits, and workers' rights are the goal of a state-corporate offensive.

Chomsky reminds us of Adam Smith's description of the principal architects of policy, who at the time were the merchants and manufacturers: "[They] have quite different interests than those of their country's population." Updating that description, Chomsky argues that they make sure that "their own interests are 'most peculiarly attended to,' whatever the effect on their own population, let alone other peoples. Nothing has changed in that regard, including the need to employ the class analysis which Adam Smith took for granted, in order to understand policy choices."

Discussing political economy thus means asking: Are we differentiating between the interests of the "'principal architects'—these are no longer merchants and manufacturers but transnational corporations and banks and so on—or are we talking about the country's population? You get quite different answers depending on which concept you choose."

The conservative Contract with America enunciated in 1994, Chomsky suggests, makes this economic and power shift clearly visible, even though it has usually been discussed more narrowly in terms of conservative attempts to reconstruct the morality of U.S. culture. The contract calls for "a greatly enhanced and much more powerful welfare state for the rich, but with punishment for the poor" and the redistribution of wealth upward.[2] It is not only Republicans, however, who advocate this version of the market but Democrats as well, as President Bill Clinton showed at the Asia-Pacific summit in Seattle during his first term. There he presented what Chomsky calls his "grand vision of the free market future" from a hangar of the Boeing Company, the largest exporter in the country. But Boeing is far from a free-market entity. It is, rather, a model of state-supported industry, a publicly subsidized private-profit corporation, as Chomsky notes: "The taxpayer pays, the profits go to private investors." Sustained by federal investment during World War II, Boeing's subsidies continued after the war, when the Pentagon "sustained and expanded the aircraft industry, the leading civilian exporter, along with a lot of other industries: metals, computers, electronics generally—almost 85 percent of electronics research and development during the '50s was paid for by the taxpayers. The profits later went to private corporations."

Such underwriting during the Cold War years was not, of course, referred to as subsidization. Chomsky quotes the first secretary of the Air Force, Stuart Symington, as having said in January 1948: "The word to talk was not 'subsidy': the word to talk was 'security.'" Though described as free-market activity, this corporate behavior is not free at all, as Chomsky suggests: "Oligopolistic competition and strategic interaction among firms and governments, rather than the invisible hand of market forces, condition today's competitive advantage and international division of labor in high technology industries," as well as, he adds, in "agriculture and pharmaceuticals, services, and major areas of economic activity in general." This advocacy of misnamed "free markets" has much less to do with democracy and free markets than with raw power, which has devastated the Third World, a "terrible story of major crimes against humanity for which we bear primary and continuing responsibility."

The insistence on accountability, a mantra raised by cultural conservatives in terms of personal behavior in the last decade, has nevertheless strategically ignored the lack of accountability on the part of transnational corporations, which "increasingly dominate the global economy... in virtual secrecy." Those responsible for major financial decisions constitute a kind of de facto government made up of the World Bank and the International Monetary Fund (IMF), the General Agreement on Tariffs and Trade (GATT) council, or the World Trade Organization, and they are controlled from the executive meetings of the G7 countries, which operate, Chomsky argues, "in technocratic insulation, free from interference by the declining parliamentary institutions and untroubled by the general public, who only have the vaguest idea of what they are up to. Their operations can be known only to a few specialists, and much in principle secret."

This technocratic insulation accompanied a general shift in investment in the United States from the position of the early 1970s, when Richard Nixon deregulated speculative capital. At the time, about 90 percent of capital investment in international exchanges was trade or investment related, and only about 10 percent was speculative investment. By 1990, the investment percentages were reversed, so that over 90 percent was speculative. The lack of democracy in this structure has too often led to a nativism dangerously crippled by the lack of a class analysis. Because of that, it has frequently turned to the ready resources of anti-Semitism and supremacist attacks on immigrants and people of color.

In a similar way, the terminology of the contemporary cultural revalorization of the family that accompanies the rhetoric of the "free market" is also misleading. Chomsky cites Silvia Ann Hewlett's study *Child Neglect in*

Rich Societies,[3] tracing the split in the last fifteen years between two approaches to children and families; on the one hand, a continental European–Japanese model and, on the other, an Anglo-American model that has had disastrous results on children and families:

> The European-Japan model, in contrast, has improved children's situations considerably, though the economic problems facing the societies are similar. Like others, Hewlett attributes the disaster of the Anglo-American model to the ideological preference for free markets. That is only half-true, as mentioned. Whatever one wants to call the reigning ideology, this form of violent, lawless, reactionary statism has nothing much to do with markets, except for the poor.

Hewlett cites a study by the U.S. Commission of State Boards of Education and the American Medical Association that found that "never before has one generation of children been less healthy, less cared for or less prepared for life than their parents were at the same age." This is true, however, only in the "neglect-filled Anglo-American societies," not in European or Japanese societies.

Understanding the effects of this internationalized economy means asking a number of questions: How is it that these elements remain so invisible to so many people? What cultural mechanisms and messages have proved so powerful in providing the kind of invisibility and lack of accountability that Chomsky identifies? In what ways are the symbolic resources of a mass-mediated culture engaged with religious belief and power? Grappling with these questions requires a move through one of the symbolic organizing structures at the heart of the resurgence of conservative religious activism in the public sphere. That is the belief that the future of the nation as well as its God-given mission in the world depends on the reconstruction of U.S. culture so that it is in tune with the natural law of the Ten Commandments and Judeo-Christian values, as natural law and biblical law are conflated. According to this belief, those values are in fact inherent in nature. Nature, when it is interpreted properly, will reveal the truths of its Creator. In this view, it is the duty of conservative Christians to re-create a national culture that matches natural law because the historical detour represented by the 1960s has led the United States away from its true identity as God's unique experiment in human history, with its divinely inspired Constitution. Because God is believed to have guided the nation's founders to its shores to establish a Judeo-Christian democracy, the United States not only has a special mission to expand its culture to the rest of the globe, but it will be harshly punished by God if it fails to do so. The basic tenets of this narrow version of natural law—such as heterosexuality, sexuality defined in terms of procreation and monogamy, woman's primary definition as mother, the naturalness of the nuclear family and the free market—are in this view inherent in human nature as well as in the nature of the cosmos.[4] As such, they should also be the fundamental ground of the legal system. It is not difficult to see why the culture wars of the 1990s were fought with such passion and such a sense of cosmic mission within this narrative of U.S. exceptionalism and apocalyptic threat.

What the contemporary culture wars hide—with their passionate denunciations of various improper groups and behavior, their attacks on workers, and their targeting of the most vulnerable members of the population, in particular children and African Americans—is the fact that democracy in the United States has become increasingly unattainable. And like the definition of markets and family, the very concept of America was long ago called into question, for it now applies to the America of "the people who count" rather than to "the geographical areas of the United States" and those of its domestic population, "some of whom may be sinking to Third World standards," while those in the Third World sink even further.

Even though the very concept of the nation is anachronistic in such an internationalized economy, nevertheless a symbolic discourse of nationalism has been one of the most important features of the religious right's influence, helping move the terms of the national discourse far to the right. This discourse has influenced many people who identify themselves as conservatives, even if not religious conservatives, but they too have actively distanced themselves from the absolutism of groups like Pat Robertson's Christian Coalition. The ability to mobilize a coherent symbolic message that is passionately grounded in one's family experiences (or at least in one's longings for such intimate and secure family experiences) has been central to the power of this discourse that elides the fact that most families are excluded from its terms and that it is primarily about "families who count." A wide range of people, many of whom would adamantly refuse to be associated with one another, nevertheless find themselves drawing on the rhetoric and symbolic language of the religious right as it circles around a relatively narrow and deceptively simple range of terms: "life," "mother," "family," "nation," "free market," "God." This is a structure that is symmetrically coherent, even though remarkably if usefully vague, a series of layered spheres that are glued together by vague passions that unite diverse interests and elide their differences by the fact that those differences need not be articulated.

In fact, for this structure to be effective, these differences must be not articulated but merely felt deeply; depth of feeling is increasingly important as evidence of truth. This is a very important point, in particular in relation to the way emotion has been historically coded as feminine and contrasted to reason, which has been more positively coded as masculine in the philosophical traditions of Western metaphysics. In a U.S. context, however, the emotions of patriotism, desire for property and gun ownership, and regional identification, for example, are likely to be unapologetically masculine. Charismatic religions, too, have always been associated with emotion, differing in this way from many other strains of Protestant belief, in particular the much more emotionally restrained traditions of New England. Yet because of the complexity of its "clarity," the symmetrical, layered structure of family, legal system, and God's universe does not constitute an unthinking, unsophisticated irrationality but might better be described as a form of superrationality, which does, however, include unconscious factors as well as conscious ones.

In attempting to understand the present political climate, a brief look at the end of the last century helps provide a historical framework for a number of issues. Nancy T. Ammerman, in Chapter 3, her history of North American Protestant fundamentalism, argues that in the early part of the twentieth century, though many Protestant churches adapted to the changes brought about by modernity or industrial capitalism, others interpreted adaptation to those changes as heresy, an interpretation repeated today in the condemnation of groups like the National Council of Churches because of its liberal agenda. Just as they publicly opposed Darwinism and the theory of evolution, religious conservatives actively opposed adaptations to modernism by mainstream churches. Particularly influential in that historical period was a conservative, militant branch of fundamentalism that had originated in the Great Awakening and in southern revivals and was influenced by charismatic evangelical groups. Though highly visible before its ostensible defeat in the Scopes trial, Protestant fundamentalism did not disappear but went into hibernation. It has reemerged from that hibernation with great strength and energy.

Ammerman's history of this movement shows how thoroughly religion has always saturated narratives of U.S. history and reminds us that in that earlier period, as now, charismatic fundamentalism defined itself as "a movement in conscious, organized opposition to the disruption of . . . traditions and orthodoxies." She identifies the four main features of fundamentalism in the United States as a belief in evangelism, biblical inerrancy, premillennialism, and separatism. The belief in evangelism joins the importance of one's own salvation to a personal responsibility to share that salvation with others. The belief in inerrancy holds that "the only sure path to salvation is through a faith in Jesus Christ that is grounded in unwavering faith in an inerrant Bible." It rests on a form of binary logic, consisting of the opposition between moral truths that are absolute and the chaos of nihilism.

A third defining characteristic of fundamentalism is the belief in premillennialism, which holds that Christ will return for a thousand-year reign of righteousness on earth. The fiery apocalyptic predictions common during the Cold War (even Ronald Reagan was a believer) have been displaced for many by a more optimistic as well as politically more pragmatic postmillennial version, influenced by a movement called reconstructionism and by dominion theology, which hold that it is the responsibility of Christians to usher in the millennium through activism rather than simply to await its arrival. And finally, fundamentalist belief is characterized by separatism, an insistence on the uniformity of belief and separation from those who do not hold those beliefs: "[The fundamentalist] would rather lose his friends than his soul. Simply getting along, not making waves, accepting the ways of the world, is not characteristic of those Evangelicals who deserve (and claim) the label 'fundamentalist.'"

The actions of the conservative religious believers of Ammerman's history were also part of a larger historical attempt to reconstruct "respectability" in that earlier period. Respectability, a concept developed in the work of the European historian George Mosse, refers to a configuration by which the middle class countered the instabilities of the rapid cultural and economic changes accompanying the shift from an agrarian base to an industrial one at the turn of the last century. Contemporary resistance to the rapid economic changes of financial capitalism and an internationalized economy resembles the efforts of the earlier period to resist modernity and helps explain the fondness of Newt Gingrich and Gertrude Himmelfarb for the Victorian era. For it was decency, Mosse argues, or "respectability," as a historically specific concept characterized by traditional values, manners, and morals, that became the carrier of the middle-class economy, the definition of nation, and the disciplinary model of behavioral standards to be applied to all: "The concept of respectability was itself part of new ways of regarding the human body and sexuality that triumphed only during the nineteenth century."[5] During the religious awakenings of the late seventeenth and eighteenth centuries, Mosse argues, in particular those of Pietism in Germany and Evangelicalism in England, the refinement of court society that led to modern manners and sexual behavior "locked [them] into place for that time and for the future as well" (5).

And it was this behavioral transition that helped pave the way for what Mosse calls the "triumph of the middle classes," which both created the traditional family and advocated its universality:

> The middle classes can only be partially defined by their economic activity and even by their hostility to the aristocracy and the lower classes alike. For side by side with their economic activity it was above all the ideal of respectability which came to characterize their style of life. Through respectability, they sought to maintain their status and self-respect against both the lower classes and the aristocracy. They perceived their way of life, based as it was upon frugality, devotion to duty, and

> restraint of the passions, as superior to that of the "lazy" lower classes and the profligate aristocracy. (5)

This particular configuration of behavior and morals, which entered into the disciplinary practices of physicians, educators, and police, required an ideal for its coherence, an ideal made available through the concept of nationalism:

> [Nationalism] absorbed and sanctioned middle-class manners and morals and played a crucial part in spreading respectability to all classes of the population, however much these classes hated and despised one another. Nationalism helped respectability to meet all challenges to its dominance, enlarging its parameters when necessary while keeping its essence intact... Through its claim to immutability, it endowed all that it touched with a "slice of eternity." (9)

That this concept of nationalism in the postmodern United States is highly contradictory was one of Chomsky's points, for like the concept of the middle class itself, in an internationalized economy the very concept of the nation has become highly problematic, the concealing of its increasingly apparent hollowness more desperate.

As another element in the turn of the century construction of coherence, religious belief and belief in the purity of motherhood and the family, in particular in the beauty and decency of true womanhood, helped establish an attachment to eternity. That attachment, however, did not disturb the dynamism of the economy, which depended on the possibility of infinitely increasing profits. Instead, the separation of public and domestic spheres was to provide the middle-class man with a secure identity and a refuge from the competition of the workplace, a refuge from which he would be able to reenter the marketplace rested and invigorated. He could thus find security and order side by side with the admonition to head out into adventure, which was represented by the dynamic and expanding market. In the midst of the rapid change man's economic activity had produced, the unfettered adventures of the marketplace could thus be assured by the "slice of eternity" represented by family, nation, and the certainty that man's activities were in accord with his true nature. As Mosse notes, the workings of nationalism and respectability "assigned everyone his place in life, man and woman, normal and abnormal, native and foreigner; any confusion between these categories threatened chaos and loss of control" (16).

The history of nationalism and the history of manners and morals were as a result thoroughly intertwined, as both depended on a distinction between normality and abnormality, between the true manly citizen and the weak or feminized abnormal one. And normality became the key element of a cultural order that would allow for economic dynamism while keeping those who benefited from capitalism safe from its ravages. Similarly, the preservation of gender distinctions was vital "in ordering a world which seemed on the brink of chaos, but which nationalism with its emphasis upon respectability was attempting to preserve" (102). And while men's passions were sublimated and directed toward a higher purpose, the public sphere of the economy found its symmetrical linkage in the nuclear family as its microcosm: "The family gave support from below to that respectability which the nation attempted to enforce from above . . . the family was a cheap and efficient surrogate for the state, controlling the passions at their source" (19–20).

At the turn of the last century, respectability also helped establish various symbolic distinctions that are being reconstructed in contemporary politics. On the one hand, respectability depended on a particular coding of the city and its "dark recesses," in which were to be found sexual excesses, vice, financial scheming, Jews, profligate artists, and those people who did not lead respectable lives, whether they were laborers or came from cultures other than those of northern Europe. On the other hand, the cultural forms of respectability mythologized the security and safety of the pastoral countryside, a nostalgic world of nature and small communities in which one might find manageability in the face of incomprehensible technological and economic change. The image of the true woman was particularly important to the distinction between the vice-ridden city and the pastoral countryside: "Woman as a preindustrial symbol suggested innocence and chastity, a kind of moral rigor directed against modernity—the pastoral and eternal set against the big city as the nursery of vice" (98).

And the entire configuration was guaranteed by manliness:

> [For manliness] was invoked to safeguard the existing order against the perils of modernity and its threats to the clear distinction between what was considered normal and abnormality. Moreover, manliness symbolized the nation's spiritual and material vitality. It called for strength of body and mind, but not brute force—the individual's energies had to be kept under control. (23)

The clarity of clear gender distinctions, like distinctions of normality and abnormality, helped seal this satisfyingly coherent structure through the manners and morals of respectability. And respectability "was as important in the perceptions of men and women as any economic or political interests. What began as bourgeois morality in the eighteenth century, in the end became everyone's morality" (191). Or at least, respectability was able to discipline behavior according to its own claims to universality, a universality to be guaranteed by a legal and cultural system in which God on high and nature below would come together in natural law.

Mosse emphasizes the importance of the resemblance between these two eras, turn of the century industrial capitalism and contemporary financial capitalism: "The analogies between past and present must have struck the reader at every turn, for this is a past that relates to everyone's experience of the present" (181). And though it is clear that any society needs cohesion, Mosse provides a warning about adopting this particular one: "Tolerance, it seems, ended where respectability began" (111).

The historical concept of respectability helps link contemporary questions of culture to a history of the senses, in which feelings, emotion, manners, and morals are linked to power, economy, and religion. The emotions have played a part in another way in the U.S. context of the libertarian features of the American common man. The historian Richard White suggests the term "plain folks Americanism" for the identity of the American common man intertwined with the myth of the West and the frontier. In particular, he emphasizes the importance of California to that myth, with California politics having served as the model for national politics, Ronald Reagan's success being the most obvious example. This form of mass-mediated Americanism, which developed in California and was influenced by both racism and the common man's opposition to non-European immigration, was also affected by the populist and libertarian traditions of those from the South and Midwest who had moved to California during the depression and who later worked in war factories. And significantly, the influence of Pentecostalism and its beliefs in traditional values, personal responsibility, and the work ethic were especially strong in southern California.

Ironically, however, the claims of plain folks Americans to be real Westerners in the 1970s, when the New Right was developing, rested on an intense construction of their own authenticity, for California's population came from everywhere else:

> Those Californians who most ardently believed in these "traditional" values were often themselves newcomers to the state. The New Right sank its strongest roots among the modern immigrants to the West who came not as a part of groups or to seek utopian ends but for individual advancement. These were the residents of the suburbs, particularly the suburbs of southern California, which were the fastest-growing and most rapidly changing section of the United States in the 1970's. Southern California was a land of migrants who were not particularly Western in origin... It would have been difficult to find a less likely site for a defense of traditional values.
>
> But the rapidity of change in southern California was, in fact, the point. The New Right prospered in southern California because the pace of change was frenetic. In southern California, except when race was concerned, boundaries seemed permeable. Ethnic and religious division mattered less than elsewhere. People were mobile; community ties were weak; and the aspirations that brought migrants to the re-

> gions were overwhelmingly individualistic and material, not much different in fact than those that had prompted the gold rush more than a century earlier. Spectacular success always seemed possible, and that made failure all the more demeaning. There was no failure as bitter as western failure.
>
> The California New Right wanted it both ways. They wanted the opportunity for material success unhampered by government controls, but they wanted government to halt social change and return society to an imagined past.[6]

Politics in California, White argues, have always foretold the direction of national politics.

The significance of the economic and political power of the West, however, has to be joined with that of another region, the South. In particular, in the case of women, the true woman of respectability, or the modern traditional woman, combined the conservative women of the suburban West and the women of a southernized GOP. In the election of 1994, all but one of the new leaders of the Republican Congress came from states that had once been part of the Confederacy.[7] This was a southern shift that had begun in the 1960s campaigns and the southern strategies of Barry Goldwater and Richard Nixon. These strategies were aimed at the disaffected white Democratic followers of George Wallace who deserted the Democratic Party because of its civil rights activities, and they essentially turned the Republican Party into a white man's party. Ronald Reagan's attacks on welfare queens, the Willy Horton ads of Lee Atwater, and David Frum's advice to attack affirmative action as a wedge issue were different versions of the same strategy.

Goldwater's presidential bid also radically undercut the influence of northeastern Republicans and empowered a new conservative coalition from the South, the Southwest, and the West. And though Goldwater carried only six states in the 1964 election, five of those were in the South. Drawing on the work of historian V. O. Key Jr., Michael Lind has dissected the cliché that southern conservatism comes primarily from angry rednecks and "poor white trash" and argues that, on the contrary, wealthy southerners, whom he refers to as southern Bourbons, have been far more influential. The effectiveness of the symbolism of ordinary plain folks Americans, however, has provided a populist image to elide that fact, and it has also provided a symbolic link between those whites who were left out of power and those whose wealth and power were symbolically effaced. This symbolic linkage joins individuals who want to be free of government regulation and taxation and wealthy individuals and corporations with the same desire. It takes the form of a Transparent American Subject, a symbolic, commonsense identification as plain folks Americans who must rebel against the federal government and the cultural elite.

Southern Bourbons, Lind argues, have long manipulated racism to retain control of economics and politics, a form of conservatism that differs from northern Whig-Republican economic nationalism that favored public investment in the infrastructure and a compromise between labor unions and business that led to high wages. The 1978 Kemp-Roth tax-cut legislation, which was based on supply-side economics and resulted in enormous deficits, was, he argues, heavily influenced by southern conservatism. And while he suggests that southern conservatism arose out of a "rigid, quasi-religious expression of the Jacksonian political culture of the Southern and Western United States," religious conservatives may go much further and make a more direct, almost literal connection between economy and religion.[8] Balancing the federal budget in that sense is made analogous to balancing one's family budget, both drawing on biblical lessons.

Contemporary attacks on government interference in the economy also have a southern model, the common southern strategy since the Civil War of favoring weak unions and low labor costs in an attempt to attract northern manufacturing to the region. This included the promise not only of cheap labor costs but of low taxes, both of which were accompanied by a crumbling infrastructure and underfunded public schools. Another southern legacy was a virulent anti-intellectualism and attacks on public education, urban culture, and secular humanism. Though there are many legitimate reasons for concerns about public education, the South had its own form of school choice during the years of the civil rights movement, when public schools were sometimes abolished by state legislatures in order to prevent integration. And finally, just as respectability in the late nineteenth century depended upon the mythology of the pastoral countryside and the small community, contemporary conservatism has been influenced by the southern ideal of the homogeneous small town, an ideal that comes together in symbolic ways with gated communities and suburban communities made homogeneous by property values. All of these are opposed, once again, to teeming cities full of perverse artists, homosexuals, immigrants, Jewish bankers and media moguls, and, as George Gilder refers to poor African Americans, welfare queens and barbarians.

The national political agenda, Lind suggests, has now come to resemble that of the southern Bourbons in other ways as well. In both Old and New South, upper-class and working-class whites were united against lowland black majorities. The Bourbon-dominated tidewater areas that were heavily black were geographically divided from the middling-to-poor white up-country of the Piedmont areas of the Blue Ridge and Appalachian mountains. In the contemporary United States, a conservative political strategy revalorizes that pattern on a national level, as conservative national political strategists imagine a nation that follows such a pattern. A "brown belt" of urban, coastal areas on both sides of the country and in lowland areas of Florida, Texas, and the rest of the South are made up of concentrations of the wealthy and minorities, both African Americans and immigrants. This brown belt is now juxtaposed to the uplands, the Rocky Mountain and northern interior states, which have relatively homogeneous populations and are characterized by less-extreme income disparities. Within the brown belt, the population is divided in two, "minority-dominated inner cities and homogeneous white suburban and exurban rings," from which one witnesses a white exodus to upland regions and an increasing abandonment of inner cities. This "national Bourbon" division, as Lind calls it, produces a dangerous alliance between "wealthy, outnumbered suburban whites in majority-nonwhite coastal states like California, Texas and Florida [and] middling whites in the Rocky Mountain and Plains states" (28). The political power of the uplands is also disproportionate because political representation in the Senate gives low-population, culturally homogeneous states the same representation as high-population states with greater diversity.

One last piece of the economic and cultural puzzle that helps frame this collection is the concept of belief, and this belief, influenced by religion, holds that certain truths are immediate, natural, and God-given, "inalienable" in the sense that they cannot be articulated because they are so deeply felt as natural and primal. In terms of understanding this belief in a particular version of the immediacy of natural law collapsed into biblical law, John Fulton has reminded us of the importance of Antonio Gramsci's analysis of religious belief and the relation between religion and power. Within the socialist tradition, Gramsci shifted the theoretical discussion away from a concentration on ideology, which had been defined as a false and mistaken view of society, a view that could be corrected by pointing out its falsity. Instead, he introduced the concept of belief, or the commitments that are lived, felt, and acted upon at a deeply emotional and affective level. Fulton suggests that in an era of postmodernity when important studies of signification, as well as the historical circumstances of an internationalized economy, have unsettled many people's sense of identity, the concept of belief can help address both the relation between social circumstances and meaning, on the one hand, and the passionate, personal yearning for meaning and agency, on the other. Belief, then, must be described not only in terms of its historical constructedness as a substitute for identity but also, simultaneously, in terms of the way it functions as an active commitment to agency: "All commitments possess an element of belief, an active conviction and commitment as opposed to a gap-filling device for insufficiencies of contemporary science."[9]

In attempting to understand belief in a way that could explain the affects, emotions, and passions of spirituality in its relation to power, Gramsci studied Catholicism in Italy, from which he developed his discussion of hegemony. By doing so, he avoided the mistakes many Marxist analysts had made, as they too had often dismissed religious belief as unenlightened superstition and overlooked the powerful sense of agency such belief provided. As Fulton argues, Gramsci took seriously "*as a source of power,* the self-understanding of religious groups and the interpretations of the world in which those groups actualize their existence" (214, emphasis in original). If the power and attractions of religion were ever to be grasped and its influence on politics understood, it was not so much the nonbeliever's view of religion that had to be understood on its own terms as that of the believer.

Yet it was not simply Catholicism that defined the effectivity of Christianity. Gramsci noted that the material conditions prior to the industrial revolution and the development of the ideology of Calvinism, especially the notion of predestination, had developed "one of the greatest impulses to practical action that the history of the world has ever had." Nature and human relations ostensibly came together "in the midst of [an] orientation to the supernatural."

Both religion and socialism, as Gramsci saw them, were forms of praxis that could oppose a rarefied metaphysical discussion by philosophers and intellectuals cut off from the realities of the political process. (It is not coincidental that Ralph Reed, Pat Robertson's brilliant deputy, learned much from Gramsci.) The active relation of religious belief to the world identified religious belief as a particularly powerful kind of social praxis; "It is part of the interior character of religion as a total praxis, a form of power and activity in society. It is this *praxis* character which marks it off from philosophy and renders it both similar and dangerous to socialist praxis" (Fulton 202, emphasis in original). What divided socialism and Christianity, as Gramsci saw it, was the fact that Christianity idealizes and individualizes "all moral responsibility and [pretends] an equality between human individuals which religion has never actually achieved."[10] And it is this characteristic of individualization that suggests that religion can never achieve such equality, for "religion in general always ends up losing sight of the social character of human actions." Socialism, on the other hand, has the capacity to provide a genuine universality and a nonessentialist theory of historical and social striving for greater equality.

Of special importance was Gramsci's focus on the way religion functioned in the everyday lives and folklore of ordinary people, in relation to what Fulton calls "the value of human cultural life in the sociological sense and of its interaction with the processes of human labor and production" (198). Production, in his usage, is both physical and mental. In relation to that observation, Fulton argues for the importance of the sociology of religion, which might help us understand, from the vantage point of the self-understanding of believers, "that which is most alive and close in the experience of the people, the beliefs, morals, and practices which express in a religious way the needs and experience of various groups of people." In this way, we might also be able to analyze the way religious belief cements experience and produces what is felt to be unmediated sense perception, experienced as spontaneous, commonsensical, natural. The belief in the immediacy of perception elides the fact that perception, or "sense," is intertwined with the social commonality of experience, with conscience, and with consciousness, all of which are historical and thoroughly enmeshed in relations of power.

A more complex analysis of emotions, belief, and symbolic resources might give us insight into the relation between the history of the senses and the history of power. And it might also show how the right seems to have thoroughly understood Gramsci's discussion of social change, though he was referring to socialism. As Fulton writes; "The advent of socialism... cannot come through the barrel of a gun, but only through '*an intellectual and moral reformation,*' a revolution of the mind and heart." A takeover could thus only happen if "an alternative hegemonic culture has been sufficiently developed among both intellectuals and the masses," and its permanence could be ensured only by "the willing participation of the people in the transformation" (199). The importance of Gramsci's work and Fulton's patient study of it show the link between the immediacy of sense perception and the effectiveness of contemporary conservatism's use of spirituality as active praxis, a sense of agency in the world. Power takes root where agency does.

The contemporary political crisis brought about by the retreat of the most powerful global economic interests from any ethical responsibility for social justice has been reinforced by the activism of religious conservatives, whose model of ethics is defined by compassion toward "people like us," with little regard for the effects on everybody else. That model, couched in rhetoric and symbolic imagery that seem simple and clear, appeals to many of the very people it makes most vulnerable. Thus any analysis of contemporary politics has to address this contradiction, which is grounded most fundamentally in the cultural and historical vacuum that Gramsci recognized:

> Religion is a need of the spirit. People feel so lost in the vastness of the world, so thrown about by forces they do not understand; and the complex of historical forces, artful and subtle as they are, so escapes the common sense that in the moments that matter only the person

who has substituted religion with some other moral force succeeds in saving the self from disaster.[11]

Notes

1. Anthony Lake, quoted by Noam Chomsky in a lecture, "Democracy and the Media," given at the University of Maryland in Baltimore, 1 November 1994, and broadcast on C-SPAN 2 November 1994. A transcript of this talk was prepared by Lesage and Kintz, condensed and edited by Chomsky.

2. Chomsky develops another facet of the contract: "The real meaning of 'free market conservatism' is illustrated by a closer look at the most passionate enthusiasts for 'getting the government off our back' and 'letting the market reign' undisturbed. Not long ago, the *New York Times* had an interesting story on these interesting phenomena. They selected a concrete example, indeed the most striking example: Cobb County, Georgia. The article appears under the heading 'Conservatism Flowering among the Malls.' That is what is happening in Cobb County, a rich suburb of Atlanta, scrupulously insulated from any urban infection so that its inhabitants can enjoy the fruits of their entrepreneurial values and market enthusiasms, defended in Congress by its leading conservative, Newt Gingrich. He proudly proclaims that the anti-government sentiments of the people of the U.S. are finally beginning to prevail over the socialist welfare state.

"However, there is a small footnote: Cobb County receives more federal subsidies than any other suburban county in the country with two interesting exceptions: Arlington, Virginia, which is part of the Federal Government, and the Florida home of the Kennedy Space Center, another component of the system of public subsidy–private profit proudly called 'free enterprise.' But if you move out of the state system itself, then Cobb County takes the prize in living off of public subsidies that are funneled through the nanny state. The leading employer in Cobb County is Lockheed Aircraft, a corporation which exists thanks to massive public subsidy. Most other jobs in Cobb County are also based on feeding at the public trough, thanks to taxpayer largesse. Meanwhile praise for market miracles is resounding to the heavens, along with calls to 'get the government off our back' as long as it keeps pouring public funds into our pockets."

3. Silvia Ann Hewlett, *Child Neglect in Rich Societies* (New York: UNICEF, 1993).

4. Interpretations of natural law are not limited to this narrow, rigid conservative version. A helpful discussion of its history can be found in Elizabeth Mensch and Alan Freeman, *The Politics of Virtue: Is Abortion Debatable?* (Durham, N.C.: Duke University Press, 1993).

5. George Mosse, *Nationalism and Sexuality: Middle-Class Morality and Sexual Norms in Modern Europe* (Madison: University of Wisconsin Press, 1985), 4.

6. Richard White, *"It's Your Misfortune and None of My Own": A New History of the American West* (Norman: University of Oklahoma Press, 1991), 606.

7. The leadership of the defeated Democrats had been from the Northeast, the Midwest, and the Pacific Northwest. All but one of the new leaders, however, were from the South: Speaker of the House Newt Gingrich from Georgia, House Majority Leader Dick Armey and Majority Whip Tom DeLay from Texas, and Senate Majority Leader Trent Lott from Mississippi. Gingrich, however, did not grow up in the South, his military family having lived in a number of places, and Armey was originally from North Dakota. Michael Lind traces this shift in "The Southern Coup: The South, the GOP, and America," *The New Republic,* 19 June 1995, 20–29.

8. Lind, "The Southern Coup," 23.

9. John Fulton, "Religion and Politics in Gramsci: An Introduction," *Sociological Analysis* 48, no. 3 (1987): 197–216. I am greatly indebted to John Fulton for the influence of his work on this volume.

10. Gramsci, quoted in ibid., 215.

11. Gramsci, quoted in ibid., 202.

2

Christian Media

Julia Lesage

Conservative religious institutions in the United States use all the modes of media technology to communicate their messages to a broad spectrum of viewers, listeners, and readers. Ironically, for many years mainstream U.S. culture has judged Christian fundamentalism primarily in terms of its resistance to modernism; for example, although the creationist position won the Scopes trial in 1925, the U.S. press and many intellectuals have long excoriated fundamentalism for its backwardness and anti-intellectualism. However, although the religious right still deals with a very narrow range of issues ideologically, in the last several decades it has built up an extensive think tank apparatus to shape public policy and has multiplied the ways by which it gets a conservative political message to a large public. By looking at the religious right through its media productions, we can evaluate the communications resources the right has to muster and the social structures within which those resources are utilized.

In Chapter 10, "Who Is Mediating the Storm? Right-Wing Alternative Information Networks," Chip Berlet describes the range of media used by three sectors of the political right: secular conservatives, the far right, and the theocratic right, which includes groups like the Christian Coalition, Focus on the Family, and Concerned Women for America (CWA). Berlet notes the many ways that right-wing institutions have built up a complex and diverse infrastructure for disseminating their perspectives outside the mainstream media, which they see as hostile to the religious right:

> The increased use of electronic alternative media in the 1980s and 1990s involved online computer systems, networks, and services; fax networks and trees; shortwave radio programs; networks of small AM radio

> stations, with syndicated programs distributed by satellite transmissions or even by mailed audiotapes; home satellite dish reception, providing both TV audio/video programs and separate audio programs; local cable television channels, through which nationally produced videos are sometimes aired; and mail–order video and audiotape distributorships.

What is particularly striking about all these conservative Christian uses of the media is that each communications outlet refers to publications or desirable follow-ups for the reader, viewer, listener, or computer user to pursue in some *other* information medium. That is, each Christian right organization or radio/television program expects to tie its audience into other outlets of information or into other uses of the media to affect public policy. In addition, a number of conservative media producers have proven to be masters of their form, most notably Rush Limbaugh in the secular sphere—as detailed by Jeff Land in Chapter 9, "Sitting in Limbaugh: Bombast in Broadcasting"—and Pat Robertson in the religious sphere, with the television program, *The 700 Club.*

I will refer several times to an extended example from *The 700 Club,* first to demonstrate how the most prominent Christian television show in the United States involves its audiences in using other media forms and later to demonstrate its emotional mastery of the medium of television. I shall also trace how other institutions on the Christian right use a variety of media outlets for their message diffusion—from think tanks to independent production companies to political action groups. Contemporary Christian media has its historical origins in entrepreneurial "parachurch" evangelism deriving from revivalism in the United States and the concomitant enterprises built up around it, particularly radio shows. Now televangelism is epitomized by the vast publishing enterprise of a figure like James C. Dobson, whose videotapes and radio programs are described by several of the authors in this book, including Eithne Johnson, Meryem Ersoz, and Chip Berlet. Although Dobson does not describe himself as a political figure, the views propagated through his media outlets coincide with those of the activist Christian right, drawing on this sector's "commonsense" view of the world shared by many conservative Christians; in Chapter 4, "Clarity, Mothers, and the Mass-Mediated National Soul: A Defense of Ambiguity," Linda Kintz draws attention to the foundation of such "commonsense" Christian ideology in essentialized gender configurations.[1] These gender assumptions have concrete political consequences, which are the subject of the last section of this chapter, in which I conclude by drawing some observations about conservative rhetorical strategies, examining as a case study the attack on homosexual rights.

The 700 Club

Pat Robertson's *The 700 Club* is the longest running news talk show on television, and it reaches a million households in the United States and about sixty other countries daily. Robertson consummately tailors his evangelism to television's pace, segmentation, and flow, and consequently his show has always been the most "televisual" of all the religious broadcasts.[2]

Each episode of *The 700 Club* appears in tandem with a news program that airs before it, *Newswatch,* a format that was previously part of *The 700 Club* proper. *Newswatch* looks indistinguishable from mainstream news, and it features Christian Broadcasting Network (CBN) reporters speaking live from all over the world. As a television production, *Newswatch* has a visual style as professional looking as that of Cable News Network (CNN); since the two networks' logos are so similar, a viewer may well confuse the Christian show for Ted Turner's news network show if *Newswatch*'s topic does not explicitly deal with religion. However, although a news talk show format also structures its hosts' activity on *The 700 Club,* the latter program emphasizes another regular feature, perhaps more important to the committed regular viewer. That is, viewers are often encouraged to call a twenty-four-hour, phone-in prayer and counseling line, also operated by the Robertson conglomerate. "Talk to us," *The 700 Club* says intimately to home viewers.

Robertson's shows have a fast-paced, entertaining style, more so than any other religious or advocacy broadcasting. No segment of *Newswatch* or *The 700 Club* lasts longer than a few minutes, and each half-hour block incorporates different genre styles and varied modes of discourse, especially in the talk show part, *The 700 Club* proper. Each daily broadcast of *The 700 Club* usually includes within it interviews with successful business people, middle-brow authors, or entertainers, whose products are also subtly pushed. Mixed with the interviews are lively dramatic reenactments of a saved sinner's life, done in a generic melodrama format, or of someone's being miraculously healed or rescued, often done in a reality television or *Rescue 911* format. The hosts read letters that contain viewers' requests to be healed of a specific infirmity, and they hold hands on the set and lead a communal call to God for healing. Pat Robertson began in broadcasting as a charismatic preacher oriented to healing the sick; both physical and spiritual healing remain a constant, popular feature of his day-to-day program structure.

It is particularly informative to examine how *The 700 Club* exploits a variety of mutually reinforcing, socially potent media formats. To elucidate these connections, I shall detail their appearance on one show, that of Friday night, 3 May 1996. On this show CBN ran self-promotional ads encouraging *The 700 Club*'s audience to engage with a number of its other media outlets.

First of all, over the course of about a week, *The 700 Club* ran an ad for a videotape, *Health Facts You Should Know,* volume 2. Part of a video series by CBN's *Newswatch* presenting investigative health reports, this particular tape deals with supposed links between MSG and Alzheimer's disease, "safe sex" and teen girls' cervical cancer, vaccines and harm to children. The advertisement's images suggest that the health video contains many scare stories about health; the ad's voice-over narrator says (and these words also appear on the screen) that it offers "facts you can trust." To receive it, viewers are asked to send "a single gift of $20 to help CBN's World Wide Ministry" and are told that they'll learn then "where to get additional reports to protect your health."

A news story about health follows this advertisement for a health video. The news story deals with people who have successfully alleviated arthritis by using nutritional supplements. Featured in the story are Christian businessman and pharmacist Bob Henderson and his veterinarian son, Todd Henderson, whose company manufactures two such supplements—Cosamin for humans and Cosaquine as a veterinary product for horses. Following that news segment, Pat Robertson tells viewers how to get a free Fact Sheet on "Arthritis Relief: New Hope through Nutrition." In general, viewers can get individual Fact Sheets, subscribe to them, or look at them on *The 700 Club*'s newest outlet, a World Wide Web site on the Internet (*http://www.cbn.org*). Since Fact Sheets are publications *The 700 Club* has offered over many years, they must elicit regular, high-volume viewer response.

Following the string of tie-ins weaving back and forth between news story, hosts' commentary, and advertisement, *The 700 Club*'s World Wide Web site, available to computer users online, is advertised on the television program's next commercial break. This ad is brief and edited to a rapid pace; it builds on the television program's two main levels of appeal, cognitive and emotional. The voice-over narration emphasizes the Internet site's important role in maintaining a community of viewers/listeners, which Christian broadcasting so carefully fosters: "Now, information you can turn to day or night . . . Talk to us."

When a computer user then visits *The 700 Club*'s Web site, he or she will notice its simple, clean visual interface. In terms of content, the site has a number of striking features. First, offering reportage, it provides a transcript of two *Newswatch* stories for each of the past thirty days, approximately sixty stories on line at a time. Another long section on the Web site has significance mainly to fundamentalists: It lists all the biblical verses referred to in the programming, tying the programming into the fundamentalist doctrine of biblical inerrancy. To give the site a personalized appeal, pictures of the show's hosts and director appear, accompanied by their biographies. Visitors to the site also have access to the very popular Fact Sheets, for which they must enter personal information such as their name, address, and phone number. This is the point at which the Web site fulfills a key function: building Robertson's lucrative and politically useful mailing list. Indeed, all the offers of free phone calls and literature on the television show serve this function, too, the political implications of which will be discussed later.

If *Newswatch* and the CBN Web site highlight their informational value, the television ad for the Web site also communicates the emotional message, "Talk to us." *The 700 Club* deftly utilizes many forms of intimate address. For example, it frequently flashes a telephone number on the screen encouraging viewers to call the many counselors who are waiting there to answer calls. In one episode of *The 700 Club,* to garner phone calls, host Ben Kinchlow promoted "a special week of prayer": "We care for you. We've got counselors standing by telephones right now. We're asking you to let us pray for you . . . and you can call in your requests to the telephone number on the screen."

We see numerous counselors talking on the phone while sitting at tables in a large room, which has a prominent "prayer clock" visible on the far wall. This consists of a large hexagonal clock with the globe as a face and with small boxes for prayer cards mounted all around it; cohost Terry Meeuwsen is seen putting prayer pledge cards in the boxes. Ben and Terry relate the kinds of prayer requests they have received, especially for family and for health. Ben notes that many of these are "just what you call impossible situations . . . We will be delighted to send you a pamphlet that will help you pray through the impossible." Ben also addresses the faithful who might not be so needy at this moment. He asks them to call, not just to ask for prayers but to pledge fifteen minutes a day when they will pray for the burdens borne by America and the world.

In 1986, when Pat Robertson first considered running for president, he said he would not run unless three million people wrote, asked him to run, and pledged financial support. Much of the history of the contemporary Christian right is the history of mailing lists and direct mail solicitation for funds. In fact, mailing lists have a very low rate of return, unless the market is very narrowly and precisely targeted. In addition, the lists go out of date at a rate of about 20 percent a year, leaving a good list "dead" after five years unless constantly updated. To keep CBN's financially lucrative mailing list up-to-date, every *700 Club* broadcast and now the CBN Internet site incorporate multiple ways for viewers/users to get "free" informational material in exchange for their name, address, and phone number. That data will be put on a mailing list and later used for soliciting funds or mounting political campaigns. In addition, the kind of "factual" information Robertson "sells" on his show either reaches the committed, his partner-subscribers, or it is presented in a slick, fast-paced, television news style; this is also true of the health videos, presumably made up of footage shot for past *Newswatch* stories about health. Furthermore, this video series is targeted demographically, designed to appeal to homemakers (Robertson's audience has more women than men) or the elderly, who may turn to religious broadcasting, especially *The 700 Club,* as a form of safe entertainment and also for its experience of community. In terms of Robertson's larger social goals, as a founder of the politically effective Christian Coalition, this media financier has access to the Christian Coalition's mailing list just as that organization has access to CBN's. These lists are highly lucrative for the religious right; in fund-raising or political advocacy drives, they can be broken down geographically and cross-listed against other lists, such as registered Republicans, for example, to find potential supporters for or against a particular issues-oriented campaign.

The 700 Club's tie-ins to multiple modes of communication have a synergy that ultimately has a political effect. Phone-ins, for example, often occur after a viewer has watched and identified with the very emotional "let's pray together" sections. A warm and caring voice answers. The caller then receives intense, gratifying, personal reinforcement for his or her *700 Club* viewership. Buying a video or getting a free Fact Sheet often puts a viewer's name on the CBN mailing list. Regular viewers may become "partners," but more important, they always get a reward for their individual contact with CBN, either something sent in the mail or a supportive one-on-one personal conversation and prayer session.

These steps indicate what direct-mail promoters have learned from refining their marketing strategies over the last several decades. Into every show, *The 700 Club* incorporates basic direct-mail marketing techniques such as these: One's best contacts should always receive something material, such as a cassette or a publication, when they respond. It's a prize offered to the small percentage of the solicited who answer the pitch. Second, tasks respondents are asked to accomplish have to be presented in very small steps, ones almost effortlessly accomplished. A very powerful persuasion tactic is to ask someone to do something that takes almost no effort at all. It makes the person feel that he or she is doing something of value, and, on the part of the organizer, it assumes that even the lazy can be stimulated to purchase something or to get involved in an organized effort (Lesage 1987). From these mailing lists, the route to face-to-face organizing, such as getting like-minded people to the polls, is relatively direct.

In Chapter 6, "Transformation of Televangelism: Repackaging Christian Family Values," Razelle Frankl describes how Pat Robertson moved from being a televangelist to being a major player in network broadcasting with the success of his Family Channel. However, Robertson has made other, less-visible moves to expand his media empire. In 1993, Robertson considered taking over the press service United Press International (UPI), but he decided that it would be too expensive to refurbish. Instead, recognizing and wanting to augment Christian radio's increasing presence and sophistication, Robertson began Standard News, a daily audio satellite feed out of Washington, D.C. On Standard News, Robertson puts out two daily audio feeds of a two-minute Christian-oriented newscast, as well as a package of prerecorded commentaries, features, and interviews that local radio programmers can use according to their needs. In this way, the information that CBN tapes each day for its television show's "news" stories serves multiple needs, media formats, and potential listener/viewerships. A story is edited on video for the television program *Newswatch,* transcribed for the World Wide Web, and perhaps reedited on audio for radio news heard on many Christian radio stations. And the *Newswatch* feature remains available to be recycled in a later "theme" video or video series. The reportage gathered for a story can also appear in print in a CBN magazine article, or it can be summarized or amplified in a *700 Club* Fact Sheet. The broadcasting arm of CBN gathers material from its in-house staff or its reporters around the world and recycles it into many other media outlets. As CBN evolved, Robertson changed from considering himself primarily a "religious" broadcaster to trying to develop the Family Channel as a leading producer of quality home entertainment. Extraordinarily well distributed on cable, the Family Channel now reaches 95 percent of all U.S. households with cable television and 62 percent of all U.S. households with television. In 1997, Robertson's media corporation, International Family Entertainment (IFE), was bought by Rupert Murdoch, with Robertson and his son moving into executive positions in the new subsidiary. IFE approved the merger, hoping through it to expand its media distribution globally.

Think Tanks and Political Activism

Another kind of conservative media distribution comes from think tanks. Apart from the Institute for Policy Studies, the left does not have think tanks with national influence. Because these policy-planning institutions are dependent on massive corporate funding, most think tanks have a political philosophy that runs from middle-of-the-road liberal to extremely conservative.

Conservative think tanks like the influential Heritage Foundation or the Free Congress Foundation, parent of National Empowerment Television (NET) network, now emphasize as integral to their mission the *marketing* of ideas. To spread their ideas, the think tanks have innovatively developed modes of distribution across a broad range of media. In Chapter 11, "Conservative

Media Activism: The Free Congress Foundation and National Empowerment Television," Anna Williams notes how Edwin Feulner, director of the Heritage Foundation, conceptualizes the foundation's mission primarily in terms of getting its ideas out: "We don't just stress credibility, we stress timeliness. We stress an efficient, effective delivery system. Production is one side; marketing is equally important."

Because of its origins and base in a think tank, NET has a top-down organizational and information-delivery style, which has a subsequent effect on political organizations that rely on its information, such as the Christian Coalition. However, not just the Free Congress Foundation, which has NET as its own media outlet, but many other think tanks develop multiple modes of outreach.

Think tanks usually maintain contact with a "resource bank of scholars and policy experts around the nation . . . to provide the media and Congressional hearings with conservative commentary" (Peschek 1987, 33). For example, the American Enterprise Institute, which has among its experts Jeanne Kirkpatrick, Robert Bork, Irving Kristol, and Antonin Scalia, puts out its own publications, runs op-ed pieces in the press, and contributes speakers to radio and television shows. Think tanks provide a visible gathering of the intellectual and professional elite and often place people in governmental policy-making positions. They also develop close contacts with the press to try to influence public opinion directly. Ironically, as Chip Berlet points out, although much think tank research is intellectually shallow, it provides a readily available source of pronouncements on national policy, a source that national news reporters regularly use. In Washington, D.C., the Heritage Foundation is known for writing timely short papers, which it hand-delivers to congressional staff people. In addition, the Heritage Foundation built a broadcasting studio in its Washington, D.C., office so talk show hosts can come to Washington and address their audiences directly from the nation's capitol (Balz and Brownstein 1996, 187).

Paul Weyrich has established two branches of NET: a subscription service for activists and NET proper, a twenty-four-hour news and information network. To widen NET's sphere of influence, each day Weyrich faxes a summary of NET's previous day's broadcasts to over a thousand talk show hosts. As Jeff Land notes in Chapter 9, "Sitting in Limbaugh," this connection between talk radio and national politics is extremely important since talk radio provides conservative Republicans and the religious right with a direct tie to millions of daily listeners, who are frequently moved by appeals to phone or fax a legislator or the president.

NET also has a close tie to religious right electoral politics and issues activism. It not only has 281 downlink sites for its television programs, but its programs appear every day on CompuServe's Political Issues Forum, where the computer user can type in questions, presumably in real time so they can be received by the program host. Extending the real-time capacities of the Internet, the Krieble Institute U.S.A. broadcasts an interactive political training conference for one day each month on NET and the Internet. The conference uses RealAudio technology to broadcast live audio via the computer site, and those who have registered for the conference can interact with the speakers by phoning an 800 number or sending a fax or e-mail. Such political training ties into and augments the two-day leadership training seminars taken by so many religious conservative activists through the Christian Coalition; on 29 July 1996, for example, the NET political training conference covered the following topics: Opposition Research, How to Topple an Incumbent, How to Run an Absentee Effort, Why Run a Third Party and What Does That Accomplish, and How to Minimize Support for a Third Party.

NET has a unique tie-in to the United States Congress since Congress has its own television production facility where legislators produce shows and television interviews free of charge. In those facilities the Republican National Committee tapes a weekly hour-long show, *Rising Tide,* which it broadcasts on NET. Newt Gingrich also puts a weekly show on NET. In fact, it is House Republican leader Gingrich who has led Republicans in Congress in developing an effective media strategy for the purposes of political action.

Starting his career as a U.S. Representative in 1978, Gingrich had a fateful conversation with Richard Nixon in 1982:

> House Republicans, [Nixon] said, had never displayed enough teamwork, aggressiveness, or interest in ideas to make them an effective counterforce in a Democratic-controlled body, and he urged Gingrich to start assembling a team of committed activists who could develop an agenda of issues around which the party could rally. (Balz and Brownstein 1996, 118)

With the goal of forging a cohesive political agenda and conservative presence within the Republican Party, Gingrich has actively used a range of mass media to transform his party into one concerned with "ideas." He began as his own video/audiocassette "publisher" in the late 1980s and early 1990s within GOPAC, a political action committee formed to develop future Republican nominees for legislative office both statewide and nationally. At that time it became his personal project to give future and current candidates the ideas, advice, and savvy of an experienced politician, emphasizing the larger picture and where they could fit into it. Gingrich sought to change his party's culture from one that was oppositional to one that believed it could win. To do this, in the early 1990s he sent unsolicited audio-

and videotapes each month to potential Republican candidates, especially in those regions where the demographics alone promised a large number of future conservative voters. In those tapes he discussed tactics, strategy, and issues; there were also lectures by or interviews with successful Republicans (Balz and Brownstein 1996, 145).

Then, in 1994, Gingrich led the political and rhetorical organizing for one of his cleverest strategic moves, the Contract with America, published on 27 September in the U.S. publication with the highest circulation, *TV Guide.* It cost $250,000; the ad's front page simply read: "A campaign promise is one thing. A signed contract is quite another." As three hundred Republicans gathered on the White House lawn for a news conference to announce the event, the right's intellectual leadership achieved one of its main goals, to control the national press agenda around legislative issues and to control the political messages discussed in the political arena. As Julia Lesage discusses in Chapter 12, "Christian Coalition Leadership Training," this tactic is known by public relations experts and campaign strategists as "framing the issues," that is, seizing control of the public discourse agenda around policy issues. Think tanks on the right had been doing this for several decades before the Contract with America, but at that point the right's agenda was communicated in terms the voting public could grasp, and the terms of the agenda became widely diffused in the national press.

Other Christian media empires have a focus different from that of the "D.C. insider," although they, too, have strong connections to national politics. Dr. James C. Dobson, whose self-help and family-advice videos are distributed primarily through Christian bookstores, has a widely heard daily radio show, *Focus on the Family.* Dobson's empire, and the use of his tapes by local churches and in the home, is analyzed by Eithne Johnson in Chapter 7, "The Emergence of Christian Video and the Cultivation of Videovangelism." I wish to point out some of his other media connections and their tie-in to his main theme—offering domestic advice and youth-oriented materials from a Christian psychologist and educator.

As one drives across the United States, the bored driver is most likely to hear a program like Dr. Dobson's *Focus on the Family* while passing through rural areas, especially on AM stations. Local Christian stations, often on AM, rely heavily on prepackaged programming, and this is why the shows like Dobson's—and Rush Limbaugh's—are so widely syndicated. Dobson's program has by far one of biggest audiences among Christian radio shows; it is broadcast daily to over 1,450 radio stations nationwide. In Chapter 8, "Gimme That Old-Time Religion in a Postmodern Age: Semiotics of Christian Radio," Meryem Ersoz locates Dobson's program within the larger context of radio used for Christian media outreach. Extending that discussion, in Chapter 9, "Sitting in Limbaugh," Jeff Land describes how the community formed by Christian radio listenership coincides with the listenership of secular talk radio, particularly fans of Rush Limbaugh's daily show.

Dobson's show, *Focus on the Family,* elicits an audience response that goes beyond just casual listening; listeners send in 250,000 letters a month, all of which are answered. Dr. Dobson has an extensive publishing empire—ten different monthly magazines go out to members of demographic groups as diverse as teens, parents, and political activists.[3] He seeks to have influence over public policy to the degree that it affects the family. His "Family Issues Alert," a weekly two-page fax, reaches 3,600 subscribers (Diamond 1996, 71; Scully 1989, E1). Dobson's perspective is always normative about family and gender, and he has played a very powerful role in the antigay struggles taking place in the United States. Dobson's facilities produced Colorado's antihomosexual Amendment 2's radio public service announcements, a campaign analyzed in detail by Laurie Schulze and Frances Guilfoyle in Chapter 13, " 'Facts Don't Hate; They Just Are,' " and the Focus on the Family organization makes radio public service announcements for campaigns in other states as well.

Dobson joined forces for a number of years with a Washington, D.C., think tank, Family Research Council, headed by Gary Bauer, formerly a member of the Reagan administration. Although the two groups still have many joint projects, the Family Research Council has separated from Focus on the Family in order to become a lobbying group and create a new political action committee without impinging on Dobson's tax-exempt educational status. Dobson's subscribers to the Focus on the Family's magazine for activists, *Citizen,* also receive a free Family Research Council monthly newsletter. Both the Focus on the Family organization and the Family Research Council promote an "ideal family" ideology. The Family Research Council, for example, does research on single-parent families or out-of-wedlock births in order to provide legislators with evidence to oppose welfare. And, as Chip Berlet notes, Clinton's proposal to lift the ban on gays in the military became the occasion for such groups as the Family Research Council to build on religiously oriented, antigay sentiment for their fund-raising campaigns. Furthermore, just as Pat Robertson's CBN mailing list helped found the Christian Coalition, according to political analyst Sara Diamond, the Family Research Council organized *Focus on the Family*'s radio-listener constituency into a group of state-based think tanks geared toward organizing the grassroots lobbying of state legislators (Diamond 1995, 250).

Focus on the Family's Internet Web site does not suggest that the organization is political. Instead, it promotes video and audio products with a specific appeal to children and youth. In contrast, the Family Research Council's site is one of the most "informational" on the Web, especially among activist sites. It electronically publishes many brief articles, searchable by topic or author. The site also posts a monthly letter from director Gary Bauer and a regular news commentary feature, *Washington Watch.* Unlike the Christian Coalition or even the Family Research Council, Dobson wishes to remove himself from directly endorsing political candidates, and his Internet site emphasizes his low-key presence in terms of drawing national media attention to himself.

Similar to Focus on the Family in its concern for domestic life is Concerned Women for America, but CWA uses a more overtly religious rhetoric. Elsewhere Linda Kintz describes the writings of CWA founder and director, Beverly LaHaye (Kintz 1997), but here it is important to note the ways that media are used by and intersect with CWA's work. The organization is structured around cohesive Prayer Chapters of fifty women: a leader and seven prayer-chain leaders who contact seven other women on a phone chain. These women not only reinforce each other through warm personal contact, they may also be members of the Christian Coalition, with which CWA works closely, and they are often asked to respond to a political issue with a "fax alert." A Christian Coalition newsletter describes the work of one such activist woman:

> Fax machines, computers and on-line information services allow Dannenfelser to do it all out of her home between caring for children and running a household. "Technology like the fax, computer and voice mail have allowed me to create a rapidly expanding political action committee while keeping my family my first priority"... With fax machines built into personal computers, a letter to the editor can be sent to every newspaper in the state at the same time. (Curtis 1995)

CWA, which claimed 600,000 members in 1992, is also prominent on Christian radio. It has a popular daily half-hour radio program featuring Beverly LaHaye, broadcast on forty Christian stations nationwide.

Sara Diamond notes the way the CWA radio programs are tied to political activism: "LaHaye's broadcasts end with action suggestions for listeners—call your Congressmember, send money to a crisis pregnancy center, find out if your school library carries one of the objectionable books named on the show" (Diamond 1995, 14). CWA's ability to call listeners into action has had a significant effect on public policy, even nationally. For example, CWA, along with the Christian Coalition, boasts that in this way they organized a drive to nominate Clarence Thomas to the Supreme Court (Reed 1994, 245–46). In a short period of time they mustered their constituency to send 100,000 petitions, letters, and phone calls to members of Congress. Now they claim success for Thomas's appointment, a political move completely unobserved by either mainstream or left and feminist media at the time.

Thus the religious right, especially at the elite level of its leadership, makes use of and builds interconnections between media. And various conservative institutions feed messages into mass media outlets. In this context, it should be noted that the Republicans in Congress deliberately exploit talk radio. Jeff Land, writing about Rush Limbaugh's audience, notes the close tie between Limbaugh's radio listeners and computer-using Internet fans; this audience of "Dittoheads," as Limbaugh fans like to call themselves, creates a community of the like-minded that has both commercial and political clout. The show delivers a predictable market to advertisers and so can command high advertising revenue. It can also agitate listeners about a specific political issue. As Balz and Brownstein note, "The affinity between host and audience made talk radio a mobilizing tool of great power. It stoked anger, sharpened resentments, personalized policy disputes, and clarified issues in a manner that reduced the middle ground" (1996, 189).

Knowing this, House Republicans have organized to take advantage of talk radio. Taking stock of this popular media format's appeal to conservative listeners, House members' press secretaries put together several hundred names of sympathetic talk radio hosts. Now, through the House Republican Study Committee's program *Talk Right,* Republican politicians "regularly send the hosts issue briefs listing GOP talking points on current issues and offering a half a dozen House Republican legislators as guests" (Balz and Brownstein 1996, 167).

The most astute critic of the rise of the contemporary religious right is Sara Diamond. In her book *Roads to Dominion* (1995), she defines how she analyzes this movement: in terms of its resources, its networks of individuals and organizations, its relation to the state, and its objectives and ideology. In writing about Christian Coalition leadership training tapes, I also reflect on the movement as such, drawing some comparisons between left and right grassroots activism. Here I wish to draw some additional comparisons between left and feminist uses of the media and those of the religious right. As indicated above, many Christian right media ventures are either well-funded televangelist ministries, raising funds from donations and sales of products, or they are tied to corporately funded think tanks. As a result, an elite coordination of message delivery characterizes the religious right's interconnected use of media forms.

In contrast, left and feminist ventures into the media are underfunded and not coordinated at all in terms of their content. Such productions include economically made documentary films and videos, occasionally shown on public television in special series like *Point of View* and often distributed through educational outlets to schools. Introducing a special issue on fundamentalist media, the editors of *Afterimage* characterize this kind of independent film/video media making:

> Informed by a combination of social and aesthetic developments (guerrilla television/street video and video as art) media activism on the left has a very different frame of reference . . . [Its foundational material conditions were] the development of portable technologies and an extensive patchwork system of public and private funding for alternative media from roughly 1965–1980 . . . [A]s Helen DeMichiel put it in Paper Tiger's *Guide to Media Activism,* "giddy and smug, passionate and righteous, alternative media activists of the late 60s and 70s dared to predict a future rosy with proliferating visions of a decentralized and creatively intelligent video democracy." It is this acknowledgment of a free-floating, democratic idealism, coupled with a loose infrastructure of modest fundraising (compared to the religious right's fundraising excess) that characterizes media activism on the left. (Kester and Love 1995, 7)

Radio activism on the left is dominated by National Public Radio, which offers daily newscasts, including "opposite" points of view to give a sense that it is "balanced."

At the elite level of left and feminist publication, independent journals have often become rather expensive quarterly or yearly publications taken over by university presses. On the level of mass distributed publications, New Left tabloid print media have lost the once energetic papers that reveled so freely in anarchist aesthetics. In the 1960s and 1970s, "underground" publications were staff owned and run, and they only had to make enough money to pay for the next printing. Now left print media is essay heavy and can be seen in publications such as *The Nation, In These Times,* or *Mother Jones,* some of which are funded by an "angel." Certain former underground-press writers publish occasional left-oriented analyses in weeklies such as the Chicago or Los Angeles *Reader.* These capitalist ventures, including New York's *Village Voice,* are advertising heavy, and the *Reader*s are given out free. These publications' readers are urban professionals; that means that many readers of the *Voice* or *Reader* pride themselves on left-leaning social views. Some independent left and feminist media ventures remain, including *Jump Cut* and *Cineaste* media reviews and the interventions into cable-access television by Paper Tiger Television and Deep Dish TV. There are still many independent video productions, few of which reach national distribution. And the spirit of this kind of production is still individualistic, often anarchist in its lack of connection to other organizations or social movements.

However, many left and feminist intellectuals have had a great impact on academic disciplines, even if just by asking the question "What were the women doing all these years?" It is, in fact, the explanatory power of left and feminist analyses that gives them such influence in academic disciplines, especially the social sciences and the humanities. Yet the religious right often sees such influence in terms of a left or feminist or gay conspiracy. Furthermore, fundamentalists have felt themselves to be cultural and political outsiders for most of the century, and it is easy to be jealous of the perceived cultural capital of the left in academia (Bourdieu 1984), although leftists and feminists are hardly coordinated in their intellectual or political endeavors, especially on a national scale.

In the same way, it would be a mistake to interpret religious right media use as either a conspiracy or a network controlled by a few elite figures. Conservative members of Congress and intellectuals in Washington, D.C., have had twenty years as a minority voice in the legislature. They have often collaborated on each other's projects and on the boards of conservative political groups or think tanks. There they strategize and constantly discuss how they might enact a conservative public agenda. Working in geographic proximity, remaining constantly aware of each other's political work, and striving to establish a strong conservative political network do not, however, add up to conspiracy. In addition, the Christian right's specific media contribution to this project has other roots, those of evangelical Protestantism.

Evangelism

As John C. Green discusses the evangelical origin of the Christian right, referring to evangelicals' strength in the 1994 elections, he emphasizes that these believers are dispersed among organizations that have little denominational hierarchy or unity:

> This tradition combines orthodox Christian beliefs with intense individualism, resulting in a highly decentralized set of organizations, including thousands of small denominations, parachurch groups, and independent churches. Even the largest bodies, such as the giant Southern Baptist Convention (the largest Protestant denomination in the country), are actually voluntary alliances of their component institutions. This environment puts a premium on aggressive, entrepreneurial leaders who can successfully compete for money, followers, and publicity with the world—and with each other. Such leaders become adept at recognizing discontent among religious people, identifying resources to respond to such discontent, and organizing the resources to bring the two together. They also become familiar with the latest communications, fundraising, and organizing techniques...Thus, the evangelical subculture is closer to the rough and tumble of American electoral politics than many other religious traditions. (quoted in Rozell and Wilcox 1995, 3–4)

Evangelicals have long participated in or collaborated with parachurch organizations, ranging from revivals to overseas missions to independent Bible colleges and religiously oriented universities. Entrepreneurial pastors have built up megachurches, especially in the suburbs, often with 5,000 to

10,000 members, that have fast-paced services that are as slick as *The 700 Club* and that include music, both gospel and Christian rock, and videos. Such entrepreneurship writ large has led to the financial success of what Eithne Johnson describes as evangelical *megacommunicators*. The megacommunicators draw on the evangelical community's longtime concern to reach out, to save the sinner. With their own particular vision and organizational skill, these entrepreneurs develop an interconnected empire of organizations, often encompassing a big-budget media operation with its own broadcasting studios, a convention and conference center that may conduct Sunday services and revivals, a series of publications, and perhaps a connected university or missionary organization. The megacommunicators have a lot of political power, and they make it easier for the conservative political movement to mobilize many people rapidly.

There's a synergy of ideological agreement, effective use of the mass media and of "narrowcasting" (targeting media to a specific audience), and political organizing. This synergy characterizes the relation between political and intellectual elites, the megacommunicators, and local, religious right political activism, often conducted through churches. A 1979 Gallup poll, conducted in conjunction with *Christianity Today,* found that 82 percent of evangelicals go to church once a week and about a third go twice or more a week. As Ralph Reed, first director of the Christian Coalition, said about this group of people as a constituency: "The advantage we have is that liberals and feminists don't generally go to church. They don't gather in one place three days before the election" (quoted in Balz and Brownstein 1996, 312).

In 1987 and 1988, U.S. teleministries were rocked by scandal, but the attention the press paid to Jimmy Swaggart and Jim and Tammy Bakker deflected public awareness from the right's steady electoral organizing, the growth of conservative think tanks, and the religious right's active participation in aiding right-wing movements in Central America, where it worked with the explicit support, indeed gratitude, of the U.S. government (Diamond 1989). In Chapter 6, "Transformation of Televangelism," Razelle Frankl traces how the teleministries recouped their former ground and in fact increased in adaptability and sophistication. She has also analyzed the roots of the televangelists' entrepreneurship in the culture of evangelism and in the permanent presence of revivals in U.S. culture.

In *Televangelism: The Marketing of Popular Religion* (1987), Razelle Frankl traces the roots of contemporary religious media enterprises in the experience gained in the promotion and management of revivals, beginning with the fascinating nineteenth-century entrepreneur Charles Grandison Finney. Finney understood that a revival has to be a *planned* event to stimulate religious fervor, something managed rationally, using psychological and organizational tricks. Some of these organizational tricks include having people come together for days of concentrated meetings, at which they are pushed to an emotional extreme, or having the entire congregation pray for the conversion of specific sinners. In his published *Lectures,* Finney said: "It is not a miracle, or dependent on a miracle, in any sense. It is the purely philosophical result of the right use of sophisticated means" (Finney 1960, 13).

Revivalist preachers were independent businessmen. They did not have to be ordained; they just heeded the call of the Spirit to go out and preach. They, like most other petit bourgeois capitalists, had to learn by trial and error and individually developed their own "tricks" to capture audiences. Thus, in the 1930s Billy Sunday made the revival format even more thrilling with his own brand of entertainment and a call to U.S. patriotism, and the 1950s saw Billy Graham filling up stadiums like Madison Square Garden and building a national radio audience. As Frankl writes about them:

> What worked well was used, what did not was dropped—this was the rationale for new practices, in direct rejection of traditional pastoral or ministerial practices. One aspect of this professional autonomy was the necessity for revivalists to build their own organizational and financial resources, which they did with a clientele of their own. (1987, 60)

As revivals and fundamentalist churches moved to urban areas, the preachers saw radio as an effective tool to publicize meetings and directly to incite religious fervor. The Federal Communications Commission (FCC) mandated in 1929 that stations provide free airtime for religious broadcasting, but that time went to mainstream denominations. From the very beginning, Christian broadcasters assumed that radio was a desirable medium with which to present their message and that they would have to pay for that airtime. Furthermore, they were usually excluded from the major radio networks, so they worked through independent stations. At the same time, although the major denominations received free airtime, they would not spend the money necessary for an expensive broadcast ministry. Finally, by 1960, two developments greatly enhanced evangelicals' broadcasting possibilities: The FCC allowed paid airtime to meet the networks' public-interest obligations, and networks granted affiliates more autonomy to sell local airtime. As Sara Diamond writes:

> Local network affiliate stations were encouraged to accumulate profits by selling "religious" air time to the highest bidder, not to broadcasters most representative of the local religious community. An up-and-coming band of televangelists was now free to devote any amount of program time to fundraising. Over time, the staid mainline religious broadcasters were unable to compete with the more flamboyant NRB [National Religious Broadcasters'] producers. The opportunity to begin to mo-

> nopolize religious television and radio tied evangelicals' media success to the production of captivating programming, an example of which was the political talk-show format pioneered by Pat Robertson's CBN, beginning in the early 1960s. (1995, 98)

Returning to The 700 Club: *Television's Emotional Appeal*

Returning to look closely at *The 700 Club* program of 26 April 1996, it is possible to analyze the ways in which *The 700 Club*'s format allows for discussion of current, that is, unpredictable, events while also maintaining a gratifyingly predictable relation to its audience. Because the show largely takes the format of discussing the news, broadly interpreted, it appeals to viewers' sense of understanding relevant world events; but it also has a deep emotional appeal. To be more precise, it has a deep *affective* appeal. Lawrence Grossberg, author of the insightful *We Gotta Get Out of This Place: Popular Conservatism and Postmodern Culture* (1992), points out that affect is not only the arena in which people can be emotionally manipulated, it is also the arena of emotional investment, commitment, passion, volition, and will. For example, the turning to Jesus that evangelists promote is seen by those within the fundamentalist religious community as an empowering event, allowing one to throw off addictions, emotional phobias and anxieties, and behavior that hurts others. If one looks closely at the structure of one *700 Club* program, it becomes clear how this very sophisticated show hails both rationality and affect on the part of its viewers. As Grossberg defines the social operation of affect, "Affect identifies the strength of the investment which anchors people in particular experiences, practices, identities, meanings and pleasures, but it also determines how invigorated people feel at any moment of their lives, their level of energy or passion" (82).

The 26 April program begins with *Newswatch,* which takes up the first half hour, followed by *The 700 Club* proper. (In this half-hour *Newswatch* section, the commentators are host Ben Kinchlow, regular Terry Meeuwsen, and staff member Lee Webb, standing in for Pat Robertson; later, in *The 700 Club* proper, just Ben and Terry share the stage since Pat has gone for the day.) This *Newswatch* broadcast contains three long, current events sections about recently breaking news. The first deals with the U.S.-brokered cease-fire in Lebanon. The Israeli Labor Party has agreed to the formation of a Palestinian state since the PLO has announced it will no longer demand the annihilation of Israel. Pat Robertson has long been a supporter of Israel, and this segment seems as "objective" as most television news, followed with little comment by the three hosts, except that Ben emphasizes that a nation has to protect its own survival and states that he hopes Israel will not sign away its rights, implicitly warning viewers about possible future treachery from Palestine.

The next story uses far more slanted language and contains as visual footage only images of Asian governmental leaders signing papers; it is about an accord between China and Russia. The commentary warns that analysts see this accord as a clear warning to the United States: China and Russia claim that the treaty lays a foundation for a new world order and thus provides a way to keep the United States from shaping world policy single-handedly. The commentary also says that for China the treaty promotes more an anti-American sentiment than a pro-Russian one since China is trying to counter U.S. influence in the Pacific. "New world order" is the story's buzzword. The term elicits the fear of "collectivism" that communism has always raised for the right, a fear that the right has also profited from for years. The story implies that the treaty threatens U.S. sovereignty or U.S. international presence, but the relation of a loss of U.S. sovereignty to a massive increase in the power and scope of multinational corporations is never discussed.

The third major current events news story carried by *Newswatch* covers the Democrats' demand to raise the minimum wage from $4.25 to $5.15 an hour. The story itself acknowledges that this is a popular proposal, indicating that Bob Dole said he might accede to it. In this way, the story proper seems relatively unbiased, presenting both pros and cons to the legislation. However, the CBN version of the demand for a raise in the minimum wage leaves out what all the other networks later spent the weekend discussing: that the Democrats' demand is an election-year ploy to embarrass the Republicans, especially presidential primary candidate Bob Dole. Such a reduction of context is frequent in all newscasts, but this reductionism is especially characteristic of CBN. With this in mind, we can reinterpret the *Newswatch* story about China and Japan, noticing that the treaty is interpreted and commented on, an attitude is proposed, which viewers are invited to take up, but the story itself is drastically stripped of any contextualization.

Earlier, *Newswatch*'s opening credits had previewed this upcoming story on the minimum wage with images of U.S. currency being run through the printing presses. Such an image bears the connotation of "false money," a connotation historically cherished by the right ever since the days of William Jennings Bryan. At the very end of the story, we see reporter Melissa Charbonneau in Washington, D.C., saying that Republicans insist that if they do give in to the bill, it will not be without negotiating for some key riders, which may include a training wage for entry-level workers, a $500 tax credit per child, or some other kind of tax reduction, such as cutting the capital gains tax. The last point, tax credit for the wealthiest sectors of the country, something corporate and upper-middle-class sectors have long fought for, is presented very quickly and then elided, not referred to at all in the subsequent talk show format discussion. In the discussion that follows, Ben makes the strongest and most interesting point, shifting the term "people" to refer to small business owners. He says Democrats always claim that they want to help "the people, but the people who will catch it in the end are those who have to ante up the minimum wage." These "people" (that is, businessmen) will only be able to do that by raising prices or laying off workers.

The *Newswatch* program then presents two feature stories, which were obviously prepared in advance; one commemorates the tenth anniversary of the Chernobyl disaster, and the other discusses UFOs and people's reported experience of being abducted by aliens. This latter segment both refers to and uses footage from very popular media narratives, the Fox Network TV show *The X Files,* and the action-adventure science fiction films *Independence Day* and *Close Encounters of the Third Kind.* The segment borrows the appeal of these shows by using footage from them, and it also gives live testimony from three people who say they were abducted: a white farmer standing in a woods by a river and two women filmed against a threatening black background. There is also synchronized sound footage of Louis Farrakhan lecturing to a crowd, describing his personally having been transported by aliens to a flying saucer and saying that the saucers will soon be seen all over major U.S. cities.

One of the women interviewed looks disreputable because she has disheveled hair and is dressed in red, which has the connotation of "loose" and which also characteristically "bleeds" in the television image. She is overweight and badly made up and at one point is seen in a store that sells UFO paraphernalia, where her presence seems to indicate "poor judgment" or "weak mind." Two statistics are narrated verbally and placed graphically on the screen: Half of all Americans believe in UFOs, and one in seven claims to have had a UFO or paranormal experience. Two British farmers who perpetrated a hoax in which strange circles mysteriously appeared in a series of fields over a number of years show how they made the patterns in the grass. They treat the deception with wry rural humor.

A UFO expert, a UFO debunker, and a theologian are interviewed. The theologian is John Weldon, author of *Encyclopedia of New Age Beliefs* (the book jacket is shown in close-up as a promo and a verification of his authenticity). The UFO expert looks a little strange, with an unusual beard, thick glasses, and a lined face; he is filmed in an unflattering, excruciatingly tight close-up. The UFO debunker, in contrast, is filmed in medium shot at his computer, surrounded by books, and in a more flattering light.

The theologian and the CBN reporter point out that the experience of abduction probably represents a manifestation of Satan, in which people have trance-like experiences and are manipulated by entities so that they cannot distinguish fantasy from reality. The more normal-looking woman says that the aliens who took her to a spaceship did a gynecological procedure on her and removed her fetus. (The mysterious disappearance of a fetus, due to the devil, also seems to be an interesting possible cover-up for or symbolic reference to a miscarriage or abortion.) The disheveled woman tells the camera that because of her experience, she lost her taste for organized religion and found something deeper inside her.

To conclude the story, the reporter walks in the field where the farmer had been interviewed earlier and says while walking: "That may be why many Christian theologians say that the UFO phenomenon is demonic, and they say that whatever UFOs are, they are best to be avoided." In this feature, *The 700 Club* cleverly introduces and does not quite condemn popular culture products. It uses UFO imagery to add to its own show's media appeal. Indeed, the reporter says to avoid UFOs, not to avoid films or television shows about the phenomenon. However, the segment clearly implies that even *depictions* of UFOs do not provide Christians with good family television or movie fare.

This feature could have been taped weeks earlier. In this show, it provides the tie-in to one of the program's regular features, the dramatic reenactment of a real-life, reformed sinner's story. To introduce this segment, Terry and Ben are sitting on a set in the ballroom of the Founders' Inn. They are presenting this segment from CBN's Virginia Beach convention center, and they have an audience of several hundred people. Ben tries jokingly to hypnotize Terry, but she resists, saying she doesn't like that kind of thing, that it has always made her edgy. Ben asks if anyone in the audience has been hypnotized. Most seem to know that it is an experience outside the acceptable range of "Christian" discourse. "There's a hand," Ben says, and a long shot shows one arm quickly dropping down from one lone audience member on the far side of the hall. The dramatic reenactment then unfolds the life and conversion of Phil Potter, stage hypnotist, who, as the narrator says, learned how he had been led down a subtle road into the occult. The segment contains within it depictions of a small farm boy's fascination with the idea of hypnosis, even though his brothers and sisters laugh at him; what looks like 8 mm movie footage of Potter's stage show, here hypnotizing a group of high school students; and shots of a hammer smashing the tools he had used. In the follow-up discussion, Ben quotes Deuteronomy, chapter 18, against imitating detestable things that others are doing, such as divination or casting spells.

Finally, the show's fast-paced, rapid-fire video logo shows a series of images that sum up the show's demographics and perhaps its audience's idealized image of itself: Pat Robertson is shown with his wife and thoroughbreds on his Virginia Beach estate; Ben Kinchlow is shown in casual clothes in a small-town "cracker" dry goods store with the elderly white couple who run it. Ben is also seen in shirtsleeves outside a rural black church, where parishioners are serving a potluck picnic. In both shots he's very warmly welcomed, almost as if he's going home to the rural South. Terry Meeuwsen is shown with children in an aquarium and in a classroom. Then Pat appears again, this time shot in close-up with soldiers at the Vietnam Memorial; a hand traces the names engraved on the black marble wall, and Pat hugs a veteran who is smiling and holding back tears. This image at the memorial is important because it is necessary to refurbish regularly the image of Pat's military career. It is as clouded as Bill Clinton's since Pat's father, a U.S. senator, reputedly had his son transferred from a troop ship bound for combat to supply duty during the Korean War (Boston 1996, 41).

The video logo closes with shots of the newsroom in action and shots of *The 700 Club* playing on a television set in a working-class living room. Lyrics of the upbeat song that run over this spot include lines such as "We believe that love endures forever and the joy can be expressed in how we live" (seen over Pat's rich lifestyle), "children bring us all together, and friendship is the best thing we can give," "someone you can talk to who will help you see it through" (at the Vietnam Memorial), and "friends you can turn to" (over the staff preparing the show).

The 700 Club self-consciously fulfills a number of functions. It serves as a televisual community for its regular viewers. It both entertains and, in the sense that Grossberg refers to above, invigorates viewers. It also sets the parameters of discourse for this viewership, both cognitively and emotionally. It signals viewers how to (or when not to) invest themselves in certain "experiences, practices, identities, meanings, and pleasures." For this virtual community, *The 700 Club* offers the pleasures of gemeinschaft, a shared set of assumptions, and a smaller and more manageable subculture that gives the comfort of security in a rapidly changing age.[4] It lets the audience have the experience of modern media and respond to the show's invitation to learn about the modern world, the secular world, within a Christian framework. And within its shared framework of patriotism and Americanism, *The 700 Club* lets its viewers explore and constantly modify what "permissible identities" might be for Christian Americans. Unlike the reductionist rhetoric of Rush Limbaugh, who also builds his own kind of virtual conservative community, this show expresses popular conflicts and contradictions within its ultimate framework of "interpretation."

Bobby Alexander (1994) has analyzed this show's unique contribution to televangelism as allowing, indeed inviting, viewers imaginatively to try out new, upwardly mobile, class-based styles in dress, language, and attitude that would allow them to raise their aspirations in class terms. Middle-class viewers can identify with the image of Pat as a rich man, "expressing joy in how he lives"; furthermore, the show regularly offers interviews with other rich people—usually men—who offer an image of the capitalist ideal of successful Christian business people. In particular, Ben Kinchlow daily offers a visual variation on the perfect picture of a rich black man. His white hair is impeccably coifed (perhaps partially straightened), and each day he appears in a new outfit, including a different suit, shirt, tie, and handkerchief. His role as fashion plate gives viewers an extraordinary visual vocabulary to teach them what it means to be a fashionably dressed man or what it might mean ideally to be a visual exemplar of a black man. Pat's style is more conservative, that of the old rich. And although Terry is a former Miss America, she demonstrates through her tasteful daily wardrobe changes what a lady dressed in colorful but conservatively tailored clothes should wear. She accessorizes with beautiful scarves and fashionable, simple jewelry. She never wears the figure-hugging clothes that other women talk show hosts do, but she usually has on long suit jackets or overblouses and skirts of modest length that deemphasize her figure while flowing gracefully as she walks.

The news shows provide a sense of being up-to-date and teach a current events or contemporary-culture vocabulary. Furthermore, this community is encouraged to get involved with extremely current media developments, particularly the use of computers and the Internet. The show offers a Christian reason to overcome technophobia. *The 700 Club* has become the vehicle par excellence for letting evangelicals enter the modern world while avoiding the feared pitfalls of "modernism."

Bobby Alexander also draws on anthropologist Victor Turner's idea that people need rituals to build and constantly reaffirm community, which they do by "performing" it. Television lets viewers constantly perform one of the key rituals of capitalism, one that reinforces Americans' most prized shared value, that is, the ritual of consumption. Turner says that performing a ritual gives people a way of relating to the world and to others, even though it seems temporarily to suspend participants from the everyday. The key ritual aspect of *The 700 Club* is its emphasis on televisual community prayer and subsequent charismatic healing. Each program has a central segment in which the hosts read letters from viewers, both from those who have been healed or spiritually called to Jesus through the show and from those who need healing. Ben and Terry describe various physical manifestations of illness, and Ben says: "We command this to heal now, in Jesus' name." Viewers and people in the audience hold hands and pray along. The whole institution of the show asserts the possibility of collapsing distance in this way and saving souls and bodies over the airwaves. Ben also requests that the saved and healed call and talk to a counselor, to share the good news, in a toll-free call. In fact, what the letters to *The 700 Club* indicate, and what televangelists have presumed all along, is that the casual viewer might just experiment and try out praying along. Whether because of a placebo effect or not, enough viewers get relief from illness, pain, and mental distress to write back, call in, and perhaps join a church. This is the motor that has driven both revivals and televangelism for years.

When they consider the political effect of televangelism and talk shows, liberal critics often focus on the obvious: how narrowly the hosts interpret current events. However, what is equally significant is that millions of listeners "authorize" a Ben Kinchlow or a Rush Limbaugh to speak for them, granting the television figures the authority of the healer, in the case of *The 700 Club,* or the authority of the mercurial iconoclast who articulates a sense of dumbfounded outrage, in the case of Rush Limbaugh. It is easy to criticize these programs for emotionally manipulating audiences and for reducing discussions of social issues to the least common denominator, but it would be a mistake not to understand the power these broadcasters have to reach large numbers of people and weave around those viewers the sense of community, of ties to others who share a moral, social, and often religious worldview. Many differences among viewers are suppressed while this sense of community prevails, but it is important that we understand how the religious right constructs a sense of community if we are to understand how it is that someone who has lost a job due to corporate downsizing, who has a gay relative or who is gay, or who has had an abortion or helped a friend or relative get one can look away from that part of his or her life to affirm the pleasure of being inside a tightly knit, moral, empowering, and secure world.

Right-Wing Advocacy Media's Rhetoric

Within its overarching project of reconstructing daily life, conservative discourse provides many consolations. It relies on familiar, ideologically coded expressions, phrased in terms that have a lasting symbolic value in the United States. In particular, conservative perspectives on social issues constantly shift the discussion to the plane of the "small world"—that of individual moral will and the family. Conservative appeals to individualism and idealized gender and family roles draw upon hegemonic structures of feeling to evoke a sense of ideological inclusion (us versus them) and thus community. This ideological project of simplification and absolutism, where only a narrow range of social positions is addressed, is described at length by various authors in this book. From a theoretical perspective, Linda Kintz analyzes the mechanisms and political implications of the religious right's drive for clarity, which results from its unquestioningly embracing natural law and the free market. Other authors—Steven Gardiner, Chip Berlet, Ioannis Mookas, Laurie Schulze, and Frances Guilfoyle—discuss these rhetorical strategies of moralizing and reductionism concretely in terms of initiative campaigns, notably in Oregon and Colorado, to limit homosexual rights.

In Chapter 14, a critique of the right-wing film *Gay Rights/Special Rights,* Ioannis Mookas refers to social developments in the United States in the 1970s and 1980s traced by Michael Omi and Howard Winant in *Racial Formation in the United States from the 1960s to the 1990s* (1994). Omi and Winant find that a key element of the right's attack on affirmative action and racial equality lies in a successful rhetorical strategy that calculatedly shifts the U.S. discourse on race from the standard of *group rights,* judged by "equality of results," back to the far older standard of an *individual's right* to equality of opportunity. To see rights as only adhering to the individual, not to a disadvantaged group, also implies that only the meritorious deserve rights and that these are individuals from morally sanctioned populations who demonstrate the will to raise themselves out of poverty or other adverse circumstances. Indeed, this concept of raising oneself by the bootstraps neatly incorporates both the ideology of individualism and that of free-market competition. Omi and Winant trace the historical basis of this regression in the public discourse around civil rights to the transformations and dislocations of the 1970s and 1980s:

> Commonly held concepts of nation, community, and family were transformed, and no new principle of cohesion, no new cultural center, emerged to replace them. New collective identities, rooted in the "new social movements," remained fragmented and politically disunited. In short, the U.S. was politically fragmented as differences of all sorts—regional, racial, sexual, religious—became more visible while economic stability and global military supremacy seemed to vanish. A plethora of interest groups, it seemed, had suddenly emerged, invoking a bewildering array of new social and political values, creating unprecedented political disorientation, and leaving the "mainstream" with no clear notion of the "common good." (1994, 121–22)

Furthermore, Omi and Winant point out that a mostly middle-class, mostly white flight to the suburbs created a population willing to tax itself for direct social services but unwilling to pay for social welfare programs. The "plethora of interest groups"[5] are now often viewed in conservative discourse as "special interests" catered to at the expense of hard-working whites, whose resentment has been stoked against group rights.

The political theme of "No Special Rights," so effectively used in the Oregon and Colorado antigay initiative efforts, was developed, according to Chip Berlet, after more than a decade of the organized right's "field testing" various media campaigns aimed at turning homophobia into a political weapon. Berlet locates the origins of this strategy in Paul Weyrich's 1981 request to his Free Congress Foundation staff member Father Enrique Rueda to research the homosexual movement in the United States. In his resulting book, *The Homosexual Network,* Rueda expresses alarm at how much this "network" has "infiltrated" many major U.S. institutions. Such a conspiracy theory has much in common with older anti-Semitic fears that rich Jewish bankers secretly control international finance; currently in right discourse around homosexual privilege, this conspiracy theory is combined with statistics demonstrating that homosexuals are more affluent and have more disposable income than the rest of the population. Ironically, such statistics were first developed by the national gay press about their subscriber base in order to attract advertising revenue, and these claims, both from the homosexual press and from the right, continue to erase the existence of poor and working-class gays and lesbians (Kahn 1993, 27).

In Colorado's Amendment 2 initiative campaign, analyzed by Laurie Schulze and Frances Guilfoyle in Chapter 13, right-wing television ads featured black speakers referring with pride to "their" civil rights movement and denouncing the extension of their legal victory to homosexuals as a group since homosexuals can freely choose their lifestyle. Similarly, the film *Gay Rights/Special Rights* draws an extended comparison between racial discrimination and discrimination against homosexuals. In the film, Lou Sheldon states: "They [homosexuals] want to be elevated... to a true minority status that would give them special rights." As Mookas points out,

> A term without any legal definition, "minority status" is actually a clever mutation of "protected classes," the legal term for discrete groups historically prevented from sharing fully and equally in civic realms such as employment, housing, and public accommodations because of bias, discrimination, or prejudice. Since we are still accustomed to thinking of minorities as primarily racial, "minority status" is employed to inflame the deeply rooted anxieties in white subjectivity over economic displacement.

Thus, the term "special" used in antihomosexual campaigns resonates with the concepts of "privileged" and "exceptional" and "tiny fraction" that conspiracy theories like Rueda's explicitly propose.

I draw this extended example not only to demonstrate how effectively the right can separate two constituencies who need to unite to defend the legal concept of "group rights"—homosexuals and people of color—but also to indicate the degree to which right discourse has shaped public discourse in the United States. That the public, legal struggle over gay rights has been definitively shaped by right-wing rhetoric can be confirmed by looking at the United States Supreme Court decision declaring Colorado's Amendment 2 unconstitutional.

The majority opinion, written by Justice Anthony Kennedy, confirms the applicability of a concept of "group rights" to homosexuals seeking political redress for discrimination; it also testifies to the *malice* expressed toward homosexuals in the initiative campaign against them:

> We find nothing special in the protections Amendment 2 withholds. These are protections taken for granted by most people either because they already have them or do not need them; these are protections against exclusion from an almost limitless number of transactions and endeavors that constitute ordinary civic life in a free society.... [L]aws of the kind now before us raise the inevitable inference that the disadvantage imposed is born of animosity toward the class of persons affected. (Kennedy 1996)

Significantly, in his angry dissent, Justice Antonin Scalia's vocabulary echoes the rhetoric propagated on the right about homosexuals. Scalia specifically denounces the "efforts of a politically powerful minority" to revise the traditional sexual mores that "seemingly tolerant Coloradans" are making a "modest attempt" to preserve. In particular, he echoes the conspiracy theories about homosexuality so carefully nourished by both mainstream religious conservatives and the far right:

> The problem (a problem, that is, for those who wish to retain social disapprobation of homosexuality) is that, because those who engage in homosexual conduct tend to reside in disproportionate numbers in certain communities,... have high disposable income, and of course care about homosexual-rights issues much more ardently than the public at large, they possess political power much greater than their numbers, both locally and statewide. Quite understandably, they devote this political power to achieving not merely a grudging social toleration, but full social acceptance, of homosexuality... The Court has no business imposing on all Americans the resolution favored by the elite classes from which the members of this institution are selected, pronouncing that "animosity" toward homosexuality... is "evil." (Scalia 1996)

The discourse propagated as common sense through a network of conservative institutions is now explicitly part of the rhetoric of the Supreme Court. And it is in both the legal sphere and the sphere of popular political activism that the struggle will continue to define the meaning of the term "rights."[6]

Notes

1. See Linda Kintz's book on this subject, *Between Jesus and the Market: Sacred Intimacy and Free Enterprise* (1997).

2. See John Caldwell's *Televisuality: Style, Crisis, and Authority in American Television* (1995) for an explication of contemporary television aesthetics.

3. Mark Schapiro (1994) describes a visit to Dobson's Colorado Springs headquarters in detail.

4. Alvin Toffler, author of *Future Shock*, is friend to Newt Gingrich and one of the gurus of the religious right.

5. See Thomas Byrne Edsall and Mary D. Edsall, *Chain Reaction: The Impact of Race, Rights, and Taxes on American Politics* (1991).

6. A number of civil rights groups are represented by our authors. Chip Berlet is a senior analyst for Political Research Associates, 120 Beacon Street, No. 202, Cambridge, Mass., 02139; for an article detailing that group's work, see Nicholson 1995, 23. Steven Gardiner is a researcher for the Coalition for Human Dignity, P.O. Box 40344, Portland, Ore., 97240. I have also drawn extensively upon the Interfaith Alliance's large (605K) document, "How to Win" (Radical Right Task Force 1994).

Works Cited

Alexander, Bobby C. 1994. *Televangelism Reconsidered*. American Academy of Religion Series, no. 68. Atlanta, Ga.: Scholar's Press.

Balz, Dan, and Ronald Brownstein. 1996. *Storming the Gates: Protest Politics and the Republican Revival*. New York: Little, Brown.

Boston, Robert. 1996. *The Most Dangerous Man in America? Pat Robertson and the Rise of the Christian Coalition*. Amherst, N.Y.: Prometheus Books.

Bourdieu, Pierre. 1984. *Distinction: A Social Critique of the Judgement of Taste*. Trans. Richard Nice. Cambridge: Harvard University Press.

Caldwell, John. 1995. *Televisuality: Style, Crisis, and Authority in American Television*. New Brunswick, N.J.: Rutgers University Press.

Christian Broadcasting Network. 1995. World Wide Web site *http://www.cbn.org*.

"Christian Coalition Presents the Contract with the American Family," 1995. Christian Coalition World Wide Web site *http://www.cc.org/cc/*, 27 June.

Christian Coalition World Wide Web site. 1996. Dates and places of upcoming spring workshops, *http://www.cc.org/cc/*, 16 January.

Curtis, Carolyn. 1995. "High Tech Activists—How Advanced Communications Are Changing the Way Pro-Family Activists Work." *Christian American*, October. Christian Coalition World Wide Web site *http://www.cc.org/cc/*.

Diamond, Sara. 1996. *Facing the Wrath: Confronting the Right in Dangerous Times*. Monroe, Maine: Common Courage Press.

———. 1995. *Roads to Dominion: Right-Wing Movements and Political Power in the United States*. New York: Guilford Press.

———. 1989. *Spiritual Warfare: The Politics of the Christian Right*. Boston: South End Press.

Edsall, Thomas Byrne, and Mary D. Edsall. 1991. *Chain Reaction: The Impact of Race, Rights, and Taxes on American Politics*. New York: Norton.

Finney, Charles Grandison. 1960. *Lectures: On Revivals of Religion*. Ed. W. G. McLoughlin. Cambridge: Belknap Press of Harvard University Press.

Frankl, Razelle. 1987. *Televangelism: The Marketing of Popular Religion*. Carbondale: Southern Illinois University Press.

Ginsburg, Faye. 1989. *Contested Lives: The Abortion Debate in an American Community*. Berkeley and Los Angeles: University of California Press.

Grossberg, Lawrence. 1992. *We Gotta Get Out of This Place: Popular Conservatism and Postmodern Culture*. New York: Routledge.

Kahn, Surina. 1993. "Tracking Gay Conservatives." *Gay Community News* 22, no. 1 (Summer): 7, 26–28.

Kennedy, Justice Anthony. 1996. Majority Opinion. U.S. Supreme Court Decision No. 94–1039, 20 May. *Roy Rohmer, Governor of Colorado, et al., Petitioners v. Richard G. Evans, et al.* Downloaded from Cornell University Law School World Wide Web site *http://www.law.cornell.edu/supct/*.

Kester, Grant, and Lynn Love. 1995. "Afterthoughts: The Right Stuff." *Afterimage* (Visual Studies Workshop) 22, nos. 7, 8 (Feb.-Mar.): 7.

Kintz, Linda. 1997. *Between Jesus and the Market: Sacred Intimacy and Free Enterprise*. Ann Arbor: University of Michigan.

Lesage, Julia. 1987. "Why Christian Television Is Good TV." *The Independent* 10, no. 4 (May): 14–20.

Moen, Matthew. 1992. *The Transformation of the Christian Right*. Tuscaloosa: University of Alabama Press.

Nicholson, Judith. 1995. "Political Research Associates and *The Public Eye*." *Afterimage* (Visual Studies Workshop) 22, nos. 7, 8 (Feb.-Mar.): 23.

Omi, Michael, and Howard Winant. 1994. *Racial Formation in the United States from the 1960s to the 1990s*. New York: Routledge.

Peyton, Jeffrey M. 1995. "High Court to Hear Colorado Case." *Christian American* (April). Taken from Christian Coalition World Wide Web site, 17 January 1996, *http://cc.org/cc/ca/ca04index.html*.

Peschek, Joseph G. 1987. *Policy Planning Organizations: Elite Agendas and America's Rightward Turn*. Philadelphia: Temple University Press.

Radical Right Task Force. 1994. "How to Win: A Practical Guide for Defeating the Radical Right in Your Community." Publication of the National Jewish Democratic Council, 711 Second Street NW, Washington, D.C., 20002. Downloaded from the Interfaith Alliance on the World Wide Web *http://www.intr.net/tialliance/index.html*.

Reed, Ralph. 1996. *Active Faith: How Christians Are Changing the Soul of American Politics*. New York: Simon and Schuster.

———. 1994. *Politically Incorrect: The Emerging Faith Factor in American Politics*. Dallas, Tex.: Word Publishing.

Rozell, Mark J., and Clyde Wilcox. 1995. *God at the Grassroots: The Christian Right in the 1994 Elections*. Lanham, Md.: Rowman and Littlefield.

Scalia, Justice Antonin. 1996. Dissenting Opinion. U.S. Supreme Court Decision No. 94–1039, 20 May. *Roy Rohmer, Governor of Colorado, et al., Petitioners v. Richard G. Evans, et al.* Downloaded from Cornell University Law School World Wide Web site *http://www.law.cornell.edu/supct/*.

Schapiro, Mark. 1994. "Who's Behind the Culture War? Contemporary Assaults on Freedom of Expression." Boston: Nathan Cummings Foundation.

Scully, Matthew. 1989. "Right Wing and a Prayer: Still Alive and Kicking." *Washington Times*, 8 November.

PART II

RELIGIOUS CULTURE IN THE UNITED STATES

RELIGIOUS CULTURE IN THE UNITED STATES

Because the term "religious right" has been used to join together very diverse interests and groups, this section includes three ways of framing both the movement's coherence and its variety, although it looks particularly at the Christian right. The first way of framing that movement is historical. Chapter 3, Nancy T. Ammerman's history of Protestant fundamentalism and evangelical movements in the United States reveals the longevity of many of the issues structuring contemporary political and cultural discourse. Though it may seem that certain issues have appeared very suddenly, they have actually emerged from the ongoing contradictions and struggles of U.S. history and cultural identity. In a related way, the criticisms of the amorality and decadence that are staples of contemporary conservative cultural politics have a long history in anticommunist activity in the United States, as Linda Kintz shows in Chapter 4, a study of the American ideology of authenticity and clarity, in particular when those are reinforced by the activism of conservative women like Phyllis Schlafly and Beverly LaHaye. The kinds of cultural messages advocated by the Christian right, when joined to a sophisticated network of electronic resources, have also fit comfortably into the simplicity of the sound bite and the instant message of contemporary media culture. And finally, the Christian right as a social movement has to be understood in a double way, as Steven Gardiner argues in Chapter 5. On the one hand, its remarkably successful national rhetoric has drawn on presumptions of homogeneity, even though the movement reveals diverse trajectories of transformation, which have constantly threatened that homogeneous message. While the Christian right's political successes have much to do with its ability to be many things to many people, its need for coalitions to achieve that breadth has also led to conflicts, for example, between economic conservatives and social conservatives. And as Gardiner shows, the more the Christian Coalition has developed the moderate language necessary for success in national politics, the more powerful has become the appeal, at the local level, of the uncompromising language of purists.

3

North American Protestant Fundamentalism

Nancy T. Ammerman

As fundamentalism reemerged in the United States in the late twentieth century after a period of apparent hibernation, no two words better captured its public image and agenda than the late 1970s term "Moral Majority," and later, in the 1990s, the phrase "family values." In 1979 independent Baptist pastor Jerry Falwell declared that people concerned about the moral decline of the United States were a majority waiting to be mobilized. He set out to accomplish that task, and since then through the Moral Majority and its successor organizations, especially the Christian Coalition, conservative voters have been registered, rallies held, and legislators elected. Ronald Reagan recognized religious conservatives as an important constituency, speaking at their rallies and inviting their leaders to the White House. And in 1988, politically active conservative pastors again had the ear of the president, Republican George Bush.[1] Currently the Republican Party is dependent on this vote to win office at all levels, from regional to national.

Pastoring churches and establishing schools were long the most likely strategies of people who called themselves fundamentalists. Not all saw politics and social change as their mission, and many had discounted such activities as useless, even counterproductive. At the same time that some fundamentalists were lobbying in the White House, others were waiting anxiously for the Rapture, the time when they would be transported to heaven. A book appeared that set 1988 as the date for this eschatological event, and many were convinced by its claims that the Jewish New Year, Rosh Hashanah, would be the appointed time.[2] Like many dates before it, this appointment with the end times went unkept, but believers were reminded again of how important it was to be "Rapture ready" and to seek the salvation of others.

Fundamentalists in North America can be found in both camps—waiting for the Rapture and lobbying in the White House—although our own times have seen an unprecedented growth in fundamentalist Christian activism in the electoral sphere. In both cases, whether anticipating the Rapture or struggling to influence state and local politics, believers have drawn on a distinctive view of the world that emerged about a century earlier. They are willing to argue that certain beliefs are "fundamental," and they are willing to organize in a variety of ways to preserve and defend those beliefs.

In the last quarter of the nineteenth century, many leaders in U.S. Protestantism were actively seeking ways to adapt traditional beliefs to the realities of "modern" scholarship and sensibilities. They were met head-on, however, by people who saw the adaptations as heresy and who declared that they would defend traditional beliefs from such change. In the first two decades of the twentieth century, the latter group produced essays that furthered their defensive cause. Among the most important was a series of short scholarly essays issued over a five-year period (1910–1915) entitled "The Fundamentals"—a name widely used to designate the threatened beliefs. In 1920, Curtis Lee Laws, editor of the Northern Baptist newspaper *The Watchman-Examiner,* wrote that a "fundamentalist" is a person willing to "do battle royal" for the fundamentals of the faith.[3] The term "fundamentalism" was both a description and a call to action, and the name stuck. During the 1920s fundamentalists actively fought against modernism in their churches and against the teaching of evolution in their schools. They lost those battles but retreated and reorganized into a network of institutions that has housed much of the conservative wing of U.S. Protestantism ever since.

However, "fundamentalist" is not synonymous with "conservative." It represents, rather, a subset of the larger whole. Fundamentalists share with other conservative Christians their support for "traditional" interpretations of such doctrines as Jesus' Virgin Birth, the reality of the miracles that Scripture reports (including Jesus' Resurrection from the dead), and Christ's eventual return to reign over this earth. Like other conservatives, they tend to support supernatural interpretations of events, whereas liberals tend to seek naturalistic explanations.

In U.S. society, conservatism in religion is widespread. In the U.S. population, 72 percent say that the Bible is the word of God, with over half of that number (39 percent) saying that the Bible should be taken literally. Almost two-thirds are certain that Jesus Christ rose from the dead. Nearly three-fourths say they believe in life after death.[4] And almost half (44 percent) could be called "creationists," since they believe that God created the world in "pretty much its present form" sometime in the last ten thousand years.[5]

Not all these people, however, are fundamentalists. Conservative Protestantism has a number of significant divisions. Among other things, not everyone agrees on that most central of doctrines: how people are saved, that is, how they make themselves acceptable to God. One branch of conservative Protestantism places primary emphasis on historic creeds of faith and membership in a church that confesses those beliefs. People are baptized, initiated, as infants into a community of faith.[6] These "confessional" churches are often conservative but are not usually the home of fundamentalists.[7]

Fundamentalists are more often found in the other, much larger branch of conservative Protestantism that identifies itself as "evangelical." For these people, only an individual decision to follow Jesus will suffice for salvation. They are concerned not only about their own eternal fate but about the destiny of those around them. They seek to "win souls for Christ" by their words and deeds, testifying to the necessity of a life-changing decision to become a Christian. They often speak of that experience as being "born again." This experience gives them a sense of personal and intimate communion with Jesus, and it often shapes their lives and conversations in noticeably pious ways.

But even the evangelical branch has significant subdivisions. Almost all black Protestants belong here, for instance, but they have developed independent traditions over two centuries of segregation that have made them distinctive from many white evangelicals. Blacks hold to many of the conservative doctrines of other evangelicals, and three-fourths of black churchgoers are in one of the black Baptist or Methodist denominations. They are likely to hold Scripture in high regard and to emphasize the necessity of being saved.

These churches were born out of the Great Awakening and the later southern revivals, and they have retained much of that evangelical heritage. But the distinctive style of African American worship and the distinctive relation of African Americans to society make the label "fundamentalist" less than apt. Theirs is a style of worship that is distinctive not for its doctrinal content but for the way in which it celebrates a separate ethnic tradition. C. Eric Lincoln has described the function of separateness as protecting the black believer from distortions that whites might introduce and as reinforcing and enhancing the very characteristics of African American worship belittled in white society. He claims that "black ethnicity denies the relevance of white styles of worship for black people and sanctions the ritual patterns developed in the churches of the black experience."[8] Theirs is not, then, a religiously based separation from a secular world but a racially based separation in which church and community are bound tightly together. In Lincoln's words: "In the black community the Black Church is in a real sense a universal church, claiming and representing all Blacks out of a tradition that looks back to the time when there was *only* the Black Church to bear witness to 'who' or 'what' a black [person] was."[9] When a black preacher speaks, he or she speaks for more than a mere congregation. In that sense, black evangelicals have yet to experience the modern secularization that has separated religious institutions from the political and economic mainstream. Theirs is not a rebellion against modernist compromises. Although they share many beliefs with other evangelicals, those beliefs function quite differently in their very different social world.[10]

Pentecostal and charismatic Christians in North America also belong in the evangelical family but are a distinct group within it. Beginning with the Pentecostal revivals near the turn of the twentieth century, new denominations such as the Church of God, the Church of God in Christ, and the Assemblies of God were formed. These emphasized "gifts of the spirit" (such as speaking in tongues and healing) as evidence of the believer's spiritual power. By the 1960s a similar emphasis on the Holy Spirit's power had also found its way into many mainline denominations, with prayer and healing groups meeting around the country in the parish halls of Catholic, Episcopal, Presbyterian, Methodist, and many other local churches. The *Christianity Today*–Gallup poll estimated that only about one-third of the nation's 29 million charismatics are in traditional Pentecostal denominations.[11] Whatever their denominational location, charismatics tend toward becoming "evangelical" in their insistence on a personal experience of salvation. But their religious experiences go considerably beyond the "rebirth" that noncharismatic evangelicals claim.[12]

Another group sometimes called evangelical or fundamentalist is the Church of Jesus Christ of Latter-day Saints, the Mormons. This group's reverence for its scripture, their disciplined way of life, and their aggressive evangelism sometimes cause them to be referred to as fundamentalist. The term "Protestant Christian fundamentalism," however, is not appropriate for most Mormons. While they share some religious and social characteristics with fundamentalists, they are certainly not Protestant. They accept few of the traditional doctrines that Protestant fundamentalists hold sacred, and their adoption of an unique sacred text, *The Book of Mormon,* sets them firmly at odds with Protestant fundamentalism.[13] In fact, in recent years Mormons have experienced a fundamentalist movement within their own ranks, with groups seeking to purify tradition and return to orthodox interpretations of their scripture.

African American churches, Pentecostals, and Mormons occupy the same general religious territory as fundamentalists. They are all conservative and evangelical, but they are still distinct from each other and from fundamentalists. Mormons have their own scripture; African Americans are defined more by race than by doctrine; and Pentecostals trust the revelatory power of experience more than do the more rationally oriented fundamentalists who seek to confine revelation to Scripture alone.

While we may be able to identify these other distinct subgroups, it is less clear whether or how we can identify fundamentalists as distinct from evangelicals in general. During most of the first half of the twentieth century, "fundamentalist" and "evangelical" meant roughly the same thing. People might use either name to describe those who preserved and practiced the revivalist heritage of soul-winning and maintained a traditional insistence on orthodoxy.

But as orthodox people began to organize for survival in a world dominated by the nonorthodox, two significantly different strategies emerged. Seeking a broad cultural base for their gospel, one group saw benefits in learning to get along with outsiders. They did not wish to adopt the outsiders' ways, but they wanted to be respected. They began, especially after World War II, to take the name "evangelical" for themselves. Billy Graham can be seen as their primary representative.[14] The other group insisted that getting along was no virtue, and they advocated active opposition to liberalism, secularism, and communism.[15] This group retained the name "fundamentalist." To this group we now turn our attention.

Central Features of Fundamentalism in North America

Evangelism

When fundamentalists describe how they are different from other people, they begin with the fact that they are saved. They clearly affirm their kinship with other evangelicals on this point. Much of their organized effort is aimed at seeking converts. They invite the "lost" to church, broadcast evangelistic messages over radio and television, print millions of pages and record millions of words on cassette tapes—all aimed at convincing the unconvinced that eternity in heaven is better than the eternal damnation in hell that surely awaits the unsaved. Preachers proclaim the hopeless conditions of lives not entrusted to Jesus, and individual believers invest much in prayer and testimony directed at the eternal fate of their families and friends. Evangelism and the salvation of individual souls remains at the heart of the message that fundamentalists proclaim to U.S. society in the late twentieth century.

Inerrancy

Fundamentalists also claim that the only sure path to salvation is through a faith in Jesus Christ that is grounded in unwavering faith in an inerrant Bible. As fundamentalists see the situation, if but one error of fact or principle is admitted in Scripture, nothing—not even the redemptive work of Christ—

is certain. When asked what else makes them distinctive, fundamentalists will almost invariably claim that they are the people who "really believe the Bible." They insist that true Christians must believe the whole Bible, the parts they like along with the parts they dislike, the hard parts and the easy ones. The Bible can be trusted to provide an accurate description of science and history, as well as morality and religion. And only such an unfailing source can be trusted to provide a sure path to salvation in the hereafter and clear guidance in the here and now. As Kathleen Boone has pointed out, fundamentalists imagine "themselves either steadfast in absolute truth or whirling in the vortex of nihilism."[16]

Such contemporary use of ancient texts requires, of course, careful interpretation. Studies of fundamentalists invariably point to the central role of pastors and Bible teachers in creating authoritative meanings out of the biblical text.[17] Fundamentalists live in communities that are defined by the language they use and the stories they tell. Community leaders, teachers in Christian schools, and Christian media personalities give shape to the way ordinary believers understand their world by offering interpretations that give the infallible text its concrete human reality. The more people are immersed in this fundamentalist community of discourse, the more easily they accept the Bible as completely accurate. They are more likely to question the validity of science than to doubt the unfailing word of God.[18]

Some aspects of modern science, of course, are not questioned (the earth's roundness and orbit around the sun, for instance). The interpretive task that fundamentalists undertake, then, requires a careful balancing of facts about the world presumed by moderns to be true with the assumption that the Bible contains no factual errors. Phrases that seem to indicate a modern view of the solar system (such as "circle of the earth") are highlighted, while statements clearly reflecting an ancient view (such as references to "waters" above and below the earth) are said to be poetic and not intended to be "scientifically precise."[19] Likewise, moral teaching in Scripture that seems to condone slavery or polygamy must be neutralized. Such teaching is neither endorsed as eternally relevant (with the notable exception of patriarchy) nor rejected as a mistake of ancient writers. Rather, such practices are deemed irrelevant to salvation, to be accepted if in keeping with the cultural custom and abandoned if not. Within any social arrangement, individuals can live fully Christian lives by virtue of their personal relationship with Jesus.

Because this idea of inerrancy is so central to the identity of fundamentalists, it is an idea that receives considerable attention and development. Theologians and church leaders worry about all the nuances of interpretation and arrive at various theories among themselves, but their worrying rarely affects the people in the pews. The primary affirmation of ordinary believers is simply that the Bible is a reliable guide for life. It contains systematic rules for living that have been proven over 6,000 years of human history. Fundamentalists are confident that everything in Scripture is true, and if they have questions about a seemingly difficult passage, they know that prayer, study, and a visit with the pastor are guaranteed to provide an answer.[20]

Premillennialism

Fundamentalists do not simply read the Bible to learn history or moral principles. They also expect to find in Scripture clues to the destiny of this world, to what will happen in the end times. From the beginning of the fundamentalist movement, traditionalists who were concerned about Scripture and doctrine were closely linked with people who were concerned about interpreting the Bible's prophecies. As a legacy of that connection, today most fundamentalists are "pre-Tribulation dispensational premillennialists." The ideas that go with that label are almost as complicated as the label, but one of the most important is the idea of the Rapture.

For fundamentalist readers of Scripture, one of the most central stories is Jesus' description of "the coming of the Son of Man" (Matt. 24:37–41): "Then shall two be in the field; the one shall be taken, and the other left. Two women shall be grinding at the mill; the one shall be taken, and the other left." Combined with words in 1 Thessalonians (4:15–18) about being "caught up together with them in the clouds, to meet the Lord in the air," a picture of heavenly escape is created. True believers will one day soon simply hear the heavenly trumpet and disappear into the sky, leaving those around them bewildered. That is the Rapture for which they seek to be ready. If the Rapture does not come before death, believers have, of course, the "hope of heaven" after death. But the Rapture might come first, meaning that even those with no reason to expect death do not know how long they have on this earth. The belief in an "any moment" Rapture, then, lends both urgency to the evangelistic task and comfort to persecuted believers.

While the Rapture is perhaps the most central feature of fundamentalist eschatology (that is, their beliefs about the climax of history), it is nearly overshadowed by the emphasis on prophecy that accompanies it. Believers are not content to know that Jesus is coming for them; they want to know when and what will happen next. For these clues they turn to the apocalyptic books of Daniel (in Hebrew Scripture) and the Revelation (at the end of the New Testament). Here there are great images of destruction and horror preceding the ultimate triumph of God. Believers interested in prophecy dissect these images to create a systematic scheme (often pictured in elaborate charts) that chronicles the Tribulation of the earth following the believers' departure, the rise of a world ruler (the Antichrist), and the final battle

(Armageddon) in which the forces of good and evil will meet. Only then will Christ establish a kingdom of peace and righteousness on this earth. That fundamentalists believe Christ will have to return before the millennium (thousand-year reign on earth) makes them "premillennialists" (in contrast to the more optimistic "postmillennialists," who thought human effort might usher in the reign of God). That they think the Rapture will happen before the upheavals of the Tribulation makes their position "pre-Tribulation." (There are also "mid" and "post" Tribulation positions, but they are less widely held.) That they divide history into such clear-cut periods, separated by climactic acts of God, is at the heart of being "dispensationalist."

Dispensationalists take their name from a reading of history that divides time into distinct periods (usually seven) in which salvation is "dispensed" in unique ways. The period from the time of Jesus' death until the Rapture is known as the "Church Age," in which salvation is by grace, obtained through belief in Jesus. In the periods before and after this age, salvation is granted differently. Therefore scriptures addressed to people in different ages may not apply to our own. Likewise, Scripture addressed to God's earthly people, the Jews, is distinct from Scripture addressed to God's heavenly people, the church. Sorting all of this out requires a good deal of effort, and many fundamentalists turn for help to the *Scofield Reference Bible* (1909) or the more recent Ryrie version (1978). Both contain extensive footnotes explaining the true intent of each passage of Scripture.

It is in these interpretations of prophecy, then, that fundamentalists depart most dramatically from a literal reading of Scripture. Prophetic words do not mean what they seem to mean to the uninitiated. Weeks are really sets of seven years, armies coming from the north refer to Soviet forces, "Tubal" is Turkey, and so forth. In these prophecies, believers discern a kind of secret road map to the unfolding of human history. They can cross-reference Scripture and the nightly news. They only occasionally set dates for the Rapture—they are, after all, repeatedly warned against that in the Bible—but they are constantly watching for the signs that it might be soon. And they distrust claims to orthodoxy made by people who do not take prophecy seriously.

Strict inerrancy, then, is taken by fundamentalists as demanding a premillennial interpretation of Scripture and attention to its "inerrant" prophecy alongside its inerrant history, science, and moral teaching. In this view, the truth of Scripture can be "proved" by its accurate predictions of future events, as well as by its practical advice about salvation and Christian living. The systematic derivation of facts and principles that is at the heart of fundamentalist interpretation lends itself to the systematic outlining of history and the future found in dispensationalism.

Separatism

The conservative orthodoxy and evangelism of fundamentalists clearly do not make them unique. As we have already seen, there are many nonfundamentalist conservatives. Even inerrancy and premillennialism are not fully sufficient defining characteristics. Among nonfundamentalist evangelicals there are inerrantists and premillennialists, but those views are both less dominant and held less dogmatically among nonfundamentalist evangelicals. And more important, few nonfundamentalist evangelicals would insist that eschatology is a critical test of faith.

The ultimate characteristic that has distinguished fundamentalists from other evangelicals has been their insistence that there can be tests of faith. Fundamentalists insist on uniformity of belief within the ranks and on separation from others whose beliefs and lives are suspect. The fundamentalist, then, is very likely to belong to a church with strict rules for its own membership and for its cooperative relations with others. It is likely to be an "independent" church, since so many of the denominations are seen as infected with apostasy and compromise. The true believer will also adhere to strict rules for her own life, shunning any person or practice that might reduce the effectiveness of her life's witness to the message of salvation. When confronted with unbelief, doubt, error, or sinful ways, fundamentalists weigh the possibility that direct confrontation might save a brother or sister from eternal damnation. If pickets at the doors of a movie such as *The Last Temptation of Christ*[21] will keep even a single soul from the fires of hell, then the effort is worth it. But if confrontation is only likely to drag the believer down to the level of the sinner, better to avoid the situation. Even if the believer might be able to witness to his buddies while they are drinking after work, the possibility for misinterpreting his presence (or even slipping into sin himself) is too great to risk. He would rather lose his friends than his soul. Simply getting along, not making waves, accepting the ways of the world, is not characteristic of those Evangelicals who deserve (and claim) the label "fundamentalist."

Emergence of Fundamentalism in North America: Retrieval of a Past

That a movement would insist on its separateness and opposition to the world around it is not surprising when that movement was born in conflict and eventually relegated to the margins of North American religion by those perceived to be in power. Much of what fundamentalism is today can be seen in conflicts that emerged in the latter part of the nineteenth century, largely in the urban, northeastern centers of U.S. and Canadian culture.

When today's fundamentalists speak of tradition or orthodoxy or "what Christians have always believed," they are most likely referring, even if unknowingly, to ideas, images, and practices that were prevalent in the late nineteenth century. It was a period that shaped them more than they often realize. Their "traditional" family values, for instance, assume as a norm the middle-class family form that had emerged from nineteenth-century industrialization with its "two spheres" for men's and women's work.[22] "Traditional" music in fundamentalist churches is likely to bear a copyright from the late nineteenth century. The doctrines they emphasize as most important are the ones they had to defend against "modernism" during that period. Even the informal network of organizations they prefer over formal denominational structure was characteristic of most of nineteenth-century Protestantism.

More subtly, the way fundamentalists think about the nature of truth reflects the view of science prominent in the period before the changes to which they responded. That view of science was, in fact, part of what they sought to preserve, namely, a way of looking at the world undistorted by human theory and open to God's design. In 1895, A. T. Pierson, speaking at a prophecy conference, put it this way: "I like Biblical theology that . . . does not begin with an hypothesis, and then warp the facts and the philosophy to fit the crook of our dogma, but a Baconian system, which first gathers the teachings of the world of God, and then seeks to deduce some general law upon which the facts can be arranged."[23]

Fundamentalism's systematic, rational approach to finding and organizing the facts of Scripture reflects the nineteenth-century scientific world from which the movement emerged.[24] George Marsden argues that both the theology and the science of fundamentalism reflect the "Baconian" view of the world to which Pierson referred in speaking of a system constructed by gathering "facts" drawn from the Bible and scientific data to be harmonized with these biblical facts. For scientists of the early modern period, such as Francis Bacon (d. 1626), the task of science was the discovery of the laws of nature. They understood the world to be organized by rational principles established by an all-knowing God and "truth" as objective and available to the "commonsense" reason of the sincere seeker. In this view, human senses apprehend facts, and reason discerns the underlying order in them. The task of science, then, is to catalog, organize, and derive theories about the true facts of the universe. By the late nineteenth century, the Baconian system was still the dominant scientific orthodoxy of the day, at least among ordinary, educated folk. It was no accident that Pierson knew something about Francis Bacon.

However, marshaled against this system by the late nineteenth century were various intellectual forces, one of the most influential of which was the legacy of the eighteenth-century German philosopher Immanuel Kant. The intricacies of Kant's critiques of pure and practical reason were lost on popular scientific culture in the United States, but they created a thought world accessible enough to challenge the Enlightenment's wholesale confidence in human reason and commonsense induction. By placing the subject at the center of the process of perceiving and knowing the world, Kant had called the entire scientific enterprise into question. Objective truth is always filtered through subjective experience and perception, he argued, and thus scientific knowledge is always shaped by the cultural and historical context in which it emerges. We cannot know "absolute realities." The "thing-in-itself" can never be apprehended but comes to us only through the welter of our sensory experiences. The order we perceive, the forms and categories through which we understand, are not demonstrably present in the natural world itself but instead are inherent in the ability of the human mind to reason.

And just as science depends on human reason, so also does moral philosophy. Kant held that an act is morally right not because of its consequences or because it conforms to any law but because it originates in a good will. The moral agent, then, must be autonomous, acting in terms of his or her own will, not God's, and the measure of his or her actions is their universalizability. We must be able to use our reason to choose actions that are good not only for our own benefit or that of our group but as a rule for all to live by.

Kant's ideas were but one element of an intellectual revolution that began to take shape in the nineteenth century, a revolution against which fundamentalists would eventually mount a counterforce. In the world of biology, Darwin proposed his theory of evolution and natural selection in *On the Origin of Species by Means of Natural Selection* (1859). In place of an orderly catalog of existing species presumed to have been created at one time in their current forms, Darwin proposed a scheme of changing, emerging, and disappearing species. Things natural, he argued, are not as they seem to be to the Baconian commonsense observer. They have a history unseen to the naked eye. The competition among species for dominance in a territory can rarely be perceived directly. Likewise, the shifting balance among creatures and their environment is not readily apparent. Nor is the static observer likely to perceive the changes from generation to generation that produce whole new species. Darwin's theory of the relations between simple and more complex organisms led him to propose that even *Homo sapiens* be seen as part of this natural, evolving order and thus as the product of natural selection (rather than a special creation). It was a theory that would make Darwin the fundamentalists' symbol of all that was wrong with modern science.

The world of society and politics was also transformed in the wake of the Enlightenment. New democratic governments and the new science of sociology began to challenge the assumption that traditional social forms reflected and followed the divine order of reality. As people experienced the upheaval attendant upon forging new political structures, they learned firsthand that human beings have a role in shaping their destinies. The French and American Revolutions were built on premises of human freedom that challenged older notions about status, participation, and the role of the church. The Constitution of the United States of America was unprecedented in the annals of political philosophy in its claim that the full rights of citizenship inhered not in the accidents of birth but in the dignity of human nature itself.

Just how broad the human role in society might be was the concern of a generation of sociologists from Auguste Comte (d. 1857) to Emile Durkheim (d. 1917). Comte proposed that humanity had passed from a stage dominated by theology and superstition into a stage dominated by metaphysics, that is, by an effort to understand the abstract forces that rule society and nature. The final stage to come, however, would be one dominated by reason and philosophy, a stage in which philosopher-sociologists would rule in enlightened fashion. Religion in its traditional forms would soon be left completely behind. Durkheim provided less speculative, but no less unsettling, analyses of human behavior. His study of suicide, for example, illustrated the power of social forces, which shape even so individual an act as suicide. Likewise, Durkheim argued, religious rituals are the expression of a group's solidarity: The very gods the group worships are projections of its own deeply felt sense of identity. Though he acknowledged that religion performed certain useful functions, he held out no illusions about its nature, stating that the morality we accept as divinely bequeathed is shaped by the very social worlds we have created and live in. In Durkheim's words, society is a reality sui generis, as potent in its unseen effects as the force of gravity.

Finally, even the inner world of the soul came under science's scrutiny. Under the psychoanalyst's watchful eye, the battle in the depths of the subconscious was fought not between God and Satan but between id and superego. Even the human personality was not what it seemed to be to the commonsense observer. It was driven by unseen forces to actions, fears, and dreams with meanings far beyond their apparent import. The human personality is shaped not by a unique act of divine creation but by interactions and traumas in the young child's life. The individual is a bundle of contradictory impulses, created and re-created by human effort.

In every area of intellectual life, then, nineteenth-century scholars were challenging two basic premises at the heart of traditional Christian orthodoxy. First they proposed that hidden forces and ancient natural processes have created and sustain human life. These are neither the commonsense, discoverable laws of a static Nature nor the cataclysmic action of an invisible God. Second, although these processes may be hidden from the naked eye, they are not, as the theists believed, beyond human manipulation and control. The moral code emerging from these challenges to Christian anthropological assumptions was direct and unadorned: We have no one to blame for our destiny but ourselves. Neither the natural origin nor human manipulation of the social, political, psychological, or biological realms conformed to previous notions about God's creation and ordering of the world. The new scientific worldview posed, in short, a challenge that could not go forever unmet.

But no aspect of nineteenth-century intellectual life proved more challenging than the turning of a scientific eye on Scripture itself. Around midcentury, German scholars had begun to study the Bible with the same critical tools being used to uncover the origins and meanings of other ancient texts. They analyzed its literary forms and its historical contexts and speculated about who really wrote which book and when. One of the most influential theories to emerge bore the names of the German scholars Julius Wellhausen and Karl Heinrich Graf. It asserted that the books of Moses (which contain accounts of the earliest Hebrew history) were in fact among the latest to be written in the Old Testament period, coming after the preaching of the prophets in the eighth century B.C. Even the history recounted in Scripture was not, according to them, what it appeared to be. These biblical scholars had great confidence that they could unravel all the apparent mysteries of Scripture. For some, angels became phosphorescence and the Transfiguration of Jesus the product of sleepy disciples and a beautiful sunset. Visions and miracles were recounted in modern terms. Biblical books were redated and stories were compared to other ancient literature. Some of these interpretations have survived, while others fell quickly by the wayside. This method of interpreting, however, became so accepted by the end of the century that "exegesis" and "criticism" became synonymous.[25]

The message of the new biblical scholars was that the Bible is neither the unique "word of God" nor the historical document it seems on the surface to be. Critical study disclosed that it is both much more and much less than it seems to the commonsense, faithful reader. It is more in that it is a record of human experience situated in particular cultural and organizational contexts. Ideas reflected in Scripture are part of a long history of ideas about the nature of the world and of human relationships with the divine. When and where they are recorded matters as much as the idea itself. Stories may have been recorded in an era very different from the one they describe, and they reflect the concerns of that later era along with the history of the earlier one. Biblical books bearing one author's name may draw from several oral traditions or have been composed by an anonymous school of disciples. Thus, Moses is no longer seen as the sole author of the Pentateuch, nor Isaiah as the single author of one seamless book. There is simply more to the Bible than meets the eye.

Yet with contextualization came the realization that the Bible was also less than it had seemed to be. If other cultures had also composed creation and flood narratives for their epics, then perhaps the words of the Bible should be considered as something less than an exact and fully authoritative divine revelation. Perhaps they are only perceived as such, accepted by believers but elusive of any absolute proof. Such implications of nineteenth-century biblical criticism would prove unsettling to the churchgoing Bible believer.

The cultural upheaval that occurred during this period was not, however, simply the handiwork of academicians. New attitudes and values were born of social and economic dislocations as well. The end of the U.S. economy's agrarian base had been foreshadowed before the Civil War. After the war, change occurred rapidly. The industrial workforce quadrupled before the end of the century. Railroads and telegraph lines made transportation and communication easier and precipitated economic expansion wherever they were built. Iron and steel were being manufactured at a record pace. New discoveries and inventions—from electricity to telephones—were changing the face of the nation. It was an age of vast growth in wealth, with huge fortunes being accumulated by men who would later be dubbed "robber barons."

Alongside the industrial boom, the forces of immigration and urbanization were transforming the social landscape, especially in the Northeast.[26] Between 1890 and 1920, 17.6 million immigrants entered this country, over half from countries where Protestantism was not dominant.[27] In 1890, four out of five New Yorkers were either foreign-born or children of foreign-born parents. These immigrants brought new languages and customs, but also new religious traditions. Catholics and Jews lived in the United States almost from the beginning, but had been everywhere a minority. The country's ethos had confirmed Protestantism as a sort of unofficial state religion. But now that was challenged by a new religious pluralism. Those who held orthodox Protestant beliefs could no longer assume that their views were shared, even by other religious people.[28]

These challenges from science, society, and the new biblical studies warranted response from the theologians and church leaders of the time. As the century wore on, some sought to redress the ills caused by unprecedented urban crowding and poverty through the Social Gospel movement. These church people wedded modern convictions about human capacity to shape nature and society to the doctrine of postmillennialism, which held that human efforts at righteous living would inaugurate the thousand-year reign of Christ. Accordingly, as evidence of righteousness they elevated fair labor practices and the provision of decent health care to the spiritual status of churchgoing. Walter Rauschenbusch (d. 1918), Washington Gladden (d. 1918), and Horace Bushnell (d. 1876) were the most effective champions of the Social Gospel. They encouraged Christians to take responsibility for the betterment of this world as a direct and necessary step in ushering in the next.[29]

Another approach to the new sociocultural conditions, often adopted alongside the Social Gospel, addressed challenges to Scripture by devising new interpretations of old doctrines. Each of the inherited Christian beliefs deemed unsupportable in the light of modern science—miracle stories, Jesus' bodily Resurrection and Virgin Birth, creation narratives—became interpreted as allegory, myth, or symbol, not as literal truth. By the 1890s, many Protestant seminary faculties were dominated by such views, and some denominations (most notably Presbyterians) began to make efforts at officially revising their historic creeds. Older beliefs about the Virgin Birth or the Resurrection would be reinterpreted to make them palatable to the modern mind. In this modernizing approach, science was taken as a reliable source of truth to which Scripture would have to adapt.

Bold innovation was also a noticeable response on the U.S. religious landscape. New movements interpreted the signs of the times and offered creative answers to the age-old questions posed by philosophy and religion. Some of them heralded a coming millennium that would bring an end to the age. Within Protestantism, such "adventist" movements flourished. William Miller was not deterred from his predilection for predictions when Jesus did not, in fact, return in 1844, and his followers rallied to become the Seventh-Day Adventists. Similarly, when Charles Russell's prediction of the end did not materialize in the early years of the twentieth century, the prediction was reinterpreted, and the Jehovah's Witnesses formed to pass prophecy on. At about the time Miller waited upon the Rapture, Mormons retreated across the western frontier to form their earthly kingdom in the desert. By the 1890s, they were content to take their place within U.S. society, seeking converts outside Utah and deepening the pluralism and variety of religion in the United States. Concern with the coming divine kingdom—in this world and in the next—was the driving force for these new movements. All adopted some new version of the millennium as their response to the challenges of this age.

Probably the most dramatic religious innovation of the day, however, was Pentecostalism. An emphasis on the Holy Spirit's power had been nurtured for a quarter century in the Keswick and Holiness movements that were spread by hundreds of evangelists from their bases in England and in New Jersey. These movements were a natural outgrowth of the revivalist piety of the day, and they nurtured many future fundamentalists as well. Millions of enthusiastic participants had prayed that they might be emptied of sin and self and filled with God's Spirit. They had gathered around the country in prayer meetings and revivals, businessmen's groups and ladies' circles. But the revival on Azusa Street in Los Angeles in 1906 brought a new dimension to the Holiness experience. There the power of the Holy Spirit was manifest in new ways, especially in practices of speaking in tongues and healing. People filled with the Spirit spoke in unknown tongues as they believed had happened on Pentecost. They also invoked divine power for healing physical infirmities, just as first-century Christians had. The news of the revival traveled quickly, as did the practices. Within twenty years, several new denominations had formed, groups in which such ecstatic religion was fostered.[30] Their response to their own longings for God's presence in an increasingly alien world led them into new experiences beyond the revivalist Protestantism from which they had come.

Each of these religious innovations, traced in barest outline here, can be seen as a response to the religious and social chaos of the late nineteenth century. Although many of the groups placed great emphasis on the strict interpretation of Scripture and a morally rigorous lifestyle, each also signaled a significant departure from the past, claiming some new truth as its revelation. Fundamentalists, too, would respond to that chaotic social environment, but their stated purpose would be restoration rather than innovation. They would take the materials of that nineteenth-century social and religious world and create a new synthesis of tradition that would carry them well into the next century.

A Developing Ideology for Fundamentalists

Those who would eventually claim the name "fundamentalist" were, then, also responding to the changes around them. Their response was not, overtly at least, innovative or adaptive but were instead an attempt to restore the purity of the faith. Conservative Protestants had a growing sense that adaptation constituted nothing less than heresy. If Jesus were not a virgin-born worker of miracles who physically rose from the dead, then how could he be other than a hoax? If the Second Coming of Jesus were not imminent, wherein lay their hope? And if the Bible could not be trusted to report the history of Israel and of the church, could it be trusted in matters of salvation? Their answer was a resounding condemnation of compromise and clear affirmation of the orthodoxy they knew.

Their affirmation, however, was different in kind from the affirmations of the generations that had preceded them. Their times would demand that the defense they mounted be innovative in its own right. Previous generations had accepted the Bible as true and had assented to orthodox dogma in a world where most, if not all, sources of cultural authority upheld those beliefs. Never again would that be the case. Those who would affirm the historical reliability of the Bible would forever after be forced to defend their affirmation. *Fundamentalism, then, differs from traditionalism or orthodoxy or even a mere revivalist movement. It differs in that it is a movement in conscious, organized opposition to the disruption of those traditions and orthodoxies.*

The New Fundamentals: Inerrancy

Fundamentalists' beliefs about the Bible therefore reflect both continuity and discontinuity with the patterns that existed before them. While it is true that most Christians before the nineteenth century had accepted Scripture as a reliable record, it was not until the latter part of that century that a doctrine defending the inerrancy of the Bible became central to Christian belief.

The story of the emergence of the doctrine of inerrancy is a mirror of the changes that convulsed the nineteenth-century Protestant world and eventually produced fundamentalism.[31] The scholarship that laid the foundation for a fundamentalist defense of Scripture was developed during the nineteenth century at Princeton Theological Seminary. At the beginning of the century, Archibald Alexander had set out to defend orthodox Calvinism against, on the one hand, the more subjective and individualistic interpretations coming from the revivals of the second Great Awakening and, on the other hand, the naturalistic assumptions of Deism. He addressed the former by insisting on the Bible's authoritative character (as against experience). He addressed the latter by asserting that everything in the Bible was in accord with scientifically verifiable truth. He assumed that science could uncover nothing that could contradict Scripture. The reader rightly led by the Spirit and the scientist rightly led by reason were bound to arrive at the same conclusions.

Alexander's student and successor at Princeton was Charles Hodge. Hodge went even further in applying Baconian science and Scottish Common Sense Realism to the study of Scripture. Scripture became a "storehouse of facts." Just as the scientist begins with facts, so does the theologian. Common Sense Realism, in turn, asserted that those facts were directly apprehended in the words of Scripture. One should not look for the ideas behind the words; truth is contained in the words themselves, words whose meanings are true and changeless, words that have the power to change lives. Hodge was able to ignore or dismiss the budding new German methods of biblical study, continuing to assume that sincere believers reading the biblical text would arrive at the same facts and the same orthodoxy.

That assumption ceased to be plausible by the time Hodge's son, Archibald Alexander Hodge, took over his father's post in theology in 1878. Working with the younger Benjamin B. Warfield, he set out to defend orthodoxy against the new challenges present in historical critical study of the Scripture. Warfield, especially, studied the critics' work carefully and addressed them directly. Still grounded in the Common Sense perspective, he looked to the Bible itself for proof of its authority and reliability. If the Bible claimed to be inspired, it could be trusted to be telling the truth, because it was, after all, inspired (a circular argument not likely to convince the unconvinced).

If his commonsense proof of inspiration was something less than formidable, his defense against critics was quite the opposite. To prove the Bible erroneous would require, he argued, that the critic prove that a disputed statement (1) was in the "original autographs" (the original texts untainted by copying and transmission errors, long ago lost and thus unavailable for inspection), (2) was intended to mean what the critic says it means, and (3) was really in conflict with a proven fact of science. Thus the orthodox interpreter had at least three lines of defense. The "scientific" facts could be wrong. The interpretation of Scripture could be wrong. Or the discrepancy could be due to errors introduced by human scribes and not present in the original.

Scripture's original writings, then, took on for Hodge and Warfield an increasingly supernatural aura. Those original autographs had to be inerrant. While human interpretations and errors may have crept in between our versions and the original, human reason could bring the texts into line with "true" science. Thus for Warfield, ironically, it was reason that must precede faith, reason that could sort out and prove the propositions of Scripture. Unlike his predecessors, Warfield could no longer assume that Scripture would prove itself. He maintained his confidence that human reason would in the end triumph, with true science and true faith ultimately pointing toward salvation and the kingdom. But it was no longer assumable that the "facts" of science and the "facts" of Scripture would be in harmony.

Warfield's successor, J. Gresham Machen, carried the rational defense of Scripture that Warfield and Hodge had formulated into the arena of the modernist-fundamentalist controversies of the 1920s. He would eventually find his old seminary too liberal and leave it to found a fundamentalist school, Westminster Theological Seminary, in Philadelphia. But the battling

Machen clearly stood on the shoulders of the Princeton scholars who had preceded him. And those scholars represented the nineteenth century's move from commonsense acceptance of the Bible's inspiration to a rational defense of it. By the end of the nineteenth century, both scholars and ordinary believers were working out ways to defend the reliability of the Bible.

Developing Organization

No movement, of course, consists solely of ideas. Those ideas must find some material form in persons, groups, publications, political activity, and the like. And those organizations are likely to have characteristic social locations, places where they make sense, places where people and ideas can come together. The places where fundamentalist ideas made sense, and therefore the locations for most early fundamentalist organization, were the urban centers of industrialized Canada and the United States—Boston and Toronto, New York and Chicago. People living in the countryside might still enjoy uniformly Protestant traditionalism, but people in cities could have no illusions about unanimous agreement on religious basics. Urban life disrupted the sense of religious continuity and tradition present in other times and places. It was in the cities that the challenge to Protestant ideas and hegemony was most clear.

Cities not only meant pluralism of belief and lifestyle; they also meant a complex division of labor. Industry and commerce occupied their niches, with public affairs and education increasingly distinct as well. Religion, too, began to be seen as serving specific, discrete functions. Its role in education diminished, as many Protestant colleges and universities became independent of their religious parents. As the nation moved from village to city, the church moved from village green to side street. Religion did not disappear or become unimportant, but it was separated from public economic and political life.[32]

It was also in the cities that organizational structures were taking shape that could become the carriers of a social movement. The activities that gave birth to and sustained fundamentalism were Bible teaching and preaching and the dissemination in written form of religious beliefs. Those activities took place in largely urban settings and gradually became distinct as an identifiable movement. In those early days, fundamentalism borrowed one organizational form, the revival, and created another, the Bible and prophecy conference. It was in those activities that leaders emerged and constituencies developed. Here ideas met the test of audience response, and ideologues worked out their compromises. As changing cities pushed people toward changing ideas, organizational structures emerged to shore up the faithful and rescue the perishing.

Urban Revivalism

Revivals had of course been an accepted part of the U.S. religious scene for 150 years.[33] The first and second Great Awakenings had created and sustained this form of emotional religious gathering, whose aim was to make people experience visible signs of God's power. Sometimes the preacher was as learned as he was passionate; sometimes he was unlettered and sensationalist. Sometimes, as in the first Awakening, revivals took place in the small towns of New England and the mid-Atlantic. Later, in the second Awakening, gatherings moved south and west onto the frontier. But always the emphasis was on individual decisions to accept God's offer of salvation, with refusal painted as having the direst eternal consequences. Sinners could look forward to judgment "in the hands of an angry God" (to use Jonathan Edwards's phrase). Such preaching effected visible changes, whether in individual converts' transformed lives or in renewed zeal among Christians. Whole communities sometimes became transformed. By the middle of the nineteenth century, the "awakening" had been institutionalized in the form of the "revival" and had moved largely to cities as its base. Even on the frontier, the "camp meeting" had become a regularly scheduled annual event rather than an unpredictable moving of divine spirit.[34]

Among the most prominent practitioners of the emerging urban revivalism was Charles G. Finney.[35] Not only a remarkable revivalist, he became a systematizer of the methods he practiced. He was the first to articulate revivalism's goal as "winning souls" and the first to set out a step-by-step method for achieving that goal and calculating its success. He urged his followers to use "any means" necessary to produce the powerful excitements that would result in revival. He matched means and results like a scientific experimenter. He also urged preachers to avoid complicated theological arguments in favor of words directly from the Bible, expressed in plain talk understandable by ordinary folk. Both the results (individual decisions about salvation) and the message (plain truths from the Bible) became democratized and taken outside the realm of institutional religion.

Finney was followed by Dwight Moody and Billy Sunday, each of whom further made revivalism's organizational structures more businesslike. Throughout the period, these preachers were touring U.S. cities, offering a message of salvation from despair and hell. Revival preachers spoke to the worries of the day—unbridled business, alcohol abuse, unassimilated (Catholic) immigrants—and offered a purification ritual both individual and communal. As drunkards, Catholics, and greedy businessmen repented of their ways, the community was reassured that their Protestant God still remained in charge.[36] The community of common sentiment and rhetoric the revivalists created was the womb from which a fundamentalist movement would emerge.

What the urban revivalists accomplished, then, was significant both for its religious consequences and for the organizational structures to which it gave birth. Here were gatherings in which people of nearly every Protestant denomination participated. No one congregation or denomination sponsored them; rather, sponsorship required cooperation. Therefore evangelism and Christian practice became more important than denominational tradition and dogma. If the participants could agree on the need for personal salvation, they would leave the details of doctrine for other times and places. At midcentury, such a lack of concern for the specifics of doctrine still seemed possible, since most of North American Protestantism could agree that personal salvation and piety were paramount.[37] Revivals, then, provided a meeting place that transcended denominational lines, bringing together potential allies in a fight that they did not yet know they would face.

Revivals also required the laity's active participation and support. Ordinary Christians gathered for weeks in advance to pray and study. They recruited potential converts and taught those converts about being Christian. They embraced a religiosity that called them to personal holiness and evangelistic fervor. Many became part of the Keswick and Holiness movements, where they learned to seek a "second blessing" that would transform them from mere "carnal Christians" to spiritual ones. Christianity in this tradition was not to be the specialized province of the learned clergy but the lifeblood of the ordinary person in business and home and school.[38]

Revivals also offered a natural activity to those concerned about prophecy and the end times. Millenarians who eagerly awaited the Second Coming of Christ wanted to save as many souls as possible before that time came. When new coalitions were later built, evangelists and premillennialists would be among the contributors.[39] Nineteenth-century revivals provided them with an early common ground.

It is no accident that during the nineteenth century, revivals moved increasingly toward an urban setting. The systematic, large-scale efforts they entailed were part and parcel of the urban industrialized world. It took a city to provide the base of support necessary for such efforts. It also took a city to provide the moral grist for the evangelist's mill. It was in cities that the ills of the day were most visible and that individuals seemed most in need of salvation, most disconnected from any source of grace. And it was in cities that Christians could organize to meet those needs. Revivals, then, had created a climate of evangelism and piety that permeated all of nineteenth-century Protestantism. They had also democratized religious practice and provided a meeting ground outside established religious structures for people not otherwise linked. Until well after the Civil War, revivals were much too widespread in practice to be characterized as unique to any movement or branch of religion. They were simply part of the religious life of the day. But their location in cities placed them strategically close to the upheavals out of which fundamentalism would arise, and their transdenominational structure laid the groundwork for alliances out of which a movement would emerge.

The Printed Word

These Bible believers who emphasized the importance of the word of God were also enthusiastic producers of their own words. This, too, helped to give shape to their movement. If they were not physically gathered in one place listening to their leaders' words, they could nevertheless share those moments' inspiration in newspapers, pamphlets, and books.[40] As efforts to communicate among scattered believers grew, the Bible League of North America added a new voice. Formed in 1903, this organization immediately began producing *The Bible Student and Teacher*. In the beginning its leaders and contributors were largely conservative Presbyterians. But as the apparent threat of modernism grew, so did its coalition of supporters. Ten years after its founding, reflecting the increased militancy of the day, the organization's name was changed to Bible Champion.

During the same period, two of the most influential publications in fundamentalism first appeared. In 1909 Oxford University Press published the *Scofield Reference Bible*. From the ideas that had developed over two generations of conferences and writing, Cyrus I. Scofield created an annotated Bible that would become the standard reference point for fundamentalists for most of the century. Where there had been competing notions about the details of Christ's return, now a consensus began to emerge as increasing numbers of people accepted Scofield's interpretations along with the literal Scripture they revered.

One year later the first of twelve paperback volumes appeared, a series entitled The Fundamentals.[41] It was a project conceived and financed by the brothers Lyman and Milton Stewart, who had helped found the Bible Institute of Los Angeles. The aim was to produce intellectually sound, popularly accessible defenses of the Christian faith. The preface to the fifth volume noted that these testimonies were being presented so that "the unbelief, which in pulpit and pew has been paralyzing the Church of Christ, may be overcome, and that a world-wide revival may be the result." The volumes would be distributed broadly to pastors, seminary professors, YMCA workers—three million of them in all.

The ninety essays the series contained ranged from defense of Scripture to doctrinal apologetics to personal testimonies. Although articles on the Bible were clearly central, the overall tone was surprisingly uncontroversial and the quality of the writers quite high. Many had earned doctoral degrees and held distinguished teaching posts. They could tackle an inflammatory topic like socialism with evenhandedness and conclude that the "church leaves its members free to adopt or reject Socialism as they may deem wise."[42] The series seemed to be important not so much because it broke new ground as because it pulled together ideas that characterized conservative Christians at the historical moment when they recognized that they would have to fight to preserve their faith. And, of course, it suggested what those conservatives might call themselves.

Fundamentalism as a Social Movement, 1915–1925

By 1915 the stage was set for fundamentalism to emerge with its own distinct identity. The upheavals of the late nineteenth century had produced a ready audience of followers. Those followers were involved in urban revivals, Keswick Holiness groups, the study of premillennial prophecies, and zeal for missions. In all of those activities they had a core of leaders whose ideas would soon be brought together into a fundamentalist movement. They had already worked out the elaborate but accessible defense of the faith that would serve them in the years ahead. In addition, those leaders were operating within an increasingly broad but distinct organizational network of schools, conferences, and publications. What might have happened in the face of increasing challenges to traditional faith was a gradual withdrawal from mainline denominations and from secular U.S. culture. What did happen was a spectacular period of conflict between fundamentalists and those institutions.

New Ideological Concerns

World War I triggered, among other things, intense interest in prophecy. Three International Prophecy Conferences were held between 1914 and 1918. Speakers examined the apocalyptic character of the times in light of the premillennialist teachings developed over the previous decades. As the birthplace of biblical critical methods, Germany seemed a natural target in a cataclysmic war against evil. At war's end the League of Nations evoked fears of the worldwide government that dispensationalists had come to expect as part of the Tribulation. And the growth of communism raised the specter of a world without God, again hinting of a Tribulation to come.

Perhaps neither the League of Nations nor communism would have seemed so threatening had they come exclusively from overseas. But the League of Nations was being promoted by the president of the United States, and in the 1919 Red Scare Communists were seen around every corner.[43] It seemed to many a time to shore up the lines of defense. Conservatives sought bastions of true belief, and they found few indeed. Even their own denominations seemed to have stepped onto a precarious slippery slope leading directly from doubting the Bible to godless communism.[44] In the postwar years, liberal Protestants enthusiastically embraced international ecumenism, hardly a trend to please those concerned about national and doctrinal distinctions. To protect Christian civilization was essential, and there was apparently no one to do it.

The chaos and tensions of the times drew believers outward, while the strength of the organizational structures they had built pushed them along. In this particular time, their message matched the needs of the culture. Those who rallied to the cause, calling themselves fundamentalists, sought to restore the true and sure belief that would keep the nation strong.

Evolution in the Schools

At the same time that fundamentalists were battling modernism in their churches, they joined forces with others to battle Darwinism in society. Ever since evolutionary ideas had come to prominence in the previous century, they had been fought by conservatives who saw each biological species (especially humanity) as God's unique creation accomplished in a historical period recent enough to be recounted in the pages of Scripture. World War I, however, gave the ideological battle new urgency. George Marsden argues that fundamentalists saw in the war the ultimate manifestation of a "survival of the fittest" mentality.[45] If one believes that the strong are destined to displace the weak, then war on one's neighbors seems only natural. The war became, then, a struggle between Christian civilization and German barbarism. Conservative minds linked the presumed German acceptance of evolution (and the role of German scholars in producing the historical-critical method of interpreting Scripture) to German aggression. Just as the United States was called on to defend Christian civilization against that aggression, so Christians were called to attack the ideas at the root of Germany's sin: evolution.

Fundamentalist concern about evolution might have remained a matter confined to religious circles had not William Jennings Bryan chosen in 1920 to take up the cause. For the next several years anti-evolutionism became a national fad. It drew together denominational conservatives and dispensational premillennialists, northerners and southerners, farmers and city dwellers. Fundamentalists organized rallies, at which Bryan spoke. People throughout the country became convinced that the future of civilization depended on banishing this atheistic and harmful dogma from the schools. And premillennialists who had thought political action useless in the face of an imminent Rapture found themselves obsessed with seeking social change.

In twenty states, as diverse as New York and Georgia, activists introduced bills in their legislatures seeking to prohibit the teaching of evolution.[46] In the Northeast those efforts never got very far. Many southern states saw real fights, but in most cases newspapers and universities could rally support among the educated public for freedom of thought. In two border states, Kentucky and Texas, the fights were especially bitter, and in Kentucky it took religious intervention to work out a compromise.[47] Yet in neither state did a law against evolution succeed. But in Oklahoma, then Florida, followed by Tennessee, Mississippi, Louisiana, and Arkansas, the outcome was the reverse: In these states anti-evolution forces got laws on the books with relatively little effort. For many in those regions, teaching evolution was simply inconceivable. Outlawing it was not difficult.

Nor would enforcement have been much of a problem in Tennessee had it not been for the intervention of outside forces. Whether John Scopes tested the law on his own or was induced to do so does not matter as much as what happened after he was charged with the crime of teaching evolution in Tennessee's public schools. The American Civil Liberties Union sent in a team of lawyers, headed by Clarence Darrow, to defend him, and the anti-evolutionists dispatched William Jennings Bryan. The result was a highly publicized clash between new and old, between science and religion, between city and country. Scopes was convicted as charged. But "in the trial by public opinion and the press, it was clear that the twentieth century, the cities, and the universities had won a resounding victory, and that the country, the South, and the fundamentalists were guilty as charged."[48]

In the days following the debacle in Dayton, Tennessee, anti-evolutionists organized furiously,[49] but their efforts were increasingly radical and marginal to the larger culture. Leaders began to fight among themselves. J. Frank Norris and Thomas T. Shields became tarnished by scandal. The racism of others was all too apparent. The Bryant Bible League, the Supreme Kingdom, and the Bible Crusaders all arose—and largely fizzled—in those years, unable to rally the nation against evolution or modernism. As Baptist and Presbyterian fundamentalists lost battles inside their denominations, they began to organize schismatic groups. After 1925 fundamentalism lost its credibility and with it the ability to rally national or even denominational support for attacks against Christian civilization's enemies.

In the battles of the 1920s, people in the United States sought for themselves cultural symbols that would make sense of the world as they now knew it. The cultural upheavals of the previous fifty years had climaxed in the Great War. And the war's anxieties lingered in the crises of the years immediately following. With its millenarian and anti-evolutionist allies, fundamentalism offered a vision of civilization restored. For a few years, early in the decade, many Protestants found that vision appealing. But after 1925 it became clear that whatever image the United States chose for its new self, it would not be the fundamentalist version of a restored Christian civilization built on an inerrant scripture.

Fundamentalism Transformed and Organized, 1925–1975

What may have appeared as the demise of a movement may better be seen as its transformation. After 1925 the culture ceased taking fundamentalists seriously as social and religious reformers. The crusade against evolution had been discredited in Dayton. Over the next few years, both Northern Baptists and Presbyterians would repulse fundamentalist attempts to impose doctrinal restrictions. People concerned about civilization's health would no longer gain a wide public hearing and would have to adopt other means. And having lost their fight to control the denominations, they would have to find other organizational bases from which to express their concerns. But fundamentalists had already built organizational structures that served to smooth the way into a new era of diminished visibility and diminished social activism.

The story of fundamentalism in the decades following 1925 is, then, a story of reorganization, but it is also a story of transformation. Until 1925 fundamentalists had thought of themselves as the restorers of Christian civilization and of orthodox religion. They had always assumed that the territory they desired to possess was rightfully theirs and only temporarily occupied by strangers. They were the true keepers of the heritage. However, after 1925 it became painfully apparent that neither mainstream religion nor the larger culture was willing to acknowledge their ownership. They had become outsiders.

Now that they were outsiders, their view of mainstream culture and religion changed. As insiders, they had been concerned with modernism as a perversion of the true faith, something to be purged from religious life. Now they proclaimed that the denominations were hopelessly apostate, no better (and perhaps worse) than the secular world. As insiders to the culture, they had fought evolution as a dangerous idea to be purged from the schools. Now they saw the entire culture dominated by non-Christian influences. They became convinced that all of society had come under the sway of ideas that excluded God, ideas they saw as forming a pattern and an ideology that they eventually termed "secular humanism."[50] In his 1946 book, *Remaking the Modern Mind,* Carl Henry wrote of the "secular philosophy of humanism" with its tenets of progress and human goodness.[51] He, and later others, would argue that Christians should be socially and politically active in an effort to reestablish Christian claims in a civilization now dominated by secular humanism.

In the face of that fact, the primary strategy adopted by fundamentalists during these years was the effort to save individual souls: the "call to evangelism" was the overarching theme of the post-1925 period. If the culture and the denominations could not be rescued, the reasoning went, then individuals must be the focus of mass evangelism and personal witnessing. Fundamentalism might have lost its public relations battles and waned as a social and political movement, but it remained lively as a force in the lives of a vast segment of the country's population. Even if orthodoxy was not welcome in the seats of cultural power, the gospel message of individual transformation and piety was quite welcome in people's everyday lives in many areas of the United States.

For those who remained true believers, fundamentalism offered a comprehensive and satisfying explanation for life's complexities. If society's condition seemed to be deteriorating, then the Rapture must be near. If there were choices to be made, then the Bible surely had the answers. Where others might be preoccupied with change and adaptation, believers could rest assured in unchanging truth. While no one could know with certainty what the future might hold, believers were proud to sing that they "know Who holds the future." Individual lives in disarray were put right by the clear rules and discipline of a fundamentalist lifestyle. While a changing, ambiguous world tossed lives and expectations about like flotsam, fundamentalists claimed an anchor in the storm. Just as their grandparents had sought scientific facts in Scripture, so these following generations sought principles to live by. Just as they continued to assume that true science and true belief could not exist in contradiction, so they also held fast to the assurance that right living demanded obedience to Scripture's rules and to the earthly authorities that Scripture commended to the believer.[52] People who chose fundamentalism chose a life of certainty in the midst of an uncertain world.

Organizations for Outsiders

Maintaining such a strict way of life and traditional way of believing demanded a great deal of people who were now outsiders to the larger culture. The movement remained alive, indeed thrived, in part because its institutional structure was so strong. The last generation's work had paid off in laying a foundation for this new phase in fundamentalism's history. Building on that foundation, both new and expanded structures emerged. It was a time of active reorganization.

New Denominations and Independent Churches

By the 1930s it was apparent that the major northern denominations were dominated by modernism and that there was little to be done to stem the tide. Fundamentalists began to face the painful, sometimes bitter, choice of separation.[53] What emerged over that decade were three basic patterns of affiliation. Some churches remained within the now-liberal denominations as a continued witness to the conservative heritage. Those churches, however, increasingly existed at the margins of their own denominations, often participating equally in the emerging network of more independent, fundamentalist organizations. Other groups of churches broke away to found new, conservative denominations. Still others chose the path of complete congregational independence.

Existing in a kind of parallel relation to these three northern paths were the large southern denominations in which conservatism still held sway. The southern churches had joined the rest of the movement in fighting evolution, but they had been little affected internally either by that fight or by other doctrinal disputes in the 1920s. The Southern Baptists and southern Presbyterians had also been little affected by the teachings of dispensationalism. To these inhabitants of a rural Protestant world, neither their church nor their culture seemed much in need of rescue. Neither dispensationalism's gloomy forecasts of religious decay nor fundamentalism's aggressive defense of Scripture seemed appropriate. Nor did it seem necessary to organize institutions to replace or supplement existing denominations. Southern churches shared a traditional, orthodox conservatism with their northern fundamentalist friends, but there was as yet little overlap in their organized activities. The primary connection between southern conservatives and northern fundamentalists existed in the person of J. Frank Norris, sometimes known as "the Texas Tornado" for his rhetorical style and incendiary personality. He pastored the First Baptist Church of Fort Worth from 1909 until his death in 1952, and during most of that time he acted as a gadfly in his own Southern Baptist Convention. He never gathered much of a following in that denomination, but he did what he could to work with Northern Baptist leaders in fostering aggressive fundamentalist cooperation. He supported the Baptist Bible Union in 1923, and he began his own "seminary" (actually a Bible institute) in 1939. In 1950 disgruntled Norris followers formed the Baptist Bible Fellowship—perhaps the most influential of the new denominations and quasi denominations emerging from the period.[54]

Those who chose more complete congregational independence often argued that the only biblical form of church organization is the local body. Any organization beyond or above that level violates Scripture. Some of the churches banded together for fellowship and cooperative ventures in the Independent Fundamental Churches of America (IFCA), formed in 1930, or the Baptist Bible Fellowship (BBF). The IFCA had its strength in the upper Midwest, while the BBF began to make inroads in the South. Many of the IFCA's members were not Baptist in background, so it offered a meeting ground with the broad interdenominational flavor of the earlier Bible and prophecy conferences. Another successor to those meetings was Carl McIntire's American Council of Christian Churches (ACCC), formed in 1941 in direct response to the Federal Council of Churches (an ecumenical, mainline organization) and the National Association of Evangelicals (a moderate evangelical organization). The ACCC too drew together a number of the new fellowships and denominations.

During this period local fundamentalist churches ranged from tiny groups on the outskirts of cities to huge metropolitan congregations. They offered their members an ideological home. When the rest of the world seemed to be living by the wrong rules, believing the wrong things, church remained the place where everything made sense. It offered people a way to understand the Bible and rules by which to live their lives. It also offered friendships and potential marriage partners, even support for hard times and help in finding jobs. Activities might go on nearly every night of the week—some evangelistic, some educational, and some just plain social. To become a fundamentalist was to join a group—a local, visible, supportive community. Living in a hostile world required nothing less.[55]

These churches' radically *local* sentiments revealed a kinship to the Landmark movement in nineteenth-century Southern Baptist life (which survives in organized form in the American Baptist Association). That movement argued, among other things, that only members of a given local church could partake of the Lord's Supper in that church and that only adult baptism by immersion in a Baptist church would count for church membership. They also argued against national organization of missions, preferring that local churches conduct their own local evangelizing.

On the issue of missions, however, the new independent fundamentalist churches differed from their Landmark cousins. These churches were eager to do mission work beyond their own locale and were quite willing to organize to make that possible. The form of organization they chose, however, was designed to protect their local autonomy and to help them ensure that no heretical missionaries would receive their support. The organizations through which they chose to do mission work were independent agencies, but ones that provided the extended support network that independent local churches needed.

Independent "Denominational" Agencies

Churches that shunned mainline denominations were not left without organizational support. For nearly a century people concerned about evangelism and Scripture and prophecy had been coming together in the revivals and conferences that had fed the activist movements of the 1920s. In the 1930s they simply took those forms one step further, expanding them and creating a loose network of church support and extension that replaced denominational affiliation.

Among the earliest U.S. and British efforts at overseas mission work, in fact, were organizations based in transdenominational evangelical coalitions. Just as nineteenth-century revivals were supported by groups beyond denominational lines, so mission work brought together sometimes disparate groups who shared an evangelistic zeal. Perhaps the most famous extradenominational mission agency, having survived since 1865, is the China Inland Mission. As the century wore on, however, independent agencies became less the rule and more the exception since much mission work came under denominational auspices. In the early twentieth century, American Protestantism, basking in the glow of its Reform-era postmillennial hopes, was eager to evangelize the world.

By the 1930s, however, the mainline denominations were struggling to keep a missionary force in the field. Liberalism did not lend itself to enthusiastic proselytizing, and money was getting tight. In 1933 conservatives (led by Machen) were so disgusted by the Presbyterian church's mission effort that they organized their own rival board.[56] That move only hastened the brewing schism in the denomination. And when fundamentalists left the Presbyterian church and other denominations, they often took their missionary zeal with them. They invested that zeal in dozens of independent mission agencies working throughout the world. At the very time that denominations were struggling, fundamentalist mission efforts grew by leaps and bounds.[57]

At the local level, evangelism and missions often took the form of the evangelistic crusade led by an independent traveling evangelist. Carrying on the traditions of Billy Sunday and his predecessors, preachers such as Bob Jones Sr. and John R. Rice pulled together a community's conservatives for an all-out effort at soul winning. They would later shun Billy Graham's similar but more ecumenical efforts, preferring to keep their evangelism unsullied by liberal associations.[58]

Special efforts were also directed at youth, especially college students. During this period, Youth for Christ (which gave Graham his start) and Inter-Varsity Christian Fellowship were thriving fundamentalist ministries. In 1951, Bill Bright started his Campus Crusade for Christ, and within ten years they had workers located on forty campuses in fifteen states. With their simplified Four Spiritual Laws version of the gospel, Campus Crusade workers sought out student leaders as well as student derelicts. They urged youth to follow God's "wonderful plan for your life," offering them fellowship and purpose in exchange for young adulthood's frequent experimentation and loneliness.[59] Smaller groups like Word of Life and Young Life targeted younger teens with camps and special programs. These parachurch youth organizations were joined in the late 1940s by efforts to begin Christian day schools as well.[60]

Another institution in this growing network of independent agencies was the summer Bible conference. An outgrowth of the Bible and prophecy conferences of the previous generation, these gatherings offered half vacation, half revival. By 1941 at least fifty different sites had Bible conferences—spread from Winona Lake, Indiana, to Red Feather Lakes, Colorado, to the Atlantic City, N.J., boardwalk.

Proliferation of Bible Colleges and Institutes

If it had not already become clear that mainstream educational institutions would not serve conservatives' needs, the defeats of the 1920s made it clear. Many Protestant colleges and universities had functioned under secular control for a generation or more. Denominational seminaries were now heavily influenced by historical-critical study of Scripture and liberal theology. The struggle at the Princeton Theological Seminary between J. Gresham Machen and his colleagues was a kind of last stand on the education front. When Machen lost at Princeton and left to found the Westminster Theological Seminary in 1929, the last major conservative stronghold seemed undone. By the 1940s, any evangelical or fundamentalist presence in major U.S. educational institutions had virtually disappeared.[61] On the one hand, fundamentalists had shunned scholarship as unimportant in the quest for souls. On the other hand, a liberal cultural establishment had shunned fundamentalists as obscurantist and obnoxious. The gulf between the two camps was growing.

Fundamentalists, however, had already begun establishing educational institutions of their own. The Moody Bible Institute in Chicago and the Bible Institute of Los Angeles were thriving. A few evangelical colleges of the nineteenth century, most notably Wheaton College in Illinois, retained their conservative orientation. Wheaton was a school with broad interdenominational ties, and its leaders had moved during the nineteenth century from centrist evangelicalism to aggressive fundamentalism.[62] During the 1930s Wheaton provided a mecca for bright young scholars who would shape the next generation.[63] Much further south, the Dallas Theological Seminary became the center for dispensationalist thought. But after the 1920s the need for new institutions grew. All over the country Bible colleges and institutes sprang up. In 1930 there were at least fifty institutes considered "true to the faith."[64]

Within the next generation, many institutes became four-year colleges, some accredited, some not. The Bible colleges were usually designed to give their students a broad base of learning—from the sciences to history and mathematics—carefully kept within the guidelines of inerrant Scripture. The subjects of the liberal arts and sciences were taught, but with a particular conservative flavor. Though there were fewer of these schools than of Bible institutes, their total enrollment doubled during the financially troubled 1930s.[65] Those that remained Bible institutes were more narrowly defined organizations designed to teach specifically religious skills and interpretations. Evangelism techniques, Bible-teaching skills, and explorations of doctrine formed the heart of their curriculum. They began with and continued to include training for Christian laity. But they also trained pastors and missionaries. They taught much more than on-site or in-residence programs. They held weekend workshops in churches, supplied guest preachers, and sponsored various other extension programs. In 1937 the Moody Bible Institute enrolled nearly 15,000 people in its correspondence programs. Bible institutes became effectively the new denominational headquarters.

Of course, these new institutions had to develop new bases of financial support and student recruitment. The increasing number of independent churches and parallel independent agencies provided that. The Bible colleges and institutes also benefited from an increased circulation of published fundamentalist communications and from innovations in the media through which that communication was received—innovations and growth that Bible institutes, in turn, helped to introduce and sustain.

Publishing and Broadcasting

A distinctive fundamentalist publishing network had begun to take shape with the previous generation. National transdenominational magazines and journals already existed, as well as large publishing houses for conservative books and Bibles. Many Bible institutes had their own magazines and other publications. As with other nondenominational institutions, growth in publications followed on the heels of conservative defeats. As fundamentalists could no longer trust or enjoy the materials they received from their denominations, they sought out new suppliers. The publishing arms of Bible institutes—most notably Moody's huge Colportage Association—benefited from this new market. Houses such as these gladly produced the Sunday school literature, books, and periodicals needed to educate the growing segment of independent churches and new denominations. Continuing in the tradition of newspaper and magazine publishing were John R. Rice's *The Sword of the Lord* (a millenarian monthly), *The Sunday School Times,* and magazines from many of the Bible institutes. Among the most widely circulated of these was probably the *Moody Monthly.* These publications kept ideas and leaders before the people, and they advertised the schools, books, and trinkets that were the material and intellectual substance of fundamentalist culture.

Fundamentalists had always sought to use modern technologies in the service of the gospel. Revivalists had developed thoroughly modern business organizations to support their message's delivery. They met in large halls equipped for the task. They became nationally organized businesses for winning the most souls most efficiently. It was only natural, then, that they would leap at the chance to move beyond personally delivered messages and printed words. When radio came on the scene, revival preachers were quick to seize the opportunity. During this era, the most popular religious radio program (indeed perhaps the most popular radio program of any kind) was Charles Fuller's *Old-Fashioned Revival Hour.* Beginning as the *Radio Revival Hour* in 1934, Fuller's program featured a skillful combination of music and straightforward gospel preaching. By evoking the rituals of old-fashioned religion, he obviously struck a responsive chord for many displaced people. In his first anniversary broadcast, he talked about the many letters he had received from "heart-broken, heart-hungry humanity, some contemplating suicide, yet hundreds have come, cheery and full of thanksgiving that they have received comfort and new hope and strength from hearing God's Word again, and hearing the songs they used to sing 'back home' with Mother."[66]

While "official" religious slots on the networks were distributed free to "official" representatives selected by the Federal Council of Churches of Christ, fundamentalist preachers were grudgingly willing to buy time, often on independent stations, for programs that sometimes proved more popular than the ones by "official" denominations. A dozen or so major national programs were joined by hundreds of local ones. They included revival-style preaching, Bible study classes, gospel music, and personalities with whom listeners came to identify in the peculiarly intimate way fostered by broadcast media.

By the early 1950s, a new medium, television, had emerged, and fundamentalists were again eager experimenters. Revivalists such as Billy Graham, Rex Humbard, and Oral Roberts were the pacesetters, adapting their usual style and format to the small screen's demands. By the 1960s, conservatives understood the broadcast media's power to create national audiences for their message. When in 1960 the Federal Communications Commission began to allow *paid* time to count toward stations' public service requirements, the desires of the stations and the desires of the preachers dramatically coincided. A surge in paid conservative religious broadcasts soon pushed mainline religions' free broadcasts into near oblivion.[67] Ministries dedicated to broadcasting slowly began to replace revivalists and Bible institutes as the "denominational" centers of the movement.

All these institutions perpetuated an evangelical view of the world, even in a time when the culture and the rest of religion seemed hostile to it. This vast, seemingly invisible, institutional empire provided a home for outsiders to the religious and cultural mainstream. These same institutions also provided the base from which revival spread into the mainstream during the 1950s and from which a reform movement would rise again in the 1970s.

Political Radicalism

Becoming outsiders meant for some fundamentalists a move toward political and cultural radicalism. The 1930s saw the rise of what Sydney Ahlstrom calls "demagogues of the right."[68] Men like Gerald Winrod and Gerald L. K. Smith toured the country preaching a message of conspiracy and hatred. Winrod had been active in the anti-evolution and fundamentalist movements of the 1920s, developing close ties to those causes' leaders and organizations. Based in Wichita, Kansas, he formed his Defenders of the Christian Faith, an organization to combat the teaching of evolution and other perceived threats to Christianity. By 1934 his journal had 60,000 subscribers. He saw the political and economic crises of the 1930s as primarily spiritual in character, signs of the coming end times. By mid-decade, he had concluded that the Antichrist would be a Jew, convinced that "a Jewish elite had played satanic roles in a divinely directed drama now drawing to a close. The modern version of this plot provided an 'exact parallel' to Bible prophecies about the last days."[69] That conclusion led to his predicting an alliance between Hitler and Stalin—both anti-Semites—his declaration that Roosevelt was really a Jew, and his adoption of the Protocols of the Learned Elders of Zion as the centerpiece of a comprehensive theory about a Jewish conspiracy to rule the world.[70] Such preachers used ideas never far below the surface of U.S. politics. They gave voice to the sentiments of the U.S. population's most marginalized and disenfranchised.

This anti-Semitism stood in stark contrast to the pro-Zionism of most premillennialists. Believing that the Jews would play a decisive role in the unfolding of the end times, dispensationalists were eager to see a Jewish state and were protective of Jewish people.[71] During the 1930s, many fundamentalist publications and mission societies began to become aware of the situation in Europe and sought to alert their readers.[72] These were people who believed that God had promised to "bless those who bless the Jews," people who placed evangelism ahead of political or ethnic considerations.[73]

Later, in the 1950s, a few visible fundamentalist leaders took up the banner of radical anticommunism. Carl McIntire, founder of the ACCC, had picked up this theme in the early days of the fundamentalist movement, but during the Cold War era his concerns found a wider hearing. His accusations against church leaders earned him a place among Senator Joseph McCarthy's helpers. He assembled lists of Communist sympathizers among the clergy and charged that the Revised Standard Version of the Bible was the product of a Red plot. His organization also helped to launch the careers of Billy James Hargis and Major Edgar Bundy, among the most visible of the anticommunist crusaders of the 1950s and beyond. Both Hargis and McIntire spread their message through popular radio broadcasts. These radical leaders were joined in 1958 by the John Birch Society in a growing crusade dominated by conspiracy theories and active in secular politics.[74]

Communism, of course, was not the only enemy identified by radical right leaders. For the John Birch Society, communism was the chief enemy, and blacks and Jews were welcomed as members. Hargis, however, was instrumental in linking white racial concerns with anticommunism and concern for religious orthodoxy. For the various Ku Klux Klans, blacks and Jews symbolized the greatest threats to white Christian civilization. For the more recent Christian Identity movement, sometimes organized into militias, only white Christian Americans can claim God's blessing as a "chosen race." And those known as Survivalists are so convinced of immanent threat that they are physically and militarily prepared for a siege. A small core of radical activists and a somewhat larger core of sympathizers have kept alive a continuing strand of fundamentalist religion tied to various racial and political conspiracy theories.[75]

Conspiracy politics, however, was not representative of U.S. religious conservatives of the time. Evangelicals were much more concerned about supporting the next Billy Graham crusade than about routing Communists from the Eisenhower cabinet. Many fundamentalists were unwilling to tolerate McIntire and his associates' political rhetoric and activities. The Orthodox Presbyterians, the Evangelical Methodists, and even the IFCA all withdrew from the ACCC in protest over McIntire's agenda.[76] While evangelicals were clearly against communism, they were also jealous of their growing acceptance in U.S. culture. The Billy Graham who regularly visited the White House could hardly be expected to embrace the conspiracy politics of the radical right.[77]

As North American fundamentalism entered the 1970s, it could draw on a rich (and sometimes bewildering) legacy of ideas, organizational forms, and relationships to the larger world. Its nineteenth-century position as keeper of orthodoxy had given way in the early part of the twentieth century to a religious and cultural battle defending that orthodoxy against modernism. With defeat in that battle, fundamentalists had withdrawn into separate territory to assess their potential as outsiders. Some had used their organizational and evangelistic skills to build an impressive religious empire rivaling the mainline denominations in institutional strength. Still expecting that Jesus might return at any moment, believers put their energy into saving souls from a decaying civilization. Some became convinced that the evangelistic task demanded some accommodation and cooperation with the ways of the world, and they slowly began to shun the label "fundamentalist." Others insisted on separatism as the only legitimate position for the defenders of truth. And a few radicals ventured into the political arena in pursuit of the kind of ideological cleansing perceived necessary to preserve the Christian heritage of the United States.

Reemergence as a Social Movement: 1976 and Beyond

For fifty years fundamentalism had been largely invisible on the U.S. political scene. A few fundamentalists had joined 1950s anticommunist crusades, but most had remained relatively inactive in politics, preferring instead to put energy into the churches and institutions that made their view of the world possible. Evangelism and missions far outweighed efforts toward social reform. However, a number of things happened in the 1960s and 1970s to mobilize fundamentalists again as a social movement. In some ways, the culture itself pulled fundamentalists into the public arena; in other ways, internal changes pushed them outward.

One cannot speak of the 1960s in the United States without speaking of rapid social change. When John F. Kennedy spoke of "new frontiers," he could hardly know just how new they would seem. The civil rights movement, simmering since the mid-1950s, burst into national consciousness in the early 1960s. Televised scenes of police beating marchers and of bombed churches began to mobilize the nation's conscience. Legislation moved through Congress mandating that black/white relations change. A century of legal segregation and three centuries of servitude were to be replaced by equal rights and equal opportunity. Such a revolution brought, of course, counterrevolution and protest from traditional whites in the North and the South. It also brought the assassination of Reverend Dr. Martin Luther King Jr., the cause's most visible leader. And his death was followed within months by Robert F. Kennedy's assassination. Along with John F. Kennedy, shot five years earlier, two more champions of justice had fallen victim to the chaos of the times.

Not only were black/white relations changing, so were the roles of men and women. Women lashed out at the "feminine mystique" that had kept them imprisoned in domestic roles. Bras were burned and new language invented, with "Ms." becoming the symbol of liberation from conventions that tied women's identities to men's. Both men and women in the counterculture youth movements preached new sexual mores under the slogan "Make love, not war." Old rules were being overturned as fast as they could be questioned by students on college campuses or demonstrators in the streets.

Their protests were given a special moral urgency by the Vietnam War. Convinced that their government was pursuing a misguided, even malevolent, policy, students sought to end the war. They burned their draft cards, fled to Sweden and Canada, and marched in the streets of nearly every U.S. city. Americans who supported the war could not understand the students' defiance, and the students could not understand many of their elders' unquestioning obedience. The students urged everyone as a matter of course to "question authority." The war would not end until well into the 1970s, but the legacy of division and distrust it spawned would go on much longer. As the 1960s faded into the 1970s, even less-radical folk were faced with the disconcerting reality that not all presidents were trustworthy. As the scandals of Watergate unfolded, people who had supported a "law and order" president were confronted with a president who broke the law. The rules of morality and leadership they had presumed to hold simply did not seem to apply.[78]

This seeming disintegration of society lent the evangelistic task extra urgency. Such chaos could only mean the Rapture was near. Such rapid change is the stuff of which sermons are made. And it is the stuff of which converts are made. Individuals often experienced cultural change as an intolerable shaking of the foundations. From burned-out hippies to disillusioned liberals to ordinary seekers, they made their way into fundamentalist churches. One of the hippies-turned-fundamentalist, interviewed by Steven Tipton, put it this way:

> One person tells you to do one thing, and the next person says to do the opposite. "Get a job, get a haircut." Or "Turn on, tune in, drop out." Or "Support the President," and someone else says, "Impeach Nixon" or "Stop the War," or whatever it is, you know. It makes you crazy. What do you do? It's typical of the world. You're in confusion. In the Lord the Word shows you what to do, and you can rest in it. You don't have to be gray.[79]

In fundamentalist churches, such former rebels found answers and order, love and stability.

If the culture as a whole remained in disarray, that seemed doubly true in the South. Just as the northern United States and Canada had experienced industrialization, urbanization, and immigration in the last quarter of the nineteenth century, so too the southeastern United States experienced those same forces a century later. From the depression onward, people were leaving their farms, but the pace quickened after World War II. At first they were more likely to go to northern cities than to southern ones, but after about 1960, the Sun Belt had its own attraction. In the 1940s the South had been two-thirds rural, but by 1960 less than half the people lived in the countryside. During that same period, gains in education and industrial base had laid the foundation for the growth that would follow.[80] By 1980 well over 10 percent of the South's urban population had been born outside the region.[81] Air-conditioning and cheap labor made it the region of choice for corporate moves and new ventures.

For the first time, migration in from other regions outstripped migration away from southern small towns and farms. The newcomers' presence and urban diversity created a pluralistic environment never before seen in the South. Alongside radical change in racial norms, southerners found themselves in a world they hardly recognized. Beliefs taken for granted in their small traditional communities had to be defended if they were to survive in this new world.[82]

The 1960s' rapid social change, then, created fertile ground that fundamentalists were only too happy to plow. Increasing numbers wanted to hear about God's truth and plan for the future. They looked around them at the chaos of the times and wondered what they could count on, where the dependable rules were. A young convert reflected on her life left behind: "There are no lines, I guess, there. You are totally free. And now I realize that lines are definitely better because you'll go too far, as much as you think you won't."[83] It was a good time for a revival.

But a social movement is more than a revival. The transitions of the 1960s and 1970s pulled fundamentalists not only into new fields for evangelism but also into new institutional and political action. The entire country, but especially the South, was ripe for a fundamentalist movement, and fundamentalists would become vital players in some massive political realignments.

The 1960s revolution had, in fact, pulled the entire U.S. polity toward new partisan alignments. The Democratic Party's hold on the South disintegrated with that party's embrace of civil rights.[84] And working-class whites outside the South also began to drop their Democratic allegiance. Both northern and southern Democrats became more interested in moral and lifestyle issues than in traditional party interests and loyalties—interested enough to vote for Republicans who caught their fancy.[85] With political choices to be made, people searched for the grounds on which to make them. At least some people began to wonder if churches might help them in that process.

Meanwhile, the U.S. government itself was creating a certain alarm in fundamentalists' minds. The retreat from Vietnam raised fears that the nation might no longer enjoy its world supremacy. Fundamentalists cared deeply about that possibility, partly because they feared communism's growth but also because they saw U.S. military and economic might as guarantors of their ability to evangelize the world. For fundamentalists, the United States has always been the "city on a hill," ordained by God as the light to the nations. From the beginning, they had been committed to foreign missions. Now they wondered if the gospel's light might go out because it would have no great chosen nation to carry it.

Their fear for the country's future was intensified by the 1963 U.S. Supreme Court decision that outlawed prescribed prayers in public schools. It seemed impossible that in this Christian nation children should be told not to pray in school. Over the next decade, the evidence mounted in fundamentalists' minds that the nation was being run by people intentionally hostile to their beliefs and determined to stamp out all vestiges of traditional religion in coming generations.[86] Attacks on home, school, and church seemed so systematic that they surely must have come from a single ideological source, identified in Tim LaHaye's popular 1980 book, *The Battle for the Mind,* as secular humanism. Among the developments fundamentalists found alarming were these:

1. A constitutional amendment was proposed that could have been interpreted so as to prevent women from fulfilling their biblical role as submissive wives, serving primarily in the household.
2. The family was further attacked as social agencies and legislatures sought to define the limits of physical punishment permitted in a father's attempts to discipline his children.
3. The IRS began to take on the task of investigating religious agencies' finances and determining what "counted" as true religion (at least for tax purposes).
4. Civil rights arguments began to be extended to those (especially homosexuals) whose lives fundamentalists deemed grossly immoral.
5. Not only could children not pray in school, they were also being taught "values clarification" and other "humanist" ideas that undermined the unwavering beliefs and traditions their parents held dear.
6. Even Christian schools could not do their work without government agencies imposing certification restrictions, which seemed to strip them of their theological power.
7. And finally, all the forces seeking to destroy traditional families and moral society seemed to converge in a court ruling, *Roe v Wade,* that found abortion a matter of private choice.[87]

Courts, schools, and legislatures seemed to dare fundamentalists to come out of their separatist institutions to defend their right to exist.

Though fundamentalist churches were enjoying the revival brought their way by increasing numbers of seekers, they were also being pulled out of their institutional subculture by broader concerns. They had a growing sense that if "God's people" did not stand up against an aggressive government in this generation, there might not be another generation of believers. The sense of urgency coming from the culture was matched by the momentum of institutional strength coming from within. In the late nineteenth century, conservatives concerned about the culture's drift into modernism had created new institutions to support their cause. In the late twentieth century, those institutions were already in place. They were, in fact, thriving.

Working-class fundamentalists of the 1930s and 1940s had given birth to a generation of middle-class children. Southerners moving to cities were also moving into greater economic resources. The people inside fundamentalism simply had more money to give to their churches, money that helped fuel the institutional boom.[88] They could afford to pay tuition to Christian academies and to send donations to television ministries. They could afford to build churches that provided services attractive to a wider and wider audience. And they could afford to get involved in politics.

Nowhere was this surfeit of organizational power more apparent than in the television ministries.[89] Television offered an enormously powerful medium for raising money, and it constantly pushed evangelists along by the sheer power of its resources. They not only raised money to stay on the air and preach the gospel; they also raised money for whatever enterprises their imagination and charisma could create and sustain.[90] Like the urban revivalists before them, these preachers built quasi-denominational complexes of institutions to extend their mission. There were colleges (CBN University, Liberty University, and the like), hospitals (most notably Oral Roberts's City of Faith Hospital), publishing houses, missions, and even amusement parks (Heritage U.S.A. being the most prominent).

Although these institutions were thriving, they were, ironically, irrelevant to the dominant culture. The standards of achievement in the two spheres were simply different, with success inside fundamentalist ranks going largely unnoticed on the outside. After two generations of separation, fundamentalists began to assess their isolation. They were tired of being ignored.[91] Their resentment can be heard in Jerry Falwell's assessment of the age: "We are living in a society today that is quite sophisticated and very educated. Ours is indeed a clever generation, but one that is suffering because men are doing what is right in their own eyes and disregarding God's immutable laws. If a person is not a Christian, he is inherently a failure."[92] As the culture pulled fundamentalists outward, then, their own economic and institutional strength, combined with a certain sense of cultural isolation, provided the fuel with which they could generate a movement for change.

The Movement Organized

Christian Academies

Following World War II, a few conservative churches began to organize their own day schools, but the movement accelerated rapidly during the 1960s. Some outsiders saw the move toward private church-sponsored schools as merely a retreat from racial integration—and some of it was clearly that—but the motivations were much larger.[93] Fundamentalists had concluded that the public schools were actively hostile to their children's faith. Now that they had the resources, they took matters into their own hands. Between 1965 and 1983, enrollment in evangelical schools increased sixfold, and the number of schools reached about 10,000. In addition, perhaps as many as 100,000 fundamentalist children are being taught at home.[94] Usually sponsored directly by one or more congregations, these schools draw primarily on members' children. They offer parents the opportunity to surround their children with knowledge in harmony with their beliefs. A mother in a northeastern city explained why she wanted her daughter in the church's academy: "I think she is going to have less options thrown at her in a Christian school than if she was in a public school, where there might be a few more things that she might have to choose about. I would rather control her environment as much as possible while she is young, until she is old enough to be let go."[95] The mother knows the Bible will be a text in every classroom, with each subject shaped by a conservative viewpoint. History is "Christian history," and economics is strictly free enterprise. Biblical words and examples even show up in spelling and math. Even more important, Christian schools operate in a disciplined atmosphere that reinforces belief, and they provide a supply of Christian friends and role models who give those beliefs plausibility.[96] Publishers have begun providing complete curricula, a widely used example being the Accelerated Christian Education series. These publishers and school administrators are proud to claim that children in Christian schools compare very favorably on standardized tests with their public school counterparts. Private schools appear to have become an entrenched part of the fundamentalist way of life. It is a way to "proclaim themselves as guardians of American culture. Caught in a world whose complexity tends to render people impotent, evangelicals have chosen to delimit their world in order to gain control over it."[97]

The Christian Right

The other major effort of 1980s fundamentalists toward gaining control over their world was their active entry into politics. Ironically, U.S. news media first glimpsed conservative religion's political potential not in terms of fundamentalists themselves but in terms of Jimmy Carter, who better fits the label "evangelical." Far from making his religion his political agenda, Carter strictly adhered to the traditional Baptist belief in separation of church and state.[98] And fundamentalists soon saw that Carter shared few of their foreign or domestic policy positions.

But 1976 was the "Year of the Evangelical" as well as the nation's bicentennial. The nation, or at least the intellectual and political elite, suddenly discovered that conservative religion had not disappeared after 1925 and that many people were willing to vote according to their moral conscience. When southerners gave their Southern Baptist favorite son a trip to the White House, pundits imagined that conservative, religious folk had newly arrived in politics. Though pundits were not quite right about this "new birth," 1976 did give evangelicals and fundamentalists a new sense of efficacy. The national attention paid to them and to the nation's moral roots boosted their growing interest in political affairs.

In truth, a political alignment of religious people, concerned about conservative social issues, was both older and newer than the 1976 election. At least since the early 1970s, people identifiable as religious conservatives had coalesced around an agenda of family-related issues. They did not yet know that they were a movement; 1976 only served to further awaken them to how ineffective it was to follow traditional religious or political labels. Jimmy Carter might be a Southern Baptist, but he was not their man. A true political movement had to await the organization of new vehicles to carry their concerns. That organization came in 1979. Some pastors of huge "superchurches" decided the time had come to organize to promote morality in U.S. life. With the help of conservative political organizers Richard Viguerie and Ed McAteer, they put together a nonpartisan political organization, the Moral Majority. Its head was to be Jerry Falwell, with other board members James Kennedy (Presbyterian from Florida), Greg Dixon (independent Baptist from Indianapolis), Tim LaHaye (conservative ideologue from California), and Charles Stanley (Southern Baptist from Atlanta).[99] Other conservative religious political groups were being organized as well—the Religious Roundtable, the American Coalition for Traditional Values, and Christian Voice—but the Moral Majority captured the public imagination (and the news media), symbolizing a revitalized, politically potent fundamentalist movement. The group built on two primary organizational bases: the independent church network in existence since the 1930s and the television fund-raising mechanisms developed to a fine art in the 1970s. With pastors as primary organizers, the movement spread quickly into their spheres of influence, often large suburban churches. And television preachers and their direct-mail fund-raising lists broadened the net further.[100]

The Moral Majority's strategy involved the full range of political activities. They distributed information through newsletters, seminars, and broadcast ministries. They registered voters and lobbied Congress. And they trained and encouraged conservatives in the fine art of running for office. No public office or bureaucratic position was too low; as political organizers, they realized that their crusade must begin from the ground up. And like the network of independent churches on which they built, Moral Majority activities often happened out of public sight, varying in form and emphasis from one location to another.

Many of these new activists are preachers, with a widely felt influence (often indirect). Even more widely felt are the messages of Christian broadcasters who in varying degrees support political involvement.[101] Those connected to this movement's political activities receive a regular flow of information about letters to write to Congress and phone calls to make in support of a bill. Conservative groups generate most of the religiously based constituent pressure felt in Washington. Conservative religious lobbies are also learning the slow, painstaking process of developing contacts, researching issues, drafting legislation—the political hardball that makes an impact on policy. Though their efforts were at first ill-timed and ineffective, as they gained experience they were able to defeat the Equal Rights Amendment (ERA) to the U.S. Constitution and to enable "equal access" legislation (for after-hours religious activities in public schools).[102]

Fundamentalist Ideas in the Political Arena

The issues around which fundamentalists have attempted to rally support have ranged from gun control and the Panama Canal to drugs and pornography. The fight against the teaching of evolution had already been revived in a new form in the effort to institute the teaching of "scientific creationism" alongside evolution. Other public school issues included efforts to reinstitute prayer in the classroom and initiatives against many forms of secular humanism. Tim LaHaye called it "the battle for the mind." Legal strategies were adopted with the premise that secular humanism is a religion (a premise given some legitimacy by reference to it as such in a 1961 Supreme Court opinion).[103]

The central theme of the fundamentalist foray into politics was to protect the traditional family, the basic unit of society. This meant a legally married man and woman, with their children, preferably supported solely by the husband's labor. From this flowed the movement's opposition to gay rights, pornography, the Equal Rights Amendment, and laws designed to protect abused wives and children. For the nation to be strong, its families should be constituted according to God's rules, rules including man's heading the family and parents' physically disciplining children. Concern for the family became most acute, however, on the issue of abortion.[104] Evoking holocaust images, pro-life speakers and writers decried the immorality that leads to unwanted pregnancy in the first place, greedy doctors who make a living destroying life, and morally bankrupt government agencies and courts that allow such a practice to flourish. Stopping the slaughter of innocent unborn babies became the rallying cry that has mobilized many previously inactive conservatives.

Abortion also became the issue that tested the limits of fundamentalist activism. In 1988 a group called Operation Rescue arose as a vehicle for the promotion of civil disobedience in opposition to abortion. The group not only picketed abortion clinics but sought to prevent women from entering. The protesters sat down, formed human blockades, and pleaded with those who came and went. When clinics obtained court orders against them, they were not deterred, and many went to jail. During that summer's Democratic National Convention, Operation Rescue demonstrators filled Atlanta's jails, many giving only Jane Doe or John Doe as identification. While leaders of the Christian Right sympathized with their cause, most drew the line at civil disobedience. Jerry Falwell, who declared himself their "cheerleader," was himself not yet ready to go to jail. Mainstream fundamentalists would stick to standard political means while this new group explored more radical measures.

The abortion issue not only divided fundamentalists into differing tactical camps, it also united fundamentalists and other religious conservatives who had otherwise shunned each other as doctrinal inferiors or heretics. Catholics, long seen as allies of the Antichrist by many fundamentalists, were embraced by those active in the pro-life movement. Other issues brought together other unlikely coalitions: Feminists joined the fight against pornography; Mormons opposed the ERA; and Jews wanted partners in supporting Israel. In the Moral Majority, Falwell adamantly insisted such partnerships were essential, boldly asserting his organization's commitment to "pluralism." Claiming that the Moral Majority did not simply foster "born-again" politics, he asserted that "the acceptability of any candidate could never be based upon one's religious affiliation. Our support of candidates is based upon two criteria: (a) the commitment of the candidate to the principles that we espouse; (b) the competency of the candidate to fill that office."[105] Falwell's Moral Majority sought a common moral ground on which conservatives could agree, attempting to maintain purity of belief alongside cooperation with those of different beliefs.

Finding common ground called for significant ideological and organizational innovation among fundamentalists. It meant playing a secular game by secular rules.[106] It also meant that Falwell and his organization quickly became anathema for believers like Bob Jones Sr., who declared Falwell "the most dangerous man in America" for his practice of forming coalitions with unbelievers. For a generation, fundamentalists had built their identity around "separation." They had built separate institutions and tried to live separate lives. They refused to drink, dance, gamble, or smoke. They dressed modestly and were careful about their associates. These were people who had condemned Billy Graham for cooperating with Lutherans and Episcopalians. They could hardly be expected now to embrace cooperation with Catholics and Mormons. Evangelism, true belief, and right living had been the only legitimate strategies for Christians anticipating the Rapture, surrounded by a corrupt world. Christians who got involved in politics were, in this view, doomed to get sullied by the dirty world into which they went.

Falwell faced the tasks of convincing fundamentalists to become involved and of explaining how they could do that without jeopardizing their Christian witness. He did so by appealing to the missionary instinct ingrained so deeply in fundamentalism. He turned these concerns around, saying: "We must stop being so negative and critical of everyone who is trying to reach people with the Gospel but does not wear our label."[107] He pointed out that Jesus had commanded the saved to preach the gospel to every nation, a command they could not carry out if that nation were Communist—a good reason to support a strong military and a conservative foreign policy. As a "chosen nation," the United States had a special role in spreading the gospel—a good reason to keep the country free and morally upright. Quoting Hebrew Scripture about the nation's need for repentance and righteousness had long been a staple of fundamentalist preaching: "Only by godly leadership can America be put back on a divine course. God will give national healing if men and women will pray and meet God's conditions."[108] Falwell took old revival sermons and gave them new implications. He did not want to give up on saving souls, but he also wanted to save the nation. He wanted to see both "spiritual revival and political renewal in the United States."

The political renewal sought by Falwell and his supporters recalls how fundamentalist reformers in the earlier part of the century sought a return to Christian civilization. Families are the basic unit of that civilization. Secular humanism is the enemy because it represents the ideological and cultural core of the institutions that now dominate society. This struggle between fundamentalists and their enemies is a very real contest to see who will define the terms of U.S. culture.[109] Secular humanists (many of whom, of course, are not very secular at all) are the intellectual and bureaucratic elite (the "knowledge class") who hold the reins of power in U.S. society. They have gained their positions through formal education and credentials—education and credentials that fundamentalists less often have. Their business requires the free flow of information and ideas. They have the power to declare that U.S. democracy requires pluralism and that separation of church and state implies excluding religion from public life. Television, news, the arts, and the educational system uphold a religion-neutral (or religion-absent) view of society. Fundamentalists are convinced that the United States must have a pro-religion culture, one in which they have a stronger voice in shaping the values and images that guide society. Theirs is an ideological battle for control of the way the United States will view its past and its future.

The ideological battle that fundamentalists wage pits them against powerful cultural enemies and forces them to reevaluate their own way of relating to the outside world. In the 1980s fundamentalism's ideological balance subtly shifted away from a premillennial pessimism to an optimism about social reform more suited to postmillennial visions. Activists were reviving myths of Christian civilization and godly dominion, myths widely shared throughout this nation's history. They did not give up premillennial ideas, but they were willing to say that eschatological ideas were "not significant" for political involvement.[110]

Crusading publicly for moral reform marked an important new phase in fundamentalist life. After several decades of focusing primarily on individual evangelism, fundamentalism again has sought collective change. Though sparked by a certain desperation about Western culture's future, the movement nevertheless exhibits that optimism present in earlier efforts to restore Christian civilization. It has drawn on its ideological roots of evangelism and mission, its image of the United States as the "city on the hill," while suppressing its heritage of dispensational premillennialism. And it has drawn on its organizational roots in independent churches, agencies, and broadcast ministries while creating new organizational forms to accommodate the broader public coalitions necessary to achieve new goals.

Changes in the South

The cultural homogeneity that had previously made a southern fundamentalist movement impossible was broken. In three decades of rapid change, the South had urbanized, its racial mores had been disrupted, transplants from the North were arriving daily, and tradition was generally in disarray.[111] Southerners who now knew that liberals existed in their midst were more likely to join political movements such as the Moral Majority and more likely to turn their Southern Baptist conservatism into Southern Baptist fundamentalism. In addition, their rising levels of income and urbanization provided resources and opportunities for mobilization not available in earlier eras. Southerners were both more concerned and more able to fight to defend the orthodoxy they remembered.

They wrote letters, offered resolutions, and otherwise voiced their dismay at the Southern Baptist Convention's perceived abandonment of tradition. They also withheld their dollars, preferring to support unofficial seminaries and missionaries untainted by the denomination's liberal drift. But their protests went largely unheard until a Texas judge, Paul Pressler, gave them some lessons in politics. He looked at the denomination's constitutional structure and noticed that the Southern Baptist Convention's presidency, always considered an honorific position, actually held the key to changing policy. Agencies, including seminaries, are run by their boards of trustees; those trustees are elected by the "messengers" (delegates) who attend the annual convention. However, the process by which trustees are nominated begins with the president, and nominees are almost never turned down. Pressler and fellow Texan Paige Patterson gathered a small group of prominent pastors who took on the task of organizing their states. Working largely unnoticed, they held informational meetings and rallies, convincing pastors and lay people that they should make a trip to the annual Southern Baptist Convention to vote for a conservative president. In 1979, in Houston (Pressler's hometown), Adrian Rogers was elected, beginning an unbroken string of fundamentalist victories.

By appointing only strict inerrantists and by passing conservative resolutions that could be used as policy guidelines in Southern Baptist institutions, fundamentalists began to put their stamp on the nation's largest Protestant denomination. Slowly the new trustees began to take office, a few more each year; and by 1987 denominational agencies were beginning to feel the results of the movement. A seminary president was forced from office, as was a Baptist editor in Georgia. Professors began to seek other employment rather than live with doctrinal restrictions. The publishing house agreed to produce a commentary series based on strict inerrancy. Mission efforts began to turn away from educational and health concerns toward single-minded evangelism and starting new churches. And the social-concerns agencies of the denomination turned firmly away from issues of separation of church and state, hunger, racism, and violence toward abortion, school prayer, and the Christian right's political agenda.[112] The movement's leaders exulted that theirs was the biggest conservative victory ever in the fight against liberalism.

New Variations on the Fundamentalists: Reconstructionists

One of the people who celebrated along with Judge Pressler at the conservative Baptist victory was Dr. Gary North, head of a small conservative think tank in Texas. In 1986 North interviewed Pressler for a tape to be distributed through his Dominion Tapes. North's purpose was to draw on Pressler's experience to provide an example for other conservatives to organize grassroots opposition to bureaucracies dominated by humanists and liberals.

Unlike Pressler, however, North belongs to a movement of orthodox Christians called reconstructionists. They seek to pose a direct threat to "the modern bureaucratic State." In their view, "Christians are called by God to exercise dominion."[113] The two primary texts on which their ideas are built are Genesis 1:26–28 (God's command to the newly created humanity to "subdue" the earth and have dominion over it) and the "Great Commission" of Matthew 28:16–20 (Jesus' charge to the disciples to "teach all nations" the things he commanded). Their movement is sometimes called dominion theology.

This movement's intellectual and theological foundations are clearly Calvinist. The "golden age" to which reconstructionists look is not the nineteenth century but the seventeenth. Their heroes are the Massachusetts Puritans who dared to establish civil law based explicitly on biblical principles. John Cotton's 1641 "Abstract of the Laws of New England" serves as their respected point of reference.[114] They also look fondly to Calvin's Geneva of the century before and to the strict Calvinists who fought Presbyterian liberalism earlier in the twentieth century. J. Gresham Machen and Cornelius Van Til, of Westminster Theological Seminary, are admired as warriors against secularism.

Reconstructionists seek to bring all life under God's rule. Christian schools are essential, a necessary step in preparing a citizenry that understands God's laws. Not only must children be properly trained in history and morality, but more advanced learning needs correction as well. The movement's intellectual elite actively produces publications to redirect knowledge in all areas, from psychology and history to mathematics and philosophy.[115]

In doing this, reconstructionists criticize and hope to undermine institutions that they see as usurping God's rightful place of lordship. Chief among the culprits is the modern state. In the reconstructionist view, it has grown far beyond its legitimate boundaries and its subjects must bring it down, like a tyrant. Government's only legitimate function is to keep the peace, with other functions constituting idolatry. The modern state, as reconstructionists see it, has substituted itself for God. Citizens have been tricked into trusting the state to care for them, rather than reserving that role for God. "Our once Christian-based civil government has become idolatrous by arrogating to itself the God-like power of permeating every aspect and sphere of citizens' lives."[116] North writes: "Civil law is not supposed to make men good; it is supposed to restrain external evil."[117] Such a stance does not, however, mean that reconstructionists are uninterested in government or unwilling to obey its laws. Reconstructionist clergy, like other fundamentalists, denounced the spread of civil disobedience in opposition to abortion (especially through Operation Rescue). In the January 1989 issue of the reconstructionist newsletter *Chalcedon Report,* Rousas J. Rushdoony wrote in opposition to the "lawless protest" of Operation Rescue's demonstrators. Though strongly arguing that abortion is a sin and unjustified under any circumstances, he also argued that Christians must obey civil law. To seek change through protest and revolution violates the Christian presupposition that change comes only through God's power.

Arguing for obedience to the law does not, however, mean that reconstructionists are indifferent to the content of those laws. They see all law, government, and social action as inherently religious. Rushdoony writes: "Every law structure or system is an establishment of religion. There can be no separation of religion and the State."[118] All such institutions attempt to mold the moral life of the culture, and all make assumptions about where the power for change lies. Reconstructionists see no neutral ground, no sphere of activity outside God's rule. One either follows God in all areas of life or does not follow God at all. One either engages in godly politics or participates in the anti-God structures that now threaten home, school, and church.

The reconstructionists' newsletter warns against the tendency of "Caucasian Christians" to condemn themselves for racism. Regular writer Otto Scott points out that it was

> Caucasian Christians [who] stopped the Amerindians of Central America from conducting their enormous human sacrifices, who ended the Hindu practice of forcing widows to sit in the midst of flames that consumed the cadavers of their husbands, who halted the slave practices of Black Africa, who lifted (though briefly) hideous despotisms in many parts of the Orient . . . [and] sacrificed their lives in a great Civil War to free black people from slavery.

He also argues that blacks in South Africa under apartheid were much better off than in some black-ruled countries in Africa.[119] Scott had made a similar effort in an earlier column to picture Spain's General Francisco Franco as a friend of Jews.[120] This revisionist history does not focus on a racist vision of the future (described as "composed of every race, assured by God of eternal life and eventual victory"). Rather, reconstructionists, like other fundamentalists, are rewriting the "secular humanist" catalog of "sins" and attempting to reclaim the goodness of the U.S. experience.[121]

Being threatened by anti-Christian structures seems to have spurred this movement into action. They fully agree with fundamentalists that government is controlled by the religious faith of secular humanism and that humanism is thrust upon ordinary people through the schools, through programs that restrict traditional family values, and even through intrusions into church life. They also agree with fundamentalists about the chaotic character of today's world. Reconstructionists disagree with some fundamentalists, however, about religion's role in public life. For reconstructionists, pietism and separatism only play into the hands of humanists, who wish to keep Christians neutralized. Like Christian right activists, reconstructionist preachers and writers urge believers to become informed and get involved. But they urge involvement with a large measure of caution against the corrosive compromises built into the political process.[122]

To counter the potential corruption of the political process, believers must keep their eye on the scriptural laws that should shape all areas of life. They should foster a "nonneutral" social order—a religiously based rule of law. For reconstructionists, in fact, laws represent not just abstract principles but detailed guidelines that are as true today as when first handed down by God. Rushdoony's Institutes of Biblical Law outline the plan, based on the covenants and law of Hebrew Scripture. Civil government is to be the servant of God, enforcing God's laws. (Among the more controversial of Rushdoony's extractions from biblical law is the suggestion that habitually rebellious children be put to death.)

The rule of law will be aided by God's judgment as well. Reconstructionists presume that a nation that so routinely breaks all of God's laws (especially by murdering millions of babies by abortion) can expect the punishment that God promises those who break divine law. Using the universe's energies, God's providence will destroy lawlessness, humanism, socialism, and the other "isms." Whatever stands in the way of Christian influence will be destroyed, clearing the way for God's people to rule. Reconstructionists look to Scripture (especially the history of Israel) as a model for God's blessing and curse. (Deuteronomy, chapter 28, is the usual source for a view of God's judgment.) Those who obey are promised both spiritual and material prosperity, while those who disobey will be either slowly or suddenly destroyed.

Implementing biblical principles in today's society requires a group willing to believe change is possible. Reconstructionism depends on a hopeful eschatology. Converts from older fundamentalist groups speak of being rescued from "Rapture fever." Theirs is now a "victory orientation": They expect that God will bless preaching the gospel by steadily adding believers. Through those believers' faithful living, the Bible will eventually become the dominant cultural force. Christians will win. They will not use force or political power to restrict nonbelievers; they will simply participate with God in a victory that God has promised.

Like their premillennial cousins, then, reconstructionists wait for a dramatic change in history. But they are not merely waiting. Because they anticipate having a role in the change, they train while they wait. Their strategy "seeks to remove the political and institutional barriers to God's law in order to impose the rule of God's law... In most instances, this must be a 'bottom-up' program."[123] People who know God's laws begin at the grassroots level to challenge a system they see as wrong. They work for laws that embody Christian morality. They practice judging all of life and the people they meet by the biblical standards that will prevail in the dominion. And despite their insistence that God is the sole agent of redemption, they support any political program that will reduce taxes, take away the power of government bureaucracy, and otherwise limit the state.

The reconstructionist emphasis on grassroots organizing to counter humanism with biblical government has found a growing audience. Its most natural home is in Orthodox Presbyterian circles, but activist Baptists and charismatics are also discovering their kinship with this tendency. Even Falwell declared himself a Calvinist, and when he was a presidential candidate Pat Robertson asserted that he considered the U.S. Constitution to be based on Calvinist principles. Robertson reportedly reads Rushdoony's publications and is commended in them. For fundamentalists like Falwell and charismatics like Robertson, the push to be active in the world has precipitated a reevaluation of their theological roots. They are now closer to the ideas of Christian social order explicit in Christian reconstructionism's version of Calvinism. In turn, the reconstructionists recognize their kinship with some activist fundamentalists and recommend organizations like Christian Voice and Eagle Forum to reconstructionist readers.[124]

Conclusions

Out of the intellectual and social changes of the late nineteenth century came a movement that sought to defend the truth of Scripture. Developing a doctrine of inerrancy and adopting dispensational premillennialism, the movement gave its followers an explanation for Christian civilization's apparent decline and a language in which to describe their traditional orthodoxy. The movement throve in the industrialized, pluralistic cities of northeastern United States and southern Canada, and it came to flower in the chaotic years following World War I. In religious and political battles during the 1920s, fundamentalist leaders sought to reassert their place as cultural spokesmen.

When they lost those battles, fundamentalists began the process of taking their place alongside many other moral communities in the U.S. cultural mosaic. They became outsiders to spheres of influence in politics, education, and the press, but they built a lively subculture in which conservative religion throve for five decades. Its religious, educational, and missionary institutions provided a home for fundamentalists who sought to maintain their purity of life in the midst of a culture they saw as dominated by secular humanism. Their primary relation to that outside culture was in aggressive evangelism, in seeking individual converts whose lives would be changed despite the deteriorating world around them. By the 1970s, however, the culture was again undergoing a moral upheaval, and the time was ripe for the fundamentalists' message of certainty. But they did not respond with just a message of individual salvation alone. They had begun to see the benefits of more actively participating in the public arena from which they had retreated. Threatened by secular humanism—seeing it not just as a deceiver stealing individual souls but as an aggressive institutional opponent encroaching on the territory they had created—they were ready to fight back.

In fighting back, late-twentieth-century fundamentalists have again created new institutions to embody their concerns. Building on the network of independent agencies and churches created since 1925, this resurgent movement has added organizations for political mobilization and influence. This organizational base is likely to serve fundamentalists well in the decades to come, whether or not conservative religion remains a visible public force, but fundamentalism is likely to remain a force in North American culture for the foreseeable future. It has built an infrastructure that is unlikely to wither, and it draws on ideas still familiar to most as major cultural symbols. For individuals, fundamentalist churches provide a haven where life makes sense. In chaotic times and places, when individuals and communities are searching for moorings, fundamentalism's certainty and clarity often are appealing. Drawing as it does on a biblical heritage deeply ingrained in the culture, fundamentalism claims to be the rightful interpreter of the stories that shape U.S. identity, and it offers a subcultural system in which those ideas can be nurtured and sustained. In revivals and local pulpits, the message of individual salvation will continue to contain a healthy mixture of exhortation to righteous living, and the righteous living espoused by fundamentalist preachers will continue to shape the vision of a good society held by those who listen.

Whether fundamentalism will remain a visible, active force in the larger culture is not yet clear. The political structures in place and the experience accumulated seem to predict that fundamentalists will have a continued role as participants in political life. Once built, institutions tend to have a life of their own, shaping the actions of those who inhabit them. In addition, the ideas being borrowed from dominion theology offer a plausible rationale for continued public involvement in a way that neither evangelism nor premillennialism ever has. It seems entirely likely that fundamentalists may take their place in the public arena alongside other previously silent minority groups. Even though they may argue that only their particular Christian view has legitimacy, they will be doing so in the context of a pluralistic democracy in which their voices will be heard and weighed against many others.

Fundamentalism in North America has been shaped by a variety of cultural, ideological, organizational, and political forces. Ideologically, fundamentalists have always emphasized widely held traditional symbols, making significant additions from newer systems of thought. They have also drawn clear boundaries between themselves and the rest of the culture, emphasizing their distinctive ways of living and unambiguous conceptions of truth. And they have been equally clear that those outside their fold needed to change, although just how that change was expected to take place has varied over time. At times fundamentalists have been content to wait for divine intervention; at other times they have sought change one soul at a time; and at still other times they have taken matters into their own political hands.

Organizationally, fundamentalists have been masters of innovation. After losing their places in existing institutions, they created a new infrastructure and have entered their current period of activism with a strong organizational base. The organizations have proven effective both in sustaining a separatist subculture and in mobilizing an activist movement. Since fundamentalists have now created specifically political institutions, their political involvement is likely to continue, whether it is highly visible or not. Once having created an organizational home, fundamentalism has proved able to enter and leave the public arena as circumstances demand.

Fundamentalism has been most politically active and culturally visible in times following major cultural turmoil. In this period, government's power has also expanded, and fundamentalists have offered both a cultural reordering and a protest against an expanding state. The mix of active and passive, individual and political responses has seemed to depend on the degree of threat that fundamentalists have perceived, the degree of potential response in the culture at large, and the strength of fundamentalists' own organizational resources. But what they can accomplish in the larger culture is limited by the pluralist legal and cultural assumptions of the United States and Canada. They can offer their vision of a good society and demand to be heard. During certain periods their message may be adopted by a wide following, but fundamentalists in North America cannot impose their way of life without the consent of the governed.

Notes

1. One strategy meeting of conservative ministers with Bush included Presbyterian James Kennedy and Southern Baptist Convention president Jerry Vines, both pastors in Florida. See S. Hastey and M. Knox, "Bush Meets with Evangelicals, Including Southern Baptist," *Baptist Press,* 4 August 1988.

2. The sources of the prediction was Edgar C. Whisenant's book *88 Reasons Why the Rapture Will Be in 1988* (Nashville, Tenn.: World Bible Society, 1988). Though admitting that he could not know the "day or hour" of the Lord's return (because of

the many time zones), he nevertheless was sure that he could calculate "the year, the month, and the week of the Lord's return" from the Bible's many end time prophecies (3).

3. George M. Marsden, *Fundamentalism and American Culture* (Oxford: Oxford University Press, 1980), 158.

4. George Gallup Jr., *Religion in America: 50 Years, 1935–1985* (Princeton, N.J.: Gallup Report, 1985).

5. George Gallup Jr., *Public Opinion 1982* (Wilmington, Del.: Scholarly Resources, 1983).

6. J. D. Hunter makes this distinction between confessional and born-again evangelicals in "Operationalizing Evangelicalism," *Sociological Analysis* 42 (1982): 363–72.

7. The notable exception, of course, is the Missouri Synod Lutheran Church, taken over by fundamentalists in the early 1970s.

8. C. E. Lincoln, *Race, Religion, and the Continuing American Dilemma* (New York: Hill and Wang, 1984), 92–93.

9. Ibid., 96.

10. On the black church, see E. F. Frazier, *The Negro Church in America,* and C. Eric Lincoln, *The Black Church since Frazier* (bound together; New York: Schocken Books, 1973); and J. R. Washington Jr., "The Peculiar Peril and Promise of Black Folk Religion," in David E. Harrell Jr., ed., *Varieties of Southern Evangelicalism* (Macon, Ga.: Mercer University Press, 1981), 59–69.

11. See S. Kantzer, "The Charismatics among Us," *Christianity Today,* 22 February 1980, 245–49.

12. Meredith B. McGuire, *Pentecostal Catholics: Power, Charisma, and Order in Religious Movement* (Philadelphia: Temple University Press, 1982); Mary J. Neitz, *Charisma and Community: A Study of Religious Commitment within the Charismatic Renewal* (New Brunswick, N.J.: Transaction Books, 1987); and Joseph H. Fichter, *The Catholic Cult of the Paraclete* (New York: Sheed and Ward, 1975) offer helpful accounts of the charismatic movement.

13. For overviews of Mormon history and practice, see Jan Shipps, *Mormonism* (Urbana: University of Illinois Press, 1985); and Thomas O'Dea, *The Mormons* (Chicago: University of Chicago Press, 1964).

14. On Billy Graham, see William Martin, "Billy Graham," in Harrell, *Varieties of Southern Evangelicalism,* 71–88. On the development of evangelicalism since the 1940s, see George M. Marsden, *Reforming Fundamentalism: Fuller Seminary and the New Evangelicalism* (Grand Rapids, Mich.: Eerdmans, 1987); and J. D. Hunter, *Evangelicalism: The Coming Generation* (Chicago: University of Chicago Press, 1987).

15. Jerry Falwell, *The Fundamentalist Phenomenon* (Garden City, N.Y.: Doubleday-Galilee, 1981), contains a discussion of the contrasts from his point of view.

16. Kathleen C. Boone, *The Bible Tells Them So* (Albany: State University of New York Press, 1989), 24.

17. Cf. Alan Peshkin, *God's Choice: The Total World of a Fundamentalist Christian School* (Chicago: University of Chicago Press, 1986); and Nancy T. Ammerman, *Bible Believers: Fundamentalists in the Modern World* (New Brunswick, N.J.: Rutgers University Press, 1987).

18. On fundamentalist ideas about the relationship between science and religion, see also S. D. Rose, *Keeping Them out of the Hands of Satan* (New York: Routledge, 1988).

19. *The Proceedings of the Conference on Biblical Inerrancy* (Nashville, Tenn.: Broadman Press, 1987) contains a number of interesting examples of fundamentalist modes of interpretation, including especially Robert Preus, "The Inerrancy of Scripture," 47–60. For a discussion of more everyday processes of interpretation in a fundamentalist congregation, see Ammerman, *Bible Believers,* chap. 4; and Boone, *The Bible Tells Them So.*

20. On the role of the fundamentalist pastor, see Ammerman, *Bible Believers,* chap. 7; and Boone, *The Bible Tells Them So,* chap. 6.

21. This 1988 film by Martin Scorsese depicts Jesus as doubtful about his mission and subject to human lusts.

22. See Hunter, *Evangelicalism,* chap. 4, on the history of the "traditional" family.

23. Quoted in Marsden, *Fundamentalism and American Culture,* 55.

24. James Barr makes this point as well in *Fundamentalism* (Philadelphia: Westminster Press, 1978), 270ff.

25. Robert M. Grant and David Tracy, *A Short History of the Interpretation of the Bible,* 2d ed. (Philadelphia: Fortress, 1984), 110ff.

26. Martin E. Marty, *The Modern Schism* (New York: Harper and Row, 1969).

27. James S. Olson, *The Ethnic Dimension in American History* (New York: St. Martin's, 1979), 206.

28. Martin E. Marty, *Righteous Empire* (New York: Dial, 1970); and Robert T. Handy, *A Christian America* (New York: Oxford University Press, 1971).

29. Williston Walker, *A History of the Christian Church,* 4th ed. (New York: Charles Scribner's Sons, 1985).

30. On Jehovah's Witnesses, see James A. Beckford, *The Trumpet of Prophecy* (Oxford: Basil Blackwell, 1975). On Mormons, see Jan Shipps, *Mormonism: The Story of a New Religious Tradition* (Urbana: University of Illinois Press, 1985). On the history of Pentecostalism, see Robert M. Anderson, *Vision of the Disinherited* (New York: Oxford University Press, 1979). And on Seventh-Day Adventists, see Gary Schwartz, *Sect Ideologies and Social Status* (Chicago: University of Chicago Press, 1970).

31. This discussion is based largely on J. D. Pulis, "Jerry Falwell and the Moral Majority: A Case Study of the Relationship between Theology and Ideology" (Ph.D. diss., Emory University, 1986). See especially chap. 3.

32. Marty, *Modern Schism.*

33. On revivals, see William G. McLoughlin, *Modern Revivalism: Charles Grandison Finney to Billy Graham* (New York: Ronald Press, 1959); and Donald Dayton, *Discovering an Evangelical Heritage* (New York: Harper, 1976).

34. John B. Boles, "Evangelical Protestantism in the Old South: From Religious Dissent to Cultural Dominance," in Charles R. Wilson, ed., *Religion in the South* (Jackson: University of Mississippi Press, 1985), 13–34.

35. Razelle Frankl, *Televangelism: The Marketing of Popular Religion* (Carbondale: Southern Illinois University Press, 1987); and McLoughlin, *Modern Revivalism.*

36. S. Sizer, "Politics and Apolitical Religion: The Great Urban Revivals of the Late Nineteenth Century," *Church History* 48, no. 1 (1979): 81–98.

37. T. L. Smith, *Revivalism and Social Reform* (New York: Abingdon Press, 1957).

38. Marsden, *Fundamentalism and American Culture,* chaps. 8–9.

39. Ernest R. Sandeen, *The Roots of Fundamentalism* (Chicago: University of Chicago Press, 1970), 174ff.

40. Norman F. Furniss, *The Fundamentalist Controversy* (New Haven, Conn.: Yale University Press, 1954), chap. 4.

41. A. C. Dixon, general ed., *The Fundamentals* (Chicago: Testimony Publishing, 1910–1915).

42. Professor Charles Erdman of Princeton Theological Seminary, "The Church and Socialism," in vol. 12 of *The Fundamentals*.

43. Robert K. Murrazr, *Red Scare: A Study of National Hysteria, 1919–1920* (New York: McGraw-Hill, 1955).

44. On the battles of fundamentalists with mainstream denominations, see Furniss, *Fundamentalist Controversy*; Stewart G. Cole, *The History of Fundamentalism* (1931; reprint, Westport, Conn.: Greenwood Press, 1971), 65–131; Sandeen, *Roots of Fundamentalism,* 250–66; and Marsden, *Fundamentalism and American Culture,* 164–95. Furniss and Cole include discussions of related controversies in the Methodist, Episcopal, and Disciples of Christ denominations. Furniss includes the Southern Baptists and southern Presbyterians.

45. Marsden, *Fundamentalism and American Culture,* 149.

46. Sandeen, *Roots of Fundamentalism,* 76–100.

47. John L. Eighmy cites the role of E. Y. Mullins, president of the Southern Baptist Theological Seminary, as important in mediating the dispute; *Churches in Cultural Captivity: A History of the Social Attitudes of Southern Baptists,* rev. ed. (Knoxville: University of Tennessee Press, 1987), 126.

48. Marsden, *Fundamentalism and American Culture,* 186.

49. Cf. Sandeen, *Roots of Fundamentalism,* 57–71; Marsden, *Fundamentalism and American Culture,* 189–90.

50. This term was popularized by Tim LaHaye in *The Battle for the Mind* (Old Tappan, N.J.: Revell, 1980).

51. Cited in Marsden, *Reforming Fundamentalism,* 78.

52. The worldview of ordinary fundamentalists is discussed at length in Ammerman, *Bible Believers,* chap. 4.

53. See Marsden, *Reforming Fundamentalism,* 41ff.

54. The story of Norris's path toward schism is told in M. G. Toulouse, "A Case Study in Schism: J. Frank Norris and the SBC," *Foundations* 4 (1981): 32–48.

55. Robert A. Baker, *The Southern Baptist Convention and Its People* (Nashville, Tenn.: Broadman Press, 1974), 356.

56. Fundamentalist congregational life is discussed in Ammerman, *Bible Believers,* chap. 6; and in Boone, *The Bible Tells Them So,* chap. 5.

57. The best discussion of institutional growth in this period is found in Joel A. Carpenter, "Fundamentalist Institutions and the Rise of Evangelical Protestantism, 1929–1942," *Church History* 49 (1980): 62–75.

58. G. W. Dollar, *A History of Fundamentalism in America* (Greenville, S.C.: Bob Jones University Press, 1973), 250ff.

59. See Bill Bright, *Come Help Change the World* (Old Tappan, N.J.: Revell, 1970).

60. Dollar, *History of Fundamentalism,* 257ff.

61. Marsden, *Reforming Fundamentalism,* 22.

62. Marsden, *Fundamentalism and American Culture,* 28–32.

63. Marsden, *Reforming Fundamentalism,* 45–47.

64. Cited in Carpenter, "Fundamentalist Institutions," 66.

65. Ibid., 68.

66. Quoted in D. P. Fuller, *Give the Winds a Mighty Voice* (Waco, Tex.: Word Books, 1972), 110.

67. Frankl, *Televangelism,* 68ff.

68. Sydney E. Ahlstrom, *A Religious History of the American People,* vol. 2 (Garden City, N.Y.: Doubleday Image Books, 1972), 418. This politically radical segment is the only aspect of fundamentalism mentioned by Ahlstrom in describing this period. Until the late 1970s, most historians treated fundamentalism similarly. Its existence as a vital religious sector was ignored.

69. Leo Ribuffo, *The Old Christian Right* (Philadelphia: Temple University Press, 1983), 114.

70. See Ribuffo on Winrod and Smith. On the political radicals of this period, see also Marsden, *Fundamentalism and American Culture,* 210; Gary K. Clabaugh, *Thunder on the Right: The Protestant Fundamentalism* (Chicago: Nelson-Hall, 1974), 83; and Erling Jorstad, *The Politics of Doomsday: Fundamentalists of the Far Right* (Nashville, Tenn.: Abingdon Press, 1970), chap. 1.

71. Weber, *Living in the Shadow,* chap. 6. See also H. Lindsey, *The Road to Holocaust* (New York: Bantam Books, 1989) for an explanation of why premillennialists should not be anti-Semites.

72. W. R. Glass, "Fundamentalism's Prophetic Vision of the Jews: The 1930s," *Jewish Social Studies* 47 (1985): 63–76.

73. Nancy T. Ammerman, "Fundamentalists Proselytizing Jews: Incivility in Preparation for Rapture," in Martin E. Marty and Frederick E. Greenspahn, eds., *Pushing the Faith: Proselytism and Civility in a Pluralistic World* (New York: Crossroad, 1988), 109–22.

74. Clabaugh, *Thunder on the Right*; Jorstad, *Politics of Doomsday*; Phillip Finch, *God, Guts, and Guns* (New York: Seaview, 1983).

75. Finch, in *God, Guts, and Guns,* estimates the total membership of such organizations at about 100,000.

76. On McIntire, see Jorstad, *Politics of Doomsday,* 27–36; and Marsden, *Reforming Fundamentalism.*

77. Farley P. Butler Jr., "Billy Graham and the End of Evangelical Unity" (Ph.D. diss., University of Florida, 1976), 160.

78. Robert Wuthnow cites these factors of national upheaval and self-doubt in "The Political Rebirth of American Evangelicals," in Robert C. Liebman and Robert Wuthnow, eds., *The New Christian Right* (Hawthorne, N.Y.: Aldine, 1983).

79. Steven M. Tipton, *Getting Saved from the Sixties* (Berkeley and Los Angeles: University of California Press, 1982), 37–38. See also R. S. Warner, *New Wine in Old Wineskins* (Berkeley and Los Angeles: University of California Press, 1988).

80. J. C. McKinney and L. B. Bourque, "The Changing South: National Incorporation of a Region," *American Sociological Review* 36 (1971): 399–412.

81. R. W. Stump, "Regional Migration and Religious Patterns in the American South" (Paper presented to the Society for the Scientific Study of Religion, Savannah, Ga., November 1985).

82. Nancy T. Ammerman, "The New South and the New Baptists," *Christian Century* 103, no. 17 (1986): 486–88.

83. Quoted in Ammerman, *Bible Believers,* 41.

84. B. Johnson and M. Shibley, "How New Is the New Christian Right?" (Paper presented to the Society for the Scientific Study of Religion, Savannah, Ga., November 1985); E. Rosenberg, "The 'New Federalism,' The 'New Racism,' and the 'New Right': Are Southern Baptists Still Captive of the Old Culture?" (Paper presented to the Religious Research Association, Chicago, November 1988).

85. See L. J. Lorentzen, "Evangelical Life-Style Concerns Expressed in Political Action," *Sociological Analysis* 41 (1980): 144–54.

86. This view is supported in Richard J. Neuhaus, *The Naked Public Square* (Grand Rapids, Mich.: Erdmans, 1984) and in several essays included in Richard J. Neuhaus and Michael Cromartie, *Piety and Politics: Evangelicals and Fundamentalists Confront the World* (Washington, D.C.: Ethics and Public Policy Center, 1987).

87. Erling Jorstad provides a helpful expanded list of the issues concerning fundamentalist activists in *The New Christian Right, 1981–1988* (Lewiston, N.Y.: Mellen Press, 1988), 6–8.

88. W. D. Sapp makes this point about Southern Baptist growth in "Southern Baptist Responses to the American Economy, 1900–1980," *Baptist History and Heritage* 16 (1981): 3–11.

89. Jeffrey K. Hadden, "Religious Broadcasting and the Mobilization of the New Christian Right," *Journal for the Scientific Study of Religion* 26, no. 1 (1987): 1–24.

90. On the technology and structure of television fund-raising, see Razelle Frankl, "Television and Popular Religion: Changes in Church Offerings," in David G. Bromley and Anson D. Shupe Jr., eds., *New Christian Politics* (Macon, Ga.: Mercer University Press, 1984), 129–38. Such fund-raising power almost inevitably invited corruption. The lavish lifestyle of Jim and Tammy Bakker eventually overstepped the bounds of what would be permitted by the courts.

91. This insight was suggested by Joel Carpenter in conversation, May 1988.

92. Jerry Falwell, *Listen America!* (New York: Doubleday, 1980), 53.

93. V. D. Nordin and W. L. Turner, "More Than Segregationist Academies: The Growing Protestant Fundamentalist Schools," *Phi Delta Kappan* 61, no. 2 (1980): 391–94.

94. D. B. Fleming and T. C. Hunt, "The World as Seen by Students in Accelerated Christian Education Schools," *Phi Delta Kappan* 68, no. 7 (1987): 518–23.

95. Quoted in Ammerman, *Bible Believers,* 176.

96. For descriptions of Christian academies, see Peshkin, *God's Choice*; Ammerman, *Bible Believers,* chap. 10; and Rose, *Keeping Them Out.*

97. Rose, *Keeping Them Out,* 10. A similar argument is made in Ammerman, *Bible Believers,* 195ff.

98. E. Brooks Holifield, "The Three Strands of Jimmy Carter's Religion," *The New Republic,* 5 June 1976, 15–17.

99. Falwell, *Fundamentalist Phenomenon,* 188.

100. Hadden, "Religious Broadcasting," and Liebman, "Mobilizing the Moral Majority," in Liebman and Wuthnow, *New Christian Right,* 50–74.

101. Frankl, *Televangelism,* chap. 9, analyzes the differing contents of the various programs.

102. A. D. Hertzke, *Representing God in Washington* (Knoxville: University of Tennessee Press, 1988), chap. 3, is an excellent analysis of religious lobbying strategies and accomplishments.

103. Jorstad, *The New Christian Right,* 28.

104. Mary J. Neitz, "Family, State, and God: Ideologies of the Right to Life Movement," *Sociological Analysis* 42 (1981): 265–76.

105. Falwell, *Fundamentalist Phenomenon,* 191.

106. A point made by Arthur E. Farnsley, "The Relationship of Belief to Institutional Location in Moral Decision Making: The Case of the Southern Baptists" (Paper presented to the Association for the Sociology of Religion, Atlanta, August 1988); and by M. A. Cavanaugh, "Secularization and the Politics of Traditionalism: The Case of the Right-to-Life Movement," *Sociological Forum* 1 (1986): 251–83; and F. Lechner,

"Fundamentalism and Sociocultural Revitalization in America: A Sociological Interpretation," *Sociological Analysis* 46 (1985): 243–60.

107. Falwell, *Fundamentalist Phenomenon,* 221.

108. Falwell, *Listen America!,* 15.

109. Donald Heinz, "The Struggle to Define America," in Liebman and Wuthnow, *New Christian Right,* 133–48.

110. Hadden, "Religious Broadcasting," 1–24.

111. On the relationship between southern social change and the Southern Baptist Convention, see N. T. Ammerman, *Baptist Battles: Social Change and Religious Conflict in the Southern Baptist Convention* (New Brunswick, N.J.: Rutgers University Press, 1990).

112. Nancy T. Ammerman, "Southern Baptists and the New Christian Right" (Paper presented to the Society for the Scientific Study of Religion, Louisville, Ky., November 1987).

113. See Gary North, *The Theology of Christian Resistance* (Tyler, Tex.: Geneva Divinity School Press, 1983), 60ff. Also see A. P. Jones, "The Imperative of Christian Action: Getting Involved as a Biblical Duty," *Journal of Christian Reconstruction* 8, no. 1 (1981): 86–131, for a list of recommended publications.

114. Reprinted in *Journal of Christian Reconstruction* 2, no. 2 (1975–76): 117–28.

115. Cf., for example, Gary North's *Foundations of Christian Scholarship* (Vallecito, Calif.: Ross House Books, 1979).

116. T. Rose, "On Reconstruction and the American Republic," *Journal of Christian Reconstruction* 5, no. 1 (1978): 34.

117. Gary North, "Comprehensive Redemption: A Theology for Social Action," *Journal of Christian Reconstruction* 8, no. 1 (1981): 19.

118. Rousas J. Rushdoony, "Biblical Law and Western Civilization," *Journal of Christian Reconstruction* 2, no. 2 (1975): 5.

119. Otto Scott, "Caucasian Self-Hatred," *Chalcedon Report* 283 (Feb. 1989): 2–3.

120. Otto Scott, *Chalcedon Report* 273 (Apr. 1988): 8–9.

121. Although the goal seems to be abolition of all racism, one cannot read these revisionist versions of white history without being reminded of the rhetoric of more radical right-wing groups.

122. Volume 8, no. 1, of *Journal of Christian Reconstruction* is a symposium on social action, and volume 5, no. 1, is a symposium on politics. See especially articles by A. P. Jones in the former and by R. Walton and Gary North in the latter.

123. North, *Theology of Christian Resistance,* 63.

124. Jones, "The Imperative of Christian Action."

4

Clarity, Mothers, and the Mass-Mediated National Soul: A Defense of Ambiguity

Linda Kintz

What happens when it is a woman who comes to embody the social at its most perverse?

—*Jacqueline Rose*

Ever since somebody ran a big old Zamboni down the infobahn, everything equals everything else.

—*Kate Clinton*

In the last several decades simplification, or the ideology of clarity, has helped move the center of contemporary U.S. politics far to the right, as it made a tidy fit with a media culture that privileges the quick, simple message over time-consuming complexities and ambiguities and that manufactures a commodified audience by ratings.[1] Simplification has, of course, long been a part of the U.S. mythology of common sense and the common man, and it has functioned as a basic element of the logic of economic rationalization in which value is ultimately equated with the simple clarity of the bottom line. In terms of contemporary politics, however, an especially important feature of that simplification has been its legitimation by the activism of conservative women, who have sealed clarity with the proper motherly face and have helped settle right-wing politics deep within the "true" nature of God-given humanity. This belief that the right-wing position is an inherent part of humanity's authentic, true identity has too often enabled right-wing conservatism to revitalize a nativist, libertarian populism that lies dangerously close to racist and anti-Semitic conspiracy theories, in spite of legitimate denials that that was its intent.[2]

Simplification takes on special importance at times of change, when technological innovation, the internationalization of the economy, and the cultural transitions of postmodernity make it all the more difficult for people to interpret a world that is moving too fast; complexity invites simplicity as a form of self-defense. Patrick Buchanan, for example, referring to the man he admired most when he was a teenager, Joseph McCarthy, describes the appeal of such clarity: "There is a simplicity that exists on the far side of complexity, and there is a communication of sentiment and attitude not to be discovered by careful exegesis of text."[3] The fact that clarity is the most highly constructed, most ambiguous concept of all, of course, means the linguistic violence on which signification rests is at risk of turning into actual violence against those members who reveal the oppressiveness of the social contract.

Before considering the activism of two influential conservative women who have been passionately involved in the construction of clarity, Phyllis Schlafly and Beverly LaHaye, I want to develop the concept of symbolic resonance as a way to describe the "communication of sentiment and attitude" to which Buchanan referred. Symbolic resonance, as I use it here, refers to a mechanism in which passionate emotions are legitimated by an overarching, male-supremacist superrationality. Under that umbrella, the combination of emotion and rationality makes empirical facts seem irrelevant (even when one acknowledges that those facts are socially constructed).

In the context of the religious right, passion with a superrational guarantee unites a wide spectrum of very different groups, many of whom would legitimately disclaim any actual contact with one other. Nested within each other like Russian dolls, however, the elements of this symbolic structure rise from the womb to the heavens, uniting God as Creator, the family, a divinely inspired Declaration of Independence and U.S. Constitution, a nation defined as God's unique experiment in human history, a belief that the unregulated free market is inherent in human nature, and a claim that the United States has a God-given responsibility to spread free-market democratic capitalism to the rest of the world. At both the beginning and the end of this clear narrative, God's judgment seals a circular logic of God, family, mother, nation, and global duty within a Judeo-Christian Book of the World made coherent from top to bottom, from beginning to end.

In studying the conservative symbolic resonance of Margaret Thatcher's England, Jacqueline Rose found that, in spite of the failures of conservative economic reforms and the resulting demoralization, Thatcher nevertheless succeeded in changing the national soul by mobilizing "a new ideological constituency."[4] Rose shows why a study of that constituency has to bring a discussion of economic interests together with what she calls a psychopolitical analysis, for only such an expanded reading can reveal

> the set of convictions which hover somewhere between an articulable belief and a fantasy in which collective self-imaginings take shape... [I]t is in the crucible of subjective identities that political histories are

> forged—the issue not one of immediate or the most obvious forms of self-interest, but of how subjects "envision" themselves... as if the fantasy component and legacy of Thatcherism could ride over all the material evidence (the worst recession, the decline if not collapse of health and educational provision, since the war). (74)

Similarly, in the United States in the same period, arguments about Reaganism often seemed to fly in the face of empirical facts and contradictions, which made no difference because the debate was not being staged on those terms. Or rather, a new fantasy component had redefined what was to be *counted* as empirical facts.

In the case of Thatcherism, Rose notes, the new ideological constituency rested on an "utter certainty of judgment that allowed Thatcher to release into our public fantasy life, with no risk of confusion, the violence which underpins the authority of the State" (59). Such certainty depended on "the repeated and central terms of consistency, persistence, and sameness, the refusal of any possible gap between reality and intent." And it relied on a very particular idea of language, "a denial of the precariousness of language itself, the insistence on the utter coherence of the word" (61). This was a word whose ostensible clarity was guaranteed by a narrow interpretation of natural law, which presumed as foundational an unambiguous definition of gender and human nature along with the absolute moral supremacy of the unregulated free market. Rose extended her study of Thatcherism to argue that right-wing ideologies, in general, gain their specific force by this refusal of contradiction or gap, as they try to "harness fantasy to reason." That is, they forcefully buttress with reason those points within the logic of the social contract where rationality is least secure, sites Rose calls the "flashpoints" of the social. On the very edge of the social, a rationality of absolute clarity both forcefully exerts itself and faces the constant evidence of its own impossibility. Its logic, then, requires that it exert itself even more strongly.

Claims of utter coherence always edge dangerously close to rationales for wars of purification because they overtly reinstate as objects of attack those elements in the social contract that have been historically repressed even if not always directly targeted, such as homosexuality, racial difference, female agency, and laboring bodies. This structure inevitably encourages metaphors of attack and warfare, for people go to war insofar as they believe absolutely in their own virtue. Drawing on the works of Sigmund Freud, Rose suggests that "absolute or total knowledge seems over and again to be offered as one cause—if not *the* cause—of war" (16). Demanding absolute clarity is also part of the structure of paranoia, in which aggressivity is projected outward onto an invisible adversary. In that structure built on fear, the paranoid person is then required to go after those enemies: "If you produce the enemy, then you must fight him" (28).

Through her motherly, nurturing figuration, the proper mother helps legitimate the deployment of paranoid fears about the family; the unquestioning clarity that she nurtures requires a cold war, even if that war goes underground, only to reemerge in the culture wars of contemporary politics. In Rose's analysis, the Cold War that followed World War II did not concern itself so much with a country's defense against an enemy as it did with the very construction of an enemy, the projection outward of an internalized, terrifying foreignness within. She quotes Franco Fornari: "War serves to defend ourselves against the 'Terrifier' as an internal absolute enemy... in this manner we arrive at the incredible paradox that the most important security function is not to defend ourselves from an external enemy but to find one" (34).

And though one stereotype of femininity claims that women inherently oppose violence, Rose suggests that Thatcher represented a different but equally powerful stereotype illustrated by such things as, for example, her support for the death penalty. That stereotype of femininity "does not serve to neutralize violence but allows for its legitimation" (59), providing the state with the symbolic figuration to legitimate the "retributive violence of... ethical absolutism." The misogynist fantasy of the castrating mother, of the punitive superego, of the terrifying omnipotent woman shadows every strong woman, and it is confusingly and dangerously intertwined with the figure of the victimized woman who has been sacrificed to seal the social contract.

Thus Rose argues that strong conservative women like Thatcher, and by extension Schlafly and LaHaye, must be analyzed as *both* fantasy and real persons, within a volatile symbolic field in which the aspect of absolute truth most rigidly guarded is absolute gender difference. Femininity here is both appealed to and denied by women like Thatcher, Schlafly, and LaHaye in a double and contradictory configuration whose instability helps feed the machinery of paranoia. In this configuration, strong conservative women have the capacity to embody the omnipotent mother while at the same time denying feminist claims to female agency. They can, in other words, act exactly like a feminist while condemning feminism. Within the symbolic space of this unstable, fantasmatic figuration that she both constructs and exploits, the modern traditional woman legitimates and, even more powerfully, embodies the social contract "in the worst of its effects" (42), both in reality and in the social imagination. And she provides an absolutist version of femininity that can then be used by a male-supremacist social contract "to draw a line around what culture will recognize of itself" while it excludes, violently if necessary, what it refuses to recognize.

In the work of Schlafly and LaHaye, an anticommunist Cold War framework joins absolutist Christianity in such a way as to code ambiguity not only as subversive to a national security state but as a Satanic force that threatens Christian civilization itself. And this Christian-anticommunist framework exhibits another characteristic of war. If a nation thinks it is fighting for freedom, Rose suggests, might it not be that it is, in fact, the *fear* of freedom, and in particular, the fear of the freedom of women by both men and women, that leads to war?

The threatened and threatening figure of the proper mother, the modern traditional woman, has also powerfully undercut the possibility of an effective class analysis in the United States by the construction of an "authentic" U.S. identity that is also symbolically, if uneasily, related to corporate interests. That identity—a clear, ahistorical, authentic Transparent American Subject—joins two different class positions: (1) the common man who considers himself to be following in the footsteps of the mythologized Founding Fathers and who resists government regulation and taxation while passionately wanting government off his back, and (2) the corporation as a legal entity or person who resists government regulation and taxation while passionately wanting government off its back.[5]

In this powerful simplification, an unstable blurring joins two very different interests. The Transparent American Subject can be *either* the multinational corporation or the common man, or both at once, for at times both speak the same language. Once again, the claim of clarity covers over an almost-liquid instability. Like the conservative woman who acts like a feminist while condemning feminism, here the victim of corporate activity often inadvertently finds himself defending corporate activity, and he is left in a volatile and uneasy position. At times, his act of resistance becomes indistinguishable from an act of support for those who helped cause his troubles. The very concept of populism is thus thrown into a symbolically loaded rhetorical field in which the common man, the anti-Semite, the supremacist, the absolutist Christian, the patriot, and the corporation as person try to occupy the same unstable symbolic subject position—and all must be guaranteed by the proper mother, who represents the control of women's freedom.

Though the activism of conservative women went unnoticed by secular analysts for far too long, many of these women have long been engaged in a sophisticated reconstruction of the United States in terms of a clarity that might be called a postmodern, purifying "folking." An abstract, idealized, but passionately held definition of nation, class, and community under the cosmic guidance of God covers over an economy defined not by national boundaries but by global corporate activity; by a middle class that exists in name only, because it is now split in two, an unskilled half having been jettisoned along with the poor from public and corporate responsibility; and by "small towns" as often as not consisting of edge cities and suburbs with privatized security services and affinities based on property values and the sameness of belief.

The modern traditionalist woman's activism and the ideology of clarity have helped produce a jammed ideological constituency—a jammed sense of history—that has lost its ability to address human mortality, physical vulnerability, laboring bodies, and difference, issues fundamental to the organization of a democratic social contract.[6]

Phyllis Schlafly was an elected delegate to three Republican conventions prior to the publication of her book *A Choice Not an Echo,* which appeared in May 1964.[7] Analyzing that book helps understand the early stirrings of what has now become a full-blown reactionary political movement; Schlafly went on to found the Eagle Forum and to serve as the cochair of Patrick Buchanan's presidential campaign in 1996. Schlafly's political positions in 1964 were located squarely in the rhetoric of simplification that now seems very familiar because of its resonance with contemporary conservative discourse: "Civilization progresses, freedom is won, and problems are solved because we have wonderful people who think up simple solutions" (81). These people "can cut through the egghead complexities in Foggy Bottom" (83). Schlafly's book, which was reprinted in June and August of that year, presaged the internal split within the Republican Party that became evident in the tepid right-wing support for George Bush and country-club Republicans in the elections of 1992. In 1964, Main Street and Wall Street opposed one another, but in Gingrich Republicanism there was an attempted realignment between Main Street and Wall Street in opposition to Washington, D.C.[8] That attempt has been resoundingly reversed, however, by the fact that the speculative economy of Wall Street now dominates economic policy.

Sara Diamond suggests the term "fusionism" to describe the way anticommunism, libertarianism, and traditionalism allowed for an integrated structure for conservative thought after World War II:

> Communism and, by extension, the liberalism of the New Deal Democrats provided the threat of an external enemy. Anticommunism provided a perspective from which both libertarians and traditionalists could see each other's points of view. Economic libertarians could see that the threat of socialism required a response more profound than mere fiscal policy or theory. Traditionalists could see that cherished institutions and moral persuasion alone could not stem the tide toward socialism.[9]

Diamond also argues that fusionism helps explain why conservatives who opposed the federal government of the New Deal nevertheless supported the federal government as represented by the Pentagon:

> The conservative movement was oppositional in that it was, tactically, more anticommunist than the administrations in power, but system-supportive in that it endorsed the prevailing strategic doctrine of U.S.

> military supremacy over the rest of the world. In contradiction to conservatives' professed goals of limiting government intervention in the capitalist economy and of opposing government attempts to achieve racial and gender equality, the movement was not anti-statist on questions of how to fight communism. At no time did the conservative movement oppose the deployment of state agencies, from the Pentagon to the FBI and CIA, to subvert and repress independent leftist political action at home and abroad. (110)

In 1964, Republicans like Schlafly came from the Midwest, the West, and the South to participate in Barry Goldwater's campaign; their activism is often forgotten in contemporary discussions of welfare reform and Medicare and Medicaid cuts, though these fights were already amply prepared for in Schlafly's arguments. Diamond also reminds us that "the conservative anticommunist movement made its initial forays into Republican politics at about the same time that the civil rights movement precipitated a major party realignment around the issue of race" (66). She argues that even though the segregationist attempts of such grassroots movements as the Citizens' Councils failed in the South, nevertheless "the mobilization of white racist sentiment had long-term political implications" and taught the lesson that "racial divisiveness could pay dividends in electoral politics" (66).

Schlafly also prefigured the strategy of simplification that Rush Limbaugh has used so successfully; her opening chapter is entitled "Who's Looney Now?" And though Schlafly was at the time highly critical of the "hidden persuaders," or the moneyed interests who engage in well-funded propaganda and duplicitous Gallup polls, her book also reveals how much contemporary conservatism has learned since 1964. As she said then:

> The advance planning and sense stimuli employed to capture a $10 million cigarette or soap market are nothing compared to the brainwashing and propaganda blitzes used to insure control of the largest cash market in the world: the Executive Branch of the United States Government. (5)

Going on to situate the argument directly in the bosom of the family, she argues that just as "every family budget in the United States was unbalanced" when Parisian dressmakers decided to make skirts shorter, similarly every family budget was also unbalanced when these "few secret kingmakers based in New York selected every Republican presidential nominee from 1936 to 1960 and successfully forced this choice on a free country where there are more than 34 million Republican voters. Fantastic? In this book we will examine the record and see how they did it" (6–7).

The historian Richard White identifies one of the dominant myths of American ideology as that of the innocent victim, like George Armstrong Custer or the pioneers, threatened by Indians; their "innocent" persecution justified retaliatory violence against the barbarians who threatened them.[10] The theme of the innocent victim draws, as well, on the symbolic weight of the Christian image of Jesus, who was also a victim unjustly persecuted. And just as Schlafly's mechanistic anticommunism repeats these themes, it also repeats a related binary opposition familiar from the ideology of post–World War I Germany, described in great detail by Klaus Theweleit.[11] There, anticommunism was linked not only with an absolutist defense of men's virility and women's motherly purity but to the issue of betrayal. The belief that Germany had been betrayed by the Armistice was linked to various categories of parasites who fed upon authentic Germans, especially weak bureaucrats and international financial conspirators. Such a linkage provided a throbbing, even seething emotional ground for feelings of rage and justifications for revenge. Barbara Ehrenreich describes that sentiment: "[They believed] that the German army had been betrayed in World War I—'stabbed in the back,' as it was so often said—by the communists, with their internationalist ideology, as well as by the vacillating socialists and other, insufficiently resolute, civilian forces."[12]

Schlafly focuses her anticommunist arguments and suspicions of a conspiracy on Roosevelt's New Deal, which she identifies as the origin of false versus real American values. The most persecuted critic of the New Deal was Robert Taft, whose language again sounds familiar: "We cannot clean up the mess in Washington, balance the budget, reduce taxes, check creeping Socialism, tell what is muscle or fat in our sprawling rearmanent programs, purge subversives from our State Department, unless we come to grips with our foreign policy, upon which all other policies depend."[13] Not only were Roosevelt's social programs redolent of communism but, according to Schlafly, Roosevelt "sold out our allies in Eastern Europe and China [at Yalta], and gave Stalin three votes in the United Nations" (46).

Her argument draws on the nativist and isolationist themes of the America First movement, for which Charles Lindbergh was a spokesman (he eventually became notorious as a Nazi sympathizer).[14] America First opposed entering World War II for reasons that complicate the myth of World War II as the "good war" that everyone supported. Schlafly repeats those reasons: "Americans did not want to go to war to battle a totalitarian system in Europe if they were to get Socialism here when it [was] all over" (39). Writing about the involvement of Pat Buchanan's father in America First, Charles Lane quotes Lindbergh, speaking in September 1941: "Only three groups are agitating for American entry into the war—the British, the Jewish, and the Roosevelt administration."[15]

In what Schlafly calls billion-dollar robberies, those interests are blamed for stealing the elections of 1940, 1944, 1948, and 1969 by causing the Republicans to pick candidates who could not win because they would not speak out about real issues. The real issues, as likely as not, had to do with communism, though they also had to do with rejecting the economic nationalism favored by America First and expanding into international markets and internationalist government policies. Though most voters imagined it was they who elected the president, in Schlafly's opinion, "the Republican presidential nominee [from 1937 to 1960] was selected by a small group of secret kingmakers" (5).

Explaining those sellouts, Schlafly begins with 1940, when the pressure from financial interests caused Wendell Wilkie to refuse to make an issue of Roosevelt's acquiescence to Stalin's invasion of Poland, Finland, Latvia, Lithuania, and Estonia. Similarly, in 1944 Thomas E. Dewey did not mention the fact that the Roosevelt administration had invited the early disaster of Pearl Harbor in order to manipulate Japan into firing the first shot and drawing the United States into the war. Dewey and Earl Warren in 1948 did not campaign on the real issue of Communist infiltration in government, Schlafly argues, though Dwight Eisenhower did so in 1952, with the result that he won on a slogan of "Corruption, Communism, and Korea." By 1960 even Richard Nixon had refused to campaign on the real issue: Kennedy's sponsorship of legislation to repeal the loyalty oath provision in the National Defense Education Act and the fact that Lyndon Johnson killed states' rights legislation that would have allowed the states themselves to punish subversion.

But though Robert Taft and other anticommunists had identified communism as the enemy, Schlafly argues that after the war, real anticommunism hardly entered the minds of bankers and others who stood to make a great deal of money out of the Lend-Lease Act, British loans, and the Marshall Plan. Postwar kingmakers had, in fact, legitimated Roosevelt's socialist activities simply because they were profitable; and thus the kingmakers would not allow a candidate on the Republican ticket "unless he has a foreign policy acceptable to the New York financiers and banking interests who profit greatly from the New Deal foreign policy" (48).

Schlafly identifies these kingmakers as a group officially called the "De-Bilderbergers," secret alliances of people in high finance and in the press who first met secretly in the Netherlands in May 1954.[16] In a small book published in 1980, *The Global Manipulators: The Bilderberg Group, the Trilateral Commission. Covert Power Groups of the West,* Robert Eringer initially distances himself from those who hold conspiracy theories about these groups, only to find himself more and more in their grip by the book's end. He begins by tracing the shadowy origins of the group in stories of the Illuminati, a secret society established in Bavaria by Adam Weishaupt in 1776, "based on the philosophical ideals of Plato" (7). Later, Eringer argues, John Ruskin revised these ideals in his teaching, and his influence led to the formation of a group of Ruskin's "disciples," including Cecil Rhodes, who founded the Round Table Group on 5 February 1881. The purpose of that group was to organize educated men of influence "to federate the English-speaking peoples and to bring all habitable portions of the world under their control" (8).

These intricate linkages to shadowy groups like the Illuminati are also part of an anti-Semitic discourse readily available on the far right. And though it is not fair to accuse Schlafly of anti-Semitism without more concrete evidence nor to suggest guilt by association, the rigidity of her monolithic anticommunist framework, which prevents nuanced investigation, makes her argument far too easily available to those who believe in conspiracy theories about international Jewish interests. She finds that those "highly placed New York kingmakers [worked] toward 'convergence' between the Republican and Democratic parties so as to preserve their America Last foreign policy and eliminate foreign policy from political campaigns" (108) and that they were heavily weighted in favor of liberal viewpoints on foreign policy and excluded those whose perspective was pro-American. Their purpose was "to get the American taxpayers to protect the kingmakers' heavy investments in England and Western Europe" (114), the primary sponsor of that strategy being the Council on Foreign Relations. And just as the kingmakers were able to control the Republican choice of candidates, so too did they control political propaganda, which included control of Madison Avenue public relations firms, national magazines, and most of the influential newspapers around the country. The *New York Times* was the "chief propaganda organ for the secret kingmakers" (83).

Blanche Wiesen Cook argues that the meetings of the Bilderbergers were, in fact, early stages in the organization of multinational economic interests, marking "a new economic power without flag or loyalty."[17] The Bilderberger meetings began the process of coordinating multinational activities in the interests of maximizing profit; the need for such structures increased as the power of multinationals increased. Those in attendance were representatives of international corporations, international banking and business interests, and, often, academics and economic theorists. Cook argues that their initial purpose was not to deal with the threat of Communist political subversion but with the threat of "the Soviet economic offensive. The Bilderbergers considered the potential danger of Soviet economic competitions as deadly to Western freedom as nuclear warfare" (342).

The proceedings of all the Bilderberger meetings were discussed by Eisenhower's cabinet and the Council of Economic Advisers. An organization that grew out of those early meetings, the Trilateral Commission, was dedicated, as Cook says, "to the liberalization of the world economy through economic integration and free trade." It was formed to encourage international interdependence and to "protect international business interests against 'the intrusion of national governments' or other nationalist pressures" (343).[18] But these multinational structures should not be seen as the counter to the imperialism of the nation-state, argues Cook:

> With corporate headquarters form Brussels to Bangkok, the multinationals are ... protected by NATO and counterinsurgency everywhere ... Although they present a challenge to the traditional nation-state, they have done little to improve the quality of life. Throughout the free world, now dominated by U.S.- and European-based transnationals, unemployment and underdevelopment prevail. Malnourishment and illiteracy increase. Locked into a phenomenal arms race that even the developed nations cannot afford, the "underdeveloped world" increasingly hosts the transnationals and is increasingly bonded to the military-industrial complex through ties of dependency, militarism, and repression. (344)

The way a critique of multinational power comes together with Schlafly's impassioned defense of U.S. sovereignty is important here. In Schlafly's narrative, these kingmakers actually saved Soviet communism from its own internal collapse after the war through a "hidden policy of perpetuating the Red empire in order to perpetuate the high level of Federal spending and control" (115). In collapsing a legitimate critique of the amorality of financial investors and the compromises of a liberal welfare state, Schlafly finds that kingmakers and socialism had become one and the same and that they encompassed every part of federal spending and all government workers. For all of these had a "vested interest in preventing—at all costs—the election of a president ... who will let the Soviet system collapse of its own internal weaknesses, who will curtail the foreign giveaway programs, as well as the level of Federal spending, and whose foreign policy will serve the best interest of the United States of America" (115).

The symbolic resonance between the 1952 Republican Party platform, quoted here from Schlafly, and contemporary conservative political discourse shows how effective that simplification has been:

> We shall eliminate from the State Department and from every Federal office, all, wherever they may be found, who share responsibility for the needless predicaments and perils in which we find ourselves. We shall also sever from the public payroll the hoards of loafers, incompetents and unnecessary employees who clutter the administration of our foreign affairs ... The Government of the United States, under Republican leadership, will repudiate all commitments contained in secret understandings such as those of Yalta which aid Communist enslavements ... We shall again make liberty into a beacon light of hope that will penetrate the dark places ... We shall see to it that no treaty or agreement with other countries deprives our citizens of the rights guaranteed them by the Federal Constitution ... There are no Communists in the Republican Party ... We never compromised with Communism

> and we have fought to expose it and to eliminate it in government and American life. A Republican President will appoint only persons of unquestioned loyalty...[and reduce] expenditures by the elimination of waste and extravagance so that the budget will be balanced and a general tax reduction can be made. (65)

Schlafly argues unapologetically that Eisenhower's victory on this platform was "aided by Senator Joseph McCarthy's television analysis of candidate Stevenson's soft-on-Communism record" (65).

Goldwater's candidacy could easily draw on the issue of betrayal. In 1964, when Nixon allied himself with Rockefeller, Goldwater, in familiar language, called the alliance "immoral" and referred to it as "the Munich of the Republican Party." That characterization helped galvanize Schlafly and thousands of grassroots activists around Goldwater's candidacy, a crucial moment in the origin of contemporary conservative activism now used so successfully by groups like the Christian Coalition: "Goldwater's victory proved that even a fortune in paid workers and hidden persuaders could not match the tens of thousands of dedicated volunteer grassroots workers who didn't stop until the ballots were counted" (91). The Goldwater candidacy, as Diamond points out, also owed much of its strength to a related aspect of the rhetoric of simplification, the racism exploited by a strategy that appealed to white southern Democrats and targeted George Wallace's constituency. Those voters opposed civil rights legislation and Lyndon Johnson's War on Poverty, both of which were put in the hands of the federal government and removed from state control.[19]

The effectiveness of this rhetoric of simplification lies in the fact that its clear structure can be easily used in a variety of different circumstances with very little adjustment, and it easily fits into an absolutist religious binary of good and evil. The lingering effects of the betrayal at Yalta and the "Munich" caused by East Coast Republicans exacerbated a sense of crisis felt by conservatives in 1964, when the U.S. faced catastrophes all around the world: in Laos, Vietnam, Cambodia, Pakistan, India, Greece, Portugal, the Congo, and Algeria. At the time, Schlafly argues, Fidel Castro was building a "fountainhead for subversion in Panama, Venezuela, throughout Latin America, and all the way to Zanzibar" (10). And just as the West had refused to read Hitler's plans for subversion in *Mein Kampf,* so in 1964 it refused to recognize that "the most important national problem is the survival of American freedom and independence in the face of the communist threat" (12).

Paranoia about possible humiliation also easily turns into a hatred of the United Nations. Schlafly cites State Department Publication 7277, which deals with the administration's plans to "abolish our Army, our Navy, our Air Force and our nuclear weapons, and makes us subject to a United Nations

Peace Force" (12). In this respect, she sees the Johnson administration as having abandoned the strategy of containment in favor of détente and interdependence between the United States and the Soviet Union while trying to force a decrease in national defense spending. All this happened, she argues, while there were Communists everywhere within the administration itself. Those Communists were located side by side with others who would be readily available as targets once communism was removed as an overt threat, even if it never disappeared but was simply recoded: "State Department Security Officer Scott McLeod listed 648 State Department employees as having had Communist activities and associations and 94 as perverts" (15).

Adding to this sense of national crisis was the fact that the Panama Canal was turned over to Panama, while "Communist-led mobs rioted in the Panama Canal Zone" and "Red agents" participated in those riots. In Panama Johnson prepared another betrayal, "another giveaway of free-world rights and territory that will rank with the tragic Roosevelt and Truman concessions at Teheran, Yalta and Potsdam" (14–15). And in listing other evidence of Johnson's socialist and perverse sympathies, she reminds us that he presented J. Robert Oppenheimer with the $50,000 Enrico Fermi Award, in spite of the fact that Oppenheimer's security clearance had been revoked by the Eisenhower administration because, to quote William L. Borden, executive director of the congressional Joint Committee on Atomic Energy, he "was contributing substantial monthly sums to the Communist Party, ... his wife and younger brother were Communists, ... he had at least one Communist mistress ... [and] he was responsible for employing a number of Communists ... at wartime Los Alamos."[20] Johnson helped precipitate the culture wars, as well, by presenting the Medal of Freedom to Edmund Wilson in 1963, even though, as Schlafly complains, Wilson had four wives and had written books "so immoral that, even under our contemporary standards, [their] sale had to be stopped in many places" (16). Wilson had also voted the Communist ticket in 1932 and the Socialist ticket in several other elections.

By now Schlafly is making two opposite arguments simultaneously (which Rose suggests is a characteristic of paranoid arguments): The United States is the greatest country in the history of civilization; in the United States, Communists and liberals are everywhere and have ruined everything. But Schlafly's book also shows how easy it is to combine her criticism of corporate activity with a monolithic anticommunism linked to a dangerous racism and anti-Semitism. They lie there fully formed and ready.

Her rhetoric, once again, sounds eerily familiar: "The kingmakers are playing for high stakes—control of Federal spending—and they do not intend to lose ... Can grassroots Americans complete in November the victory they started winning in July?" (120–21).

Schlafly's book was written in 1964. She later became a leading figure in the opposition to the Equal Rights Amendment (ERA) and abortion, issues that found many women passionately drawn into activism for the first time, their participation framed in terms of religion, prayer, and action. Tracing Beverly LaHaye's description of the founding of Concerned Women for America (CWA)—which LaHaye sees as the counter to the National Organization for Women that claims to speak for all women—helps show how powerfully Schlafly's arguments have been incorporated into the concerns of many conservative women. Framed in terms of a rigid, absolutist definition of gender, the centrality of the family becomes an authentic, unquestioned truth capable of arousing deep passions that override contradictions. And LaHaye's proper feminist, the modern traditional woman, will be situated directly within the passionate frame of anticommunism described by Schlafly.

In her book *Who but a Woman?,* LaHaye situates the need for women's activism within an apocalyptic narrative, which suffered a catastrophic interruption caused by feminism.[21] Like communism, feminism is characterized as not only subversive but even Satanic. LaHaye describes a sense of crisis so great that women have been required to do double duty. Of course they have had to continue to make their families their first priority, but because the dangers caused by feminism impacted so directly on those families, their role as proper Christian and conservative women *required* that they also take action in the public sphere. This is a strategically powerful move, joining both prayer and action to the reconstruction of the primary role of women as mothers. By providing women with an identity and a form of solidarity based on their commitment to families under threat, this apocalyptic narrative has rescued them from the banality to which secular culture often consigns the housewife and mother. They were and are to be heroines: "Courageous women have been known to save a nation" (9).

LaHaye compares the extent of the crisis faced by the United States to another crisis in which women were called upon to act in the public sphere, this one in the 1960s in Brazil, which was supposedly threatened by a Communist revolution. And events in Cuba exacerbated the sense of hysteria. Like Schlafly, LaHaye collapses concern with moral corruption into the simplified language of anticommunism: "The nation was ruled by morally corrupt men who had allowed themselves to be manipulated by communist subversives" (9). As in Schlafly's narrative, this threat of communism also framed the crisis faced by Americans, just as it provided a model for combating it. In order to counter the Communists, LaHaye tells us, businessmen in Brazil established a television station, educational campaigns, and intelligence and information networks.

Yet a closer look at that period in Brazil finds the Goulart government in power, a Socialist rather than a Communist government, though this is a distinction that makes no difference in such an implacable binary rhetoric.[22] At the time, priests and Catholic lay people were involved in Peasant Leagues in the countryside. Their work included literacy projects and health education, among other activities, and were part of the social justice work of liberation theology. Aided by the groups LaHaye describes and by a crackdown by the pope on progressive priests and bishops, the government was overthrown by the military, which went on to set up a police state that relied on death squads, torture, and human rights violations. It also shut down the Congress, eliminated the vote for mayors and governors, censored all media, and expelled labor leaders and progressives, one of whom was Paulo Freire.[23]

LaHaye does not tell that part of the story, although the right's moral policing has, in fact, been closely tied to violent elements, semi-acknowledged by official power, that police "undesirable elements." Ignoring that part of Brazil's story, which she found in *Reader's Digest,* LaHaye goes on to argue the importance of women in Brazil's "democratic" victory over communism, which she attributes to the fact that their activities were not monitored so closely by the government as were men's; as mothers, they were given wider leeway.[24] Though she will later argue that feminists have overly generalized the term "women," here she universalizes "women" to refer to conservative women of the landed gentry and the aristocratic business class. The Campaign of Women for Democracy developed a powerful strategy of "cells," or women's chapters, throughout the community; organized protest meetings and debates; and distributed leaflets and pamphlets throughout the country. They also organized a "March of the Family with God toward Freedom" that drew over 600,000 women in its support, with a slogan of "Family, tradition, property." Their activity taught LaHaye a lesson:

> This nation which God has given us, immense and marvelous as it is, is in extreme danger. We have allowed men of limitless ambition, without Christian faith or scruples, to bring our people misery, destroying our economy, disturbing our social peace, to create hate and despair. They have infiltrated our nation, our government administration, our armed forces and even our churches with servants of totalitarianism.[25]

The activities and prayers of Brazilian women, in LaHaye's telling, saved their country from a bloody Communist revolution: "Who but a woman could have led such a successful educational campaign against Marxism?" (13).

And it is precisely this call that she issues to conservative women of America, who face an equally dire threat: "Some feminists are becoming more and more open about their true objectives: lesbianism, Marxism, and extreme social change... In Brazil, the subversives called themselves Communists; in America, they may call themselves feminists or humanists. The label makes little difference, because many of them are seeking the destruction of morality and human freedom" (14).

In one fell swoop, the rhetorical frame of simplification has placed the template of clear anticommunism onto the fragmented, confusing diversity of economic and social change and made it manageable in terms of women's duties as mothers. Though Nancy T. Ammerman, in her history of Protestant fundamentalism (Chapter 3 in this volume), argues that fundamentalists in the United States were rarely overtly anticommunist, arguments like LaHaye's show that the defense of absolute moral values, located within a structural binary framework of good and evil, makes many fundamentalists and evangelicals anticommunist in spite of themselves.

Motherly identity is also lifted out of the realm of domestic boredom into the global sphere of anticommunist heroism and public duty, and U.S. women are now assigned every bit as much responsibility as the women of Brazil. LaHaye has here provided a defense of agency, even a permissible form of aggression for women in the public sphere. Though secular feminists are demonized because they exhibit manly aggression, in this arena aggression is legitimately feminized by being symbolically recoded. It is now aggression in the interests of the family, carried out by a proper mother:

> Someone once remarked that perhaps it is because God has implanted in a woman's heart and mind an aggressiveness that shows itself most obviously when her children or husband is threatened. Even in the animal kingdom, we see examples of lionesses fighting to the death to protect their offspring, and normally docile mother dogs will become vicious when they sense that their puppies are in danger. (15)

Thus, because women have a God-given mothering instinct at the very core of their being, they will seek to protect, comfort, and serve. Simultaneously they also have a legitimate instinct to be aggressive and active, because aggression and activity have been carefully situated within the family: "They see their families and lives coming under attack and they cannot remain passive" (16).

LaHaye then constructs a clear narrative about conservative women's reaction to the chaos and threat of feminism and socialism by recounting the shock and dismay caused by the National Women's Conference in November 1977 in Houston, at which, she argues, 20 percent of the delegates were conservative women, though the convention was controlled by the following radical groups: the National Organization for Women (NOW), the American Civil Liberties Union (ACLU), the League of Women Voters, the

Women's Political Caucus, ERAmerica, the National Federation of Business and Professional Women's Clubs, the Citizens Library Council on the Status of Women, the National Gay Task Force, Church Women United, American Association of University Women, the Women's Alliance Coalition of Labor Women, and Common Cause.

The conservative women were shocked, nauseated, and finally enraged, as was LaHaye, when she heard the stories of the convention from one of the women who had attended:

> Those feminists had managed to convince Congress to spend five million dollars of our tax money to hold state conventions and then this grand finale at Houston, which seemed to be a Marxist/lesbian circus, manipulated and controlled from the beginning by a dissident group of feminists who were demanding federal intervention into our lives. (29)

That passionate emotional reaction, joined to Schlafly's superrationality, marked the beginning of LaHaye's intense, increasingly sophisticated activism and the founding of Concerned Women for America (CWA): "My nausea soon changed to rage, and I determined in my heart that I would do whatever was necessary to raise up a standard of righteousness against feminism" (29). She realized that she and other religious women like her had, in fact, been so busy trying to be good wives and mothers that they had not noticed what had been going on; they "had been completely ignorant of the social forces that threatened to destroy our families and our nation" (29). It was time for them to emulate the women of Brazil and "get busy and do something to oppose the feminist movement—or any movement that purposed to destroy the sanctity of our homes" (29).

After the shock of the National Women's Conference, she and other women began to organize, first holding coffees with other women in southern California and then incorporating CWA in 1979, developing a national organization with state and local chapters and prayer groups, and finally opening an office in Washington, D.C., to help lobby Congress: "We are here, hundreds of thousands now, telling the world that feminism is a false view of the world" (31). And that false view had even more direct links to Marxism, she learned, for through the influence of Marxists in the United Nations, Jimmy Carter had allowed the United States to be drawn into observance of the Declaration of the Rights of the Child. Her research revealed that this declaration had first been proposed in 1959 by the United Nations: "In this seemingly harmless declaration, the United Nations has mapped out a strategy for 'nationalizing' all children of the world. A careful reading of this document leads me to believe that the U.N. does not support the basic unit of society, the family" (35). The United Nations figures in most absolutist conservative schemas because of its perceived threat to the two things that cannot be compromised: the rights of parents and national sovereignty.

But though opposing the nationalization of children's rights, she defends nationalism against the internationalization of control over families, for even more dangerous than the U.N. plans for the International Year of the Child was its attempt to "liberate children from the poisoned atmosphere of nationalism, training all the children of the world to favor international socialism" (36). Framing the crisis in this way feeds directly into heroic victimization and provides tremendous energy for resistance because the danger is located so close to home: "If we, as Christians, were to fall under the authority of the United Nations' Declaration, all of us would probably lose our children—simply because of our Christian beliefs" (37).

By the time Jimmy Carter called the White House Conference on Families in 1980, part of "the never-ending attack on the family by the feminist/socialist/humanist coalition in America" (43), conservative women had begun to organize against it, forming a National Pro-Family Coalition, chaired by LaHaye and her husband Tim. This coalition, which included 150 pro-family, pro-life, pro-American organizations, eventually staged walk-outs and finally held an Alternate White House Conference in 1980 in Long Beach, California, drawing up a statement of principles written by Dr. Onalee McGraw of the Heritage Foundation.

The momentum from this effort carried over into opposition to the ERA. That struggle was prolonged and successful for the right, and it provided a vast training ground for women activists, who opposed it as a "cleverly disguised tool to invite total government control over our lives" (53). According to LaHaye, the ERA threatened to lead to unisex restrooms, integrated prison facilities, the legalization of homosexuality, the requirement that women register for the draft, the abolition of sodomy and adultery laws, the abolition of requirements that husbands support their families, the loss of a wife's rights to her husband's social security benefits, the abolition of single-sex schools, the jeopardizing of churches and church colleges because they refused to admit women or homosexuals to the clergy, and the establishment of abortion as a constitutional right.

After the Scopes trial in the earlier part of the century, secular thinkers and activists had assumed that religious conservatives had disappeared; they discovered that instead of disappearing, the political religious right had gone into hibernation and had grown. Similarly, after conservative women were mobilized in the ERA battles, they for a while faded from view; they spent the time patiently establishing women's groups and prayer chapters, as well as antipornography and right-to-life campaigns, many of which have provided the carefully organized grassroots networks into which, along with the churches, conservatism has inserted its political organizing. LaHaye again reminds us how powerfully women's intimate fears have been framed within the world-historical workings of anticommunism:

> I felt as though an alien force had invaded the state capitol and was seeking to overthrow it. A humanistic force is dividing this nation into warring politics and social camps. We no longer think of ourselves as Americans but as conservatives, liberals, feminists. I believe many of our social problems have been fomented by conscious agents of communism. They have simply carried out communist doctrine: divide the nation into warring classes in an effort to weaken us, sap our strength, and destroy us. (62)

For, she quotes Karl Marx as having said: "Humanism is the denial of God and the total affirmation of man... Humanism is really nothing else but Marxism" (63).[26]

It is a very short move from Schlafly's anticommunist worries about the nation to LaHaye's passionate defense of women to the neat inevitability of Irving Kristol's equally passionate defense of the market economy in *Policy Review,* the monthly journal of the Heritage Foundation, a corporate-funded think tank. The founders of the Heritage Foundation include Paul Weyrich, of National Empowerment Television and the Christian Coalition, and Joseph Coors, a former John Birch Society member and union opponent. The Heritage Foundation was instrumental in framing the public policy discussions that led to the Contract with America; it also conducted the workshop for congressional representatives newly elected in 1994.

Kristol's words give a rationale for joining the Red danger of Schlafly's anticommunism to LaHaye's defense of the family: "If you de-legitimize this bourgeois society, the market economy—almost incidentally, as it were—is also de-legitimized. It is for this reason that radical feminism today is a far more potent enemy of capitalism than radical trade unionism."[27]

The neatness of this framework fits comfortably into a mass-mediated culture, a fit that should not be surprising given that advertising, the commodification of information, and right-wing common sense have developed out of the same historical circumstances.[28] Though conservative activists attack the media for its violence and immorality, the values that media and the rhetoric of simplification share may be far greater than the issues that separate them.[29] For both find common cause in universalized definitions of the market and the family, grounded in a definition of the true nature of the individual as a subject of capitalism, which expresses God's plan and man's deepest nature.

Though Jean Baudrillard's analysis of media culture has been justifiably criticized for its misogyny and pessimistic abstraction, nevertheless his discussion of the concept of the hyperreal makes an important link between the logic of commodified simulacra and the rhetoric of simplification in its absolutist forms. For both are based on a paradoxical structure: The reproduction of the Same must be guaranteed in the form of certain foundational values, while the infinite circulation of that Sameness must also be assured. On the one hand, the logic of commodified simulacra depends on an infinite increase in profit guaranteed by a static definition of the "market." And on the other hand, the rhetoric of simplification depends on the infinite increase of symbolic resonance guaranteed by a static definition of "family" and values. The aim of interpretation in both systems is to rediscover in nature what one already knew would be lying there waiting to be found because both market and family are guaranteed by natural law.

Keeping the foundational values the same while providing for infinite circulation thus depends on the perpetuation of a jammed representational imaginary within which the maturation of democracy is stalled. That jammed representational imaginary, or social imagination, is characterized by a logic of simulation in which identical units of meaning are produced: "genetic miniaturization is the dimension of simulation."[30] That is, what the social imaginary has to work with are units of meaning that are *structurally* the same, even if the contents of these units are different, and the circulation of these structural units constructs what we come to think of as the real: "The real is produced from miniaturized units, from matrices, memory banks, and command models—and with these it can be reproduced an indefinite number of times" (204). In this way, the argument about what is real or true or absolute "no longer has to be rational, since it is no longer measured against some ideal or negative instance. It is nothing more than operational... It is a hyperreal, the product of an irradiating synthesis of combinatory models in a hyperspace without atmosphere" (204).

Because these units merely have to be circulated again and again in their structural similarity and because democratic discourse is supposed to take place within this representational space, we find in this space no atmosphere of ambiguity in which a democratic imaginary might, in fact, develop. And yet, within that representational space, we do find the intense passions and emotions of a superrationality, a closed atmosphere of emotion that reinforces its unchanging structure because the "feelings" aroused by absolute values and by media imaginary produce a real that feels more real than our ordinary lives.

The rhetoric of simplification, when it is joined to the hyperreal of mass-mediated culture, proves to be particularly effective. For within the space of the simulacrum where the difference between the real and the copy long ago disappeared, the mythologizing rhetoric of simplification finds a comfortable place to do its work of "substituting signs of the real for the real itself" (204). We do not have to return to the bad old days of claiming that there is a clear distinction between real and copy, however, to insist that within this new blurred representational space our analysis will have to make finer distinctions within the field of signs. For while it is liberatory to deconstruct the constraints of absolutist identities, we are also operating within the blurred framework of paranoia and its backlashes and must proceed very carefully in recognizing the need for solace during frightening times.

The hyperreal, Baudrillard argues, is part of a system of death, but this time it is not death as an inherent part of life, as Rose argued. It is, rather, the absolute *denial* of death and mortality in "anticipated resurrection." Here in the absolute rule of the bottom line, the purity of absolutist religion, and the passions of anticommunist patriotism, nothing is left to chance, to accident, to sheer arbitrary coincidence on the way to the pure abstractions of profit or the pure transcendence of evil. In this mass-mediated, religious, anticommunist hyperreal, there is room only for "the orbital recurrence of models and the simulated generation of difference" (204).

And in a curious way, Baudrillard's classic analysis of Disneyland is now even more relevant in terms of the rhetoric of simplification, a prescience borne out by Disney's merger with ABC and its role as one of the principle arbiters of the media monopoly.[31] Disneyland, Baudrillard argued, might best be defined as a "miniaturized and *religious* reveling in real America." By this he does not mean that Disneyland constitutes a simple imitation or simulacrum of America, even though it is obvious to everyone that on one level, it is precisely that, a make-believe America. However, the fact that Disneyland openly and overtly constructs itself as an imitation America makes other kinds of make-believe invisible. As he says: "Disneyland is there to conceal the fact that it is the 'real' country," that what we think of as "America" is also a myth, "just as prisons are there to conceal the fact that it is the social in its entirety, in its banal omnipresence, which is carceral" (205). If "real America" is a myth and if the "real" produced by that myth is experienced in ways that are more intense, more "real" than the real, then we are left with no way to point out the difference between myth and real. And what is more, because of that inability, the very belief in a certain unquestioned version of reality, a definition of reality as unchangeable, is paradoxically preserved.

Like Disneyland, the commodified image and the absolutist rhetoric of simplification operate as "deterrence machines" that reinforce the fictions of "real" America, that keep it locked within its "network of endless, unreal circulation" without "space or dimensions." Disneyland and the rhetoric of simplification, like an absolutist reading of the biblical Book of the World, thus provide an "immense script and a perpetual motion picture" (205), whose exegesis excludes the ambiguity of unknowing.

The fact that corporate media interests and absolutist Christians occasionally find themselves in conflict overshadows this structural linkage between the simulacra and the rhetoric of simplification. They also find common ground in another feature of information culture, what Julia Kristeva calls the "refuge" provided by both the media and the rhetoric of simplification to counteract the complexities of postmodernity. Within the logic of the commodified image and the rhetoric of simplification, the psychic working-through that might allow people to mature and deal with disruption, foreignness, and mortality are short-circuited not only by absolutist values but by a social imaginary defined by profit. Though there are images everywhere, paradoxically that surfeit of images produces a failure of representation in which "both the producer and the consumer of images suffer from lack of imagination."[32]

Just as we have encountered a renewed interest in nationalism at a moment when national boundaries have been made increasingly irrelevant by transnational corporate activity, Kristeva asks a similar question about a resurgent interest in religion in an era of mass-mediated culture:

> As for the renewed interest in religion, we have reason to wonder if it stems from a legitimate quest, or from a psychological poverty that requests that faith give it an artificial soul that might replace an amputated subjectivity...Actions and their imminent abandonment have replaced the interpretation of meaning. (7)

If increasingly hegemonic media corporations rob us of imagination and if the rhetoric of simplification leaves us in a jammed, adolescent imaginary space capable only of dealing with cosmic wars of good and evil, we are left with a difficult project that may require a number of refusals, one of which is a refusal to take refuge, another the refusal of binary reasoning. But we also have to refuse to overlook the yearning for solace on the part of people caught up in an age of incomprehensible change.

An ideological constituency, a different kind of soul than that achieved by the uncompromising, warlike rhetoric of clarity or the commodified simulacra of media, both of which exclude the very atmosphere a democratic social contract needs, might follow from a recognition of the crucial importance of ambiguity. Ambiguity in this sense can be interpreted as the inevitable and unavoidable interruption of mortality into thought. Or as Jacqueline Rose argues, thinking "mimics the falling apart of the body it both celebrates and mourns" (20). The mourning of mortality, she argues, initiates thinking and gives us access to abstraction, but it also severs us "once and for all from any certainty of thought."

The status of ambiguity grounds two thoroughly different definitions of the social contract. One of those, the right-wing version discussed here, showed a seemingly inexplicable concern for what was going on in the esoteric realms of academia, as the right sensationally accused postmodern theorists, who insisted on the importance of textual exegesis and deconstruction, of creating a climate in which nihilism and relativism made ethics impossible. Yet Rose's insight and the unsettling dangers of the ideology of clarity suggest something quite different. Ethical behavior seems far more likely to be grounded not in certainty but in what she refers to as the rigorous, thoughtful process of *unknowing*. While Schlafly, LaHaye, and Buchanan advocate "a simplicity on the far side of complexity," where ambiguity is condemned as the mark of the Satanic, the Communist, or the perverse, Rose's unknowing reads ambiguity as signs of strangeness and difference, as evidence of mortal and vulnerable human bodies that are put at risk by the violence of grand symbolic and abstract certainties.

These different versions of ambiguity frame two fundamental questions. Is ethical behavior really possible when absolute clarity is the basis of interpretation? Is democracy?

Notes

1. See Eileen R. Meehan's study of television ratings, "Why We Don't Count: The Commodity Audience," in *Logics of Television: Essays in Cultural Criticism* (London: BFI, 1990), 117–37.

2. Patrick Buchanan's political campaigns are an example of this. His criticisms of the General Agreement on Tariffs and Trade (GATT) and the North American Free Trade Agreement (NAFTA), as well as his recognition of the circumstances of blue-collar workers, are rare in Republican politics. Yet his political message is one of purity, attacking not only mysteriously hidden financial interests but welfare recipients, immigrants, gays, and feminists.

3. Charles Lane, "Daddy's Boy," *The New Republic,* 22 January 1996, 25.

4. Jacqueline Rose, *Why War? Psychoanalysis, Politics, and the Return to Melanie Klein* (Cambridge, Mass.: Blackwell, 1993), 46.

5. In discussing the symmetry produced by this revision of history, I often use the term "America" in spite of its historical imprecision and in spite of the fact that though the United States claims that term for itself alone, there are many other nations in North and South America. It is hard, however, to convey the powerful synthesizing effects of this nationalist narrative without using one of its key resonating terms, "America." The differences between the nativist branch of the Republican Party and the corporate one, differences that can sometimes be elided in this single symbolic space, show how crucial the production of that transparent symbolic space is.

6. In discussing the growing resistance among conservative Christians to the politicizing of religion by the Christian Coalition, E. J. Dionne quotes Walter Shurden, a professor at Mercer University in Georgia. Dionne criticizes the narrowness of the Christian Coalition's compassion and refers to those sentiments as the "dwarfed affections and stunted sympathies" of Christians who "extend their feelings only toward those who are just like themselves." E. J. Dionne Jr., "Hijacked Faith," *The Washington Post National Weekly Edition,* 3–9 June 1996, 29.

7. Phyllis Schlafly, *A Choice Not an Echo* (Alton, Ill.: Pere Marquette Press, 1964).

8. See Kevin Phillips's tracing of this historical development in *The Emerging Republican Majority* (New Rochelle, N.Y.: Arlington House, 1969), *The Politics of Rich and Poor: Wealth and the American Electorate in the Reagan Aftermath* (New

York: Random House, 1990), *Boiling Point: Republicans, Democrats, and the Decline of Middle-Class Prosperity* (New York: Random House, 1993), and *Arrogant Capital: Washington, Wall Street, and the Frustrations of American Politics* (Boston: Little, Brown and Co., 1994).

9. Sara Diamond, *Roads to Dominion: Right-Wing Movements and Political Power in the United States* (New York: Guilford Press, 1995), 31.

10. Richard White, *"It's Your Misfortune and None of My Own": A New History of the American West* (Norman: University of Oklahoma Press, 1991).

11. Klaus Theweleit, *Male Fantasies,* vol. 1: *Women Floods, Bodies, History* (Minneapolis: University of Minnesota Press, 1987).

12. Barbara Ehrenreich, Introduction to Theweleit, *Male Fantasies,* vol. 1, ix.

13. Robert Taft, quoted in Schlafly, *A Choice Not an Echo,* 26.

14. Sara Diamond quotes Lindbergh: "Instead of agitating for war, the Jewish groups in this country should be opposing it in every possible way, for they will be the first to feel its consequences. Tolerance is a virtue that depends upon peace and strength. History shows that it cannot survive war and devastation. A few far-sighted Jewish people realize this, and stand opposed to intervention. But the majority still do not. Their greatest danger to this country lies in their large ownership and influence in our motion pictures, our press, our radio, and our Government" (quoted in *Roads to Dominion,* 24).

15. Lane, "Daddy's Boy," 19.

16. Robert Eringer, *The Global Manipulators: The Bilderberg Group, The Trilateral Commission. Covert Power Groups of the West* (Bristol: Pentacle Books, 1980). Schlafly's spelling differs from that of Eringer or Blanche Wiesen Cook.

17. Blanche Wiesen Cook, *The Declassified Eisenhower: A Divided Legacy* (New York: Doubleday and Company, 1981), 342.

18. Cook quotes David Rockefeller's description of the Trilateral Commission: "The Trilateral Commission now has about 300 members from North America, Western Europe and Japan. About one-quarter are from the U.S. and include not only business people, but labor union leaders, university professors, and research institute directors, congressmen and senators, media representatives and others. There are about as many Republicans as Democrats, and most regions of the nation are represented . . . The Trilateral Commission does not take positions on issues or endorse individuals . . . It holds meetings . . . and assigns task force reports that are discussed . . . Reports have dealt with different aspects of world trade, energy resources, the International Monetary System, East-West relations and more" (343).

19. Charles Lane tells of Patrick Buchanan's influence during that period, when he was a speechwriter for the Nixon administration. He bragged to Leonard Garment, White House counsel, about a speech he had written in 1970 for Spiro Agnew, which urged Nixon not to enforce court orders requiring that southern states desegregate their schools. Such a refusal to enforce those orders would, Buchanan said, "tear the scab off the issue of race in this country." He also argued at the time that "the ship of integration is going down; it is not our ship; it belongs to national liberalism; and we ought not to be aboard" ("Daddy's Boy," 23).

20. Lewis Straus, quoted in Schlafly, *A Choice Not an Echo,* 16.

21. Beverly LaHaye, *Who but a Woman?* (Nashville, Tenn.: Thomas Nelson, 1984).

22. Part of the problem with describing this rhetoric is that my own description threatens to become as monolithic as the one I follow. Of course there are many differences among the positions held by conservatives. However, without taking the risk of showing how this rhetoric functions as a unifying force strengthened precisely

because it can remain vague, with its vagueness reinforced by emotional passion, it is hard to understand its power.

23. The connection to Latin America was extensive. The growth of the contemporary Christian Right owes much of its success to the sophisticated electronic and grassroots networks developed during the Congressional prohibition of contra funding. These private and religious organizations were, in many cases, encouraged and supported by the Reagan administration.

24. LaHaye gets her evidence from an article by Clarence W. Hall, "The Country That Saved Itself," *Reader's Digest,* November 1964, 143. Jean Franco has discussed the special nature of women in Catholic countries in Latin America in "Killing Priests, Nuns, Women, Children," in Marshall Blonsky, ed., *On Signs* (Baltimore, Md.: Johns Hopkins University Press, 1985), 414–20.

25. LaHaye's quote of the Brazilian women is drawn from Clarence W. Hall, "The Country That Saved Itself," *Reader's Digest,* November 1964, 143.

26. This genre of books is notorious for its lack of scholarly documentation. Here LaHaye's note identifies her source: Karl Marx, *Economic Politique et Philosophie,* vol. 1, 38–40. There is no publication information, and in her many other texts, I have seen no indication that she reads French.

27. Irving Kristol, quoted in Mark Gerson, "Battler for the Republic: Irving Kristol's Terrible Swift Pen," *Policy Review* 62 (Fall 1992):57.

28. See Jennifer Wicke's study of the historical links between advertisement, literary forms, and American ideology, *Advertising Fictions: Literature, Advertising, and Social Reading* (New York: Columbia University Press, 1988) in the Social Foundations of Aesthetic Forms series, edited by Edward Saïd.

29. There is, of course, an extended critique of monolithic descriptions of mass culture and its hegemonic influence, descriptions like those of Jean Baudrillard and Theodor Adorno. Their monolithic versions have been opposed by those who want to reclaim the liberatory possibilities of subversive readings and the pleasure available to spectators from conditions of reception that are highly varied. While recognizing those critiques, however, it is also important not to lose sight of the powerful structural impulse toward sameness.

30. Jean Baudrillard, "From *Simulations,*" in Antony Easthope and Kate McGowan, eds., *A Critical and Cultural Theory Reader* (Buffalo: University of Toronto Press, 1992), 204.

31. In terms of the structure of the media monopoly, see the entire issue of *The Nation,* 3 June 1996.

32. Julia Kristeva, *New Maladies of the Soul* (New York: Columbia University Press, 1995), 10.

5

Through the Looking Glass and What the Christian Right Found There

Steven Gardiner

For now we see through a glass, darkly; but then face to face: now I know in part; but then shall I know even as also I am known.
— *1 Cor. 13:12*

First, there's the room you can see through the glass— that's just the same as our drawing-room, only the things go the other way.
— Through the Looking-Glass and What Alice Found There

If it were possible for Ralph Reed, speaking on behalf of the Christian right, to send a message from the May 1995 cover of *Time* magazine back to journalists and scholars of the movement circa 1990, he might well have echoed Mark Twain's famous witticism about the rumors of his death having been exaggerated. By 1989 the national press had all but lost interest in the Christian right as a political force.[1] The failure of Pat Robertson's presidential bid, combined with the Jimmy Swaggart and Jim Bakker televangelist scandals and the election of country-club Republican George Bush, seemed even to friendly observers to have taken the wind out of the movement's political sails.[2] Finally, in the context of the late 1980s, Jerry Falwell's anticlimactic folding of the once-mighty Moral Majority seemed to many like an appropriate epilogue to the Reagan era.[3]

Meanwhile scholarly interest in the Christian right began to focus on what has been referred to as its "transformation." Sociologist Jerome Himmelstein, political scientist Matthew Moen, and historian William Berman—among others—noted such a process, characterized by growing political sophistication and secularization. The Christian right was also moving away from Washington-based direct mail lobbying aimed primarily at Congress and toward grassroots and Republican Party activism.[4]

With the exception of those writing for a larger audience of anti–Christian right activists, notably Sara Diamond,[5] academics also tended to see in the Christian right's "transformation" evidence of its declining influence, citing declining national press coverage as indicative of this. Moen's treatment of the transformation theme, for example, is for the most part carefully nuanced, noting that the Christian right in the late 1980s was far from dead. Nonetheless he opined:

> Unfortunately for its leaders, the Christian Right will probably be pushed further out of the realm of political influence . . . as the 1990s unfold. Why is that the case? The Christian Right's ability to affect the national public and legislative agendas will diminish. It will do so because the movement lost much of its distinctiveness as a political force over time, rendering it less able to capture the attention of policymakers and the imagination of the media.[6]

Other academics have been less circumspect. Political scientist Robert Booth Fowler, for example, has written of the Christian right: "My argument is that it failed, and failed badly, and that there are lessons for the future about evangelicalism and politics that may be learned from this experience."[7]

What virtually no one in either journalistic or academic circles anticipated in the late 1980s and early 1990s was the rise of the Christian Coalition—the transformed Christian right organization par excellence.[8] In fact, from the vantage point of 1995, one of the most striking features of books and articles published on the Christian right between 1989 and 1992 is that they fail to mention the Christian Coalition.[9] (However, they showed a certain nostalgia for the Moral Majority.)

I do not necessarily mean this as a criticism—or at least not a serious one—but mention it to remind ourselves just how difficult it is to predict which organizations and movements will rise and how far. Social movements have a disconcerting way of having unanticipated consequences.

Still, the basic theme of the transformation of the Christian right is a powerful one; it was embraced by academics in the late 1980s and by journalists following the 1992 (or 1994, for the truly unimaginative) elections. Besides describing an empirically demonstrable process, the idea of a transformation fits the expectations of social movement theory.[10] Few things in the realm of politics and social interaction are certain, but the changing character of social movements over time (and their eventual demise as social movements) seems to be one.[11] A social movement, by definition, involves *extraordinary* political activity on the part of some significant portion of a definable segment of a population. Therefore, social movements are effectively self-limiting in duration. Eventually the political work of the movement is left to a relative handful of professional activists, as the majority of participants return to the routine of their lives.

However, the exact nature of the changes wrought as a social movement "matures" are historically contingent. Observers of the Christian right have until recently focused on its increasing political sophistication, as reflected in the use of less vitriolic rhetoric, willingness to compromise, and recognition that efficacy requires working in coalition with like-minded organizations. Ralph Reed's demand for a "place at the table in the conversation we call democracy"[12] *is* a far cry from the Christian right's rhetoric of the early 1980s to "Christianize America" and "put God back in government." The transformation of the Christian right, however, has not been as monodimensional as the academics' focus on professionalization and secularization might lead us to believe. It is true that the Christian Coalition under Reed has taken pains to moderate its image and reach a modus vivendi with the existing power structure. However, other organizations, particularly those at the state and local levels, adamantly stick to core Christian right issues—for example, abortion and homosexuality. These organizations refuse to compromise, and they flirt with the militant ideas of the conspiratorial far right, as I will discuss in detail below.

My thesis is that there is a growing distance between the rhetoric and policy positions of the Christian Coalition's national leadership and those of other Christian right organizations, particularly organizations at the local level. These differences reflect more than the national leadership's "heightened sensitivity to language."[13] Real ideological and organizational conflicts are emerging, placing increasing stresses on the Christian right as such, and these stresses may ultimately lead to its disintegration. As a corollary to this thesis, I will argue that academics' operational bias toward studying national organizations, as opposed to local ones, has obscured the bifold nature of the Christian right's transformation, since such studies both gloss over emergent conflicts and examine professionalization and institutionalization rather than ideological entrenchment and what I will call "lateralization."

I do not want to repeat the prognosticative errors of the recent past and pronounce the end of the Christian right as a political force, and I cannot predict either where any of the existing organizations might end up or how much power they might wield along the way. What I am suggesting is that we take a closer look at the nature and various *trajectories of transformation* observable in various parts of the movement and examine how those various parts interact. Such an analysis will provide a better understanding of the Christian right as it exists today and a sense of where it is headed.

Changing Definitions

When Thomas Atwood's article "Through a Glass Darkly: Is the Christian Right Overconfident It Knows God's Will?" was published in the Fall 1990 *Policy Review,* the Christian right's "transformation" was already well underway.[14] But if the points he made were not wholly original, Atwood's article was still a bellwether of sorts, offering the first synthesis of "transformed" Christian right thinking. Atwood's prescriptions for a more politically effective Christian right presaged developments in the Christian Coalition and its programs as articulated by Ralph Reed.[15] Therefore, it is useful to take Atwood's piece as a point of departure for discussing the continuing transformation of the Christian right in the 1990s.

Atwood, erstwhile controller of Pat Robertson's 1988 presidential campaign exploratory committee, starts with the premise that in the late 1980s a certain malaise struck the Christian right. He writes: "Conservative charismatics, Fundamentalists, and other born-again and Evangelical Christians were briefly confused and demoralized"[16] by the failure of the Robertson campaign, the collapse of the Moral Majority, the televangelist scandals, and the slow response to the Supreme Court's *Webster v. Reproductive Health Services* decision.[17] "But," Atwood argues, "the Evangelical Right is back, better organized for state and local politics and less dependent on highly visible national leaders."[18]

Atwood places front and center the move from Washington-based "paper tiger" organizations to grassroots campaigns "against federal funding of obscene and blasphemous art," the then-anticipated introduction of "major pro-life legislation in all but a few state legislatures in 1991," and the punitive targeting of state legislators who vote against such legislation.[19] However, Atwood also acknowledges that

> most of the movement's victories so far have been defensive—protecting the tax-exempt status of Christian schools when the Internal Revenue Service threatened to take it away, protecting the religious liberty of students who wanted to form voluntary after-hours prayer groups at public schools, pressuring Presidents Reagan and Bush to name Supreme Court justices who would overturn *Roe v. Wade,* stopping public funding of abortion and abortion counseling, stopping convenience stores from openly displaying pornography, stopping state and local "gay rights" legislation in many jurisdictions.[20]

And he goes on to prescribe what the Christian right must do if it is "to move from cultural isolation to cultural leadership" and thereby assume "leadership positions in government and mainstream politics."[21]

First, Atwood counsels, the Christian right must stop overestimating its strength. "A common fallacy during the 1980s," he writes, "was to cite Gallup polls indicating that between 50 million and 80 million Americans call themselves 'born-again Christians,' as if this self-description somehow equated to acceptance of the Evangelical Right's political agenda."[22] Reviewing survey work done by the Free Congress Foundation and by George Gallup Jr. and Jim Castelli in their 1989 book *The People's Religion,* Atwood affirms the generally conceded diversity within the evangelical world. He concludes that "the Evangelical Right probably numbers in the millions rather than the tens of millions."[23] This conclusion about the Christian right's baseline strength, though difficult to verify, is of vital importance in understanding the movement's successes and failures and the nature and direction of its transformations.

Difficulties in estimating the movement's numerical strength arise from the vagaries inherent in arriving at an operational definition of the entity called the "Christian right." Social movements do not issue membership cards, making it difficult to know whom to count. Consider, for example, the case of the Oregon Citizens Alliance (OCA), one of the most successful of the state-level Christian right organizations.

Founded in 1987, the OCA has risen to regional prominence through sponsoring a series of anti–gay rights ballot measure initiatives. The OCA claims approximately 3,000 dues-paying members. This figure is roughly equal to the number of contributors to the organization's various political action committees as identified in contribution reports filed with the Oregon Secretary of State's office.[24] The OCA also claims a mailing list of 160,000, and year after year it manages to collect the 100,000 plus signatures needed to place initiatives on the ballot *without* resorting to paid signature gatherers.[25] Active membership in the OCA, including leadership and volunteers, probably numbers no more than a few hundred people. At the other extreme, OCA electoral efforts have attracted between 13 percent (for a 1990 OCA-sponsored gubernatorial candidate) and 52 percent (for a 1988 initiative rescinding an executive order banning discrimination on the basis of sexual orientation in public employment) of the vote.[26]

OCA members and supporters obviously exist on a continuum, according to the degree to which they identify with or support the organization. The case is further complicated by the fact that individuals who engage in activities that would seem to place them unmistakably within the OCA orbit—contributing funds or gathering signatures, for example—often subsequently deny having any association with it.

The problem of deciding who is and who is not part of the Christian right is an even thornier one. In addition to all the factors involved in deciding who is part of a specific local group like the OCA, in the case of defining the movement as a whole the would-be analyst must also decide what groups and what issues to include as definitional criteria.

To say that support for a social movement and its various representative organizations exists on a sliding scale is something of a truism. However, the way we decide to put the definitions into operation is not trivial, either for those trying to understand the Christian right or for those working for or against it. For example, if we settle on a loose definition, equating a Christian right with tens of millions of members, associates, and potential members—

in effect, something like a majority of the active electorate if not the population—then we are likely to anticipate rapid, profound results. If such results do not occur, we must explain why not. Contrariwise, a tight definition of the movement, including only the members of organizations unequivocally part of the Christian right and their active supporters—those who contribute money or attend events—yields more modest expectations and a complementary need for the analyst to explain any outstanding successes.

The choice of a "loose" or "tight" definition of the Christian right is somewhat arbitrary. However, I would argue that something akin to Atwood's estimate of the Christian right's strength, reflecting a tight definition, has been incorporated into the planning of movement organizations. It leads to a more powerful understanding of the way that the Christian right interacts with U.S. politics.

What They Found There

If the real base of support for the Christian right numbers in the millions rather than the tens of millions, Atwood argues, the movement "cannot achieve much political influence without forming coalitions."[27] In fact, it has been argued that the work of the then-nascent Christian right in coalition with the New Right helping to elect Ronald Reagan marked a high point of early Christian right influence.[28] The reality of the 1990s, however, is that the end of the Cold War—with its unifying ideology of anticommunism—has made coalition work trickier between economic conservatives and the social conservatives of the Christian right.[29]

Atwood makes this point implicitly; he urges the Christian right to seek coalitions with religious conservatives outside of the white evangelical community, including conservative Catholics, orthodox Jews, and the black church—a theme Ralph Reed would later emphasize.[30] Even more to the point, Atwood takes the movement to task for a series of what he refers to as "theological errors" that have prevented it from working in coalition with secular conservatives. These errors include cognitive immodesty, compromise, failure to provide "servant-leadership," and misuse of "the language of redemption."

Atwood's "theological errors" are exhortative, meant to persuade the recalcitrant to "get with the program." The first of such "errors," "cognitive immodesty," gives rise to the title of his paper and indirectly to that of this chapter. He writes:

> Conservative Evangelical activists are now notorious for displaying an overconfidence in their ability to discern the Divine Will at any time, in any situation... Evangelical theologian Carl F. H. Henry said it well when he criticized the Evangelical Right for "its confusion of the in-

> errancy of Scripture with the inerrancy of its own interpretation and application of Scripture."[31]

As an antidote Atwood offers what he calls an underpreached scriptural verse: "For now we see through a glass, darkly; but then face to face; now I know in part; but then shall I know even as I am known."[32]

Atwood emphasizes the need to engage forthrightly "the ideas of non-Evangelicals or liberals or even other Evangelicals or conservative Republicans with different views." He bemoans as inappropriate to politics the attitude of the bumper sticker that proclaims: "God said it, I believe it, that settles it." He says that instead "the American people expect to hear policy issues openly and publicly debated; indeed they need those kinds of debates in order to make well-considered decisions."[33]

Cognitive immodesty, Atwood argues, leads to an unwillingness to compromise, his second theological error. He explains that Christian right activists have been guilty of inappropriately applying to politics the same kind of absolutism they appropriately apply to religious doctrine. Recounting his own experience at the 1990 Fairfax County, Virginia, Republican Convention, Atwood writes of a delegate "who was told that he was 'not a Christian' because he was supporting the 'wrong' candidate for county chairman."[34]

This kind of unbending political orthodoxy, Atwood tells us, has led Christian right activists to take hard-line positions on virtually every issue. More important, it has led them to refuse to compromise on tactics.

Rather than define and pursue a realistic, achievable agenda of incremental progress, conservative Evangelicals have expected too much too fast, sometimes displaying an almost martyr-like relish for taking extreme positions without concern for results.[35]

Writing an exhortative, corrective article, Atwood comes down firmly on the side of conventional wisdom: Go along to get along.

In social movement politics things are never quite so simple. Never monolithic even at their most vigorous, social movements tend to bifurcate as they mature, often repeatedly, with one faction moving toward the status quo—and hence becoming the movement's "mainstream"—while other factions remain "pure" and "true to the vision," often pursuing innovative or violent tactics. John Brown, the Black Panthers, and ACT-UP are all relatively well-known historical examples of social movement factions (or representatives thereof) that veered away from the mainstream; closer to the Christian right are Paul Hill and the signers of his Defensive Action list[36] at a tactical extreme and the reconstructionist movement at an ideological one.

The interactions between a maturing social movement's various factions are always complex. On the one hand the very existence of movement factions means that some are perceived, correctly or incorrectly, as more "radical" or "dangerous" than others. The perceived differences between factions gives those in power in society an incentive to negotiate with and often to accommodate the mainstream faction. From the other factions' point of view, this is perceived as "selling out," "co-optation," and "heresy." Further, the innovative, confrontational, and often-violent tactics of the "factionalized" portion of the movement keep the movement in the public eye; these factions' pure vision and energetic activism act as a magnet for new recruits. On the other hand, because the more purist factions have a tendency to commit all of Atwood's theological errors (or secular equivalents thereof) and to embrace confrontational and even violent tactics, they increasingly become an embarrassment to the mainstream of the movement.

A maturing social movement's bifurcation or factionalization by no means brings about predetermined results. In the U.S. context, the expectation is that the mainstream portion of the movement, having reached a modus vivendi with the powers that be, will become either part of a "governing coalition," in the U.S. sense of an elective majority, or part of the "loyal opposition" and will divest itself of social movement energy and become institutionalized. Other factions are expected to disintegrate into vainglorious rhetoric, conspiratorial accusations, increasingly esoteric infighting, and real or symbolic martyrdom.

There is no guarantee, however, that such a course will be followed. It is entirely possible that one of the social movement's "extremist" factions will end up leading a successful revolution or ally itself with an emergent power in an effort to outflank its mainstream rivals. The movement's various factions often reserve for each other their most vitriolic condemnations; they echo medieval Christian distinctions between "heretics" and "infidels," the former being infinitely worse than the latter because they turned away from the light of "true religion."

Another way to talk about a social movement's factionalization as it matures is to consider not a single "transformation" but multiple transformations resulting in various factions that interact in complex ways. Once again, consider the OCA and the way it has interacted with the Christian Coalition.

The OCA, founded in 1987, two years before the Christian Coalition, in December 1991 became the only preexisting statewide organization to take the step of actually becoming an official chapter of the Christian Coalition. Then–Christian Coalition national field director, Guy Rodgers, described "the OCA as a 'model' of the kind of organization that Christian Coalition is building in other states." OCA chair Lon Mabon returned the compliment, stating: "They have the same vision and aggressive spirit as OCA."[37]

The cordial relationship between the two organizations would quickly sour in spite of the fact that the Christian Coalition contributed $20,000 to the OCA's 1992 anti–gay rights Ballot Measure 9 effort.[38] By January 1993 the two organizations were feuding. The position of chair of the Oregon Republican Party was up for election, and the OCA was pushing the candidacy of conservative businessman Bill Witt. Witt had been a board member of the Oregon Christian Coalition, which had been founded as an entity separate from the OCA in the fall of 1992 but with a board stacked with OCA insiders. Following advice from the Christian Coalition, he resigned his board position to run for the GOP chair position. When it became clear that Witt would lose a close race to "compromise" candidate Randy Miller, Witt and Mabon argued vigorously. Mabon asserted that Witt's resignation from the Christian Coalition board had been a mistake and that Witt had caved in to the forces of compromise and thereby failed to offer a distinctive alternative; Witt maintained that holding such a position would make him unacceptable to most moderates and even mainstream conservatives, whom he would need to win.[39]

In July 1993 the two organizations would quietly go their separate ways, offering vague explanations about how it was too difficult for a young, growing organization to be a chapter of another.[40] It was clear, however, that the two organizations increasingly had different visions. At the time of the OCA–Christian Coalition crack-up, Ralph Reed wrote that the "pro-family movement has limited its effectiveness by concentrating disproportionately on issues such as abortion and homosexuality."[41] The OCA provided a veritable organizational definition of just such disproportionate concentration. In 1988 the OCA had effectively launched itself with a successful initiative campaign to rescind a gay rights executive order, and in 1990 it pushed an initiative to virtually ban abortions in the state. In 1992 the OCA pushed an anti–gay rights initiative to amend the Oregon Constitution; though that amendment was defeated, it received 45 percent of the vote and a majority in twenty-one of Oregon's thirty-six counties.[42] In 1993 the OCA launched two dozen local anti–gay rights initiatives in towns and counties it perceived as sympathetic, and it managed to win in virtually every case.[43]

The OCA's strategy of expending most of its energy on the core Christian right issues of homosexuality and abortion has had mixed results for the organization. Though Ralph Reed has argued that "to win at the ballot box and in the court of public opinion . . . the pro-family movement must speak to the concerns of average voters in areas of taxes, crime, government waste, health care, and financial security,"[44] the OCA has achieved both notice and notoriety with its high-profile ballot measures. It has even gained a measure of grudging respect from the establishment with its no-compromise stance. In fact, the amount of attention the OCA has received is impressive. In 1991 the *Oregonian,* the newspaper of record in the state, mentions the OCA in 165 articles; in 1992, 647; in 1993, 464; and in 1994, 401. To put this in perspective, in his survey of the *New York Times* index between 1980 and 1989, Mathew Moen counted a *total* of 244 entries for ten of the most prominent national Christian right groups of the 1980s.[45]

Most of the media attention lavished on the OCA and its ballot measure initiatives in the early 1990s was decidedly negative, eventually leading to the OCA's organizational position not to talk to the largest newspapers in the state—a decidedly odd stance for any political group. Furthermore, the first half of 1995 has shown a dramatic decline in the amount of media attention the OCA received, with only sixty-one mentions in the *Oregonian* through the end of August. Yet, as I will argue below, this has hardly been the result of the OCA's moderating its rhetoric or positions.

Consequences of a Moderate Proposal

Atwood's third theological error is what he refers to as "servant-leadership," in scriptural terms, aiming at the "dominion mandate," or "the triumphalist idea of Evangelical Christian rule, of 'putting the righteous in authority' as an end in itself.[46] This is a notion influenced by Christian reconstructionism, a controversial theonomic form of neo-Calvinism. Against what he calls a "widespread" dissemination of dominionist ideas, Atwood argues that such "triumphalism is in conflict with Christ's own definition of leadership: 'Whoever would be great among you must be your servant, and whoever would be first among you must be slave of all.' "[47]

As Atwood is arguing against dominionist ideas, his purpose is clearly Republican. He makes this quite explicit, writing:

> Conservative Evangelical activists who have been most successful at getting and staying ahead in the Republican Party have done so by quietly and diligently earning the trust and respect of both conservatives and moderates. This has been happening with greater frequency as the Evangelical Right's experience grows. But those Evangelical Right activists who have won GOP leadership simply because their faction controlled a majority have lost influence when their newcomer fellow activists failed to sustain their political involvement.[48]

Here Atwood is slightly disingenuous. It is probably too much to ask of anyone in the political world to favor a compromise coalition over a majority. Yet he does have a point about the difficulty of obtaining a stable majority, which goes back to the fact that the baseline numerical strength of the Christian right is relatively small. There is also an important subsidiary point that he does not make: The Christian right has been actively opposed, even by conservatives, whenever it has attempted to govern *in its own right* rather than as part of a coalition. The OCA discovered this when T. J. Bailey, a member of its executive board, was elected chair of the Oregon Republican Party in 1987—when the OCA was still virtually unknown. Bailey was defeated by moderate John Frohnmayer in 1989 as the OCA's negative image grew and it became known for its uncompromising stances.[49]

The Christian Coalition is increasingly seen as the Christian right's representative in the governing Republican coalition. For this reason, the Christian Coalition has certainly made efforts to distance itself from dominionist, reconstructionist, and "Christian nation" positions, at least at the national level. In his 1994 book *Politically Incorrect*—fawningly reviewed not only by Christian right leaders like James Kennedy and Christian Coalition founder Pat Roberson but by Bob Dole, Newt Gingrich, Jack Kemp, and William Bennett—Ralph Reed writes:

> Religious conservatives do not want a "Christian" nation, a "Jewish" nation, or a "Moslem" nation. They want a nation of strong families and basic goodness that respects the right of all individuals to express their faith and which does not prohibit faith to inform the laws that govern society.[50]

Reed's words are aimed both at the Christian right's liberal critics and, by implication, at the dominionists and reconstructionists to whom those critics try to link groups like Reed's. And in spite of the fact that nowhere in his book does Reed deign to discuss Christian reconstructionism directly, the reconstructionists clearly perceive that they are among his targets.

In a review of Reed's book in the reconstructionist journal *Chalcedon Report*, Jay Rogers writes:

> Pluralism is defined as each person having an equal voice in a democratic process. This has become the battle cry of Ralph Reed: "*All we want is equal time!*" Either he is ignorant or he is lying. Most politically active Christians *don't* want equal time with homosexuals, abortionists, animal worshipping pagans, witches, radical feminists and pornographers. We want them silenced and mercifully disciplined according to the Word of God [emphasis in original].[51]

Yet in spite of the fact that certain factions within the movement see the Christian Coalition's positions as a betrayal, many liberal and left critics tend to see these compromising positions as disingenuous, no more than a facade. Reed's protestations notwithstanding, liberals argue, what the Christian Coalition actually does is to train activists in the techniques of "guerrilla politics," or how to have the maximum impact on the process even with relatively few numbers.

At a 28 October 1995 Christian Coalition training seminar held in Tacoma, Washington, the tension between dominionist and nondominionist themes emerged within the organization. The seminar distributed a new edition of its *Training Seminar Manual*, which admonishes coalition members against taking dominionist positions. However, at least one seminar trainer, Ellen

Craswell, seemed ready to embrace such positions. A flyer promoting her gubernatorial campaign distributed at the event is titled: "God's Principles of Social Order and Morality Are Effective with Everyone." The flyer goes on to say: "Defying these principles has left a devastating wake of crime, broken homes, battered, abused and abandoned children, sexual immorality, drug and alcohol problems, corrupt government, reckless taxing and spending, counterproductive welfare programs and deficit."

Craswell, honored in the past by the Washington Christian Coalition,[52] founded a Christian right Washington state political action committee called IMPAC. IMPAC's 1994 promotional flyer described the group as "a Political Action Committee designed to put Bible-believing Christians in leadership in our state. Genuine, long-term reform will come only when Bible-believing people are making, interpreting and enforcing our laws." Not surprisingly, one of the original advisory board members of IMPAC was R. J. Rushdoony, the founder of Christian reconstructionism.

This does not "prove" that Ralph Reed and the Christian Coalition are acting disingenuously as they distance themselves from dominionist positions, but it does highlight the contradictions within the movement. The Christian Coalition can distance itself from organizations like the OCA and factions like reconstructionism, but even within its own organizational structure it is constantly faced with the potential difficulty that its membership is drawn extensively from the conservative evangelical subculture, which has been energized not by a broad-based and pluralistic vision but by a narrow and triumphalist one.

As Atwood denounces his "theological errors," he criticizes the Christian right's "overuse of redemptive vocabulary and concepts in public policy arguments, which imply, contrary to Christian teaching, that the state has a redemptive capability."[53] Under a section titled "Reformed Rhetoric," he even makes so bold as to offer a series of suggestions, including: "Use scriptural references more judiciously"; "Keep discussions of 'spiritual warfare' to a minimum"; and "Calm down fund-raising communications."[54]

Such suggestions find their apotheosis, so to speak, in the Christian Coalition's "Contract with the American Family." Self-consciously cast in the mode of the Republican's "Contract with America," the Christian Coalition's "contract" takes up the very issues Reed highlighted in 1993: taxes, education, religious freedom, and so on. The statement led National Public Radio commentator Nina Totenberg to muse: "I'm beginning to think that Ralph Reed is more Republican than Christian Coalition."[55]

Criticisms of the Christian Coalition's "accommodationist" positions are not just coming from reconstructionist sectors. Relatively secular right-wing organizations have characterized the Contract with the American Family as prima facie evidence of a sellout to the powers that be. William Norman

Grigg, an activist in the far-right John Birch Society, for example, has written that the Christian Coalition under Reed has attached itself to the Republican Party in the same way that "unions, feminist groups, and the self-designated civil rights movement have battened on to the Democratic Party."[56] Grigg quotes Judy Brown, president of the American Life League, as saying of the Christian Coalition: "I am horrified. It's terribly disappointing. The outcome of such failed pragmatism will be more dead children."[57] In a similar vein, Robert Knight of the Family Research Council told the *National Catholic Register*: "It seems as if they are embarrassed by the very issues that brought them to the dance."[58]

The point is that although the Christian Coalition increasingly seems to be *represented* as typical or symbolic of the Christian right as a whole, the movement is far more complex. Certainly national organizations like the Christian Coalition and James Dobson's Focus on the Family have professionalized the Christian right's public image and infused it with increased political sophistication, but at the same time other organizations have continued to push traditional Christian right issues. And even when organizations have moved away from the "language of redemption," this does not necessarily translate into a move away from dominionist positions.

To revisit the OCA one last time, it is noteworthy that in this organization a form of "secular dominionism" seems to have arisen. In fact even from its earliest days the OCA was firmly rooted in what it refers to as "the politics of confrontation."[59] OCA chair Lon Mabon has written:

> A movement is made by people like you and me, taking action on a daily basis—energized by having the courage of their convictions. It is doing everyday what you know to be right. That is why the Citizens Alliance nickname is "The 82nd Airborne" of the pro-family conservative movement. We are going to stand publicly for what is right in any and all situations, even if we stand alone. Don't let the liberals scare you off with mere words; this is a *culture war*. It is a battle between what is false and what is true. Between what is right and what is wrong. Between what is good and what is evil.[60]

The OCA demonstrated this confrontational politics in the campaign for chair of the Oregon Republican Party in January 1995 when it ran its own "pro-family" candidate against popular conservative incumbent Randy Miller. Mabon was outraged when the OCA candidate was defeated 73 to 46, going so far as to name "traitors," including the 1990 OCA candidate for governor, a major activist in the Oregon Right to Life Committee, and a former OCA staffer, who presumably voted for Miller.[61]

The OCA generally refrains from quoting chapter and verse as a basis for political activity, but it retains a movement ethic that in 1995 has begun to seem, if not monomaniacal, at least rigidly fixated on homosexuality (especially) and abortion. Once again it is pushing initiatives toward the 1996 ballot aimed at curbing gay rights and limiting abortion, in spite of the fact that the Oregon media, and presumably the Oregon electorate, have grown weary of the seemingly endless fights on these issues.

This is not the end of the story, however. If the OCA has cast itself as " 'The 82nd Airborne' of the pro-family conservative movement," in the process it has not fallen from grace. The OCA remains a force within Oregon politics, even if it clings to homosexuality and abortion with what increasingly seems like desperation and even if it refuses to compromise. Yet as an organization it is on a different tangent of transformation than the Christian Coalition. For if the OCA has steadfastly refused to embrace the watered-down message and agenda promulgated by Reed, there is at least some evidence of a willingness to embrace the ideas of the conspiratorial far right.

This tendency toward support for the ideas of the so-called militias and the Christian Patriot[62] movement has been most in evidence in the *Oregon News-Leader,* a bimonthly conservative newspaper founded with OCA backing and edited by OCA communications director Scott Lively. In the December 1994 issue, OCA research director Pat Smith worried about the "One World Government," using the work of far-right conspiracy monger and militia promoter Jack McLamb as a basis for her claims.[63]

More recently the *Oregon News-Leader* has published editorials rhetorically asking if the militia is the last means to save the Constitution: "The militia is armed and getting more so, and they don't care who knows it. All you have to do is look around and see what's going on."[64] The author tells us about the manifold ways "in which they [Congress] are causing the downfall of this country":

> #1—They don't honor the treaty to protect our borders. They let every non-citizen and illegal alien come in and either get on welfare or, if they are Japanese, Asian or Korean they are given a 3% loan to get into business. #2—Let's not forget affirmative action ... #5—If anyone doesn't like what they do, and if they amass any kind of substantial following, they send in ATF agents to annihilate them. Case in point—Randy Weaver.[65]

I do not mean to suggest by pointing out these references to far-right conspiratorial ideas that they are typical of OCA positions. They are not. The point is that, as in the case of the internal picture of the Christian Coalition, there are tensions emerging within the OCA organization that suggest the possibility of further fragmentation. Within the body of OCA activists and sympathizers, the message of far-right conspiratorialism, with its metaphysical classifications of society into ultimate good and ultimate evil, has a certain appeal. And this appeal sounds all the more sweetly the more the national Christian right leadership is perceived as moderating and compromising.

Notes

1. Mathew C. Moen, *The Transformation of the Christian Right* (Tuscaloosa and London: University of Alabama, 1992), 147. Moen examined indexes of the *New York Times* between 1980 and 1989 for entries on ten Christian-right organizations: American Coalition for Traditional Values, American Freedom Coalition, Christian Voice, Concerned Women for America, Family Research Council, Freedom Council, Liberty Federation, Moral Majority, National Christian Action Coalition, and Religious Roundtable. He found that the aggregate number of "hits" declined steeply from fifty-three in 1980 and eighty-five in 1981 to four each in 1988 and 1989.

2. Thomas C. Atwood, "Through a Glass Darkly: Is the Christian Right Overconfident It Knows God's Will?," *Policy Review* 54 (Fall 1990): 44–52.

3. Laura Sessions Stepp, "Falwell Says Moral Majority to be Dissolved," *Washington Post,* 12 June 1989.

4. Jerome L. Himmelstein, *To the Right: The Transformation of American Conservatism* (Berkeley: University of California Press, 1990); Moen, *Transformation of the Christian Right*; William C. Berman, *America's Right Turn: From Nixon to Bush* (Baltimore, Md., and London: Johns Hopkins University Press, 1994).

5. Sara Diamond, *Spiritual Warfare: The Politics of the Christian Right* (Boston: South End Press, 1989).

6. Moen, *Transformation of the Christian Right,* 144.

7. Robert Booth Fowler, "The Failure of the Religious Right," in Michael Cromartie, ed., *No Longer Exiles: The Religious New Right in American Politics* (Washington, D.C.: Ethics and Public Policy Center, 1993), 57.

8. The rise of the Christian Coalition was not the only factor revitalizing the Christian right in the 1990s. Other factors helped to raise the Christian right's national profile. These include the emergence of other politically sophisticated organizations—particularly Focus on the Family—the election of a Democratic president against whom the movement could pit itself in 1992, and the subsequent, not unrelated, election of Republican majorities in both houses of Congress. Equally important, and usually neglected in academic and national journalistic analysis, was the rise of local and state-level Christian right groups that have arguably had a greater impact on public policy and agenda setting than the national organizations have ever had.

9. There are two index entries for the Christian Coalition in Moen's *Transformation of the Christian Right,* none in Berman's *America's Right Turn,* and none in Himmelstein's *To the Right.* The popular press was no more perspicacious: The *New York Times* index has no entries for the Christian Coalition in 1989, four in 1990, none in 1991, six in 1992, thirteen in 1993, twenty-two in 1994, and twenty-nine through the first half of 1995—a pace that matches that of Moral Majority in its heyday.

10. Michael Lienesh, "Christian Conservatism as a Political Movement," *Political Science Quarterly* 97 (1982): 403–25; Mayer Zald and Roberta Ash, "Social Movement Organizations: Growth, Decay, and Change," *Social Forces* 44 (1966): 327–41. More generally, see Sidney Tarrow, *Power in Movement: Social Movements, Collective Action, and Politics* (New York: Cambridge University Press, 1994); and for a useful critique and overview, see Daniel A. Foss and Ralph Larkin, *Beyond Revolution: A New Theory of Social Movements* (Boston: Bergin and Garvey, 1986).

11. Foss and Larkin, *Beyond Revolution.*

12. Ralph Reed, *Politically Incorrect: The Emerging Faith Factor in American Politics* (Dallas, Tex.: Word Publishing, 1994), 24.

13. Gary Bauer in a 14 June 1989 interview with Mathew Moen, quoted in *Transformation of the Christian Right,* 133.

14. Atwood, "Through a Glass Darkly."

15. Ralph Reed, "Casting a Wider Net: Religious Conservatives Move beyond Abortion and Homosexuality," *Policy Review* 65 (Summer 1993): 31–35.

16. Atwood, "Through a Glass Darkly," 44.

17. The Supreme Court's *Webster* decision returned partial control of regulation of abortion to the states.

18. Atwood, "Through a Glass Darkly," 44.

19. Ibid.

20. Ibid., 45.

21. Ibid.

22. Ibid.

23. Ibid., 45–46.

24. Val Burris, "The Social Base of Christian Right Activism" (Unpublished work, University of Oregon, 1993), 5.

25. Burris, "Social Base of Christian Right Activism," 6.

26. S. L. Gardiner, *Rolling Back Civil Rights: The Oregon Citizens Alliance at Religious War* (Portland, Ore.: Coalition for Human Dignity, 1992).

27. Atwood, "Through a Glass Darkly," 46.

28. Emmett H. Buell, Lee Sigelman, and Clyde Wilcox, "An Unchanging Minority: Popular Support for the Moral Majority, 1980 and 1984," *Social Science Quarterly* 68 (1987): 876–84.

29. Gardiner, *Rolling Back Civil Rights,* 11–12; Himmelstein, *To the Right,* 6–7.

30. Reed, "Casting a Wider Net," 32.

31. Atwood, "Through a Glass Darkly," 47.

32. 1 Cor. 13:12, quoted in Atwood, "Through a Glass Darkly," 48. Unintended ironies abound in politics, but it is difficult not to see wry humor in Atwood's use of 1 Corinthians as a scriptural source with which to remind the Christian right of the need for interpretive humility in an imperfect world, given the preoccupation of 1 Corinthians with sexual themes. The Greek city of Corinth was dedicated to the goddess Aphrodite and was best known in the ancient world for its temple prostitutes and sexual promiscuity. Much of the text of 1 Corinthians consists of Paul warning about the dangers of sexual sin.

33. Atwood, "Through a Glass Darkly," 47.

34. Ibid., 48.

35. Ibid.

36. Paul Hill is the excommunicated Orthodox Presbyterian minister who has been convicted of murdering a Pensacola, Florida, abortion provider and his escort; the Defensive Action list was a statement formulated by Hill and signed by other anti-abortion activists arguing that the murder of doctors who perform abortions should be considered "justifiable homicide."

37. Oregon Citizens Alliance, "OCA Becomes Oregon Christian Coalition Chapter," *The Oregon Alliance,* December 1991, 1.

38. Gardiner, *Rolling Back Civil Rights,* 37.

39. As reported to the author by Portland-based freelance writer Robert Sullivan, who witnessed the argument between Mabon and Witt at the 1993 Oregon Republican Party Convention.

40. Sura Rubenstein and Jeff Mapes, "OCA, Christian Group Split," *Oregonian,* 18 June 1993.

41. Reed, "Casting a Wider Net," 31.

42. Burris, "Social Base of Christian Right Activism," 5. Ballot Measure 9, the OCA's 1992 antigay initiative, would have amended Section 41 of the Oregon Constitution: "(1) This state shall not recognize any categorical provision such as 'sexual orientation,' 'sexual preference,' and similar phrases that includes homosexuality, pedophilia, sadism or masochism. Quotas, minority status, affirmative action, or any similar concepts, shall not apply to these forms of conduct, nor shall government promote these behaviors. (2) State, regional and local governments and their properties and monies shall not be used to promote, encourage, or facilitate homosexuality, pedophilia, sadism or masochism. (3) State, regional and local governments and their departments, agencies and other entities, including specifically the State Department of Higher Education and the public schools, shall assist in setting a standard for Oregon's youth that recognizes homosexuality, pedophilia, sadism and masochism as abnormal, wrong, unnatural, and perverse and that these behaviors are to be discouraged and avoided," Gardiner, *Rolling Back Civil Rights,* 44.

43. Coalition for Human Dignity, "OCA 'Surrounds the Cities,'" *Dignity Report,* 1 April 1994, 1.

44. Reed, "Casting a Wider Net," 31.

45. Moen, *Transformation of the Christian Right,* 147.

46. Atwood, "Through a Glass Darkly," 48.

47. Mark 10:43–44; Matthew 20:26–27, as quoted in Ibid.

48. Atwood, "Through a Glass Darkly," 48.

49. Gardiner, *Rolling Back Civil Rights,* 21.

50. Reed, *Politically Incorrect,* 132.

51. Jay Rogers, review of *Politically Incorrect,* by Ralph Reed, *Chalcedon Report,* February 1995, 39.

52. Devin Burghart and Steven Gardner, "Caught in the Wider Net: The Christian Coalition of Washington on the Road to Victory," *Dignity Report* (Summer 1995): 16.

53. Atwood, "Through a Glass Darkly," 50.

54. Ibid., 50–51.

55. As quoted in William Norman Grigg, "Right Problems, Wrong Solutions," *The New American,* 26 June 1995, 4.

56. Ibid., 6.

57. Ibid., 5.

58. Americans United for the Separation of Church and State, *Church and State,* April 1995, 5.

59. H. L. Richardson, "Winning through Confrontation and Positive Politics," *The Conservative Digest,* May-June, 1988; republished in OCA promotional literature.

60. Lon T. Mabon, "Confrontational Politics: Building Movement," *The Oregon Alliance,* June 1995, 1.

61. Lon T. Mabon, "Pro-Family Movement Setback," *The Oregon Alliance,* February 1995, 2.

62. "Christian Patriot" in this context is "a term of self-reference for a broad spectrum of the Far Right. Christian Patriots constitute the largest portion of the white supremacist movement in contemporary America. Christian Patriots generally hold to a literal interpretation of both the Bible and the constitution, but unlike most Christian fundamentalists, they also believe in a monolithic conspiracy (sometimes centuries old) directed against white Christians. For most Patriots, Jews are ultimately behind this conspiracy, although they may work through a variety of front organizations such as the United Nations, the Trilateral Commission, the Bilderburgers, etc.," Robert

Crawford et al., *The Northwest Imperative: Documenting a Decade of Hate* (Portland, Ore.: Coalition for Human Dignity, 1994), A-2.

63. Pat Smith, "One World Government: Myth, Conspiracy, or Reality?," December 1994, B-1.

64. D. A. Oaks, "The Militia—Last Means to Save Our Constitution?" *Oregon News-Leader,* August-September 1995, B-1.

65. Ibid.

PART III
POPULAR CONSERVATIVE MEDIA

POPULAR CONSERVATIVE MEDIA

Cable television, videotapes for home and group viewing, radio stations, and talk radio programs are all areas where Christian media producers have made dramatic inroads since the early 1980s. Some of these productions are popular fare for mainstream listeners and viewers as well as for the conservative Christian community. For example, as Razelle Frankl shows in Chapter 6, Pat Robertson has developed from one of the most successful televangelists to a mainstream television entrepreneur, establishing the Family Channel on cable television. Family Channel executives tell Frankl how they select programming to be consistent with family values, finding in the Western, for example, a model of ethical behavior and heroism.

Less visible is the dramatic growth and diversification of Christian publishing, the spread of Christian bookstores, and the rise of a new form of evangelism that Eithne Johnson in Chapter 7 calls "videovangelism." In these bookstores, one finds a plethora of family advice books and books and videos for children. Partly this is because these bookstores serve as outlets for the burgeoning Christian home schooling movement. With an even wider audience, Christian family advice videos are shown in churches and homes, and these have been the brainchild of one video producer and distributor, Dr. James C. Dobson, whose tapes, entrepreneurship, and widespread influence Johnson describes in detail.

Christian evangelical use of the radio has a long history, but recently Christian radio stations have proliferated and modernized their formats, garnering a huge listenership. In Chapter 8 Meryem Ersoz offers a theoretical discussion of radio's potential pleasures and emotional impact, and she analyzes the sophistication of the contemporary new style of Christian programming. In Chapter 9, Jeff Land analyzes the career and rhetorical style of Rush Limbaugh, a media celebrity whose show is regularly broadcast on Christian stations. Limbaugh, according to Land, creates a communal feeling among his fans, who often call themselves "Dittoheads" to express their oneness in attitude with Limbaugh and with each other. Such a sense of community is consistent with the sense of community many gain by listening to Christian radio on a regular basis and by participating in other aspects of a Christian lifestyle.

6

Transformation of Televangelism: Repackaging Christian Family Values

Razelle Frankl

Televangelism after the Bakker/Swaggart Scandals

Before our eyes, Pat Robertson gracefully ages on *The 700 Club*. Less visible are Christian television's incremental adaptations, new messages, and new alliances that signal shifts in its leadership, programming, delivery systems, and organizational structures. Other broad changes in Christian television relate to new technologies, economies of scale, and national conservative political activism. Not only is religious broadcasting (both evangelical and mainstream) taking new forms to retain its traditional audience, it also wants to grow by attracting new members. In part, religious broadcasters are becoming more commercial and more accessible to those who are not born-again Christians. Furthermore, contemporary televangelism is global. Christian conservative uses of electronic communication embrace many forms of communication, yet these new directions in media systems and uses of technology are barely discernible, even to students of the mass media. In order to understand the relation between media and public policy and how media can influence viewers' attitudes, it is very important to try to understand the shape, interrelationships, and influence of Christian broadcasting, even as it is extended into areas that may not seem related to broadcasting at all.

Historically, some of these changes are directly related to the new developments in Christian broadcasting, specifically televangelism, that occurred after the fall of Jim and Tammy Faye Bakker and Jimmy Swaggart. In 1987, I wrote in *Televangelism: The Marketing of Popular Religion*:

> For the time being, the electric church can be expected to become an even stronger societal force, [but] there are inherent limits to its growth which can eventually slow down its spread... [In addition, if] the television audience remains relatively stable, competition among televangelists is likely to become even more fierce than it is now... Unabated, such a competitive struggle raises the possibility that internal factors—poor management, overexpansion, scandal or fraud, or dissension—might force some of these televangelists out of the picture. (Frankl 1987, 149–50).

Indeed, this is precisely what happened in spring 1987. The trials of the Bakkers and Swaggart revealed the extent of televangelism's poor management and dissension. Jim Bakker received a forty-five-year sentence and a $500,000 fine for defrauding his PTL ("people that love" or "praise the Lord") followers by selling more shares in his Heritage Village, U.S.A., resort than he had space available and thus enriching his and Tammy Faye's lifestyle with cars, homes, and jewelry. Bakker's sentence was reduced to eighteen years, then eight, of which he served only five (Garfield 1994). The *Swaggart v. Gorman* trial demonstrated the venality arising out of market competition in a stable or shrinking market. A New Orleans jury found that Swaggart, his ministry, and its attorney plotted to spread lies to damage Marvin Gorman's reputation, emotional well-being, and ministry. Gorman was awarded $1 million plus $9 million to his bankrupt ministry ("Swaggart May Appeal Jury's Award," *Chicago Tribune* 14 September 1991). Both Swaggart and Bakker were defrocked as a result of the scandals (Poloma 1989, 217). As I will explain in detail, these scandals led the National Religious Broadcasters (NRB) to institutionalize changes in teleministries and for all religious broadcasting by emphasizing ethical accountability for funds.

What were the responses of the eight major televangelists[1] and of the NRB to televangelism's changing fortunes? Initially, televangelist organizations reduced purchases of airtime and downsized and reengineered their operations. Oral Roberts, for example, gave his law school to Pat Robertson's Christian Broadcasting Network (CBN). The hospital founded by Roberts opened one floor and then closed. Rex Humbard Ministries, the first teleministry, closed. His family did not want to continue producing programs. Jim Bakker's PTL empire and his Heritage Village, U.S.A., a Christian resort and television network, were lost in bankruptcy proceedings but have since risen from financial disaster. The resort was reorganized by a Malaysian developer and the operation of the hotel and golf course were farmed out to the Radisson Corporation to be resurrected as the Radisson Grand Resort (Garfield 1994). Bakker's television network was divested and is now the Inspirational Network. Looking at how things stand since the fall, we see that of the eight televangelists, only Pat Robertson, Robert Schuller, Oral Roberts, and Jerry Falwell still retain a national identity, albeit in a significantly different manner than before the fall. Of the remaining four, Swaggart and Robertson continue their programs but only after "downsizing their organizations and reducing their purchase of air time from commercial stations and broadcasting on cable as a cost-saving method... Christian Broadcasting Network suffered a staggering 33 percent drop in donations [in one] month—a total of $10 million—and may have to cut its budget" ("Evangelical Crunch," *Philadelphia Inquirer,* 10 May 1987).

A new kind of hybrid televangelism flourishes. Many forms of Christian broadcasting are now supported by a new and flourishing growth of varied Christian enterprises and productions, not least of which are the Christian Coalition (of which Pat Robertson is president and Ralph Reed was executive director), videocassettes, talk radio, bookstores, Web sites,[2] and teen-oriented music. Together these enterprises are fed by and reinforce the hybrid social movement of the religious right. Pat Robertson has taken a unique path away from the televangelism of the 1980s. He has expanded his enterprises from *The 700 Club* and CBN to include a major corporation, International Family Entertainment, Inc. (hereafter referred to as IFE), which he and his son Tim acquired in 1990; an accredited institution of higher education (Regent University); and a grassroots political action organization (the Christian Coalition). Robertson's two seemingly disparate endeavors (religious Christian broadcasting and IFE, or the Family Channel) stem from his use of the televangelism hybrid, and they reflect similar social agendas, which I will explain in detail later.

National Religious Broadcasters' Response to Scandals

When the NRB established as its priority restoring credibility to televangelism and to religious broadcasting in general, it set the stage for the recovery and transformation of televangelism. Its members must now comply with financial standards set by the Ethics and Financial Integrity Commission (EFICOM) and must also open their boards of directors to include "outside directors." Scandals such as those with PTL and Jimmy Swaggart Ministries in part occurred because family members and perhaps a few friends constituted their boards.

David Clark, then-president of the NRB, stated in 1991 that viewers would "fade away" if the perception of trustworthiness were not part of televangelism's message. He predicted that "wherever financial, moral, or spiritual ambiguity remains, we will see a continuing decline in audience size and giving" (1991b, 3). Seemingly in response to Clark's editorial, the 6 October 1991 broadcast of Robert Schuller's *Hour of Power,* promoting a book by Norman Vincent Peale, informed viewers that Dr. Peale had contributed his profits and 80 percent of viewers' contributions directly to Crystal Cathedral Ministries.

The NRB's EFICOM and its predecessor, the Evangelical Council for Financial Accountability (ECFA), were established as a Christian broadcasters' self-regulating accountability committee. According to Clark (1991b):

> [In 1991] 106 NRB members [are] fully certified with EFICOM. Another 91 ministries are considered to be in good standing and do not need to further qualify because of their limited income. In addition, 96 ministries are members of the Evangelical Council for Financial Accountability (ECFA), a sister accountability organization for ministries. It is working well today.

A few ministries withdrew from NRB rather than join EFICOM (Clark 1991a).

In Clark's opinion, the crisis in confidence deriving from the scandals strengthened both EFICOM and ECFA as organizations (1991b). In 1995, NRB's process of requiring financial accountability for members entered its second phase, replacing EFICOM with the ECFA. Nonprofit organizations with annual broadcast-related incomes or expenses of $500,000 or more must meet the standards of the ECFA, which is a separate group.

With the shift in viewing habits from broadcast television to cable television in the 1980s, televangelists purchased less network airtime. Then, with their restored credibility, many reassessed their previous marketing strategies. In the 1980s ministries looked for alternative sources of funding, shifting from product sales to consolidation of market share (see McKenna 1991, 70, for an explanation of this strategy). This same game plan has accounted for many organizational mergers in the communications industry, aiming for vertical integration, including acquisition of production companies as well as delivery systems for their products.

Pat Robertson exemplifies this strategy, both producing *The 700 Club* and owning the cable network to carry it. From this cable network, the Family Channel and a variety of other enterprises developed: CBN television productions; CBN University (now Regent University, comprising graduate schools in business, communication, law, and public policy); CBN Publishing, offering a "Superbook Audio Cassette and Coloring Book" for children ages four to eleven; "Sing, Spell, Read, and Write," an instructional system for children in primary grades; and Video Tracts "designed to be used by the individual or as a key element in a church's or organization's overall evangelistic outreach." CBN travel and Operation Blessing became separate endeavors, as did America Benefits Plus.

The NRB has championed such vertical integration, especially in the light of retaining access for local Christian stations as television began shifting from networks to cable channels. Cable operators, Christian broadcasters worried, might not be required to carry public interest programming. It was such "public interest" access to television during the "golden age" of the 1970s and 1980s that enabled televangelists to buy airtime after decades of being shut out by mainstream denominations (Frankl 1987). Thus, a major, ongoing NRB task is constantly to monitor changes in communications regulations so as to retain access to this valuable resource.

NRB membership has grown and continues to show signs of vitality, such as the affiliation of media producers and broadcasters with denominations (for example, the Assemblies of God), which continue to grow into big businesses in their own right despite very loose organizational control over individual churches. "Sales from [mail order ventures, publishing, and video production] enterprises exceeded $29 million last year... Video centers produce sermons aimed at the nation's 200 religious television stations. Although the Assemblies do not own any of the stations, most air the videos and church services" (Johnson 1990).

Mergers of denominational broadcasting facilities signal televangelism's recovery and growth. Family Net—a television network originally owned by the Old Time Gospel Hour, Inc., and Liberty Broadcasting Network, Inc.—developed in part to reduce the need to purchase airtime for the *Old-Time Gospel Hour*. Family Net, carried primarily by television stations, has now been acquired by the Southern Baptist Radio and Television Commission (RTVC) as a second television network to enhance RTVC's outreach, along with the Association of Christian Television Stations (ACTS) satellite network, which reaches about three-fourths of its 10 million households through local cable channels. With this merger, the Southern Baptist Convention is in a strong position to barter for airtime.

About 740,000 cable households were added to the viewing audience through these acquisitions, and 13.2 million households will be able to receive the television stations that carry Family Net. Cable systems serving 2.8 million homes also transmit the programming of some of the television stations. "We believe that this combination of ACTS and Family Net will make it possible for almost one-fourth of the television households in America to receive the gospel messages carried by the two networks" (Media Focus, *Religious Broadcasting* 1991, 36).

Just as corporations and businesses adjust to market shifts, regulatory changes, and new technologies, televangelists adapted successfully, particularly in reformulating marketing plans. Well before the public became aware of scandal, televangelists began using new marketing strategies (cf. Frankl 1987). Partly they were reacting to the fact that they had a stable audience, which is appealing to advertisers, and partly they were responding to mainline religious groups' criticisms of them. Dominant religious groups accused televangelists of failing to be good Christian stewards, wasting monies that should have been spent on direct services for parishioners or the needy. Moreover, critics asserted that a television experience was not religious expression, since it lacked theological dialogue, rituals, prayers, and other aspects of denominational religion. At that time, televangelists' switching to cable, bartering, and downsizing represented their best short-term response to facilitate recovery. However, as good businessmen for the Lord, they are by training attuned to look for signs of success. And that success has come in part from their capacity to readjust constantly, while making certain to stir religious enthusiasms, as Charles Grandison Finney, the original urban revivalist, taught.

Full Recovery of Religious Broadcasting (1995)

The NRB theme, "An Unchanging Message to a Changing World," was most appropriate for its 1995 Fifty-Second Annual Convention and Exposition, an international event to help those in the religious broadcasting field. Evident was a renewed religious broadcasting industry composed of the electric church and networks of religious broadcasters with claims to worldwide audiences. With credibility restored, NRB membership has increased to approximately eight hundred religious broadcasting organizations, up 12 percent since January 1991. Of these, thirty-one are international members. The membership is divided among program producers (52 percent), station owners or operators (45 percent), and agencies (39 percent). Data from NRB's 1995 *Directory of Religious Media* show a large increase in the number of full-time radio stations over the period from 1972 (399) to 1995 (1,328); the number of full-time television stations increased from 1977 (10) to 1994 (207) but decreased in 1995 (163). This change in absolute numbers may simply reflect a consolidation of the market and does not indicate the size of the audiences or how many programs are produced.

The trend toward niche marketing, that is, developing program formats for specific audiences, has influenced radio as well as television programming. Staples from the televangelism era of the 1980s like the *Hour of Power, Old-Time Gospel Hour,* and *The 700 Club* constantly update their content, not their format. For example, now they use more crossover and inspirational music. Both radio and television formats offer special programs that appeal to black and Latino audiences. Much more than preaching, there has been a blossoming of Christian music radio shows featuring gospel music, contemporary Christian music, and Christian country music. There are also inspirational and news talk shows. Clearly, some broadcasters are bridging Christian and secular markets with their success in Christian music (Dawidoff 1995, 40–44, 66, 68–69, 72.). For many years the NRB in their educational sessions discussed packaging programs for niche markets, and this year the convention even had a session that covered programs using public service announcements to attract "secular" generation X viewers.

According to a 1994 *New York Times* article, Christian broadcasters, fringe players in the radio industry just twenty-five years ago, appear to be holding on to the impressive gains they realized during the 1970s and 1980s, when the religious format enjoyed a surge in popularity. In 1996, religious programming was the third most common radio format, alongside country and adult contemporary. In 1993, for the fourth consecutive year, almost 1 in 10 American radio stations identified their programming as "religious" (Kelleher 1994).

New Communication Structures and Technologies Used in Religious Broadcasting

New technologies include satellite links, digital recordings, and interactive TV, as well as converging technologies—computers and telephones, television, radio programs, and faxes. The word "technologies" means more than equipment. The term also refers to new arrangements and social relationships to spread the gospel. Thus the 766 displays crowded on the Grand Ole Opry's exhibition floor at the 1995 NRB convention showcased new equipment, product diversity, and new cooperative ventures with secular businesses. Christian publishers who displayed their diverse products (Moody Press, Zondervan, NavPress, Thomas Nelson, and Bethany House) also featured video- and audiotapes.

Converging and merging media were exhibited. TV and radio networks exhibited their programming (USA Radio Network; Skylight Satellite Network; Inspirational Network, formerly PTL; and Reach Satellite Network). AM and FM radio and several satellite vendors offered their services (NPR Satellite and Orion Atlantic) for uplinks and digital audio equipment, needed for distributing and sharing programming. In addition to the dazzling hardware and professionally produced radio and television programs, ancillary services for religious broadcasters were proffered. Travel agents, working with the Israel Ministry of Tourism, CBN Travel, and other organizations, advertised group trips to the Holy Land. The exhibits demonstrated the large variety of business services available for Christian broadcasters, for example, comprehensive marketing services, Timothy Plan (a mutual fund), Optimum Health (health products), Messenger Christian Calendar Premiums, Discover Card Services, Franklin Electronic Publishers, and Sony Professional Media.

The Christian Interactive Network and Christianity on Line have established "links" into the computer world of "cyberspace" as a forum for prayer, information, support, education, and furtherance of the "Great Commission" (from a Christian Interactive Network brochure). These are reached through Compuserve. Greater numbers of secular firms are exhibiting and working with the NRB members in mutually beneficial relationships as Christian broadcasters continue using varied means (such as the latest digital editing systems) to achieve quality programs and products and spread the word.

At prior NRB conventions, Robertson's CBN and Bakker's PTL bought exhibit space promoting their networks and production facilities. PTL, as an organization, no longer exists. Inspirational Network replaced PTL broadcasting functions, and Heritage Village, U.S.A., has become a separate entity, which did exhibit and appears to be expanding. What had been Robertson's CBN is now IFE, which owns the Family Channel and carries *The 700 Club.* Ben Kinslow, host of *The 700 Club,* spoke at the 1995 convention; in relation to the Robertson enterprises, there were displays for Operation Blessing, CBN Travel, and Regent University, which announced the first Ph.D. program to use distance learning. As Robertson now runs a commercial television network, he had no place at the NRB convention. He turned to commercial broadcasting trying to make his network the dominant international broadcasting system for family entertainment in this secular marketplace of popular culture.

Technology and Marketing in a Transitional Era

All electronic media and the people who own and operate them have entered a turbulent period of conflict and readjustment. New technologies and new combinations of delivery systems are constantly being introduced and are challenging current Federal Communications Commission regulatory practices, which have been based largely on discrete television channels.[3] As I mentioned before, the NRB sees as part of its mission keeping a constant vigil on new broadcast technologies and on changes in the regulatory environment. In the 1980s the major teleministries concerned themselves with sales pitches and market share tactics, watching the Nielsen and Arbitron ratings and their relative positions as top religious broadcasters (Frankl 1987). Several televangelists sought to make themselves less dependent on donors by centralizing and customizing technical services for evangelists with smaller viewing audiences. They made and promoted educational videos and books; they taught churches and Christian special interest groups how to improve their communications, managerial, and fund-raising skills. Such services were in the past the province of denominational headquarters; in effect, entrepreneurial Christian producers decentralized production of the "religious product" so that access to it would now reside in individual ministries. Religious broadcasting as an industry continues to be dominated by independent evangelical organizations, and perhaps by the needs of Christian special interest groups (for example, the teen audience for music or the Christian Coalition), while denominations' role in the growth of religious broadcasting continues to decline.

One unintended consequence of these newer technologies is the proliferation of delivery systems that fragment former mass markets. There are now too many producers, too many choices for the viewer. With today's "telecosm" combinations (that is, television and computers), production companies can customize a variety of messages for specific audiences. The problem for producers now becomes one of establishing and retaining a large enough share of the audience to make their enterprise financially profitable. Because there are so many bewildering choices, producers *must* create a feedback loop, not only to establish dialogue with their audiences but to create credibility for their organizations. When the NRB made the restoration of credibility and accountability to religious broadcasting a primary objective, they also facilitated the use and gave credibility to the producers of these new delivery systems.

Cable continues to attract more and more viewers. In 1976, 92 percent of the prime-time television audience watched three networks. By 1991, that audience was down to 60 percent and continues to dwindle. Today, the prime-time share of the big three broadcast networks (ABC, CBS, and NBC) has dropped to 57 percent, while the cable prime-time share has increased to 23 percent, up from 6 percent in 1985 (Winfrey 1995). Cable and other forms of video expanded in part due to their innovative programming. Satellite transmissions also expand viewers' choices. In this way opportunities for religious programmers have grown, as has competition with other religious programs. Video- and audiotapes provide supplemental delivery systems for instructional opportunities and are important tools for the Christian home schooling movement. In higher education, Liberty University uses video as integral to its distance learning program for nontraditional students. And at the graduate level, Regent University is starting a long-distance Ph.D. program using satellite transmissions.

George Gilder, a conservative futurist, predicts that within the next decade we should expect major changes in electronic media:

> The terminals on our desks and televisions in our living rooms will give way to image-processing computers, "telecomputers" that will not only receive but also store, manipulate, create and transmit digital video programming. Linking these computers will be a worldwide web of fiber-optic cables reaching homes and offices... Telecomputers would make it possible for the originators of distinguished or special offerings to reach a substantial audience anywhere around the globe at any time. It would allow advertisers to reach the specific audiences most receptive to specialized products... The culture will change from a mass-produced and mass-consumer horizontal commodity to a vertical feast with a galore of niches and specialties. (Gilder 1991, 150, 160, 161)

This vision of Christian communication assumes a computer society, or a society in which those with computers are the most important part of the market. According to Gilder:

> In essence telecomputers will harness the full imaginative and sensory faculties that allow people to be most intuitive and creative. People will be able to talk face-to-face, travel in imagination around the globe; they will be able to show, not just tell. They will be able to call up audiovisual illustrations, transmit dynamic pictures, navigate through architectural designs and databases like pilots. (Gilder 1991, 151)

Think of the opportunities for teleministries. Instead of telephone banks, interaction with viewers or listeners occurs during the program. Viewers would transcend not only studio boundaries but national ones. Instead of phone banks and computerized mailings, personalized programming—electronically billed—only awaits regulatory willingness and capitalization. The technology exists. In fact, cheap desktop publishing and fax systems require little cash and already permit people with a religious or political mission to send and receive religious and political messages. (In particular, individuals on the extreme right have taken advantage of inexpensive fax machines and the Internet to disseminate their messages.)

Paradoxes abound in this scenario. On a social level, the user is alone when connected to the Internet. In that sense, the number and variety of messages, the oversaturation of images, sounds, and information, may offer society only the new face of alienation. The agenda still remains in the hands of the broadcaster, who is responsible for limiting ideas, dialogue, and discussion. Christian broadcasters want interactive communication, yes, but managed and focused.

There is no question that religious broadcasters eagerly use new forms of media. One example is *Beverly LaHaye Live,* with Concerned Women for America's president Beverly LaHaye as host. This nationally syndicated one-hour program airs live from the nation's capital and brings a Christian perspective to late-breaking news affecting families and citizens with traditional moral values. Airing at 3 P.M. eastern standard time, *Beverly LaHaye Live* frequently gives its listeners timely political information, which it asks them to act on. As program producer Chuck Merritt noted:

> One day Senator Bill Armstrong's office called us minutes before air time, and the Senator came on live to explain an amendment he was sponsoring. The amendment was coming up for a 5 P.M. vote. This gave the listeners an opportunity to call the U.S. Capitol and voice their opinions instantaneously. (Media Focus, *Religious Broadcasting* 1991, 34)

The entire telecommunications industry is undergoing structural changes toward the vertical integration of delivery. For example, in summer 1995 two major mergers were completed: Disney Entertainment with ABC and MCI Communications Corporation with Rupert Murdoch Corporation. According to Rupert Murdoch: "No one has put together the right building blocks—

programming, network intelligence, distribution and merchandising—to offer new media services on a global scale" ("Murdoch and MCI Joining Forces," *Philadelphia Inquirer,* 11 May 1995). The Ted Turner (CNN) and TimeWarner merger created an even larger vertical and horizontal industrial enterprise than the Disney and ABC and MCI and Murdoch mergers. The reason for these mergers is that media corporations want to survive all the configurations of media delivery that are currently just possibilities. To that end, they want to control as much "product" as they can for the greatly expanded, worldwide, media delivery systems of the future. Given the plethora of delivery systems and the uncertainty about which configurations will dominate, broadcasters are thinking about all potential changes and making decisions aimed at maintaining as much flexibility as possible in their options. Since the old regulations do not fit the new technologies, these mergers are also being forged as the industry is awaiting new regulatory provisions. Whether the delivery system is fiber optics for pay-per-view or cable or direct-to-home satellite, the opportunities for future television programming will occur in the context of a 200-channel delivery system. Specialized channels or purchased, internationally distributed, satellite television programming slots could easily be used, for example, for short courses on topics such as parenting and health, subjects appealing to families.

Changes in information technologies, delivery systems and industry structures require new marketing strategies. Electronic communication is and will be increasingly international in scope. Furthermore, media logic influences all of popular culture. TV formats and media literacy are part of viewers' cognitive maps, creating what Altheide and Snow (1991, 207) designate as media culture. Because our culture is so imbued with media, other events in our lives are enhanced by the degree to which they imitate TV. Perhaps more than any other group seeking to sway public attitudes and individual beliefs, religious broadcasters first began to learn this lesson with the diffusion of radio in the United States and have understood this aspect of television from their initial uses of the medium.

Not only have televangelists adapted popular TV formats, they have also promoted a parasocial sense of extended family and community using memberships or visits to religious and social complexes like Heritage Village, U.S.A. When parareligious organizations such as the teleministries offer new electronic relationships between viewers and their ministers without the formality of church walls, they lack the settings of human interaction that all churches have and also the church's accountability. The ministry can be all "front stage" to the consumer with the "back stage" revealed only marginally. Learning and interaction are shifted and take place more quickly than in a traditional setting. In the mass media, unbounded institutions and organizations have eroded relationships between viewers and listeners and the producers of messages.

> The difficulty in distinguishing between televangelism as video theater and televangelism as religion is what has made televangelism a consummate form of media culture. This is not simply religion being telecast to a viewing audience, it is a new form of religion—a television religion in which religious experience as a cultural phenomenon is 'informed' by television format criteria... The major cultural change is essentially a matter of practicing and experiencing religion and morality through the formal properties of television as opposed to the traditional formal properties of the church and ecclesiastic organization. (Altheide and Snow 1991, 214, 216)

Most commonly, however, organizers within the evangelical community promote a parasocial sense of the extended family through direct mail and conferences and courses sponsored by the various ministries. More recently, making members feel like part of a community through direct contact via phone banks and direct mail is a tactic refined by conservative Christian groups seeking political office.

Such varieties of contact with "consumers" may seem predictable marketing developments for Christian media producers, but there are other motives for seeking a wider audience. When religious broadcasters articulate their mission as establishing a more nonsectarian base, they downplay theological interpretations for ecumenical moral appeals. Their message shifts to Christian cultural values and morals. For many viewers, Jerry Falwell remains doctrinaire while Pat Robertson is concerned with influencing culture and daily life. Of course, in another interpretation, Robertson is simply a "businessman for the Lord" (to quote Billy Sunday). Currently his role is as leader in the cultural struggle waged by conservative Christians, largely via the Christian Coalition, and supported by an effective media apparatus, which has become such an integral part of U.S. social and political life.

A good example of the way televangelism has been transformed by an entrepreneur's riding the crest of the changes in the U.S. communications industry is the transformation of Pat Robertson's television business. With great economic and political acumen, Robertson transformed his media empire from *The 700 Club* and CBN into IFE. Three factors contributed to this transformation: new communications structures and technology; history and Robertson's adaptive response to the televangelism scandals; and his own business skills, drawing on the marketing experience of the religious right. These factors have created a context that Pat Robertson has used very skillfully to develop a complex set of interrelated organizations. He recognizes the value of and utilizes all the proliferating forms of electronic communication, having seen early on the degree to which the media are a ubiquitous, familiar aspect of contemporary social life. By establishing the first Christian network, he learned further how to control television as a uniquely and highly profitable resource for religious ends. In a past generation, Charles Finney taught evangelists to stir religious enthusiasms with plain speech and dramatic appeals to individuals who, as Finney argued, were "free to choose salvation." As a religious broadcaster with a clear focus and an ethos of "use any means" (derived from Finney), Robertson has now mobilized large numbers of constituents and become a multimillionaire.

Televangelism, the thriving religious right, and the changes in their use of electronic communication have occurred out of the view of the mainstream and, significantly, out of the view of liberal politicians and the liberal press. The Christian right has built an infrastructure to try to place Christian culture center stage in the United States. Their efforts are now most successful at the grassroots level, electing school board members and government officials and pushing in the courts for strict "Christian" interpretations of the Constitution. The public seems to separate these public battles from televangelism. Even the press, who work within the mass media, continue in their writing to use old perceptual boundaries and structures to make sense of and organize the changes in the media world. Media categories such as news, arts, entertainment, and politics are still called upon to focus our attention and our behavior, but such categories exclude other structures that do not fit our current way of understanding the media synergy and that, moreover, do not fit our cognitive maps.

Our mental maps primarily make sense of and give meaning to our lives, but they also have consequences for our daily behavior, determining our interests, how we use our time, and even the people we associate with. As media analyst Joshua Meyrowitz explains, television has created cognitive boundary changes that have altered individual behavior and perceptions by setting new links among people and places, new ways of storing and retrieving social information: "*Where* one is has less and less to do with what one knows and experiences. Electronic media have altered the significance of time and space for social interaction... We must expect a fundamental shift in our perceptions of our society, our authorities, and ourselves" (Meyrowitz 1985, viii).

What most people do not recognize in a conscious way is how the electronic media have changed our *religious* cognitive systems. In contemporary life, according to Robert Wuthnow, the media and, in an expanded way, much of electronic communication now point to "new modes of religious identification, new distinctions in the web of religious interaction, alterations in the lines of moral obligation that define religious communities, changes in the categories that are taken for granted in religious discourse" (Wuthnow 1988, 10).

The Family, Television, and the New Right

To return to Pat Robertson as the exemplar of religious broadcasting today, it is important to note how he uses the family as the central organizing metaphor of his programming. By focusing on the family as his main reference point, he also creates an effective marketing strategy, for this metaphor forges the necessary link he needs to audience demographics. He has repackaged religiosity and politics in *The 700 Club,* for example, to incorporate two familiar genres, the news program and the domestic melodrama, and he does this by formulating most of the show's material around topics and emotions related to family life. Such an emotional link weaves viewers into his televisual community, where his programming and form of entertainment fulfill his patriarchal role as "good provider." For example, he uses the metaphor of the family in all its shadings to establish a tie to needy viewers, who receive direct counseling and prayer from *The 700 Club.* And the same metaphor as the basis for programming offers a rationale for parents to turn to the Family Channel for daily entertainment and education, even to use it as an electronic baby sitter.

The Family Channel and IFE offer Robertson a much subtler way to deliver his religious-political messages. Furthermore, his emphasis on the family as a central organizing concept for programming coincides with the symbolic manipulation of "family" by the contemporary conservative social-political movement. Robertson's personalized address to viewers was developed over the years on *The 700 Club.* Now his expanded vision of domestically appealing programming furthers his goal to make IFE globally dominant.

The Family Channel repackages the Christian family ideal into daylong "quality" family entertainment. Such entertainment has a strong emotional appeal. Its aim is to enter the heart first and then the mind to form emotional connections and, as the producers hope, even to shape viewers' personalities. Morally, the Family Channel has as its aim reinforcing viewers' beliefs in the possibility and desirability of a strong family supporting each other in a hostile world. With pro-family values established as its programming measure, the Family Channel is the countervailing entertainment system to both Disney and Nickelodeon, the other family television networks. In effect, Robertson is engaged in popular culture wars, fighting for "Christian family values" and seeking to build young audiences around family messages.

The new Christian right posts as a cornerstone of its philosophy and political strategizing that the family is the basic unit of society, essential for contemporary society's survival, and that strengthening the Christian family can help the United States recover its greatness. As a unifying political symbol, the family "stands as 'a means to recover a lost meaning as well as a lost past.' What's more, all other issues can be subsumed under the 'pro-family' label: the teaching of evolution, prayer in schools, abortion, traditional roles for women, sex and drugs, pornography, and so forth" (Donald Heinz, in Hadden and Shupe 1988, 60).

Most members of the New Christian Right see enemies of the family everywhere, working to destroy this holiest of institutions. Titles commonly found in a local Christian bookstore convey a strong element of defensiveness: *Attack on the Family; The Battle for the Family; How to Protect the Family; Rape of a Nation*; and *Listen, America!* The Christian lifestyle desired by the religious right should, it feels, permeate schools, work, politics, and entertainment, in short, all those activities that socialize the family. Such a lifestyle is enhanced with interactive television, which has changed the religious boundaries between producers/preachers and audiences.

Beyond exploiting the family as a social and cultural symbol, Pat Robertson has been a leader in showing how television production values can spread the word by using the full panoply of entertainment formats: music, drama, talk shows, and a strategy of niche marketing to attract Christian families and reinforce their values. The Family Channel targets a variety of age groups as well as ethnic and racial groups. Content has evolved from a focus on saving souls to a focus on social and political concerns such as pro-life messages,[4] abstinence from premarital sex, and attacks on homosexuals—"pelvic politics" (Poloma 1989). Robertson deals with all these issues as relating to the traditional family pattern (that is, married, heterosexual, with children, father dominant). Early in his career, Robertson went from religious broadcaster to Christian broadcaster, learning very skillfully how to utilize the media, inserting religion into traditional and popular programming formats rather than adapting the medium to the religious message. He incorporates his messages into all his activities. As he continues on this path, he uses existing institutional structures, imbuing them with his religiously grounded ideology and values to maintain and energize the social movement of the religious right.

The Family Channel is owned by IFE. As self-described in its 1994 annual report, IFE is an advertiser-supported basic cable television network that provides family-oriented entertainment programming, one of the nation's largest basic cable television networks, currently reaching approximately 95 percent of all cable households and 63 percent of all television households. IFE is a leader among basic cable networks in the development of original programming. The Family Channel provides high-quality entertainment programming and related products that emphasize traditional values and that can be enjoyed by the entire family.

The quality of the programming on the Family Channel remains of constant concern for IFE's Board of Directors (Report to Stockholders 1994). Promoting a pro-family agenda is more complex than just mythologizing the nuclear family. Translating this agenda into programming must avoid the obvious pitfalls of boredom and limited audience appeal. Realizing that "the network's brand identity is not as clear or definable as it can be ... [the Family Channel] has launched an innovative advertising campaign ... [B]ased on the theme, 'one channel celebrates the extraordinary power of the family,' these contemporary ads deal with the changing definition of the traditional family." (Report to Stockholders 1994, 10). The annual report clearly states the company's decision to increase audience size and advertiser base, rational steps for a television network.

As a subtext, keep in mind that though Christians eagerly use broadcasting as a vehicle to get the word out and to persuade, broadcasting requires stories and context. Stridently opposed to the messages of the secular media on a multitude of family issues, Robertson gives voice to pro-family sociopolitical messages through his stories and programming. In their gatherings and in their writings, Christian broadcasters characteristically rail against many social institutions, giving voice to a litany of "sins": "great waves of sex," abortion, media violence, liberal court rulings on pornography, and intrusive government in schools and the workplace. Robertson and his ilk view these social problems as intrusions and attacks on the family. As Hadden and Shupe explain, social movements, in this case Christian conservatism, need to identify one cause-and-effect around which to focus their efforts: "First they chose the hallowed family as the focal point around which virtually all other issues could revolve" (1988, 59–60). "Secular humanism" is often named as the villain, and the government, media, and schools are seen as the carriers of secular humanists' influence. Robertson's response to this paradox in the movement—vilifying the media yet using it to convey the message—is that he has always aimed to provide the viewer with an alternative message, both religious and secular.

Trust and loyalty are deeply held parts of mainstream organizational culture. So, too, among members of Christian organizations, these values aid in establishing a core that will resist the establishment. Religious broadcasters establish trust and loyalty with their viewers for several reasons. As independent revivalists, fundamentalists' tradition comes from that of religious dissenters or nonestablishment groups. Severely criticized by established denominations, they have had to protect themselves. Their stance is reminiscent of that of Charles Finney, the first urban revivalist and the author of the handbook *How to Conduct Religious Revivals,* who personally suffered the wrath of his denominational peers when he popularized religion with unbridled emotionalism. Because they work outside the mainstream, televangelists have a strong need for a sense of being identified within their community as Christian. Excluding non-Christians and non-Christian lifestyles reinforces trust for televangelists within the religious community and builds distrust for those outside of it. Family and church members are always seen as more trustworthy than strangers. As fundamentalists, televangelists partake of a religious family whose maintenance requires constant vigilance within the group and in relation to outsiders. Anything less could threaten the community.

Another dynamic that sets televangelists apart is that teleministries are family businesses, with wives part of the professional team and other family members engaged in the work of the ministry. Family members add stability to the organization. In general, a major strength of family firms is their long-term perspective. Participation by family enlarges the audience potential. Younger members attract younger viewers; wives serve as role models for other women. Family members, on-camera, add credibility and legitimacy to the program and the organization. Off-camera roles are important as well. Frances Swaggart controls administrative details; Arvella Schuller is executive producer of the *Hour of Power.* Sons and daughters preach, work, and contribute to the ministry in many different ways. On camera, Robert A. Schuller preaches and is prepared to assume his father's place. So too, Richard Roberts, son of Oral, has developed a music ministry to succeed Oral Roberts's Healing Ministry. Timothy B. Robertson is president, chief executive officer, and a member of the Board of Directors of IFE.

Family firms have a major marketing advantage in their consistent image and product loyalty. This enables them to plan for the long run. Product association with the family name, such as Levi jeans and Ford automobiles, ties consumers to these products and establishes reliability and trust. It reduces the risk for the general consumer, who wants to be assured that the product, whether an aspirin or a religious message, is consistently the same (Frankl 1990). In addition, the family business is part of the moral-political message of the New Christian Right. It represents family traditionalism and individual economic libertarianism. Christian families working together are visual icons, part of the "system of meaning" produced by the New Christian Right for religious broadcasting.

Media's "Businessman for the Lord"

Historically, key factors have contributed to shaping CBN into the media giant of IFE and the Family Channel in particular. An aggressive regulatory and political climate followed the Bakker and Swaggart scandals. The U.S. Internal Revenue Service then investigated the finances of all religious broadcasters. U.S. Representative J. J. Pickle (D–Tex.) held investigatory hearings on not-for-profit organizations, calling on Congress to take notice of these large enterprises that operate with little more than the tax officers' supervision. Because he had been legally challenged by the IRS, Robertson was fearful of IRS intervention when the Family Channel became profitable; his response to the investigation was to establish a separate for-profit corporation.

Although the initial impetus to its founding was a legal one, inside the organization, the development of the Family Channel and IFE stems from Pat Robertson's charismatic leadership and unique sense of mission. Robertson is a charismatic Pentecostal, believing in gifts of the Holy Spirit. As an entrepreneur, he is also a "charismatic" leader, a concept adopted from leadership studies, especially Max Weber's studies of traditional religious organizations. According to Conger, charismatic leaders "create among subordinates a compelling desire to be led in the direction of the vision" by "linking the vision to values that are central for their audience. They simultaneously suggest a return to values that are already cherished and link these old but important values to future goals in order to heighten their meaningfulness" (1989, 31).

Robertson personifies such a leader, exuding "self-confidence, conviction, and expertise, dedication to the cause, and a concern for followers' needs" (Conger 1989, 32). In addition, with the use of the Family Channel and its family-friendly fare, he is building trust in his organization and at the same time institutionalizing his charisma.

The Robertson organizations are legally established not-for-profit and for-profit entities that seem stable and financially secure. They all feed into and reinforce the work of each other. The first not-for-profit was CBN University, now Regent University, consisting only of graduate schools in the fields of law, divinity, communications, counseling, government, and business. Its promotional materials explicitly state that Regent promotes a "Christian worldview and values in the student's professional education." Regent is gaining a credible reputation, in part, by sending its graduates to secular and religious organizations. Robertson, according to Harvey Cox, "subscribes to a postmillennial eschatology in which Christians—at least the ones who share his views—are called upon to try to assume positions of power wherever they can in order to build a more righteous and God-fearing society" (1995, 66). Coupled with postmillennial theology is the dominion crisis, whereby "Christians perceive God's dominion over this land to be threatened... At the heart of its proponents' anguish is the belief that America, this special place in God's divine plan, has stumbled again" (Hadden 1987, 7). It follows that "believers are entitled to 'dominion' over all the world's major institutions" (Cox 1995, 66), and according to Cox, the vision of an "entire nation run at all levels by the faithful is what inspired Robertson to rename his universiy 'Regent'" (Cox 1995, 66). Robertson's vision also created a complex system of companies, regardless of their legal status as not-for-profit or for-profit organizations. Operation Blessing is an international outreach ministry providing flood and medical relief that "could bring millions to Christ." In addition, he established political action committees, the Christian Coalition, the American Center for Law and Justice, and a number of for-profit firms in addition to IFE (see Figure 1).

Figure 1. Transformation of *The 700 Club:* Building Religious Identity through Television, Business Relations, and Political Action. A Hybrid of Urban Revivalism and Television

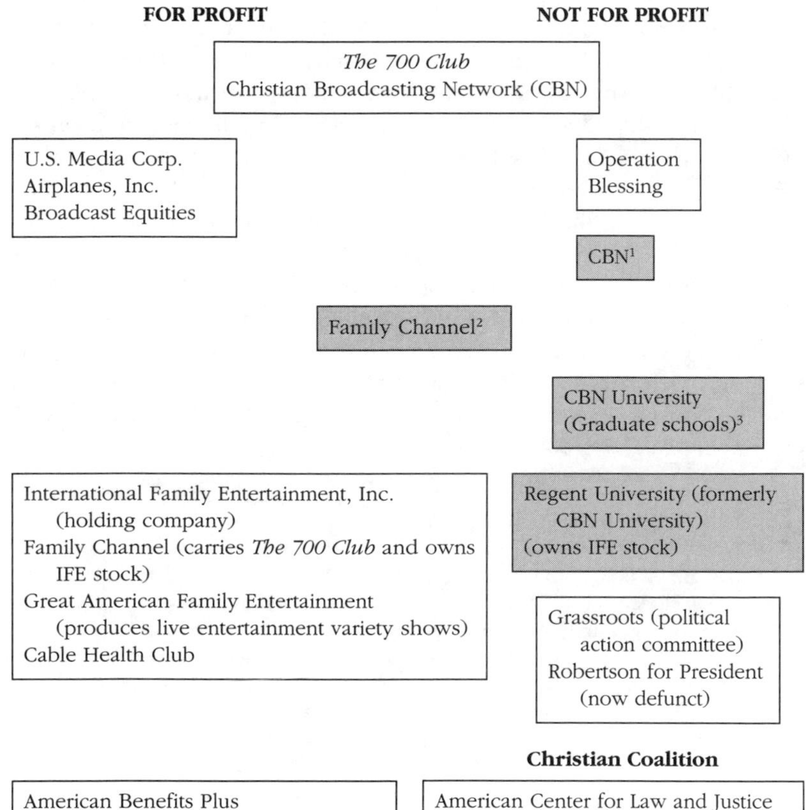

1. Became the Family Channel in 1981.
2. The Family Channel, in its earlier incarnation as CBN, started our as a not-for-profit organization. In 1981, the Family Channel became a for-profit organization.
3. The graduate schools comprise colleges of business, communication, law, and public policy. Regent University to date has no undergraduate programs.

Reminding us of radio evangelist Billy Sunday, who described himself as a "businessman for the Lord," Pat Robertson extends his Christian mission to several other businesses for the Lord. Robertson personifies the charismatic entrepreneur described in management studies, setting new goals and developing successful enterprises and diverse spin-offs; and if he fails, he tries something new. His early legal and business training were useful here, as was his knowledge of the workings of the U.S. Senate and the principles of finance. These he learned from his father, Senator A. Willis Robertson, who was sent to Congress when Pat was two years old. Senator Robertson, an expert on taxation and banking, in 1958 became chairman of the powerful Senate Banking and Currency Committee (Harrell 1987, 14). Like many other charismatic leaders, Pat Robertson has difficulty releasing control and leadership to his sons or other executives, preferring to remain active in his many endeavors. There is little question that he is still a major participant in these endeavors as chairman of the Board of Directors of IFE and as chairman of the board and chief executive officer of Family Channel, Inc.

Robertson's leadership and vision provide unique talents for linking the Christian right to broadcasting. In the 1980s, Robertson identified himself as both a broadcaster and a businessman. In *The Plan,* he describes his work as a web of relationships with one goal in mind: to reach as many people as possible with his sociopolitical messages. Rejecting the request to enter politics, he says:

> And furthermore, I like the job I have. It provides a pretty good platform for addressing the needs of the country. I'm not sure public office would be a promotion... The Christian Broadcasting Network (CBN) had grown from a seventy-dollar beginning to a multifaceted enterprise that included the nation's fifth largest cable television network. CBN University is a fully accredited graduate institution with five colleges, including a law school. CBN also has a major private sector relief agency called Operation Blessing; a highly effective literacy program, "Sing, Spell, Read and Write"; international broadcast operations and relief centers serving millions in twenty-seven nations; and 700 Club Crisis Counseling Centers responding to more than two million calls for help each year. I felt I could do more good there than anywhere else, including the presidency of the greatest nation in the world. (Robertson 1989, 20–21)

I was fortunate to visit and interview five executives at Family Channel corporate headquarters as a professional colleague of the dean of the Communication School and of former staff and faculty members. We talked about the Family Channel and its transformation into a for-profit network. Several executives were familiar with my book, *Televangelism,* and were aware that a number of Christian communications schools were using it. At the same time that his media empire underwent name changes—from CBN to the Family Channel—Robertson distanced himself from being a religious broadcaster and began to identify with the role of entrepreneur. These steps taken during the 1980s are explained by Douglas B. Stewart, the Family Channel's director of research and media,[5] as eliminating on-the-air confusion between the television network and the parent organization:

> *The 700 Club* program came up, and at the end of the program, in the credits it would say "Christian Broadcast Network, copyright 1981." And then, you'd close that credit and then here comes an ID that says "CBN Cable Network"... we needed to change the name of the channel to something that had a much clearer, stronger identity in the marketplace. So that's when we decided on the Family Channel name. And initially, it was the CBN Family Channel because we didn't want to alienate our viewers or confuse them further. Because all of a sudden, you know, it happens overnight, all of a sudden you've got this CBN Cable Network that's been out there 10 years and the next day it's the Family Channel.

According to Doug Stewart, CBN grew partly as a result of studying television viewers. In 1988 when the Gallup organization interviewed a random sample of U.S. television viewers, it found that they were "generally pretty dissatisfied with what they were getting" in regards to "the values that TV was portraying." After that study, the Gallup organization specifically looked at CBN in depth, wanting "to know the whys." As CBN had already learned, as a cable network it had an identity crisis: Viewers saw it both as a ministry organization and a local TV station.

The description of the development of the network illustrates how its managers learned from each step taken. Doug Stewart explains that the satellite network was initiated at first as part of a financial decision to save distribution costs:

> But then, when they realized that they had this 24-hour-a-day signal out there, and basically anybody in the country with a dish could pick it up... they changed the format to family-oriented format where they offered some old re-run series, and other things in addition to the religious programming that began to be pretty popular.

CBN Cable Network separated itself out to distinguish the satellite system from the Christian broadcasting ministry. This move not only clarified the cable network's identity but also enabled it to refocus its mission to develop as part of the cable television industry. Now operating in and appealing to two worlds, it found new opportunities to develop audiences and revenues. Advertising revenues, according to Doug Stewart, started about 1980 and supported the network for six or seven years. After 1987, the organization began charging cable operators about six cents per subscriber. Revenues from cable subscriptions and advertising accelerated, becoming almost as great as donations to *The 700 Club*.

Stewart confirms: "So all of a sudden you had this situation where you had a charitable corporate entity that owns this for-profit business over here... So what they felt like they probably should do was go ahead and sell off the network or split it off, form a separate... [interrupted]."

At this juncture, challenges from the IRS led to the new public organization, IFE. Paul Krimsier, IFE's senior vice president for programming, told me IFE's goals are to "create program schedules that multi-generations of families can watch together—and not be made uncomfortable." Krimsier has been in the music and entertainment business his entire career, earlier working with Turner Broadcasting. I asked if he, as a Christian professional, experienced value conflicts working in television. He replied that instead of conflicts, he saw opportunities for people with spiritual values:

> And I think the communications industry, entertainment industry is very attractive to a lot of people because it does have so much of an impact on people's lives; they spend so much time with it. But I don't think we've divorced ourselves from the spiritual heritage of it, but we're trying to reach a broader goal of providing comfortable yet stimulating television to families in the US and around the world. And, if we can be good at that, it can provide an arena in the family unit where they can talk about issues, including spiritual issues, and come to some conclusions on their own. So, I don't sense a stress or dilemma in it. I sense a real comfort in knowing who I am and knowing what I would like to bring into families' households.

The Family Channel seeks technical excellence and high production values. It also seeks to balance its entertainment aspects with core moral values. The producers are not certain that *all* Christians will be comfortable with their programming selections, but the professional need for new shows pushes them to take risks. As Krimsier explains, the use of rap music to accompany a show on families in south central Los Angeles might make small-town America uncomfortable, but, he adds, "I think it's valuable for people to be exposed to other cultures and other experiences like that. It's hard to always do something that's going to be entertaining and stimulating and not make some people uncomfortable."

Family Channel executives have consistently emphasized that they are not exploiting sexuality or violence for profitability. When they brought back Westerns in 1981, these films were selected because of their low cost, and the organization planned to set them aside for better programming in the future:

> However, instead of that, they caught on like wildfire and we're still looking for more instead of trying to get rid of them. *The Virginian,*

> *Bonanza, Gunsmoke,* things like this. Of course there's going to be some violence. But, it's always to the same end—which is to bring the bad guy down and the good guy always wins. You always know the good guy's gonna win. They are morality plays. But you will see things on television today that would appear to cast the violent person, or the criminal, or the murderer, as the good guy, as the one to be emulated... [The tendency is] more and more toward glorifying the bad guy, the criminal, the murderer, whatever he might be, the international terrorist. So there seems to be that trend of "stretching the envelope."

Pat Robertson saw international opportunities very early and proclaimed "his ministry as a harbinger of world wide revival" (Harrell 1987, 77), buying (in 1968) a radio station in Bogota, Colombia. By 1987 Robertson's *700 Club* was on radio and television in over sixty foreign nations. In 1982 he acquired a television station in Lebanon (Harrell 1987, 76) and today retains a presence in Israel. Currently, IFE is pursuing expansion into international markets aggressively. It engages in international co-ventures on an ongoing basis, offering the appeal of broad-based family entertainment. Media enterprises from other cultures now want to emulate the Family Channel's approach. Representatives from Latin America, Europe, and Korea have consulted with Krimsier about the enterprise's organization and demographics. When I questioned Krimsier about this kind of international expansion, he said that although at first it seems to us that the U.S. popular culture is different, these other societies value the family as a core unit in their societies. He said that the Koreans, for example, "have very strong and clear family units." Krimsier reiterated that U.S. films are very popular abroad, even if U.S. viewers perceive "foreign" films as difficult.

In selecting a programming mix for children, Krimsier said: "We need to have a blend of programming that consists of programs people are already aware of and have an affinity to watch and programs we're developing that we believe in and value either as entertainment or stimulating in one way or another. We're trying to bring the children's programming to include that mix. We have *Popeye* on the air—that's a program that people have a very strong awareness of and are quick to either watch or not watch."

Krimsier was very clear about the type of children's programming that IFE found acceptable; for example, Babar and Madeleine are not only entertaining but have "good values." An added asset of much popular children's merchandise is that it is "nice stuff," not exploitative of children. *The Wizard of Oz* was rejected as unsuitable because it "could be frightening," and IFE does not want to present wizards, demons, and fortune tellers in a positive light. In general, IFE is careful not to show characters of any spiritual nature without parents being able to participate in the viewing process. As the Family Channel positions itself in the rapidly growing children's market, it differentiates its objectives from Nickelodeon's, clearly wanting the whole family involved in viewing what is seemingly a children's network.

The business team developing the Family Channel is proud of its accomplishments, gaining recognition as a major cable network providing entertainment. A key point to remember is that the Family Channel's agenda is not hidden. The IFE business team is well aware of the public and professional beliefs that graphic sex and violence on TV are harmful, especially for children. They also know that Christian families want more and more movies and videos with family-appropriate messages. And it is because the organization has had such success as a mainstream media enterprise that it is the darling of the Christian right, who admire it for explicitly setting out to program a countervailing culture and making money in doing so.

The financial and organizational growth of IFE is impressive. In its 1993 annual report to stockholders, IFE reported total revenues for the second quarter of $43,883,000—a 37 percent increase over the same quarter in 1992. In the 1994 report to stockholders, Tim Robertson wrote: "Total operating revenues for 1993 increased 56% to $208.2 million"; however, the value of stock declined from $0.70 to $0.49 per share (Report to Stockholders 1994).

In 1993 two additional cable networks were started by IFE: Family Channel (UK) and the Cable Health Club, twenty-four-hour health and fitness network. IFE already owned MTM Entertainment, Inc., which develops, produces, syndicates, and distributes television series and other programs worldwide. Its film library includes such series as *Hill Street Blues, The Mary Tyler Moore Show, The Bob Newhart Show, Remington Steele, Lou Grant,* and *St. Elsewhere,* all once shown on network TV. They will use those that are deemed suitable. With the expansion of the number of channels, there is a "constant pressure to buy or develop new shows as well as TV movies and Specials . . . IFE also entered the live family entertainment industry in 1993 with the purchase of a majority position in Calvin Gilmore Productions, Ltd. of Myrtle Beach, South Carolina" (Report to Stockholders 1994).

According to the theologian Harvey Cox, the love affair between conservative religion and the electronic media is the most significant recent religious event in the United States: "Television has given new life to a dying ideology" (in Litman and Bain 1989, 329). Barry Litman continues: "From a mass communications perspective, the critical message is that theoretical frameworks based on concepts of mass audiences and common denominator programs are outdated analytic tools for studying the audiences of religious programs in particular and for minority taste programs in general" (Litman and Bain 1989, 330). More than television, radio, film, and print, the forms of electronic communication that are termed the New Media and that are used in religious broadcasting include the old forms plus low-powered TV, audiotapes and discs, interactive TV, computing networks, and World

Wide Web sites. When I asked Family Channel executives about future uses of technology, representatives mentioned taking advantage of home videos and offering programs on pay-per-view, which might entail "either producing or buying some family feature films to establish Family Channel in this market" (Krimsier).

IFE is also exploring opportunities for new networks, perhaps, according to Krimsier, one with the forty-five-plus age group as its demographic target:

> I think we could do a good job with having 4 or 5 different networks of various degrees of demographic targeting. I would really like to get into—have a network that's 45 plus targeted. That's going to be a real growth opportunity for cable and for advertisers and I think that, at that point, we've got an audience that's a little less fad-driven and a little more looking for substance and for consistency in the entertainment and information choices they have. And I think we could do a good job with that.

The Family Channel recognizes that new media means new parasocial interactions. Media personalities and content (that is, programming) are intertwined and in some respects are interpersonal communications between broadcasters and audiences. The Family Channel is positioned for the long term to be the dominant family entertainment system. They define their role as engaging audiences with their definition of Christian family, and they seek to imprint this message around the world as a countervailing popular culture in a crass and secular humanist media culture.

Postscript

Since this essay was submitted for publication, Rupert Murdoch, in June 1997, successfully merged one of his subsidiaries (Fox Kids Worldwide—FKWW) into IFE. Murdoch bought IFE for $35 per share, a deal roughly valued at $1.9 billion. Pat Robertson will be cochairman of the Board of Directors, and his son will continue as president and CEO.[6] The Robertsons will have a noncontrolling ownership in the new subsidiary. The move was approved by IFE's Board of Directors, which cited "vertical integration among content providers" and possible loss of competitive advantage in the "multichannel environment" as reasons for agreeing to the merger. The board saw the merger as a way to "enhance [IFE's] access to content, globalize existing products and expand its existing channels of distribution."[7]

Not only will the family retain ownership, but Robertson has also provided an endowment for *The 700 Club* and Regent University since they will own preferred stock in the new subsidiary, thus having a supply of investment income to carry them for years to come. The merger means financial security and a permanent place for the Robertson empire in the television industry. As a TV enterprise, with Murdoch capital and international holdings, IFE will be able to produce more original material as well as to buy additional product to compete in the new digital environment. As I have shown in this chapter, the Christian message has been mainstreamed, and IFE, as a content provider, will have more opportunity to broadcast it all over the world.

Notes

In grateful appreciation to David Stephan, graduate assistant par excellence, for his diligent pursuit of the most arcane reference.

1. Pat Robertson, Jimmy Swaggart, Jim Bakker, Robert Schuller, Jerry Falwell, Oral Roberts, Rex Humbard, and James Robison.

2. A cursory search of the World Wide Web will find the homepages of the Christian Coalition, CBN, the Family Channel, and the Campus Crusade for Christ, with links to many other sites and resources.

3. See *Telecommunications Act of 1996,* 104th Congress, 2d Session, S.R. 104–230. The conference report by Larry Pressler tries to foresee possible difficulties with the merging of cable, telephone, and online services. The act passed early in 1996.

4. Pro-"innocent"-life, according to the Christian Coalition's Contract with the American Family on their Web site. Apparently it is not a contradiction to oppose abortion and favor the death penalty because unborn fetuses are presumed innocent and convicted capital offenders are presumed guilty (see Christian Coalition Presents the Contract with the American Family, at *http://www.cc.org/publications/ca/speech/contract.html*).

5. Interviews were conducted at the corporate headquarters of the Family Channel on 28 July 1992 in Virginia Beach, Virginia, with Earl Weirich, vice president for public relations, Paul Krimsier, senior vice president for programming, Douglas B. Stewart, director of research and media, and Larry W. Dantzler, vice president and chief financial officer.

6. See *http://www.comlinks.com/news/sji524.htm.*

7. International Family Entertainment, Inc. *Information Statement,* 12 August 1997.

Works Cited

Altheide, D., and R. Snow. 1991. *Media Worlds in the Post-Journalism Era.* New York: de Gruyter.

Clark, D. 1991a. "Cable Crucial to Future of Christian TV Broadcasters." *Religious Broadcasting* 23, no. 10: 3.

———. 1991b. "Recovering Confidence Hinges on Accountability." *Religious Broadcasting* 23, no. 9: 3.

Conger, J. 1989. *The Charismatic Leader: Behind the Mystique of Exceptional Leadership.* San Francisco: Jossey-Bass.

Cox, H. 1995. "The Warring Visions of the Religious Right." *The Atlantic Monthly,* November, 59–69.

Dawidoff, N. 1995. "No Sex. No Drugs. But Rock 'N' Roll (Kind Of)." *New York Times Magazine,* 5 February, 40–44, 66, 68–69, 72.

Frankl, R. 1987. *Televangelism: The Marketing of Popular Religion.* Carbondale: Southern Illinois University Press.

———. 1990. "Teleministries as Family Businesses." *Marriage and Family Review,* special edition, 15 nos. 3, 4: 195–205.

Garfield, K. 1994. "Bakker Faces an Uncertain Future." *Philadelphia Inquirer,* 1 December.

Gilder, G. 1991. "Into the Telecosm." *Harvard Business Review* 69, no. 2 (March-April): 150–61.

Hadden, J. 1987. "Religious Broadcasting and the New Christian Right." *Journal for the Scientific Study of Religion* 26, no. 1: 1–24.

Hadden, J. K., and A. Shupe. 1988. *Televangelism: Power and Politics on God's Frontier.* New York: Henry Holt and Company.

Harrell, D. 1987. *Pat Robertson: A Personal, Political and Religious Portrait.* San Francisco: Harper & Row.

Johnson, R. 1990. "Heavenly Gifts Preaching a Gospel of Acquisitiveness, a Showy Sect Prospers." *Wall Street Journal,* 11 December.

Kelleher, J. 1994. "Christian Radio Stations, Riding a Wave of Change, Keep Their Popularity." *New York Times,* 10 January.

Litman, B., and E. Bain. 1989. "The Viewership of Religious Television Programming: A Multidisciplinary Analysis of Televangelism." *Review of Religious Research* 30, no. 4: 329–43.

McKenna, R. 1991. "Marketing is Everything." *Harvard Business Review* 69, no. 1 (January-February): 65–79.

Media Focus. *Religious Broadcasting.* 1991. 23 (March): 36.

Meyrowitz, J. 1985. *No Sense of Place: The Impact of Electronic Media on Social Behavior.* New York: Oxford University Press.

Poloma, M. 1989. *The Assemblies of God at the Crossroads: Charisma and Institutional Dilemmas.* Knoxville: University of Tennessee Press.

Report to Stockholders. 1994. International Family Entertainment, Inc., 2877 Guardian Lane, Virginia Beach, Va., 23452.

Robertson, Pat. 1989. *The Plan.* Nashville, Tenn.: Thomas Nelson.

Winfrey, L. 1995. "Cable TV Makes Gains as Networks Lose Viewers." *The Philadelphia Inquirer,* 17 August 1995.

Wuthnow, R. 1988. *The Restructuring of American Religion: Society and Faith since W.W.II.* Princeton, N.J.: Princeton University Press.

7

The Emergence of Christian Video and the Cultivation of Videovangelism

Eithne Johnson

Throughout this century, evangelical Protestants have cultivated a specifically Christian culture through "parallel institutionalism."[1] While their parallel media industry—with radio, film, and television programming—has been crucial to the maintenance of Christian culture in a predominantly secular society, conservative Protestants have been motivated by their "faith in technology" to spread their salvation message through new communication channels, to reach beyond their cultural separatism.[2] With cable and satellite access, televangelists have increased the power of the Christian media industry while increasing the visibility of a conservative, Christian-identified lifestyle. As William Martin observes, televangelism has been instrumental in "serving notice to the nation that evangelical Christians are no longer content to be treated as a backwater minority, but are a force with which to reckon—socially, politically, and theologically."[3] Through more aggressive marketing and media use, ministers and professional lecturers have found new ways to define and build the conservative Christian market segment. Given the demographic profile of VCR owners, Christian video draws on a more prosperous, lifestyle-conscious audience than does religious television.[4] Certainly, audiences for religious television and video overlap; however, born-again Christians who own VCRs are also motivated to shop for specialty tapes that appeal to their lifestyle interests. Such videos include devotional and inspirational lectures, dramatic movies, musical performances, exercise (even "blessercize") workouts, and, most notably, guidance for living as a conservative Christian. No longer content to remain culturally separated and marginal, conservative Christian leaders seek to nationalize their religious value system by claiming that it adheres to the "traditional" Judeo-Christian heritage of the United States. Across their media outlets, these leaders have rallied support for their "civil war" against an alleged conspiracy of secular humanists—Democrats, liberals, gays, and feminists—who, they charge, have attacked the "traditional" institutions of church and family.

Although religious television has been the subject of much research, Christian video has been neglected by media scholars. Much as televangelism became famous for its flamboyant figures, Christian video serves to popularize another media personality: the professional lecturer specializing in Chrisitian lifestyle issues. Marketed as "mastercommunicators" and "megacommunicators," these lecturers are identified here as "videovangelists." Like televangelism, videovangelism is a predominantly therapeutic discourse.[5] Though some conservative Christians avoid clinical therapy because it is based in secular culture, Christian video is practically synonymous with one pious psychologist with a penchant for melodramatic oratory: Dr. James C. Dobson. Dobson is a marginal figure in national culture, having served on various committees during the Reagan administration, but he is a powerful figure in conservative Christian culture as the head of the Focus on the Family ministry and as a popular radio broadcaster.[6] In 1992, Focus on the Family, based in Colorado Springs, Colorado, had an estimated income of $78 million.[7] As of 1995, that estimate had risen to $101 million.[8] In Bill Moyers's report on the "New Holy War," he describes Colorado Springs as "Vatican West."[9] For Protestants, Colorado Springs is a good example of the regional and economic power concentrated in conservative evangelical hands through the maintenance of separate culture industries. Looking at the top ten ministries in Colorado Springs in 1993, Steve Rabey observed that "together these groups bring in $357 million in income annually, employ 2,400 people, and spend $33 million on local payroll."[10] Moyers mentions that Focus has also become the target of criticism for its alleged role in political activities, including the promotion of the antigay Amendment 2 in Colorado. Given Dobson's militant attitude in the conservative Christian "culture war," it is no coincidence that Focus has counted among the directors on its board people associated with the Republican establishment, including Susan Baker, whose husband, James Baker, served in the Reagan and Bush administrations, and Donald Hodel, former secretary of the interior (1985–1989) and secretary of energy (1982–1985). Dobson has welcomed into his radio studio former "education czar" William Bennett and the founders of the Alliance Defense Fund, including Bill Bright of Campus Crusade for Christ and the Reverend Don Wildmon.[11] According to People for the American Way, Dobson was deliberately chosen from among the conservative Christian leadership to replace Jerry Falwell as the symbolic leader for the religious right.[12] With its many subministries, Focus on the Family actively supports coalition building and church-based community activism for ultraconservative causes. Although Dobson claims that he does not use Focus to support any political campaigns, it is clear that he urges his supporters to align with conservative Republicans.

To understand videovangelism, the first section in this chapter traces the emergence of Christian video by following Dobson's migration from the periphery to the center of conservative Christian culture. Dobson's success as a media personality not only parallels the development of Christian video but also coincides with the resurgence of religious belief in general and of the religious right in particular. Targeting the "traditional" family through his videos, books, magazines, and radio programs, Dobson's blend of behavioral psychology and religious faith may be especially appealing at this time because it converges with dominant market trends in self-help and spirituality, both of which are therapeutic discourses. The second section examines these talking head videos and their melodramatic therapeutic narratives for Christian audiences. The expansion of Christian-identified consumer culture attests to the significance of what is considered one of the top ten "megatrends" for the 1990s: "religious revival."[13] Conservative ministers and megacommunicators are reaching out to the larger community by adopting a "consumerist approach" that engages with contemporary lifestyle issues.[14] Along with officially political organizations, such as the Family Research Council (Gary Bauer), Concerned Women for America (Beverly LaHaye), the Eagle Forum (Phyllis Schlafly), and the Christian Coalition (Pat Robertson), Dobson's Focus on the Family lobbies for grassroots—especially suburban middle-class—support for the nationalization of the conservative Christian value system. In their book and companion video series, *Children at Risk,* Dobson and Bauer describe their "culture war": "Instead of fighting for territory or military conquest, however, the struggle is now for the hearts and minds of the people. It is a war over *ideas.*"[15] By studying Dobson's media productions in relation to the proliferation of Christian consumer culture, we might understand how this conservative pop psychologist has positioned himself as a crusader for what he calls the "beleaguered, exhausted, oppressed, and overtaxed family."[16]

The Christian Series Film and the "Dobson Effect"

> Many churches have for years used films in ministry... An even larger number of churches are expected to use and produce video as part of their ministries. And video's impact is already being felt in the body of Christ. Just as printed Scripture, organs, light bulbs, and audio amplifiers have affected and changed local congregations, so too the video cassette recorder will continue to have an influence on the way we live and communicate the Gospel.[17]

When the consumer VCR was introduced in 1975, Christians had already established film, music, and publishing businesses oriented toward the religious market segments. For many years, Christian film companies and ministries, such as the Reverend Billy Graham's World Wide Pictures, created inspirational pictures for educational and evangelistic purposes. In recognition of such efforts, the Christian Film Distributors Association (later changed to Christian Film and Video Association) issued annual Crown Awards for films that "glorify Jesus Christ."[18] The business consisted mostly of rentals to churches through "film library" distributors. Occasionally, exhibitions were arranged in mainstream theaters for dramatic features, in particular by Graham's ministry. By the late 1970s, the Christian film industry experienced difficulties because of increasing costs and the lack of highly profitable exhibition outlets. According to the industry's publicity printed in *Christianity Today,* two interrelated phenomena were instrumental in changing the industry's direction: consumer home video and the "talking head" series film.[19]

With video, evangelical entrepreneurs envisioned a new angle for communicating the gospel, but this medium required different distribution strategies. They began by duplicating their existing films onto tapes, which were then offered through the film libraries to the church market for ministers to use. However, it soon became clear that the home market offered a more profitable target. Since the existing film distribution channel—a network of film libraries—was designed to serve churches, it could not easily be used to reach home consumers. In 1982, *Christianity Today* reported that Graham's World Wide Pictures "announced plans to make several of its films available on videocassette" through Christian bookstores.[20] The booksellers' direct link to consumers had already created the opportunity for Christian publishing houses to diversify. By 1982, Word, Inc., a Texas-based company, had played a significant role in "the Christian record and book publishing industries."[21] Just as World Wide Pictures moved to sell its tapes in selected bookstores, Word introduced Word Home Video, a "tape rental library of 40 programs," to affiliated bookstores across the country.[22] Included in this new video "library" was Dr. James Dobson's first series film, *Focus on the Family.*

According to Rolf Zettersten, Dobson's biographer and former employee, this series film had its genesis in 1978 when Word approached the psychologist about videotaping his Christian lifestyle seminars scheduled in San Antonio, Texas.[23] By this time, Dobson had published some books and audiotapes, primarily about children and parenting, through Christian-identified publishers and had received enough attention in the target audience to make him a favored lecturer. As a result of this popularity, Dobson quit his academic psychology career to devote his time to Focus on the Family, a nonprofit organization founded in Arcadia, California, in 1977. According to one of the original founders, Peb Jackson:

> The early meetings of the Focus Board dealt with concepts that are unrelated to what the ministry is doing today. None of us held that vision. Here is why we incorporated as a nonprofit organization. Dobson's seminars were drawing 2,000 to 3,000 people per weekend, who each paid about $12 for tickets. Thus, $24,000 to $36,000 was generated at each of these events, less expenses. Dobson didn't feel it was right to accept the huge income for himself, and we wanted to funnel the extra money to other ministries.[24]

Since that time, Focus has supported Dobson's efforts to get his advice to Christian families produced and distributed through various media in order to spread salvation and to raise funds for various ministry projects related to the mission of "strengthening the home." Zettersten maintains that Dobson made a commitment that Focus would be a "Christian ministry" and would avoid any "secular opportunities."[25] This decision served the purposes of Christian book publishers and contributed to their growth, particularly in the religious and later the recovery market segments. Tyndale House published Dobson's *Dare to Discipline, The Strong-Willed Child, What Wives Wish Their Husbands Knew about Women,* and, through its Living Books division, *Dr. Dobson Answers Your Questions: Marriage and Sexuality,* compiled from earlier books. Focus used money from Dobson's books to support a syndicated radio program featuring the psychologist and Christian guests. The ministry also produced television programs for Dobson.

Word, Inc., not only published several Dobson books—*Straight Talk to Men and Their Wives, Love Must Be Tough,* and *Parenting Isn't for Cowards*—but also produced his first series film, *Focus on the Family,* in 1978. When asked to tape the San Antonio lectures, as Zettersten writes, "Dobson thought it was a bad idea."[26] Oriented toward the church market, the lectures were designed to be screened sequentially during services in order to promote discussion and reflection. According to Zettersten: "Since a 'talking head' series had never been produced for the church market, his publishers were more uncertain of the risks than they let on. They weren't sure if pastors would be willing to devote seven Sunday night services to a series of practical films on family living."[27] Apparently, many churches welcomed the tapes because the Dobson/Word products are credited within the industry for starting a trend in series films featuring expert speakers who, like Dobson, are not necessarily ministers. The success of the Dobson/Word series helped expand the market for Christian film and video generally and for "Dr. Dobson" specifically. *Christian Film & Video* magazine reported that by 1987 it was estimated that the *Focus on the Family* series had been rented more than 50,000 times and seen by over 40 million people.[28]

By 1984, Word was described in the Christian media industry's publicity as "the most active trendsetter in series films."[29] Esther Ellington, then president of the Christian Film Distributors Association, likened the appeal of such series to the popularity of serial television. [30] The comparison is noteworthy because the Christian media industry wanted to be more competitive with mainstream media in order to attract new believers and to strengthen their market share. Like serial television, one advantage of the series formula is that it extends the product over separate viewings. Christian distributors rent or sell a series as a package or by the individual film or tape. Unlike televangelism, home video does away with the need for potentially embarrassing pleas because the donation or rental fee for the product is made in advance of viewing. Like serial television and routine church attendance, the Christian series film generates a feeling of familiarity because the audience sees the same featured speakers in several segments. Moreover, the established infrastructure of the Christian media industry had already prepared the ground for repeat screenings, especially in churches. Distributors slash prices in the summer to give ministers something with which to compete against other seasonal attractions. As a result, films continue to circulate for many years. Video technology helped extend the lifespan of Christian films because it enabled distributors to re-release them on tape. For example, Mark IV Productions' *Thief in the Night,* a dramatic trilogy created in the 1970s and based on the biblical concept of the Rapture, made the fall 1993 top-ten list of hit videos compiled by the Christian *Bookstore Journal.*

In 1986, Word advertised the release of another "powerful six-part series," *Turn Your Heart toward Home,* with Dobson lecturing on the topic of parenting. Initially available only for church exhibition, in its first year it "eclipsed the first series by twice the viewing rate."[31] Independently reviewing the series, Mark Fackler, then-editor of *Christian Film & Video,* issued this criticism:

> Some churches may be called to patience with the opening sequence in each film, a cavalcade of sentimental Americana: an army private trudges homeward to the embrace of his farm family, with cutaways to mom's jam jars and 1930s-era toys. It's touchingly irrelevant, and does not at all connect with the vast problems of family disintegration among America's ethnic and racial minorities.[32]

Although Fackler found this representation of Americana provincial and anachronistic, the *Turn Your Heart toward Home* series appealed to large numbers of Christian viewers, reportedly so many that with six hundred prints in circulation, Word was hard pressed to meet the church market demand.[33] Zettersten offers this explanation for the popularity of these series: "Like his books, Dobson's films offered 'how-to' advice that met real needs, and pastors found that the series helped to swell church attendance."[34] But the church audience was only a small part of the vast market that could be tapped by home video.

In the evangelical spirit, the Christian film industry wanted to reach a larger audience; in the capitalistic spirit, it paid to copy the series film formula. By 1987, publicity indicates that the industry was grappling with two problems: how best to exploit the consumer market for home video and what to make of Dobson's "blockbuster series," which monopolized that market.[35] As summed up in "Industry on the Move," the "Dobson Effect" was correlated to the following phenomena: series and seminar films on "the family," "greater emphasis on personal emotional needs," and "the sudden popularity of speech films, or 'talking head' pictures." Aware of the special appeal of inspirational speakers within the culture and the cheaper costs for lecture-based films, Word became known for producing and distributing pictures featuring what the company calls "mastercommunicators," including, as the publicity puts it, "Joyce Lansdorf, Charles Swindoll, Keith Miller, Anthony Campolo, and Josh McDowell in series films tackling topics ranging from sharing one's faith to finding the right vocation."[36] Describing this trend in *Christian Film & Video,* reviewer Randy Petersen points out:

> Of course, a dozen other companies churned out Dobson clones. To be fair, most of these films, featuring an expert giving practical counseling on family or personal matters, had value in their own right. But there's no question that Dobson had unearthed a huge market for this kind of film, and everyone was trying to capitalize on it.[37]

While the series film formula accounts for some of the appeal of Christian videos, the talking head style for conveying expert advice has proven very attractive to the religious market. How is it that these videovangelists speak to and for their audiences as Christians? Dobson's popular tapes provide more insight into the therapeutic intent of videovangelism.

Conservative Therapeutic Spirituality for Christian Families

> Churches had always looked for film dramas with a message. Why not forget the drama and just offer the message? The "talking head" format revived by James Dobson's 1978 "Focus on the Family" film series did just that. But it also changed the message from evangelism to family management. This hit a hot button for Christians.[38]

Because Christian films had been created for church exhibition, the minister or lay leader played an important role in organizing screenings and facilitating discussions in response. Thus, Christian films were intended to support local ministries rather than to compete with them. In comparison, ministers were threatened by televangelism's popularity because they feared it would replace church attendance and siphon off resources. Given this situation, it is plausible that the talking head aesthetic initially achieved prominence because it provided ministers with a product that looked like a Christian TV show but could be provided by the local church. However, these videos do more than supplement ministers' services; videovangelism has made it possible for a variety of experts on Christian lifestyle issues to reach audiences inside and outside churches. Since the VCR reached optimal market penetration fairly rapidly, the success of the Christian talking head video must be related to both its availability and its significance to the home audience. In fact, the popularity of Christian video correlates with the discursive shift evident in Christian media: Once dominated by doctrinal and dramatic narratives, they now offer more and more self-help and how-to narratives. This shift appeals to audience familiarity with mass culture's therapeutic narratives, from advertising to talk television.

In *Tele-Advising,* Mimi White considers the significance of therapeutic discourses ("talking cures") on television generally and on *The 700 Club*'s televangelism specifically. According to White: "Self-identity and social recognition within familial and consumer networks hinge on participation in the process of mediated confession."[39] Although Protestantism holds that faith is professed by the individual believer, who then joins with others to form a congregational community, the expert authority figure has been accorded an important role among conservative evangelicals in mediating faith. According to Robert Liebman, evangelicals share Baptist beliefs but they differ in ecclesiology: Evangelicals place more authority in the individual pastor; they value local autonomy; they emphasize the "planting" of churches; and they support the growth of megachurches.[40] Because evangelicals value outreach, lay speakers can become respected experts among Christian audiences. Televangelism dramatizes participation in this therapeutic confessional process by inciting public professions of faith in Jesus Christ: By identifying oneself as a born-again Christian, one becomes healed and joins the "Body" of believers. As White puts it: "On *The 700 Club* the force of confession as a discursive strategy is associated with religious rituals and melodramatic narratives."[41]

For these reasons, it is not surprising that "Dr. Dobson," as he is popularly known, could build a multimillion dollar media enterprise based on giving spirtual-therapeutic advice to Christians. Emphasizing hierarchical authority figures, Dobson claims that his loving yet disciplinary method for Christian child rearing can provide the domestic solution for social problems, which he blames on secular society's disdain for the "traditional" family. Referring to social unrest in the 1960s and student activism especially, he writes: "The *primary* cause of this pervasive disrespect for authority: parents in the western world generally failed to instill responsible attitudes when their children were small . . . The second most influential force in the rise of disorder has been the school."[42] According to this evangelical psychologist, respect for authority and leadership, in relation to hierarchical gender roles, must be rigorously instilled from infancy to adolescence.

That Dobson's appearance on tape initiated videovangelism and motivated the growth of the religiously identified video market points to his cultural significance as an expert on conservative Christian lifestyle issues. Reviewing Dobson's impact on the film and video industry, Chris Franzen spoke with Gil Moegerle, then–senior vice president in charge of film production at Focus on the Family: "Dobson's first series, says Moegerle, 'rewrote the history of religious films. Nobody knew, back in 1978, if churches would rent a film series featuring a man standing and talking'—the phenomenon known as the 'talking head' among skeptics in the media."[43] In 1982, Word produced and distributed Dobson's series *Straight Talk to Families,* which was created from excerpts of Dobson's previously syndicated TV series. According to Linda Easter's review for *Christian Film & Video,* the program was designed in the "talk show format."[44] That same year, Word also distributed Dobson's *Sex and the Family.* As described by Dean Ridings for *Christian Film & Video*: "In a television-program setting with Dobson sitting casually on a stage, announcer Gil Moegerle moves a microphone throughout a modest-sized audience."[45] Released on home video, these programs show Dobson counseling his studio audiences on family matters and child rearing from a conservative Christian perspective. He refers to his academic training in psychology to authorize his advice, yet he also frames that advice as stemming from the highest authority. Unlike his later videos, this talk show format allowed for participants who voiced disagreement with his ideas. In comparison, videovangelism privileges the expert, who addresses an audience whose reaction appears to be unanimously positive, as represented through reaction shots of emotionally expressive faces and, when permitted, participation that supplements the videovangelist's perspective.

In 1986, Focus on the Family established production and distribution outlets for videos featuring Dobson and others. When it was announced that Focus had created its own film-production division, film rentals were "down 30% below" the previous year's level, suggesting enormous risk for the ministry.[46] However, Focus was determined to target the home video market "aggressively."[47] Not only would the ministry offer products to the church segment, but also it would advertise directly to the underexploited home video market, especially through Dobson's popular radio broadcasts. In addition, the film division would develop products based on feedback from Dobson's radio audience. In a 1987 article for *Christian Film & Video,* Franzen reported that "Moegerle uses much of the response from the radio program to inform his future film projects. 'From a marketing standpoint,' he said, 'you start the project with test marketing already done.'"[48] Thus, Franzen noted, "Focus has its own instant audience poll."

Focus's first release was apparently motivated by the mail received in response to a radio program featuring Harold Morris, who became a born-again Christian while serving time in prison. In 1987, Focus released *Twice Pardoned: An Ex-Con Talks to Teens,* a two-part series featuring Morris. Reviewer J. Stephen Lang writes: "Just when I thought I was thoroughly burned out on the testimonies of prisoners who turned to the Lord, I found myself almost tearful listening to Harold Morris speak of prison life and his conversion."[49] Notably, homosexuality is among the "painful" images Morris recounts of prison life. The industry responded very favorably to the series; the Christian Film and Video Association bestowed three awards on *Twice Pardoned*: "Best Evangelistic Film," Best Film Series," and "Best Individual Non-Dramatic Presentation" for Harold Morris.

The next release may well have been motivated by radio-audience response to another topic that was guaranteed to elicit strong reaction at the time. In *Pornography: A Winnable War,* Dobson delivers a "full-length" (fifty-eight-minute) presentation inspired by his tenure on the Meese Commission. In his review, Fackler says that Dobson "nearly chokes at some places recalling testimony by victims of sex abuse and the pornographic environment in which they live. Camera shots to the crowd of 300 listeners catch gasps of shock and anger, tears and restrained horror at hearing how the 'other side' lives."[50] To capitalize on such reactions among home viewers, Focus publicity offered an "action kit," provided at no charge, so that "you can mobilize your congregation to become involved in this fight" against pornography. To personalize the problem, the promotional materials reiterate Dobson's claim that "pornography destroys families."

As the Dobson/Focus tapes indicate, television's talking head aesthetics have had an influence on the aesthetics of videovangelism: Both privilege the speaker's direct address to an audience (inside and outside the visual frame). While Christian critics frequently fault Dobson/Focus videos for lacking scriptural or doctrinal depth in their rhetoric, they are assuming that the content alone is meaningful. In fact, the formal properties of videovangelism must also be considered. For Christian viewers, the special significance conservative evangelicals ascribe to higher authority figures is formally replicated by the space accorded to the communicator in the talking head video. In the hierarchical structure of the conservative evangelical church, the pastor is the focus of congregational attention; similarly, in these Christian tapes, the videovangelist is situated in front of a studio or seminar audience, whose members are routinely shown in close-up responding dramatically to the expert's words. That the orator appears to elicit vivid, emotional responses from audiences reproduces the melodramatic nature of Christian evangelism. That these emotional responses are commented upon and even criticized by reviewers points to their significance.

Some examples of audience and reviewer reactions to Focus videos have been quoted above. As Fackler describes Dobson's delivery: "He is heavy on tear-jerking anecdotes. Carry tissues to avoid embarrassing red-eye when the lights come on."[51] Referring to an interview with British documentarist Norman Stone, Lang notes that Stone criticizes such displays as "con tricks." According to Lang's elaboration on this opinion, evangelical enthusiasm "has led Christian filmmakers to become propagandists, swaying audiences with schmaltzy music and an overemphasis on emotion."[52] But this is precisely the point of the genre: Tears and laughter are significant to videovangelism as a melodramatic discourse rooted in Christian conversion.

Framed as spiritually based psychological advice, Dobson's narratives illustrate the melodramatic process through which Christian identity is produced in relation to sinfulness, which is associated with secular culture and the (alleged) persecution of Christians. In Dobson's view, Christian parents struggle with "strong-willed" children who are "at risk" in secular society; Christian teenagers fight to preserve their virginity or their drug-free bodies in secular humanist schools; and "traditional" marital relations are challenged minimally by gender-based misunderstandings and maximally by extramarital temptations. In that these narratives share a common structure in their appeal to pathos, they belong with what Linda Williams identifies as "body genres." Discussing film melodrama as an example of a "body drama," Williams writes:

> In these fantasies the quest to return to and discover the origin of the self is manifest in the form of the child's fantasy of possessing ideal parents in the Freudian family romance, in the paternal fantasy of possessing the child in maternal or paternal melodrama, and even in the lovers' fantasy of possessing one another in romantic weepies. In these fantasies the quest for connection is always tinged with the melancholy of loss.[53]

The Christian foundational story is pure melodrama. Not only are the "original" human parents lost, but they precipitated the fall from grace for all subsequent generations. Since Christian identity is constructed in relation to the loss of contact with God the originator, one must become "born again" through accepting Jesus Christ as savior. Through his martyrdom, he came to embody human sinfulness. For believers, human flesh is always-already sinful and willful. Considering disobedience in children, Dobson suggests: "Perhaps this tendency toward self-will is the essence of 'original sin' which has infiltrated the human family."[54] For conservative Christians, the representation of the body—especially in relation to the family formation—has become increasingly a matter for social activism, for engaging a secular culture that is perceived as morally sick. Dobson's style of videovangelism provides a spiritual-therapeutic discourse, a "talking cure," framed as a heartfelt conservative response to changes in sex and gender roles.

Religious instruction has always offered techniques for mastery over the corruptible body. Dobson's books and videos (which echo and excerpt each other) promote behavioristic self-help techniques centered on the body, especially corporal punishment of children. For videovangelism, signifying Christian identity through the representation of the individual body and the Body of believers is important cultural work. Regarding the process of representing the body in literature, Peter Brooks explains: "The sign imprints the body, making it part of the signifying process. Signing or marking the body signifies its passage into writing, its becoming a literary body, and generally also a narrative body, in that the inscription of the sign depends on and produces a story."[55] That analysis can be extended to videovangelism: The cross-cutting between shots of the videovangelist and of the audience signifies the marking of their bodies in terms of the spiritual-therapeutic narrative structure of Christian salvation. The "megacommunicator" signifies the patriarchal body whose lineage is traced from God to pastor to expert. This is coupled with the studio audience, whose bodies signify the living church, the Body of believers formed by the congregants. This discursive coupling can also be seen to replicate the hierarchical gender relations adhered to by conservative Christians: The expert occupies the actively performative masculine body position and the audience occupies the passively responsive feminine position. But this does not mean that emotions are strictly gendered. Indeed, videovangelism—precisely because it is a melodramatic body genre—allows for women and men, speaker and listener, to express deeply felt, religiously validated emotions, which are otherwise typically disparaged. Regarding audience reaction in the Focus production *A Man Called Norman,* the reviewer reports: "At one point [Mike Adkins] got them laughing, but in a second tears well in their eyes. Viewers become part of the audience as well."[56] This remark suggests that successful videovangelism effects an emotional alignment between the audience inside the frame and the viewer outside, thereby bringing them together in the Body. If a salvific effect can be attributed to the spiritual-therapeutic structure of videovangelism, it may be because this body genre's signifying process symbolically produces that saved ground for the "born again" between the sacred body of the lost Christ and the profane bodies of secular culture.

"Blood Money" for the Culture War

While the church traditionally stands for the Body of Christ, Christian media make it possible for Evangelicals to unite symbolically no matter where they are located. According to Quentin Schultze, the "mythos of the electronic church" invites Christians to "hope that the world will indeed become a better place because more people will receive the message of the gospel."[57] For such audiences, videovangelism offers inspirational advice for living as a conservative Christian in a sinful, secular world. As reported in *American Demographics,* born-again Christians "are inclined to see religion as a personal process to be lived, instead of a product to be passively consumed."[58] Many Christian products are marketed to appeal to this evangelical sense of process, emphasizing the habitual practice of faith in all aspects of life, including consumption patterns. Christians may find the series film formula especially appealing in terms of their lived experience as believers. Christian film and video advertisements emphasize the importance of repeated viewings. Multiple screenings are necessary in order to inspire new viewers, who may not yet be "saved," as well as to remind repeat viewers of the experts' messages. These ads frequently invoke the inspirational and educational aspects of the series and their proven emotional appeal. According to James Davison Hunter, the relatively recent standardization of spiritual products, such as Christian study guides, books, and videos, represents a cultural "accommodation" to the effects of "privatization" and "individuation" brought on by modern life.[59] Thus, conservative evangelicals seek to counter the perceived ill effects of privatization and individuation by adhering to concepts of family and community expressed traditionally through doctrinal teachings and increasingly through consumer-oriented self-help and how-to advice for Christian living.

Although Focus on the Family is not organized as a commercial business, it depends on financial transactions. According to Dobson: "We consider the contributions we receive to be 'blood money'—sent from loving people who have sacrificed to make their gifts possible."[60] All videos, magazines, audiocassettes, daily planners, and books are available through the mail to consumers for tax-deductible donations. In this way, Focus on the Family carries on a tactic that Evangelicals learned from neoconservatives. As right-wing strategist Richard Viguerie puts it: "Direct mail is the life blood of the New Right."[61] In contrast to televangelism's highly visible and potentially embarrassing appeals for funds, direct mail ministries make their case directly to subscribers. On the one hand, this suggests a more limited market; on the other hand, it is a strongly motivated market. Focus's products are also available for purchase through the network of Christian bookstores. As Brad Edmondson notes: "Christian-book buyers represent the highly religious, highly motivated end of the evangelical movement."[62] Given that these bookstores supply many tapes, the Christian home video market may represent the core of the conservative evangelical culture. This audience is most likely to see itself in the content of the spiritual-therapeutic narratives offered by videovangelism, which represents them and their children as victims of a sick secular society for which salvation, discipline, and clean living are the cures. As for the formal properties, the effects cannot be easily measured, but this melodramatic body genre specializes in providing moving experiences for its audiences. Whether or not audiences outside the frame are receptive to the evangelical mission, they may still identify with the audience inside the frame as it responds positively to leadership espousing a conservative value system.

With the emergence of home video, the Christian film and video industry is faced with a dilemma: To grow, it must attract a wider audience and offer competitive prices, but this requires higher-quality productions and the dilution of the evangelical message for the mass market. Following on the "Dobson Effect," the proliferation of videovangelists—including ministers, athletes, teachers, and humorists—attests to the multiplicity of media personalities engaged in the cultivation of Christian culture. Although many of these speakers become professionals in such work, they tend to maintain the appearance of amateurs—regular folks moved to share their advice about Christian life. Tapping into the seemingly vast market for therapeutic discourses, the videovangelist has come to play an important role in mediating faith as a consumer service to its target audience. That "family management" advice should be so popular among conservative born-again Christians indicates its appeal to the broadest demographic grouping: families with children. Thus, Dobson directs his attention to issues of marital relations, parental authority, child rearing, gender roles, and critiques of materialism, referring frequently to personal anecdotes about his own family. Dobson's spiritual-therapeutic discourse melodramatically authorizes the Christian nuclear family with its particular subjectivizing effects: father, mother, and children in the hierarchical roles assumed by the fundamentalist interpretation of the Bible.

However, in this capitalistic society, the conservative Christian identity is considered one lifestyle choice among many. The pressure to market a religious value system through consumer products may serve subjectivizing effects that are multiple and contradictory: They may define and empower Christian identities, yet their dispersal across regional and competing commercial affiliations may undermine attempts to nationalize their conservative beliefs. Phillip Hammond argues that "insofar as evangelicalism promotes upward mobility or develops increased attraction for the middle classes, it must become 'respectably mainstream' and therefore more tolerant of moral styles other than its own."[63] Indeed, Focus appears to be engaged in market diversification, which may dilute its message. Two versions are frequently offered of the same tape: One excludes overtly religious messages and the other retains them for the core Christian audience. (See the Appendix to this chapter for titles.) If once the Christian industry was known for its "substandard product," Focus has changed the industry's reputation, in part by providing more products that look like mass media fare. As Lang points out, changing negative opinions about Christian fare "can only be done by producing films and TV programs that respect audiences' intelligence and do not come across as mere propaganda. And quality must be present, for secular audiences today will not tolerate shoddy production or poor story lines."[64]

With its Scripture-free versions, Focus's Educational Resources division exploits product diversification and targets secular institutions that are not supposed to promote specific religious ideas. Exact details are not made public, but Focus on the Family's publicity claims that 10,000 schools have used its videos. These include *Twice Pardoned, Teacher of the Year* (with Guy Doud, who was honored by Ronald Reagan), and *Sex, Lies, and the Truth,* billed as "a revealing look at the myth of 'safe sex'" (Focus publicity). Another strategy to extend product life comes from the re-release of older series in new packaging; for example, *Pornography: Addictive, Progressive, and Deadly,* the seventh part of the *Life on the Edge* series, uses a large part of *Fatal Addiction,* Dobson's interview with serial killer Ted Bundy. Similarly, Dobson sold *Where's Dad?,* adapted from the original *Focus on the Family* series, to the Pentagon. According to a *Christianity Today* news report, "Col. Edmond Solymosy, director of the Army's Family Action Plan, called the film 'a building block on which we've based our entire program. It is an instrumental part of our philosophy to provide wholesome, functional role models for our men.'"[65] The video was also purportedly "required viewing for all service wives at all U.S. Army bases around the world."[66] This acceptance of Dobson's product within at least one wing of the military under the Reagan administration comes as no surprise given Dobson's conservative beliefs. Although Christian critics fear that Focus on the Family's Scripture-free videos represent a sellout to secular society, Dobson remains committed to the promotion of conservative Christian culture. As Dobson told Moyers on prime-time television: "We firmly believe that we're involved now in one of the most incredible cultural wars that has ever occurred in western civilization." This statement is more than melodramatic oratory; it is a "blood money" sales pitch to anyone—whether at home, in a church, or on an Army base—who opposes abortion, homosexual civil rights, gender equality, welfare, freedom of speech, and the separation of church and state.

Acknowledgments

Parts of this essay were originally presented as a conference paper at the Society for Cinema Studies, March 1994. Thanks to Henry Jenkins for many helpful comments on that paper. Thanks also to those who supplied me with information about Christian media, especially Mark Fackler and Mark Tuttle for generously providing back issues of their publication, *Christian Film & Video.*

Appendix: List of Single and Series Videos from Focus on the Family

*Indicates that secular versions are available

Children at Risk, featuring Dr. James Dobson and Gary Bauer; two-part series

Common Cents: Training Your Children to Manage Money, featuring Ron Blue

Fatal Addiction, featuring Dobson interviewing Ted Bundy

Focus on the Family, featuring Dobson; seven-part series

Learn to Discern, featuring Bob DeMoss; two-part series

Life on the Edge: Preparing for the Challenges of Adulthood, featuring Dobson; seven-part series (part 7 excerpts from *Fatal Addiction*)

A Man Called Norman, featuring Mike Adkins

**Molder of Dreams,* featuring Guy Doud; two-part series

Pornography: A Winnable War, featuring Dobson; issued in two versions

Preparing for Adulthood, featuring Dobson; four-part series

A Question of Worth, featuring Dobson

**Sex, Lies, and the Truth,* featuring Dobson and professional athletes and actors

Turn Your Heart toward Home, featuring Dobson; six-part series

**Twice Pardoned: An Ex-Con Talks to Teens,* featuring Harold Morris; two-part series

**Classroom of the Heart,* featuring Guy Doud

**Teacher of the Year,* featuring Guy Doud

Fiction for Children

Adventures in Odyssey, series, based on radio drama series

McGee and Me!, series, live action and animation

U.S. Army

Where's Dad?, featuring Dobson (excerpts from *Focus on the Family* series)

Notes

1. James Davison Hunter, *American Evangelicalism* (New Brunswick, N.J.: Rutgers University Press, 1983), 56.

2. Quentin Schultze, "The Mythos of the Electronic Church," *Journal of Communication* 4 (1987): 246. Conservative Christians include not only evangelicals but also fundamentalists, who share the former's doctrinal beliefs but may not necessarily be involved in evangelism. Schultze offers this definition of evangelical drawn from George Marsden's work: "I mean by 'evangelical' those Christians, from whatever denominations or religious background, who emphasize (1) the Reformation doctrine of the final authority of Scripture; (2) the real, historical character of God's saving work recorded in Scripture; (3) eternal salvation only through personal trust in Christ;

(4) the importance of evangelism (proclaiming the gospel of Christ to others) and missions; and (5) the importance of a spiritually transformed life."

3. William Martin, "Giving the Winds a Mighty Voice," in Robert Abelman and Stewart M. Hoover, eds. *Religious Television: Controversies and Conclusions* (Norwood, N.J.: Ablex, 1990), 70.

4. Most research on televangelism has pointed to a "dispossessed" audience composed of older, lower-income religious people who watch a lot of television. See Robert Wuthnow, "The Social Significance of Religious Television," in Abelman and Stewart, *Religious Television,* 87–98.

5. Mimi White, *Tele-Advising: Therapeutic Discourse in American Television* (Chapel Hill: University of North Carolina Press, 1992).

6. Focus on the Family is called a ministry because it is a nonprofit Christian organization, not because Dobson is a minister. According to his biographer, Rolf Zettersten, Dobson gained national notice during Jimmy Carter's presidency when he "served on the task force which summarized the White House Conferences on the Family," for which he "received a special commendation" from the president in 1980. During the Reagan years, Dobson served in several roles, including appointee to the National Advisory Committee to the Office of Juvenile Justice and Delinquency Prevention, 1982–1984; consultant to White House staff on family matters, 1984–1987; cochairman of the U.S. Army Task Force Staff, 1986–1988; appointee to the Meese Commission on Pornography, 1985–1986; appointee to the Attorney General's Advisory Board on Missing and Exploited Children and to the Panel on Teen Pregnancy Prevention, 1987. Rolf Zettersten, *Dr. Dobson: Turning Hearts toward Home* (Dallas: Word Publishing, 1989), 182.

7. Steve Rabey, "Focus under Fire," *Christianity Today,* 8 March 1993, 48.

8. Gustav Niebuhr, "Advice for Parents, and for Politicians," *New York Times,* 30 May 1995.

9. *Bill Moyers' Journal: The New Holy War,* Journal Graphics transcript, Religious Issues Index; phone (800) 825-5746.

10. Rabey, "Focus under Fire," 48.

11. Reverend Don Wildmon is best known for his campaigns against explicit language and imagery, targeting the music and television industries. For more information on Bill Bright and Campus Crusade for Christ, as well as evangelical involvement in global politics, see Sara Diamond, *Spiritual Warfare* (Boston, Mass.: South End Press, 1989). For a critical perspective on right-wing political history, see Sara Diamond, *Roads to Dominion: Right-Wing Movements and Political Power in the United States* (New York: Guilford Press, 1995).

12. People for the American Way, press release for report "Focus on the Family; Extremism Cloaked in the Rhetoric of Family Values," 20 May 1993, 1; available from People for the American Way, c/o Carol Blum, Mary Conway, and Mike Mitchell, (202) 467–4999 or People for the American Way, 2000 M Street NW, Suite 400, Washington, D.C., 20036.

13. See Stephen W. McDaniel and John J. Burnett, "Targeting the Evangelical Market Segment," *Journal of Advertising Research,* August-September 1991, 32. Referring to this "megatrend," as identified by John Naisbitt and Patricia Aburdene, McDaniel and Burnett observe: "Although some advertisers have been successful targeting this market through the growing number of Christian media alternatives, the greatest impact can perhaps be made through secular media."

14. Kenneth H. Sidey, "Boomer Boom and Bust," *Christianity Today,* 16 August 1993, 14. Sidey critically examines the ways consumer-oriented evangelicals, such as

Reverend Bill Hybels, have adopted "seeker" strategies to attract congregants: "Hundreds of churches across the country have redesigned their programs to meet the wants and needs of Boomers. By offering a mix of contemporary music, drama, practical messages, and networks of support groups and social services, they have coaxed Boomers into the sanctuary—which is now called anything but a sanctuary." In this way, Hybels, who serves on the board of Focus on the Family, cofounded the prosperous "megachurch," Willow Creek Community Church in suburban Chicago, which draws an estimated 16,000 people to its weekend services. See "The Spirit behind the Mega-Church Movement," *The Boston Sunday Globe,* 18 February 1996.

15. James C. Dobson and Gary L. Bauer, *Children at Risk* (Dallas, Tex.: Word Publishing, 1990), 20 (emphasis in original).

16. Ibid., 23.

17. Mark H. Tuttle, "Film Vs. Video: Which Should You Choose?" *Christian Film & Video,* May-June 1987, 7.

18. David L. Winters, "How the Crown Awards Are Changing," *Christian Film & Video,* September-October 1988, 7.

19. The term "series film" refers to episodic segments devoted to overarching topics. Typically, these are video productions, not necessarily films in the technical sense.

It is very difficult to get information directly from Christian media industries. Therefore, I have had to rely on their own publicity as well as independent observations, when available. The publicity materials include several Special Advertising Sections in the evangelical magazine *Christianity Today*: "Video Goes to Church," 19 September 1986; "Industry on the Move," 17 April 1987; "Hard Questions and Entertaining Answers," 18 September 1987; "How to Use Christian Video," 21 September 1987; "Fast Forward," 22 April 1988; "America's Favorite Home and Church Videos," 28 October 1991; and "Oases in the Video Wasteland," 27 April 1992. Observations that are defined as independent from the industry are derived from various sources, including news and articles in *Christianity Today* and reviews and articles in *Christian Film & Video,* an informative magazine that ceased printing (because of a lack of advertising support from the Christian media industry, according to its former editor, Mark Fackler).

20. Carol Thiessen, "What's That on Your TV Screen?" *Christianity Today,* 7 May 1982, 27.

21. Ibid.

22. Ibid.

23. Zettersten, *Dr. Dobson,* 96–97.

24. Ibid., 95.

25. Ibid., 111.

26. Ibid., 97.

27. Ibid.

28. Chris Franzen, "Dobson Brings the Family into Focus on Film," *Christian Film & Video,* January-February 1987, 7.

29. "How to Use Christian Video," *Christianity Today,* Special Advertising Section, 21 September 1987, 42.

30. "How to Use," 40.

31. Franzen, "Dobson Brings the Family into Focus," 7.

32. Mark Fackler, *Turn Your Heart toward Home,*" *Christian Film & Video,* January-February 1987, 3.

33. Franzen, "Dobson Brings the Family into Focus," 7.

34. Zettersten, *Dr. Dobson,* 97.

35. "Industry on the Move," *Christianity Today,* Special Advertising Section, 17 April 1987, 50, 54–55.

36. "How to Use," 42.

37. Randy Petersen, "What's Ahead for Christian Film and Video: Trend Watch for the 1990s," *Christian Film & Video,* March-April 1989, 1.

38. Petersen, "What's Ahead," 1.

39. White, *Tele-Advising,* 8. It should be noted that White is referring to confession as a discursive relation, following on Michel Foucault's work. Whereas Catholics practice a ritual of confession, evangelical Protestants believe in professions of faith. Although they entail different subject positions and practical situations, they can both be said to function within Foucault's theory of confessional discourse as a power/knowledge relation inciting one to speak the requisite "truths."

40. Robert C. Liebman, "Mobilizing the Moral Majority," in Abelman and Stewart, *Religious Television,* 61.

41. White, *Tele-Advising,* 135.

42. James C. Dobson, *Dare to Discipline* (Wheaton, Ill.: Tyndale House, 1974), 88 (emphasis in original).

43. Franzen, "Dobson Brings the Family into Focus," 7.

44. Linda Easter, "*Straight Talk to Families,*" *Christian Film & Video,* January–February 1989, 5.

45. Dean Ridings, "*Sex and the Family,*" *Christian Film & Video,* March–April 1989, 5.

46. Franzen, "Dobson Brings the Family into Focus," 7.

47. Moegerle, quoted in Ibid.

48. Ibid.

49. J. Stephen Lang, "*Twice Pardoned,*" *Christian Film & Video,* November-December 1988, 3.

50. Mark Fackler, "*Pornography: The Winnable War,*" *Christian Film & Video,* March-April 1989, 4.

51. Fackler, "*Turn Your Heart toward Home,*" 3.

52. J. Stephen Lang, "Christian Films: A Concern for Truth," *Christian Film & Video,* September-October 1985, 1.

53. Linda Williams, "Film Bodies, Gender, Genre, and Excess," *Film Quarterly* 44, no. 4 (Summer 1991): 11.

54. James C. Dobson, *The Strong-Willed Child* (Wheaton, Ill.: Tyndale House, 1981), 17.

55. Peter Brooks, *Body Work: Objects of Desire in Modern Narrative* (Cambridge: Harvard University Press, 1993), 3. Brooks, *Body Work,* 5. He suggests that scholars should address a range of bodies, from sacred to profane, in literature; by extension, the same course should be pursued with other media.

56. Dean Ridings, "*A Man Called Norman,*" *Christian Film & Video,* January-February 1989, 3.

57. Schultze, "The Mythos of the Electronic Church," 255.

58. Brad Edmondson, "Bringing in the Sheaves," *American Demographics,* August 1988, 30.

59. Hunter, *American Evangelicalism,* 74–75.

60. Zettersten, *Dr. Dobson,* 105. Here he quotes from the "policies" written by Dobson for Focus on the Family. Distinguishing himself and the ministry from unscrupulous practices and unsavory stereotypes, Dobson states that he will not use contributions for himself or for lavish expenses.

61. Quoted in Jerome Himmelstein, "The New Right," in Robert C. Liebman and Robert Wuthnow, eds., *The New Christian Right* (Hawthorne, N.Y.: Aldine, 1983), 28.

62. Edmondson, "Bringing in the Sheaves," 31.

63. Phillip Hammond, "Another Great Awakening?" in Liebman and Wuthnow, *The New Christian Right,* 219.

64. Lang, "Christian Films," 8.

65. "All Active-Duty U.S. Soldiers Are Expected to See Dobson Film," *Christianity Today,* 5 October 1985, 100.

66. "How to Use," 42.

8

Gimme That Old-Time Religion in a Postmodern Age: Semiotics of Christian Radio

Meryem Ersoz

What hath God wrought?
—*first words sent over an American telegraph line, 24 May 1844*

The year was 1984, and my parents enjoyed the comforts of economic privilege. But my mother, a product of the morally strict 1950s, harbored oddly anachronistic ideas about commodity deprivation as a way to build character in her own children. So, though she gave me a brand new car as a lavish high school graduation present, she stubbornly insisted that it be equipped only with AM radio. If I ever questioned her logic as she imposed this sort of minor privation on me, she would offer the same laconic, incontrovertible reply: "Because it's good for your soul."

Perhaps she was right.

I have a long-standing interest in religious radio broadcasting, which was born of necessity and fueled by shameless, voyeuristic fascination. As the daughter of a lapsed Moslem and an equally lapsed Protestant/Catholic mongrel, I evaded the trappings of most formal religion. Instead, the church with which I became most familiar was the "electric church,"[1] as Ben Armstrong has called it. When I drove through West Virginia and Ohio on my way to college, my puny AM radio picked up only one radio signal on the western side of Wheeling, West Virginia. The programs were hosted by a rural preacher who dubbed himself "the Blind Evangelical." With the car as my cathedral, I could while away an hour or two listening to Bible stories and biblical messages before his West Virginia twang evaporated into static fuzz or was gradually displaced by AM bubblegum.

Even then, I was already too radicalized—already too queer, too feminist, too bicultural—to embrace a Christian religious message, but I was still interested in how the message was conveyed. I understood the irony of listening to "the Blind Evangelical" on a blind medium. What did it matter that God's messenger was blind if, in fact, I could not see him anyway? If he were blind, radio was able to conceal the "real" facts about his physical makeup from his listeners; if he were not blind, what (or whose) interests were served by claiming blindness?

That same year, as I read *Antigone* in a political science class, I learned that the Blind Evangelical had been invoking a stock image like Tiresias, the blind seer who built his reputation on a paradox: He was the prophet who gained insight because he lacked vision. This Blind Evangelical had found grace through faith, as had the wretch in "Amazing Grace," who "was blind but now I see." I learned that an archetype could draw on recognition and familiarity; here it naturalized the disjuncture between the person I could not see and the Blind Evangelical's persona, the person he claimed to be. I had "seen" this character before, even though I had never "seen" him in actuality.

Driving for several hours through a flat Ohio landscape with little else to occupy my attention, I probed postmodern questions about what constitutes the "real" in the age of technological reproduction, although I did not yet have a critical vocabulary to explain them.

Christian broadcasting has changed considerably since its backwater days in the outer provinces of the AM bandwidth. Its volume and its audience continue to grow, and its presence has been diffused across both the AM and FM dials. The most recent *Broadcasting and Cable Yearbook* tallies 1,178 (597 FM and 591 AM) religious radio stations, which places religious radio as the seventh most common programming format.[2] An article published in *Christianity Today,* however, claims that Christian radio ranks third, behind only country and adult contemporary stations. The National Religious Broadcasters (NRB) counts a total of 1,600 stations that follow a Christian format.[3] Despite these statistical discrepancies and even if the true figures fall somewhere between these assessments, Christian religious radio programming has established its own media kingdoms within what Lee de Forest, one of the earliest pioneers of radio broadcasting, once described as an "Invisible Empire of the Air, intangible yet solid as granite."[4]

As Christian radio programming has grown in numbers, it has also changed in its practices. The stereotype of the lone male preacher delivering a long-winded fire-and-brimstone sermon, peppered by an occasional number from a gospel or church choir, fails to capture the complex ways that contemporary Christian radio programming has been modernized. It has now assimilated the practices of adult contemporary stations into its own broadcast practices. The programming model on which the Blind Evangelical based his format still exists; many local Christian programs fit that stereotype. But there is another very different kind of format that prevails, one that has to do with Marshall McLuhan's claim that "the medium is the message." If he was right, the question to be asked about Christian radio today is how the paradigmatic shift in broadcast practices has changed the religious message being delivered.

That shift is illustrated by the fact that a growing number of FM Christian radio stations are implementing new methods for delivering the message of a highly politicized and archconservative Christianity. These new Christian radio channels are associated with a conservative, grassroots political movement that *Business Week* magazine has dubbed the "New Populism." According to the magazine, New Populism has crystallized around issues important to both secular and religious conservatives, whose political bedfellows include America-firsters, militant moralists, Perot-style independents, and economic nationalists.[5] These diverse interest groups have found a willing mouthpiece for their agendas in a particular segment of the Christian radio broadcast community, where they broadcast a "traditional values" message using sophisticated, even identifiably postmodern, broadcasting forms and techniques.

One of the difficulties of analyzing either the Christian right as a political movement or Christian radio programming, however, is that neither is monolithic. Attempting to pinpoint the particular demographics of the Christian right can be as difficult and confusing as attempting to posit the monolithic audience for Christian radio's message.[6] This chapter will attempt a close analysis—or "close reading"—of the broadcasting practices of one representative radio station in particular, KRKS Denver/Boulder, as a way of understanding the message of conservative Christian politics vis-à-vis its use of radio as a medium.

Any consideration of current broadcasting practices must begin by considering the relation between the Christian kingdoms of the radio and the larger "Invisible Empire" of radio that Lee de Forest anticipated since the very beginnings of radio broadcasting. The presence of Christian programming may be significant, but the entirety of the "Invisible Empire" of modern radio broadcasting is still more vast. There were more than 11,543 radio stations on both AM and FM bandwidths reported in the United States in 1993. There are more than 576 million radio sets in use in the United States alone. Also, of the combined advertising revenue statistics most recently compiled by the Television Bureau of Advertising and the Radio Advertising Bureau, radio accounts for only 24.6 percent ($8.8 billion) of the total advertising revenue generated by both media combined. Though it is true that television produces substantially more advertising dollars, it is interesting to note that an overwhelming percentage of the funds ($6.899 billion) generated by radio are obtained at the local, rather than the national, network level.[7] The national advertising spotlight remains firmly focused on television; radio reveals itself as a primarily local—perhaps even grassroots—medium.

These statistics, which reveal the vastness of the Invisible Empire of radio and the significant place that Christian radio occupies within it, beg a series of questions. How has a medium as powerful and pervasive as radio escaped serious critical attention until recently? How has the Invisible Empire somehow remained invisible to the scrutinizing gaze of critical analysis? And similarly, how has a programming format as potent as Christian radio managed to colonize the commercial dial without drawing significant attention to itself?

It is not only Christian radio, of course, that has been ignored but radio in general as a discrete medium. As R. Murray Schafer points out, radio "lacks an exegetical apparatus for external analysis." It is an undertheorized medium for which "a meta-language by which it can be adequately described" has failed to develop.[8] Just as I, as a teenager, lacked the vocabulary to articulate the blind preacher's paradox, radio studies within the academy are similarly impoverished. There are few theoretical frameworks for discussing the cultural work performed by radio. A critique of Christian radio is, therefore, already doubly blind at the outset because of the lack of critical tools and vocabulary available for discussing either the medium or its messages. To do a close reading of a particular radio station's broadcast seems tantamount to analyzing a book with no definition of what constitutes literature. As a result, this chapter is driven by a two-pronged impulse to reconceptualize radio in terms of both theory and practice. In the next section, I will consider radio in terms of its importance as an object of study and analysis, arguing that Christian radio has paradoxically co-opted and absorbed postmodern broadcasting techniques in order to transmit "traditional values" ideologies. This is a practice that can be seen through a close reading of radio station KRKS Denver/Boulder ("where the Word is the Rock"). Before a close analysis of a particular case study can take place, however, it is necessary to take a closer look at the Invisible Empire and see what factors have permitted the blind medium to remain invisible.

Given the number of radios sold, the local distribution of advertising dollars, and the radio stations currently broadcasting, radio has the ubiquity of a god. It is everywhere in ways that television is not. Of the 576 million radio sets previously mentioned, only 64 percent of these sets are used in homes. Television, by comparison, is a relatively domesticated medium, with 93 million sets operating primarily in homes.[9] One of the paradoxes of radio is that because it is located everywhere, colonizing both public and private space in more or less equal measure, it resides nowhere in particular, which makes the process of locating or isolating its presence in the culture extremely difficult.

In terms of the sheer presence of the physical apparatus, radio far outstrips television, even if it is less visible and less prestigious. The editor of *Channels of Discourse Reassembled,* a volume of television criticism, claims that television's invisibility results from the "intricate ways it is woven into the everyday lives of so many people."[10] In his view, television's invisibility to media critics is related to the fact that it is a seamless and naturalized part of daily routine; its importance as a cultural artifact "remains invisible."[11]

Radio clearly has this problem to an even greater degree, but it is also characterized by a second level of invisibility to analysis in that it is almost exclusively studied as one element under a broader, more monolithic umbrella known as "the media," which conceptualizes radio as part of a system rather than understanding radio's unique position within the system. As a result, scant attention is given to radio as a discrete medium with a specific power structure of its own. Radio, unlike television, is thus not analyzed as an independent system of signification that merits its own theoretical apparatus.

The elision of radio from media studies is not surprising, since media studies privilege spectacle. In a society in which direct experience is displaced by mediated visual representations of experience—what Guy Debord calls the "society of the spectacle"—vision has become "the privileged human sense which the sense of touch was for other epochs."[12] We are, as Chris Jenks suggests, bound by the tautological nature of our "visual culture"[13] wherein "visual ability has become conflated with cognition."[14] In visual culture, seeing is knowing and knowing, seeing. Writing in the 1930s, Rudolf Arnheim had already acknowledged the privilege of vision as the primary sense in a technologically mediated modern age: "The sensory preponderance of the visual over the aural in our life is so great that it is very difficult to get used to considering the aural world as more than just a transition to the visual world."[15]

This sort of anthropomorphizing discourse has framed the study of film, in which the discussion of film and its apparatus is almost ubiquitously couched in terms of its "look" or the "gaze." Jean-Louis Baudry points out that film apparatus functions as a prosthetic equivalent for the human eye, representing a type of cyborgism that stands in for the spectator's own vision as "secondary organs, grafted on to replace his own defective ones."[16]

However, radio apparatus does not appear to work this way. It does not mediate the sort of "spectatorial reciprocity," or the "returned gaze,"[17] that Winston Wheeler Dixon points out takes place between the spectator and the characters on the screen in film or television. It replicates sound, not vision, yet this capacity is not usually discussed in terms of radio's ability to duplicate a human sensory function. Though there has been much critical discussion of television's ability to approximate a particular human sense, there has been little analogous consideration of radio apparatus in such terms. It does not seem to elicit the same degree of fascination for the critic.

To counteract this invisibility may require developing a model that relates it to the human sense of hearing, which will involve asking a number of questions. Can there be a model for aural radio "spectatorship," or is the medium completely blind? Can there be a different model or models of human sensory experience upon which we can build a theory of radio? And can this theory mediate praxis?

To answer this last, perhaps most important, question, we need to turn back to the Blind Evangelical, who solicited listeners by using a recognizable metaphor, the paradox of the blind seer. The deployment of this metaphor took place within a specific semiotic field—the grainy AM signal, the long, uninterrupted sermons, the choir music; the lack of commercials—that "hails" listeners (in the Althusserian sense).[18] It also allows listening subjects to recognize that indeed they are listening to an easily distinguished and recognizable package, Christian radio broadcasting, and can trust that format to meet certain predetermined expectations in regards to programming.[19]

But the semiotic signals of Christian radio programming have been radically restructured in recent years, scrambling those expectations. Radio station KRKS Denver/Boulder exemplifies a new signifying system for Christian radio programming, a system that has grown out of postmodern broadcast practices. There are several paradoxes implicit in this shift. For instance, 94.7 KRKS colonizes what is one of the strongest signals on the FM dial, rendering it more "visible" or available to a broader and more mainstream audience base. KRKS maintains a conservative "traditional family values" message while appropriating the format of an adult contemporary station, a practice that makes the messenger station more visible, higher profile, more available, and yet makes the message itself less visible. This repackaging of Christian radio makes it less discernible from its secular, adult contemporary counterparts and unhinges it from the formatting precedents established by prior religious broadcast programming.

Radio station KRKS is a pastiche of programming devices borrowed from a variety of adult contemporary stations and reinscribed within its own conservative Christian political and religious context. Its station identification signature is "The Word is the Rock, 94.7 KRKS" (or its shorthand derivative, simply "94.7 The Rock"), a phrase pronounced by a deep, male voice and followed by the heavy, thudding echo of a rock dropping. In a broadly religious semiotic system, this signature contains obvious biblical resonances.

The Rock is an image that establishes continuity between the Old Testament God ("He is the Rock, his work is perfect," Deut. 32:4) with the New Testament Jesus ("they drank of that spiritual Rock that followed them: and that Rock was Christ," 1 Cor. 10:4). In a biblical context, the Rock serves as an image of solidity, foundation, salvation, and perfection.[20]

In the signifying structures of adult contemporary stations, however, "the Rock" has been used as a signature to identify rock-music format stations. In the context of current adult contemporary broadcast practices, "rock" music has heteroglossic associations. On the one hand, it is affiliated with the iconoclasm of youth culture, rebellion, irreverence, and antiestablishment sentiment; and on the other, it represents the interests of a multibillion-dollar mainstream music industry that co-opts these values to promote consumer interest in its own products. "The Rock" and references to rock music in general, in a secular context, contain an implicit tension. It is seen as simultaneously marginal and mainstream in the field of musical signification and history, a feature that makes it easily manipulable by a radical right that touts so-called traditional family values. KRKS conflates and manipulates these contexts with and against each other to resignify the meaning of their own signature, invoking a standard conventional signature image and reproducing it in a Christian context. To a listener running the tuning dial in search of a conventional, secular rock music station, the audible difference is virtually indistinguishable. In terms of listening practice, it is not unusual to hear politically liberal consumers complain that they have repeatedly let the dial rest on KRKS for several minutes before realizing that the station was a tool of conservative ideologues.[21] This packaging represents a radical rupture with prevailing stereotypes of Christian religious radio broadcast practices while maintaining the easily identifiable imagery of a mainstream adult contemporary station.

This one seemingly small detail, the station identification signature, reflects the station's larger practice of co-opting secular adult contemporary broadcast tactics in service to its Christian message. The station, for instance, hosts a weekly program called *A Look at the Charts* with host Victor Cooper, a weekend countdown of contemporary (Christian) music hits that imitates the secular rock and roll tradition begun by the peerless Kasey Kasem in his weekend radio broadcast of the *American Top 40.*

KRKS has aired short messages on topics such as how to budget money that are imparted through the voice of an elderly gentleman who sports the persona "Harv Pauley," an obvious intertextual reference to popular radio personality Paul Harvey, popular host of *The Rest of the Story.* In a broader cultural semiotic field, Harvey's reputation and iconic status as a reporter and storyteller for the nation represent longevity, stability, and public trust; "Harv Pauley" evokes and co-opts this imagery in service to producing "a

Money Minute from Christian Financial Concepts." Also included in the programming format for KRKS is a regular feature entitled *Golden Years Theater,* whose commercial tagline "Let's hearken back to the years when radio was truly Theater of the Mind" invokes a nostalgic reenactment of 1940s and 1950s serial broadcasts that once appealed to a broad secular audience but that are recontextualized by KRKS as a means of reinforcing the politics of a traditional family values message.

Christian radio programming has also capitalized on the immense popularity of the radio talk show format. Talk radio—interactive radio—abounds throughout the KRKS programming week, serving up fare from "the undisputed king of Christian radio,"[22] James Dobson and his daily *Focus on the Family* program, as well as offering a slate of lesser-known talk show personae.

The advantage to airing talk shows on stations such as KRKS is that these products are translatable into direct political action. *Christianity Today,* for instance, reported that on 24 February 1994 one million callers, incited by several Christian talk radio programs, "jammed the House of Representatives' phone lines to protest HR 6,"[23] a bill that could have jeopardized home schooling privileges. As a result of direct action, Congress overwhelmingly amended the bill, prompting *Christianity Today* to speculate that "the effective alliance between Christian radio and largely conservative Christian activists may foreshadow their influence on the issues of health-care reform, abortion, and countless other social issues."[24] ABC's *Day One* newsmagazine claims that James Dobson's *Focus on the Family* generates over $100 million in contributions and can mobilize more direct political action and "deliver more bags of mail" through his radio broadcasts than Pat Robertson can through his television broadcasts of *The 700 Club.*[25]

The "Invisible Empire" of Dobson's radio broadcasts is, by his own admission, vast, broadcasting two-and-a-half hours each week, over 12,000 times in North America and 4,000 times across the world. Its affiliated magazines are sent to 3–4 million people per month, Dobson's own letter is mailed to 2 million people a month, and he is published in 500 newspapers each week.[26] If Dobson represents the political mobilization possible through a single daily half-hour talk show, it is difficult, then, to imagine the extent of the political clout wielded by the burgeoning number of radio stations like KRKS, which encourage the aggregation of these sorts of direct action-oriented Christian talk radio programming into a monolithic forum.

One other notable programming feature is the segmentation of the message. KRKS, like any adult contemporary station, has segmented its own programming by breaking broadcast messages into smaller increments. Commercial spots are brief. Talk show formats and extended regular features[27] are broken down into seven- to fifteen-minute time segments interspersed with commercials, station identification, public service announcements, and so on. All of these segments, however, reinforce a monolithic broader message: a conservative Christian values ideology that distinguishes it from other commercial radio stations. The segments themselves are differentiated in terms of their form (such as talk show, sermon, commercial), but in terms of the message these various forms attempt to convey, there is no distinction. The message remains homogenous, while the medium itself attempts to maintain a surface heterogeneity.

This broadcasting strategy of invoking conventional images and recognizable icons as a means of achieving a seamless format echoes the practice of my Blind Evangelical. This strategy naturalizes the presence of religious broadcasting on the FM dial through the conflation of conservative Christian radio messages with secular adult contemporary broadcast practices.

At the same time, however, this new packaging reflects a rupture from the conventional expectations for the style of religious radio that the Blind Evangelical represents. The pretense at a mimetic replication of the trappings of a church setting has been cast aside by stations like KRKS; gone are the long, uninterrupted sermons, the lone male preacher, the church choir. As the message itself is cloaked in contemporary imagery and broadcast practices, the station itself, the messenger, is rendered more visible to a broader consumer base.

A discussion of broadcast practices is one useful way to discuss radio (particularly Christian radio) in terms of its visibility or invisibility, but it still does not address the question of why radio has been excluded from the anthropomorphizing discourse that characterizes studies of visual media. In turning over the question of Christian radio's (in)visibility, I think it is equally important to consider whether or not the medium can be adequately theorized in terms of its blindness or its gaze.

Rudolf Arnheim pointed out that the listener supplements radio's lack of visual imagery by drawing on the mind's eye or calling upon the imagination to fill in the gaps, a process that explains how the presence of a "blind evangelical" can be accepted by the listener without drawing attention to its own irony. Arnheim noted that this phenomenon was "worth investigation,"[28] but he resisted pursuing this line of thinking himself, instead arguing that radio constitutes an entirely new realm of experience, a "world of its own."[29] In Arnheim's view, radio is not a means of communication based on filling in a lack or deficiency but instead represents a wholly new and complete mode of sensory experience, "an entirely unexplored form of expression in pure sound," which he conceptualized using the phrase "blind hearing."[30]

This paradoxical concept of "blind hearing" helps to explain why radio is such a compelling medium for delivering a Christian religious message.

R. Murray Schafer is not the first theorist to note that God is the original radio broadcaster, the original invisible, disembodied voice proclaiming a message across the ethers.[31] Before there was light, the necessary condition of vision, God, the original broadcaster, had to proclaim: "Let there be light" (Gen. 1:3). Standard biblical exegesis recognizes that prior to vision, before there could be vision, there had to be something else: "In the beginning was the Word, and the Word was with God, and the Word was God" (John 1:1). But given our visually oriented culture, it is easy to accept John Berger's assumption that "seeing comes before words"[32] without questioning the history of this assumption, that is, without considering ways in which our visual orientation is a product of modernity and not necessarily a first principle of epistemology. The Christian broadcaster, for instance, operates from a different epistemological assumption, that the Word precedes vision. Faith is a function of hearing and believing; in other words, belief precedes miracles, the visual manifestations of faith. Berger, on the other hand, takes his cue from a psychoanalytic model in which vision forms language structures, eliding the fact that the mother is "broadcasting" to the child before the child can even open or focus its eyes. The Christian broadcast similarly is designed to bring listeners to faith through the power of the Word.

This investment in an epistemology that privileges words before sight is hardly naive and does not operate outside of the prevailing visually oriented epistemological hierarchy, however. A close reading of one of James Dobson's *Focus on the Family* broadcasts reveals that the conservative Christian broadcaster is deeply aware of the power of postmodern self-reflexivity. Dobson knows how to use the culture's master tools, the visual media, to build his Master's house and is perfectly capable of manipulating and subjugating the visual media, the camera eye, the gaze, in service to the "blind hearing" of radio.

In October 1995, Dobson devoted three days of his half-hour daily talk show to dissecting a fifteen-minute segment from ABC's *Day One* newsmagazine. *Day One* interviewer John Hockenberry conducted a seventy-five-minute interview with him as part of the process of researching *Focus on the Family*. Dobson agreed to the interview with the stipulation that it could only take place "if they permitted us to put a video camera behind theirs and videotape them videotaping me so that we could have a record"[33] of the entire seventy-five minutes of the interview, which Dobson then reproduced on a videocassette entitled *Day One: The Truth* and then offered to his own consumer audience in exchange for "a gift of $7.00."

The layering of media in this image is remarkable—the ABC camera recording the interview, the *Focus* camera recording the recording, the radio serving as the larger panoptical device for depicting this image, and the direct marketing strategy. By assimilating all these images within his own broadcast, Dobson converts a potentially damaging television interview into a product designed to defuse the power of the television broadcast image and to generate additional revenue for the Focus on the Family coffers. Dobson manages to undo his television competitors by out-commodifying them, by offering himself up to commodification by the television industry and then repackaging their product for his own use.

Dobson says that "we weren't quite sure what the media would do," justifying this practice on the grounds that the so-called monolithic liberal media can't be trusted. He uses "the media" in this phrase to place himself and his own radio and direct marketing empire on the margins of the media power structure. The fact that radio, as I discussed earlier, is publicly perceived as a degraded, less powerful form of media than television fuels the logic behind Dobson's claim. It is the public perception of radio within the semiotic field of "the media" that gives Dobson the license to cast himself as the radio David doing his best to combat the Goliath of television when in fact Dobson is hardly a "little guy." Dobson proves remarkably savvy about postmodern tactics for self-reflexively absorbing the power of one medium within another. He uses the Word to absorb and defuse the power of the panopticon, the camera's consuming and controlling gaze.

His cohost, Mike Trout, admits Dobson's insider knowledge of media power structures when he says: "You've been with the media long enough that you knew there were some things that you were able to do and so were able to come back at what was presented on Thursday night." Interestingly, both men invoke this phrase, "the media," but in oppositional contexts. Trout represents Dobson as an insider with special knowledge that can be used from the outside to chip away at the phantasm of what they both perceive to be a monolithic liberal media. But clearly, *Focus on the Family* broadcast practices contradict that entire notion by claiming "less" visibility from within an enormous media empire.

A second strategy that Dobson uses to defuse the power of the ABC newsmagazine's camera gaze is to play the soundtrack from the segment aired on television on his own radio talk show. Dobson fragments and weakens the narrative integrity and semiotic structure of the television broadcast by divorcing image from sound. Dobson's plan is "to comment on this feature a piece at a time," stopping the tape periodically and overlaying the television soundtrack with his own radio broadcast commentary.

Also, Dobson reinserts parts of the taped interview that were left out of the television broadcast but are intact on his own seventy-five-minute interview tape. His intent is to make the "invisible" portions of the interview visible to his listening audience by reinforcing the primacy of words over visual imagery, countering what he perceives is a misrepresentation of his organization. ABC's *Day One* attempted to reveal the breadth of the political power and influence generated by the Focus on the Family media machine. Dobson's reaction is to downplay his political role, claiming that he doesn't solicit or endorse politicians but, rather, makes himself available to let politicians know what his listeners want. His aspirations, he emphasizes, are spiritual, not political, and he claims that the interviewer "just could not accept the fact that somebody could be this visible and not want to do anything with it." He has an uncanny knack for both downplaying and reinforcing the extent of his visibility as a media icon with a remarkable degree of simultaneity.

Dobson spent three days reworking the ABC *Day One* segment on his own talk show, devoting a disproportionate amount of radio broadcast time to assuming control of what he himself admitted was "an honest effort to describe the ministry of Focus on the Family" in its fifteen-minute television segment. Managing to downplay his motives for devoting so much airtime to this issue of his perception of ABC's misrepresentation, he claims: "I just thought it would be an interesting thing to show how television newsmagazine programs are constructed and to help people be a little more skeptical of what else they see." The irony of this statement, of course, is that radio broadcasts are equally constructed or, in the case of this particular broadcast segment, reconstructed. What is equally interesting about this passage is Dobson's exhortation to be skeptical of vision, to be suspicious of what is seen, and to trust instead in the word, his word.

Radio, the blind medium, asks us to believe what we hear, rather than what we see. And Christian radio, in particular, can illustrate that an epistemology that is based on "blind hearing" does not necessarily forsake the hegemony of vision. The way power is distributed through the medium of radio intertwining both its presence and absence with the simultaneity of its invisibility and its visibility is summed up in the *Day One* announcer's description of James Dobson: "He's one of the most powerful men in America, but few people know his name."

A project of developing a semiotics of radio in general and of Christian radio in particular thus has to begin by describing it in terms of the anthropomorphizing discourses that initially draw on images like visibility, invisibility, blind hearing, blind medium to conceptualize the apparatus, the medium, and its message. The notion of "blind hearing" is, perhaps, a useful conceptual tool because it recognizes that radio calls for a reevaluation of subjective experience in relation to the apparatus, and it considers radio as a discrete experience, separate from other forms of media. But such a model has also been limited by those who have begun to develop it by the fact that earlier studies have presumed a listener whose listening practices are stripped of the facts of ongoing, multiple, and simultaneous sensory experiences that invade the experience of listening to the radio. Just as Arnheim does, most of our models for considering radio have posited the listener as the "passive standardized man."[34] The flaw in Arnheim's concept of "blind hearing" is that it erases the fact that listeners cannot shut down their other senses. Radio is a synesthetic experience in which ongoing multiple sensory experiences are inherently mixed and intertwined; these floating signifiers of human speech are not detached at all.

In a more contemporary analysis of radio, Julia Loktev describes the way radio becomes a part of the whole experience of "just staring straight ahead into the video game called the road."[35] Her analysis acknowledges the way sensory experiences are multiple and inextricably braided. The visual agitation of the moving vehicle is synthesized with the aural bombardment of the radio into a "video game" in which visuals and sound are working in tandem to produce a subject who is, in Loktev's own words, "infinitely antsy."[36] Her interest in what is produced by radio has nothing to do with its programming content and everything to do with enhancing her own sense of aggressiveness through this synesthetic fusion of exterior and interior sensory experiences. Loktev's listener, unlike "passive standardized man," is neither passive, standardized, nor, for that matter, male.

As my chapter began with an image of a woman driving down the road, it also ends there. By contrast, a semiotics of radio must begin by conceptualizing radio in relation to a common series of images for describing its anthropomorphic characteristics. It must, however, certainly not end there.

Notes

Thanks to Lee Scriggins for her assistance with radio research.

1. Ben Armstrong, *The Electric Church* (New York: Thomas Nelson, 1979), 1.

2. Statistics from the *Broadcasting and Cable Yearbook* do not distinguish between "religious" and "Christian" stations, meaning that stations representing "other" religions, such as the occasional Jewish station, for instance, are included in these figures. *Broadcasting and Cable Yearbook, 1994* (New Providence, NJ: Bowker, 1994).

3. John W. Kennedy, "Mixing Politics and Piety," *Christianity Today,* 15 August 1994, 42–46.

4. Lee de Forest, *Father of Radio: The Autobiography of Lee de Forest* (Chicago: Wilcox and Follett, 1950), 2.

5. Lee Walczak et al., "The New Populism," *Business Week,* 13 March 1995, 72–78.

6. Even a demographic study cannot account for the regular listening practices of the oppositional listener. For instance, I have talked with a number of leftist political activists who are avid listeners of Christian radio, in part to "keep up" with what the opposition is "doing." But I would also speculate that the phenomenon of the voyeuristic (dis)pleasure that listeners and viewers take in the sensations of dislike and distaste is entirely underexplored terrain.

7. *Broadcasting and Cable Yearbook, 1994,* 3.

8. R. Murray Schafer, "Radical Radio," in Neil Strauss, ed., *Radiotext(e)* (New York: Semiotext(e), 1993), 295.

9. *Broadcasting and Cable Yearbook, 1994,* 3.

10. Robert C. Allen, "Introduction to the Second Edition: More Talk about TV," *Channels of Discourse Reassembled* (Chapel Hill: University of North Carolina Press, 1992), 5.

11. Allen, "Introduction," 6.

12. Guy Debord, *Society of the Spectacle* (Detroit: Black and Red, 1983), 18.

13. Chris Jenks, "The Centrality of the Eye in Western Culture: An Introduction," in Chris Jenks, ed., *Visual Culture* (New York: Routledge, 1995), 16.

14. Ibid., 1.

15. Rudolf Arnheim, *Radio,* trans. Margaret Ludwig and Herbert Read (New York: Arno, 1971), 136.

16. Jean-Louis Baudry, "Ideological Effects of the Basic Apparatus," in Philip Rosen, ed., *Narrative, Apparatus, Ideology* (New York: Columbia University Press, 1986), 295.

17. Winston Wheeler Dixon, *It Looks at You: The Returned Gaze of Cinema* (Albany, N.Y.: SUNY, 1995), 134.

18. For an extended discussion of hailing, see Louis Althusser, "Ideology and Ideological State Apparatuses," in *Lenin and Philosophy,* trans. Ben Brewster (London: New Left Books, 1971).

19. Radio programming formats are somewhat akin to the concept of genres in film or literature. The *Broadcasting and Cable Yearbook* categorizes stations by format type—country, religious, adult contemporary, and so on—which are recognizable by their style and their aggregation of conventions specific to their particular format.

20. Additional biblical references relating the image of the Rock to the power of God include 2 Sam. 22:3; Psalms 18:2, 18.46, 89.26, and 95.1, Matt. 16:18; and 1 Cor. 10:4.

21. This assertion is based on a casual polling of my own acquaintances, all oppositional listeners living in Colorado, who have admitted that at one time or another they have mistaken KRKS for a secular adult contemporary station and felt "tricked" or "deceived" into listening to conservative Christian messages by the radio station's co-optation of standard conventions.

22. Dobson has nearly twice as many listeners as any other Christian radio talk show host. Kennedy, "Mixing Politics and Piety," 42–43.

23. Ibid., 42.

24. Ibid.

25. From an ABC *Day One* broadcast that aired 28 September 1995. This reference and all subsequent references to the *Day One* broadcast are taken from the *Focus on the Family* broadcast of the *Day One* soundtrack on 30 September 1995.

26. These figures were quoted by James Dobson during the 30 September 1995 *Focus on the Family* broadcast.

27. Out of respect for the church atmosphere and tradition, perhaps, sermons are usually exempt from the practice of segmentation and generally are aired in full, without interruption.

28. Arnheim, *Radio,* 137.

29. Ibid., 137–38.

30. Ibid., 226.

31. Schafer, "Radical Radio," 291.

32. John Berger, *Ways of Seeing* (London: Penguin, 1972), 7.

33. This reference and all subsequent references to *Focus on the Family* broadcasts were taken from a weekend segment of *Focus on the Family* that aired on KRKS on 30 September 1995.

34. Arnheim, *Radio,* 260.

35. Julia Loktev, "Static Motion, or the Confessions of a Compulsive Radio Driver," in Strauss, *Radiotext(e),* 204.

36. Ibid., 205.

9

Sitting in Limbaugh: Bombast in Broadcasting

Jeff Land

> *The alphabet of living is capable of forming a nearly infinite number of combinations, or situations. Yet some people never acquired more than the spelling of one word: ditto, reducing all singularity to commonness.*
>
> —*Abraham Heschel*

Rush Limbaugh dominates the cultural and political landscape of the mid-1990s. With consummate skill he presents himself as an entertaining, optimistic spokesperson for "traditional American values" through a dizzying array of media: radio, television, books, advertisements, cassettes, the monthly *Limbaugh Newsletter,* personal engagements, and Internet conference groups. In his impact on current government policies, in the passion he elicits from his audience, and in the effortless manner he popularizes a curious, some might say pathological, pastiche of postmodern social Darwinism, he has no peer.

Whether the ideals of family, religion, and profit are divinely sanctioned, as he would claim, or simply evoked as part of the media ratings game, the manner in which Limbaugh blends them have struck a chord: "Rush is a great American success story. He has made millions, because he found a way to publicly state what most people (the mainstream) have believed and wanted to say all along, but have not had the opportunity to do so. Rush gives us that voice, and I will support him."[1]

The sincerity of his supporters indicates the depth of conservatism within our political culture; most Americans *do* cherish many of the ideals that Limbaugh promotes, even if certain of those ideals themselves do not jibe easily with other deeply held beliefs.

The contours of Limbaugh's right-wing populism were first articulated in the national presidential campaigns of George Wallace in 1968 and 1972.

The virulent racism of the governor's earlier years was recoded as an attack on federal government welfare policies, cast in the name of giving decent, hardworking (white) Americans their due. Wallace's attack on big government—never big business—as an expression of working-class or middle-class interests was consolidated in the regime of Ronald Reagan, during whose presidency government tax policies effected a massive upward redistribution of wealth. Like Reagan, Limbaugh is a master of artificial authenticity, deploying a rhetoric that seamlessly weaves together apparently contradictory positions: Patriotism is exemplified by attacking the government; wealthy white men are the most beleaguered members of society; workers ultimately benefit by capital flight; gender equality destroys the family. Limbaugh, who is not subject to the same public accountability as an elected official, broadcasts his ideology three-and-a-half hours daily (the three-hour *Rush Limbaugh Show* and a half-hour late-night TV show) over radio and television with constant self-deprecating references that no one should take his positions too seriously. After all, he is only an entertainer.

Before assessing the substance of Limbaugh's politics head on, one does well to consider the reach of his gospel, undergirded by his reinvention of the moribund medium of talk radio. A devoted fan—perhaps with a team of elves—transcribes Limbaugh's three-hour call-in radio show each day onto the Internet. (Some of these highly detailed narrative expositions reach up to twenty-five double-spaced pages.) These postings are prefaced by these useful figures:

> December 30, 1994—It's now day 52 of America, the Way it Ought to Be, [that is, since the landmark 1994 Republican electoral victory] and 773 days after Bill Clinton's election, but Rush is still on the air with 665 radio affiliates (with more than 20 million listeners weekly worldwide), 250 TV affiliates (with a national rating of 3.7), and a newsletter with nearly 500,000 subscribers.

Limbaugh's first book was on the *New York Times* hardback nonfiction best-seller list for fifty-four consecutive weeks, with 2.6 million copies sold, but fell off the list after Simon and Schuster stopped printing it. The paperback version of *The Way Things Ought to Be* was on the *New York Times* paperback nonfiction best-seller list for twenty-eight weeks. His second book, *See, I Told You So,* was on the *New York Times* best-seller list for sixteen weeks and has sold over 2.45 million copies.[2] (Other sources indicate that his cassettes, which sell in the quarter million range, are among the most popular in the exploding field of "talking books.")

This survey leaves out the many (thousands? tens of thousands?) fans on the Internet who avidly use their computers to further enlarge the range of Limbaugh's ideas on several very active conference groups. His ascendancy in the world of mediated politics shows no sign of diminishing. As he reminds his audience daily: The ratings continue to go up, up, up.

How has Limbaugh accomplished this? One must first examine his use of radio as the primary medium spreading his message. Within a commercial media universe that ceaselessly eviscerates the historical specificity and context of current events, call-in radio has until now distinguished itself for a certain dialogic honesty. As one writer argued, the format has provided "a poignant vehicle" for a range of participants to discuss "the alienation of urban life."[3] Call-in radio models a potential alternative to the passive transmitter/receiver paradigm of broadcasting, an alternative that invites the listener's more active engagement. Even should the host of a talk radio show hang up the phone or bleep out some particular verbal indiscretion, the premise of the format has been that every listener, regardless of political predisposition, is invited to participate in a public forum. This sliver of democratic communication within the mass media is now shrinking even further, a victim of the ideology of a new generation of hosts whose sanctimony enables them to insist that their wisdom need not be contested by any random listener, as well as of the improvement in telecommunication technology that provides refined filtering and screening of callers. Limbaugh is not alone in this trend toward diminished dialogue, but he remains its most visible and pernicious exponent.

The three-hour *Rush Limbaugh Show* highlights the shifting structure of the traditional radio call-in format: The increasing nationalization of the programs via the use of 800 numbers, the paucity of callers actually reaching the air, and the sophisticated computerized phone-stacking arrangements all alter the basic generic forms. On Limbaugh's programs those elements of reciprocity in which host and caller meet as equals in the electronic public sphere have been erased. Operators carefully screen each caller to ensure ideological conformity, as Limbaugh brags: "Bo Sneardly [the flow director] is now answering phones to see who is qualified to speak with me." Most listeners who are given a clear path to the air simply offer their immense appreciation for the work that Limbaugh does, agree with one of his comments—"Ditto"—and then hang up.

This chapter begins with an overview of the path that "the harmless little fuzzball," as Limbaugh calls himself, took reaching the apex of media celebrity in the past decade and half. It then considers a vexing problem that an analysis of Limbaugh necessarily confronts: Can one speak of a unified project within the blend of ironic megalomania, humorous musical skits, assaults on "liberalism," and pious invocations of Judaeo-Christian or American or Republican or conservative values that fill radio, television, the Internet, and the print media in the name of Limbaugh? With which aspect of "Rush" do his callers and fans absolutely agree when they begin each phone call with "Ditto"? I conclude by evaluating various forms of criticism leveled against his project.

Those opposed to Limbaugh's political agenda might concede two things at the start: First, he has shown staunch commitment since childhood to the values he currently preaches. (Whether he practices them is an issue addressed below). Second, Limbaugh has worked tirelessly to reach the fame he has achieved. His unquestionable skill in shaping the aural environment of his radio program with music, comic routine, political commentary, and dialogue with listeners was honed over many years of apprenticeship in the brutally competitive world of commercial radio.

Limbaugh's politics were forged in his family environment.[4] Born in 1951, the son of a conservative Republican lawyer in Cape Girardeau, Missouri, Limbaugh (Rush III) has only drifted rightward from the ideology that his father vigorously espoused. Heavyset and reportedly somewhat anxious about his self-presentation as a teen, "Rusty" began his career as a part-time rock and roll DJ in high school at a small AM station in his hometown. In a rebellion against the career plans of his upper-middle-class family, he eschewed higher education, dropping out of a local college in 1971 after one year in order to pursue employment in broadcasting (only after receiving a questionable medical deferment from the draft for a pilonidal cyst). Although remaining doggedly Republican in his politics, he found a niche in the world of rock radio, moving from job to job while honing his patter under the pseudonym "Jeff Christie." As one commentator noted, his current popularity with younger white males stems in no little part from the rock sensibility that infuses his current program, filled as it is with hooks and jingles effortlessly woven into the fabric of the three-hour "talk radio" show.[5]

Archival tapes from the mid-1970s from a Pittsburgh, Pennsylvania, station display Limbaugh's emerging routine. They show him simultaneously emphasizing and mocking his own skills ("I can do this [work the mixing board] with one hand tied behind my back") and the initial use of the stock phrase "excellence in broadcasting" to describe his project; in the early 1990s he would christen his media conglomerate the EIB (Excellence in Broadcasting) Network. A voracious reader, always well versed in current events, "Jeff Christie" would provide glib commentary on the news spoken between and over the music he was hired to play. This skill proved a mixed blessing. Often chastised by management for voicing his contentious conservative opinions in the mindless environment of top-40 radio, he led an itinerant life, moving from job to job. He was able to leave the formulaic world of the DJ for the more demanding role of talk show host for a Kansas City, Missouri, station in 1978, but within months his bombastic style and reactionary politics led to another job termination.

Forsaking radio for a stint in the publicity department of the Kansas City Royals baseball team, Limbaugh went into a four-year hiatus from broadcasting, during which time his first marriage ended and a second one began. Financial difficulties plagued him. For his work with the Royals, Limbaugh kept close contact with the media world in Kansas City; when he was let go by the team following a shift in management, he used his network of friends to find a position in the news department of a local radio station in 1983. Fired once again in 1984, after ten months, for excessive commentary in what was supposed to be a straight newscaster position, his career prospects appeared dim.

This period of personal and professional turmoil has become foundational in the narration of his own biography. These years in Kansas City, so he now posits, enable the media star currently earning tens of millions of dollars a year to possess a unique understanding of the daily plight of working-class people. His critics should not dismiss this claim. Limbaugh has undeniably mastered a vocabulary capable of speaking to anxious working- and middle-class listeners, a vocabulary that comes from some direct experience with the fragility of the current job market.

Limbaugh's rise from personal and economic hardships has also provided him with the "objectivity" for mythologizing his own ascent:

> My story is nothing more than an example of the Original American Ethic: hard work, overcoming obstacles, triumphing over enormous odds, the pioneer spirit... I've been on every rung of the economic ladder. I've been fired six times. I've been hopelessly in debt... I've also been near the top. I've seen life from all sides. Because of this, my own experience is particularly instructive... [N]o matter what your status in life, you can learn about what's possible for you in this country by studying me. And if you attain even a fraction of my level of excellence, you will have arrived.[6]

As he explains elsewhere, even when mired in the most dire straits, he never lost faith in his ultimate capacity for "greatness."

After losing his radio position in Kansas City, fate smiled. Morton Downey Jr., who would later receive national fame for vituperative attacks on women, gays, and others, uttered an on-the-air slur against "Chinamen" and was summarily fired from his position as host of a talk show at Sacramento, California, radio station KBFK. A colleague of Limbaugh from Pittsburgh was the station manager. Needing a rapid replacement for Downey, he invited Limbaugh to audition for the job, which Limbaugh was immediately offered.

Limbaugh had, at last, a pulpit from which he could freely speak his mind about whatever topic happened to interest him. KBFK news director Tyler Cox recalled: "Between the phone response and the street talk about the show, the numbers skyrocketed. I would go to chamber of commerce meetings, the Lions Club, and people wanted to talk about Rush. It was one of those magical moments."[7] In four years in Sacramento, Limbaugh perfected the skill of combining outrage, cynicism, humor, and commentary (and lots of brief musical clips) into a highly polished program that clearly connected with an audience. Ad rates for *The Rush Hours* tripled within a short period.

In 1988 Limbaugh attracted the attention of Ed McLaughlin, a former president of ABC Radio Network who was then working as an independent syndicator of national radio programs. A personal meeting dispelled McLaughlin's reservations about the pomposity of Limbaugh's style (which McLaughlin initially "couldn't stand"), and plans were drawn to bring Limbaugh to New York with a program packaged for national syndication. Tapes of the Sacramento show convinced station managers around the country that Limbaugh's brash, political insouciance could capture an audience. In a short time, McLaughlin succeeded in marketing Limbaugh to over fifty stations, more than enough to attract enough advertisers to ensure initial profitability; 1 July 1988 was Limbaugh's last show in California before moving to Manhattan and the premiere his of new, national, two-hour *Rush Limbaugh Show*. The contract for the first year guaranteed him $150,000 annually.

From this moment success followed success. Though the new program was slow to make an impact in the highly competitive New York daytime market, stations throughout the country reported immediate, dramatic audience response and increase. Arbitron ratings for 1990 showed that over one million listeners tuned in to *The Rush Limbaugh Show* during an average fifteen-minute segment, making Limbaugh one of the more prominent voices in national politics overall. Within four years, his audience would multiply exponentially, as new stations, now around the globe, continued to join the Excellence in Broadcasting Network.

McLaughlin used a highly successful strategy in bartering *The Rush Limbaugh Show* to stations that showed interest. No up-front costs were involved; all a station needed to do to receive the show was to guarantee that a certain number of commercials, often read by Limbaugh himself, would be included in each program. EIB then used each new station to augment its ad rates based on ever-expanding audience "penetration." Each local station also retained the opportunity to sell several of its own slots each hour, highly lucrative minutes with the nation's most visible gadfly. By 1995, the competition in certain markets for carrying the Limbaugh show—with over six hundred affiliates—was so great that stations offered to pay a fee for the right to air the show, altering the original formula.

Limbaugh's immense prestige within the media profession derives not from his politics but from his single-handed revival of daytime talk radio, a genre that in the late 1980s appeared to be altogether moribund. Now the fastest growing format in radio, ad dollars and audience figures approximately doubled between 1988 and late 1994 to over 1.5 billion dollars, with new hosts and programs following in the wake of the trail that Limbaugh and McLaughlin blazed. Before Limbaugh's success, the audience for talk radio, especially for the nationally syndicated hosts such as Arthur Godfrey or Paul Harvey, was made up mostly of homebound older listeners. Limbaugh, and the new generation of hosts who have followed, appeal to a much younger, more mobile population who tune in the programs in their car, at work, or in the hundreds of restaurants around the country featuring "Rush Rooms," restaurants that publicize the fact that diners need not miss their favorite program if they choose to eat out. In 1992 *Broadcasting Magazine,* featuring a story on Limbaugh and his audience, quoted a Detroit radio executive describing his baby-boom listeners: "They have short attention spans. They want to be entertained. They are turning conservative. And Rush is a mirror image of that."[8] (It is also claimed, however, that Limbaugh does not have the number or caliber of advertising clients that the size of his audience might attract. His strong ideological slant has deterred certain sponsors who have no trouble affiliating their products with, for example, Paul Harvey. That his contract as promoter of Florida orange juice was terminated after one year is an example of the difficulty Limbaugh has faced parlaying his success into the field of marketing.)

In one oft-cited capstone to his dizzying ascent, Ronald Reagan wrote Limbaugh a letter in 1992: "Thanks for all you're doing to promote Republican and conservative principles. Now that I've retired from active politics, I don't mind that you've become the number one voice for conservatism in our country." (At the time, Reagan perhaps did not know that the new paragon of conservatism had not found the time to register for the vote before 1988 and thus never had the opportunity to cast his ballot for the Gipper.)

Of the different lessons that Limbaugh learned in his path to fame, none was more important than an abiding belief in his own rectitude. Outside of the Christian broadcast networks, it is difficult to find any parallel in the media landscape where a host so constantly invokes privileged access to the truth to which he testifies and his audience bears witness. Rather than finding this sanctimonious approach offensive, a vast audience responds vigorously to Limbaugh's boast; listeners attest to their devotion every time they begin conversations with "Ditto" or "Megaditto from Akron, Ohio."

For a noninitiate, the intensity of this adulation may seem difficult to fathom. The auditory surface of any given Limbaugh radio program is a collage of editorializing, music, and calls (and about twelve minutes of ads per hour.) The substance of Limbaugh's gospel is a contemporary right-wing Republican interpretation of American society, leavened by his "rumpled, avuncular" humor. Although claiming to be a future-oriented, dynamic, optimistic creed, this ideology remains inherently reactionary, with a latent vicious and racist core. It derives its animus from the accurate perception by a vast number of working, middle-income Americans that their economic status is increasingly shaky. Limbaugh, himself no stranger to employment difficulties, expertly channels this anxiety away from its corporate substratum toward politics.

If 80 percent of the citizens fear they are losing ground financially, Limbaugh, like Wallace and Reagan, deftly connects their distress to both hypothetical and real failures of liberalism, national government, and the 1960s counterculture (now that the "Evil Empire" can no longer be demonized). Limbaugh himself becomes the model of what is possible: the possessor of enormous wealth resulting from hard work in a free, competitive market. Though they actively promote a dizzying array of ethical platitudes and books of virtue, the moral center of gravity for Limbaugh and his minions remains the vaguely Calvinist notion that wealth is the manifest sign of the pious. This is complemented by a devotion to the market and capitalism generally as the most perfect means of distinguishing the "elect."

If "decent, hard-working Americans" are not receiving their just reward, for Limbaugh, echoing Wallace, the reason must lie in a system that channels wealth toward the so-called undeserving. At the heart of Limbaugh's dogma is an unceasing attack upon the national commitment to equality. Rebelling against the Declaration of Independence, Limbaugh hearkens to an aristocratic sensibility that hierarchies of wealth and power are natural and efficacious. As Alexis de Tocqueville observed 150 years ago, U.S. democracy is a highly unstable situation in which the sovereign rights of individuals to act autonomously remain in dynamic tension with the collective commitment to equality. It is against this uniquely American synthesis that Limbaugh battles mightily, noting, with Tocqueville, that government policies that establish a more level playing field inevitably inhibit those who wish to begin the game with a wide lead.

The state as the primary agent fostering the ideal of equality within U.S. political culture—via taxes, social policy, or education—thus becomes the most important target of attack. Beginning with the premise that the pursuit of equity is socialist, Communist, or liberal, *The Rush Limbaugh Show* derives the litany of conservative complaints. Feminism—gender equality—is vile because it undermines the family unit, the center of moral training. Welfare—income redistribution—promotes a culture of indolence. Affirmative action—social equality—undermines honest evaluation of individual excellence. The failures of public education are beneath contempt. (After some vulgar satire about AIDS and the "Gerbil Report" brought about an immense outcry, Limbaugh has by and large steered clear of gay bashing.) Warning against the liberal "fascism of compassion," Limbaugh schools his audience to become champions of the heroic individual, inoculated against feeling guilt for the unfortunate circumstances in which some folks happen to find themselves, a situation inevitably blamed on their own lack of initiative and desire.

Unlike his great media predecessor Father Charles E. Coughlin, Limbaugh rarely voices his own substantive ideas about policy in his broadcasts. Indeed, his political ideas taken out of context are decidedly unoriginal and could hardly on their own serve to propel him into the public limelight. His "analysis" of welfare, affirmative action, socialism, feminism, public education, or the liberal "agenda" paint complex social and historical transformations in broad outline: "The last three decades are replete with examples of 'compassionate' liberal legislation that have brought harm to those segments of the population they were enacted to help—not to mention to the taxpayers in general."[9] His capacity for close scrutiny and attention to detail are reserved for parody, invective, and attack. (The possibility that the "free market" might itself be corrosive of the "natural" order of the family and other centers of ethical training is a historical question never a subject for the host's quips and jibes. This is an issue to which I shall return.)

If the content of his political message is unremarkable, *The Rush Limbaugh Show* has distinguished itself for two characteristics: One is the economic and technical transformations the show itself has wrought in the genre of talk radio; the second is the unique rhetoric Limbaugh has perfected, balancing indignation and megalomania into a seamless whole. For three-and-a-half hours a day, Limbaugh choreographs several dozen registers of huffiness and outrage into a tightly woven presentation of the day's news, a performance that is undeniably amusing; this serves as the "ironic" foil to his obsessive self-aggrandizement.

To be sure, his show may at times contain spirited debate about topical issues concerning, for example, the timing of the Federal Reserve Bank's interest rate increases, the presidential race, or questions over which conservatives are divided, such as ratification of the General Agreement on Tariffs and Trade (GATT). Limbaugh is at his best in these discussions; he has a nimble grasp of the sweep of current events, he has a wide range of informants in and out of government, and he can be an entertaining source of trivia about debates within the conservative ranks on topics such as Robert Dole's presidential ambitions. But unlike in earlier talk show programs, there is almost no airing of different ideological perspectives. For example, articulate environmentalists do not have the chance to speak over the air about CFCs and the ozone hole (which Limbaugh claims is purely a result of natural phenomena and hence no cause for concern). Nor, given the premise of the show—that Limbaugh is the most talented and perspicacious mind in the universe—need there be.

In one of the more thoughtful articles on Limbaugh's politics, Jon Meacham outlines the corrosive cynicism about the very possibility of democracy that is promoted by Limbaugh's umbrage. Placing "Limbaughism" within the orbit of the 1980s, the "Me Decade," Meacham argues that "Limbaugh comes out of a selfish world and urges self-absorption on the self-absorbed."[10] Although he calls himself, among other appellations, "the Doctor of Democracy," Limbaugh's aggressive and relentless attacks on government do little to foster intelligent civic understanding. As Meacham argues, a polarized, self-absorbed electorate splintered into mutually incompatible special interests is ill prepared to provide the necessary direction on major government policy.

Beginning with the assumption that liberals have succeeded in corrupting society generally, Limbaugh spearheads a response that is never less than vicious. There are, for example, countless elements of misogyny in his attack on feminism. ("The feminist movement was created to allow unattractive women access to the mainstream of society.")[11] His famous buzzword "feminazis," which he leveled at leaders of the movement, occasioned such a backlash that he was forced to plead that it was meant as an attack only on vociferous pro-abortion advocates. In a radio show in January 1995 he attacked the Antioch College dating codes attempting to establish guidelines for sexual etiquette. In classic Limbaugh style, he chastised this highly publicized gesture toward "politically correct" dating rituals: How dare any liberal college bureaucrat impede red-blooded men from exhibiting their "primal instincts"?

In his attack on feminism, as with so many of his other pronouncements, Limbaugh plays on his listeners' preconceptions and fears. As Walter Lippmann (quoting William James) explained incisively seventy years ago, the currency of the emerging mass media would be stereotypes: "All strangers of another race proverbially look alike to the visiting stranger... A diffuse blur and an indiscriminately shifting suction characterize what we do not understand."[12] Lippmann argued that the print media and the emerging wireless showed little interest in revealing the world as it is encountered in all its manifold intricacies. As daily life became increasingly disjointed, the media response was to fabricate a cosmos of stereotypes. The media's emerging function was not to work as an aperture presenting a realistic vision of the "world outside" or "the scene of action" (in Lippmann's terms) but, rather, to garner as large an audience as possible to deliver to its advertisers. The media's ability to do this increasingly relied on stereotypical representations (male "primal instincts," for example) that served to manipulate the audience's predispositions and latent anxieties.

This modernist critique retains its full force as an analysis of Limbaugh. For example, in telling a listener that Antioch College dating regulations were doomed to failure because they constricted the male "primal instincts," it is extremely doubtful that Limbaugh either had read the codes or studied the subsequent effects they may have had on student behaviors. He had no desire to engage in the practical, "real" issues at hand but, as is his habit, used a listener's comment to mock and attack the feminist premise of the right to control one's body—an ideal that flies in the face of "human nature" according to the radio host.

Limbaugh's engagement with feminism—if engagement is what one can call it—provides in miniature certain of the key features of his use of the standard tropes of conservatism. The patriarchal stereotype is deployed in a typical two-step manner: Foundational is the claim that there exists a natural—biological or genetic—order to social life ("primal instincts") which should never be subject to political regulation; second, this order is so manifest that it needs no justification. As with certain forms of religious psychology, one either recognizes the transparency of "the" truth, or one does not. For this reason, dissident callers are essentially extraneous on the program. There is no middle ground from which to engage debate because Limbaugh's presentation overall is not an "argument"; he does not present a thesis and evidence in order to convince someone that the world happens to be a certain way—that the women at Antioch are deluded about the real nature of mating habits, in this example.

The "analytic" style Limbaugh uses is well presented in the title of his second book: *See, I Told You So*. Liberals, feminists, and deluded college professors may persist in believing that social relations are historical artifacts and hence subject to human will—"dating codes," affirmative action, governmentality most generally—but they have not yet realized that at "the end of history" politics has assumed a new, digitized form of either affirmation or rejection.

Yet if suspicion of the liberal policies fostered under our system of self-government is one foundation of Limbaugh's creed, he never wavers in unabashed, obsessive promotion of himself as exemplar and oracle. On any given broadcast he alludes to himself dozens of times: as the single source of information his audience needs, as the only broadcaster telling the truth about politics, as America's most intelligent talk show host. ("Monday through Friday I do three hours of the most sophisticated, spontaneous, entertaining, and informative talk show radio in the universe.")[13] It may well be thought that this is another aspect of his postmodern iconoclasm. How can anyone take seriously the social commentary of someone who needs to preface every remark with a reference to his own infallibility? He must be mocking his own pretentiousness, one is forced to conclude. Like John Lennon's casual if rather impolitic remark that the Beatles were more popular than Jesus, Limbaugh's stream of pieties seem both heartfelt and utterly ridiculous simultaneously. ("I realized early on how right I have been about so much.")[14]

This ongoing balance, effortlessly achieved in each program, between passionate ideological conviction and overwhelming self aggrandizement are delicately poised at the foundation of Limbaugh's performance.

At the center of Limbaughism remains the particular ambiguity of his appeal: Is he a radio entertainer who uses current politics as the source of his comic material, or is he a populist using the media to spread the political gospel with a growing legion of adherents who either agree with his self-assessed brilliance or tolerate it as less significant than his overall message?

In an Internet posting, one "Dittohead" provides a reading or "decoding" of Limbaugh's allure, paradigmatic precisely in its ambivalence as the writer gyrates from politics to entertainment and back to ethics as he tries to account for Limbaugh's popularity:

> His fans, to be sure, are in agreement with Rush's overarching political perspective. Rush has won. The goal was never to effect social change. The real goal was to have an entertaining and successful talk-radio program—his way. You cannot get higher than number one. Everything else that occurs as a result is simply gravy... Rush's message is hard to swallow. It reintroduced individual decency and goodwill, stripped from us somehow over the past 40 years. It redefines compassion and makes it a personal quality instead of a government function. His message explodes in the face of everything we learned about how to achieve social balance. Above all, it taps into simple central beliefs we learned to hold in disdain. This explains Rush Limbaugh's phenomenal success—he restores to us good qualities we had lost.[15]

It is important to trace the labyrinthine logic in this encomium. It displays in miniature many of the contradictory elements both of Limbaugh's performance and of the way his act is perceived.

The precedent condition is that his fans agree with the political line. This identification ("Megaditto") enables Limbaugh to translate any attack on his politics or his program into an attack on his audience. However, politics is separated from "social change" in order to argue that the "real goal was to have an entertaining and successful talk-radio program—his way." The more grandiose ideological or political project is cast as supplemental—"simply gravy."

Yet though the writer argues that having an entertaining talk show is the "real goal," the closing sentences are actually much more revealing. This ethical claim that Limbaugh "taps into simple central beliefs" is one of the key clues to his massive appeal. Rather than alleviating the social problems that unequal distributions of wealth and privilege bring about, progressive social experiments, according to this ideology, have the devastating effect of snuffing out the spark of individual initiative while degrading basic standards of excellence.

Limbaugh has mastered the art of radio to disseminate the message of the essential goodness of the common person who can effect change if only allowed the freedom from the mindless bureaucracy and tax policies of the liberal state. He speaks of unleashing the latent individual compassion and goodwill now submerged under the embrace of big government. If one's capacities or career prospects are now blocked, then there is a simple cause: a bloated federal government, supported by its theft of "our" tax dollars, promoting a quota system that stymies personal initiative. As an explanation of white working-class resentment, the argument about the inherent injustice of "quotas" has remained a stock item in the appeal of reactionary populism for almost three decades. It resonates with such a large audience not on its merits alone, nor on any incipient racism in the U.S. body politic, but because of the larger economic framework in which it is embedded.

Linking the libertarian and populist elements in Limbaugh's discourse is an unceasing argument about the failures of the taxation system. ("I am morally opposed to taxes. The more I know about them, the more I see they are used for social experimentation.")[16] While the attack on "social experimentation" is another broadside against equality, its articulation within a harangue against taxes is significant. The federal government *has* failed to maintain a progressive tax system, with the result that wealth accumulates for those perched at the commanding heights of the economy. Middle- and lower-income wage earners *do* find themselves shouldering an increasingly greater tax burden for ever-diminishing government programs.[17] Thus, when Limbaugh inveighs against the government's fiscal policies, he is able to speak as a populist, publicizing a broadly held, accurate perception that the welfare and redistributive operations of state no longer serve the general interests of the great majority of the population.

Yet if it is populism, it is populism that hearkens to only one element in the historical populist critique that scrutinized imbalances in power in both the state and the corporate world. Absent altogether is any analysis of the realm of the economy proper, most especially the large-scale corporate and financial institutions that, far more than the state, might plausibly be held responsible for the loss of "decency and goodwill." Though Limbaugh inveighs ceaselessly against all forms of taxation, there is no critique of the larger macroeconomic factors at play in the contemporary geopolitical scheme. His searing indictment of social welfare plays into an undeniable anxiety felt by low- and middle-income workers in the United States confronting competition from both technological shifts and a global workforce. With the sustained attack on organized labor that began with the Reagan administration and the subsequent squeeze on the income growth of the majority of workers, ever more people in society yearn for some explanation for their apparently diminished life prospects.

Prior forms of populism, both of the right and the left, would excoriate both business (and Jewish bankers) as well as government for the economic burdens shouldered by the common man. This is not the case with Limbaugh, who, as his support for both the North American Free Trade Agreement (NAFTA) and GATT demonstrates, might be considered relatively friendly toward major corporate interests. After ruling out the economy itself as the site of social dislocations that have a potential or actual deleterious effect on the career prospects and wages of large sectors of his audience, what could be a more likely villain than large government, identified with the liberal welfare state? Sapping individual wealth and motivation, this state's primary raison d'être is defined as taxing honest, hard-working Americans in order to subsidize a stratum of indigents unwilling to pull themselves up by their own bootstraps.

The most elaborate compendium of Limbaugh's exaggerations, lies, and misstatements is Fairness and Accuracy in Reporting's (FAIR's) ongoing catalogue of inaccuracies from Limbaugh's books and programs.[18] FAIR's researchers have chronicled an ever-expanding list of faux pas ranging from remarks about health care to his mischaracterizing a school essay by Chelsea Clinton. This scrutiny has forced Limbaugh to retract or clarify his thinking on certain issues. If the question were simply getting to the core of whether America's poor are as well off as the European middle class, or whether the actual number of acres of forest land in the United States is currently greater than it was two hundred years ago—two points that Limbaugh has erroneously argued—one could at some point end the discussion with the appropriate data.

Yet even when forced to concede on certain mistakes, Limbaugh successfully uses his ratings as a gauge not simply for the popularity but also for the inerrancy of his overarching world view. His skill in manipulating stereotypes, combined with his listeners' insistence that the "real goal was to have an entertaining and successful talk-radio program," perpetuates a "know-nothing" attitude that mitigates the need for objectivity. As was Reagan in his effortless weaving of war movies and actual warfare, Limbaugh is surrounded by a Teflon shield, minimizing the impact by critics chronicling his "reign of error."

Indeed, his response to attacks by "the liberal press" is the claim that, alone of those working in the media, he deals with the truth. An example is detailed in an Internet summary worth quoting at length to discover how Limbaugh, and his audience, have handled his critics in the press:

> On Rush's TV show last night, Rush showed Sam Donaldson saying that he listens to Rush Limbaugh while at his New Mexico farm because Rush is entertaining; however, Donaldson then claimed the "new media," which Rush represented, never reports stories, but just yells at people, telling them just opinions.
>
> Donaldson then claimed that he, as a reporter, for the most part told people the facts and the truth, saving his personal opinions for his appearances on the David Brinkley show. He then ended up condemning the new media for not "getting its facts straight" like he and others in the mainstream news supposedly do.
>
> After Rush showed this clip, he responded on his TV show by saying that in his 4,000 or more hours of being on the air, he has had at most 43 "factual errors" alleged against him, and even that number is highly inflated. Rush thus would be more than happy to stack his record against anyone else's in the mainstream media. Rush then, though, pointed out that the reason Donaldson was discussing what Rush does was because Rush is doing the job that the media is no longer doing but should.
>
> This reminded Rush that one of the reasons his show is so successful is because the American people have such a huge distrust of the mainstream media.[19]

Keep in mind the claim that "Rush is doing the job that the media is no longer doing but should." His great success in casting his unabashed partisanship as the precondition to understanding the informational content of his program helps puncture one of the great sacred cows of the liberal media, namely, that the press should, and *could,* stand above ideology, reflecting as objectively as possible a true state of affairs that it neutrally reports. Limbaugh is at his most honest when he admits that he traffics in stereotype; this acknowledgment expertly neutralizes the chorus of attacks based on factual error.

Limbaugh is a textbook case of the proposition that one knows and judges the world only from a particular basis; one's "report" on any given state of affairs is directly affected by a range of circumstantial factors, subject to revision based on shifting ethical, political, geographical, and biographical standpoints. Though Limbaugh would hardly wish to be considered a materialist, his critique of the mainstream press is not all that different in form from what might come from a radical critic such as Noam Chomsky: The liberal bias of the media is ever more pernicious precisely in that it disguises its own stake in writing the rules of the game. Limbaugh refuses this gambit, making no pretense that his broadcasting is not ideologically situated. By celebrating his own bias, he is able to do the job that "the media is no longer doing but should."

To say this is hardly to argue that Limbaugh's ideological predisposition enables him to make more reasoned judgments about the nature of current events. There is no guarantee that simply making manifest one's own stake in competing claims over the nature of the real is itself enough to ensure informed or more truthful accounts. Arguing that one's standpoint is a decisive factor in producing "knowledge" does not eliminate the need for sifting and judging the evidence.[20] What it does potentially allow for is both a more honest form of debate about the practices of the media as well as closer scrutiny of the ethics of the self-proclaimed "smartest man in showbiz."

It is precisely in Limbaugh's relentless insistence on joining his principles, his observations, and his biography into a unified platform that one might begin the task of critique. Rather than attack his objectivity, one might cast greater scrutiny on his rhetoric and ethics. Can Limbaugh reconcile the claim that "morality is not defined by individual choice," that there are "thirty-five undeniable truths of life,"[21] with the equally strong affirmation that he personally is the arbiter of those truths, the supreme individual "chooser" of just which aspects of ethical understanding count and which do not. Limbaugh constantly refers to a "higher" source in justifying his position: "If there are no ultimate standards of behavior that descend from God, and if morality is merely individual choice, then life itself has lost its greater meaning."[22] Yet how does one come to those standards? "With my background, *I* am uniquely qualified to address [these issues]."[23] Unlike great conservatives of the past like Edmund Burke or Tocqueville, whose attempt to naturalize ethics relied on complex historical or religious argumentation, Limbaugh's imaginary relationship with God enables him to dispense with sophistry of this sort.

Is it possible to puncture Limbaugh's balloon, to measure him by his own ethical standards? How might one read the biography of someone who is a master of ad hominem attacks and professes to be the personal yardstick of excellence by which others should be measured "against the grain," as it were? A critique in this vein would quickly reveal that Rush has been incapable of acting on many of those thirty-five undeniable truths: a 1971 draft evader espousing the supreme value of U.S. military might; a thrice-married fellow with no children holding dear the virtues of family; a greatly overweight person, famously lazy and indolent in his private life, presenting a gospel of personal responsibility; a believer in divinely ordained morality attending no regular church; a nonvoter most of his adult life claiming honorary membership in the new Congress. While this list could continue, each item would demonstrate the same "contradiction": Limbaugh is extremely liberal in the application of the gospel he preaches.

Notes

1. Harold E., posting on the Usenet newsgroup alt.rush-limbaugh, 14 February 1995.

2. John Switzer, posting on the Usenet newsgroup alt.rush-limbaugh, 19 February 1995.

3. Murray B. Levin, *Talk Radio and the American Dream* (Lexington, Mass.: Lexington Books, 1987), 145.

4. What follows is based primarily on the Paul Colford's admiring biography *The Rush Limbaugh Story* (New York: St. Martin's, 1993).

5. Colford, *The Rush Limbaugh Story.*

6. Rush Limbaugh, *See, I Told You So* (New York: Pocket Books, 1993), 9–10.

7. Quoted in Colford, *The Rush Limbaugh Story,* 65.

8. "AM Radio's One-Man Come Back" *Broadcasting Magazine,* 4 May 1992, 55.

9. Limbaugh, *See, I Told You So,* 217.

10. Jon Meacham, "What Will Rogers Could Teach the Age of Limbaugh," *Washington Monthly,* February 1994, 18.

11. Colford, *The Rush Limbaugh Story,* 184.

12. Walter Lippmann, *Public Opinion* (New York: Free Press, 1965; originally published 1922), 54.

13. Limbaugh, *See, I Told You So,* 3.

14. Ibid., xiv.

15. Posting on the alt.R-L.usegroup of 5 January 1995. For the purposes of this chapter, I used the daily conversations on the Internet as a better source of information of the psychology of Limbaugh's fans. Unlike his shows, whose callers are highly screened, the more or less open access to the Internet means that opinions pro and con confront each other.

16. *The Rush Limbaugh Show,* 21 February 1995.

17. Donald Barlett and James Steele, *America: Who Really Pays the Taxes?* (New York: Touchstone, 1994).

18. Steve Rendall et al. *The Way Things Aren't: Rush Limbaugh's Reign of Error. Over 100 Outrageously False and Foolish Statements from America's Most Powerful Radio and TV Commentator* (New York: New Press, 1995).

19. Posting on the Usenet newsgroup alt.rush-limbaugh. 23 January 1995.

20. See William James, *Radical Empiricism* (New York: Library of America, 1992).

21. Limbaugh, *See, I Told You So,* 81.

22. Ibid., 83.

23. Ibid., 286 (emphasis added).

PART IV
RELIGIOUS RIGHT ADVOCACY MEDIA

RELIGIOUS RIGHT ADVOCACY MEDIA

Advocacy media varies in its form according to the power of those who diffuse it; different levels of funding influence the choice of propaganda medium and how it is distributed. Chip Berlet points out in Chapter 10 that secular conservatives have traditionally had more corporate funding than those spreading an explicitly religiously oriented political message, and so the secular right has access to think tanks and often to government advisory positions to get its proposals enacted, especially on economics and foreign policy. Another sector of the right, the "theocratic right," as Berlet calls it, uses both mainstream media and alternative media forms, such as documentary film and video, printed fliers and direct mail materials, fax machines, and phone trees, to promote a Christian-oriented society; like secular conservatives, these groups work within the electoral system; in fact, most of the groups discussed in *Culture, Media, and the Religious Right* belong to the theocratic right. Berlet also discusses the media activity of the "hard right": ultraconservatives, often promoting overtly racist, anti-Semitic, and homophobic messages. Since these groups on the hard right do not have the financial resources of the secular right or the theocratic right, they often use the Internet for communicating their views, and Berlet details some of the specific hard right sites on the Internet at this time.

In Chapter 11, Anna Williams presents the career and influence of one of the major figures on the theocratic right, Paul Weyrich, who now runs a satellite television station, National Empowerment Television (NET), out of Washington, D.C. NET offers regular shows by Concerned Women for America (whose work was described by Linda Kintz in Chapter 4), an economist from the Heritage Foundation, the National Rifle Association, and Newt Gingrich, who gives a daily report on government. NET describes itself as "interactive," but such interactivity is limited to the opportunity for listeners to phone in during certain shows. The information circulated nationally by NET is important for right political organizing in terms of influencing governmental policy (for example, on-air speakers can elicit faxes and phone calls to key elected officials on a moment's notice) and teaching electoral campaign strategies (for example, Christian Coalition members often meet to watch and discuss certain shows).

Julia Lesage, in Chapter 12, analyzes a series of leadership training tapes used by the Christian Coalition, noting these tapes' electoral "savvy" and the potential effect such training and face-to-face organizing might have on coalition activists. The Christian Coalition has been especially effective in establishing good relations with the mainstream press, and its leadership training tapes present a methodology for "framing" issues in a way that will win public favor for the conservative Christian viewpoint, now no longer presented using "theocratic" rhetoric. The consequences of such kinds of framing as they have been worked out in campaigns against homosexual rights are analyzed by Laurie Schulze and Frances Guilfoyle in Chapter 13 in regards to Colorado's anti–gay rights initiative, Amendment 2, and by Ioannis Mookas in Chapter 14 as evidenced in a propaganda film, *Gay Rights/ Special Rights,* comparing the gay rights struggle to African Americans' civil rights movement. As described by Linda Kintz, codified gender role definitions are part of the symbolic structure that unites the religious right, so it is no accident that these electoral initiatives against homosexual rights have elicited the active support of all three sectors of the right—the secular right, the theocratic right, and the hard right.

10

Who Is Mediating the Storm? Right-Wing Alternative Information Networks

Chip Berlet

Discordant themes of right-wing political ideology illuminate center stage action as public discourse shifts stage right. The success of the political and religious right in shaping public debates is in part due to a network of right-wing institutions that package and disseminate their propaganda using diverse modern technologies. Some right-wing information outlets have general public visibility, such as the *National Review,* Rush Limbaugh's radio and TV talk shows, the *Washington Times* newspaper, and to a more limited extent, Pat Robertson's *700 Club* TV show. The vast majority of right-wing media, however, seldom step from behind the curtain into the spotlight of mass culture; instead, they circulate backstage among specific subcultures. Nevertheless, the depth and diversity of alternative right-wing media have played a leading role in building a mass base for the reactionary backlash movements now negotiating the script changes for the U.S. political drama.

Change in the societal tug-of-war can be assisted by ideas, elections, or actions. In all three realms, the role of popular and elite information dissemination is critical, but the role of alternative media in this important process is often overlooked. The major mainstream media in the United States include corporate print media, with a core of nationally distributed newspapers, magazines, and books, and corporate electronic media, with a core of commercial radio and television stations, many of which carry nationally syndicated programs through networks.

The term "alternative media" has traditionally referred to dissident, topical, regional, and campus-based newspapers, magazines, newsletters, and journals; small topical or ideological book publishers (often with distribution primarily through mail-order catalogs); and small public, nonprofit, noncommercial, or college-based radio and TV stations. The underground and alternative press of the left and social liberation movements is better known, but right-wing alternative media also flourish. There are also millions of pamphlets, fliers, tracts, brochures, and other printed handouts and direct mail materials that play a role in popular propaganda and are a form of alternative media. The production of alternative printed matter has flourished in part due to the increased availability of powerful yet easy-to-use desktop publishing software for designing and typesetting print materials, coupled with high-speed photocopying and relatively inexpensive "quick-copy" offset printing. These new technologies have especially assisted in the creation of alternative small-run counterculture newsletters and magazines that call themselves "zines."[1]

The increased use of electronic alternative media in the 1980s and 1990s involved online computer systems, networks, and services; fax networks and trees; shortwave radio programs; networks of small AM radio stations, with syndicated programs distributed by satellite transmissions or even by mailed audiotapes; home satellite dish reception, providing both TV audio/video programs and separate audio programs; local cable television channels, through which nationally produced videos are sometimes aired; and mail-order video and audiotape distributorships.

What we call the political left and right include a variety of electoral political organizations, ideology-forming intellectual institutions, and mass-based social movements. Right-wing media, especially religious right media, may have fired the first semantic salvos in the culture war against the left, but it is first necessary to ask the question: What is left and right? Sara Diamond has offered the most concise definition, one that covers the widest variety of right-wing tendencies: "To be right-wing means to support the state in its capacity as *enforcer* of order and to oppose the state as *distributor* of wealth and power downward and more equitably in society. Throughout the history of U.S. right-wing movements, we . . . see this recurring pattern as one organization after another worked to bolster capitalism, militarism, and moral traditionalism."[2] Intent and effect are separate issues when studying social and political movements. For example, movements that pursue supremacy and power often rationalize it as promoting justice and democracy; this is especially true with forms of right-wing populism.[3]

In this chapter, the term "secular conservative right" refers to primarily electorally focused conservatives, neoconservatives, and reactionaries primarily motivated by issues involving economics or foreign policy and operating within the electoral system. Institutional examples include the American Enterprise Institute, the Hoover Institution, the Heritage Foundation, the American Security Council, and the Center for Strategic and International Studies. Secular ultraconservatives in groups such as the Reserve Officers Association and the John Birch Society anchor the right wing of this sector.

The term "theocratic right" refers to primarily theologically motivated reactionaries, usually Christians, who seek to impose on secular society their religious views on morality and culture but who still are operating within the electoral system.[4] Christian nationalism is a resurgence of the theocratic Calvinistic vision of settlers in the Massachusetts Puritan colony who banished free thinkers as heretics.[5] Institutional examples include the Christian Coalition, the Free Congress Foundation, Focus on the Family, Concerned Women for America, and the Traditional Values Coalition.

The term "hard right" refers to right-wing dissidents and revolutionaries primarily motivated by reactionary ultraconservatism, regressive populism, white racial nationalism, or xenophobic chauvinism rooted in white supremacy and anti-Semitism. Institutional examples include the Liberty Lobby and Aryan Nations. This sector includes the regressive populists in the patriot and armed militia movements, out to the far right, consisting of overt race-hate groups and organizations with revolutionary agendas, including various Christian Patriot formations, and groups promoting racist forms of Christian Identity.

Many groups in all three sectors have at least some philosophical roots in orthodox versions of Calvinistic Protestant Christianity, especially support for heterosexual patriarchy, individualism, and a free-market economy. The WASP has its sting. There is overlap at the margins of the sectors, and some ultraconservative political ideologues such as Pat Buchanan and Sam Francis draw from all three tendencies. Nonetheless, the secular conservative, theocratic, and hard right branches of the right each have distinguishing characteristics and operate as self-conscious movements.[6] There is a tremendous range of information exchange taking place within the long-standing and emerging right-wing alternative media, but not all sectors of the right use alternative media in the same way.[7]

Since the secular and theocratic right have greater access to corporate media, their use of alternative telecommunications media, although extensive, has been a less significant mode of information exchange than in the hard right. This is especially true with online computer networks, fax networks, and shortwave radio broadcasts. One reason the hard right devotes greater resources to alternative media is that their ideas are generally excluded from the corporate mainstream print and electronic media. In response, some hard right propagandists have developed coded rhetoric that avoids hot-button words and phrases. Among the topics where the hard right has been successful in repackaging its supremacist views for popular consumption are the Holocaust, alleged genetic differences in intelligence between races, fears over depleted tax resources drained by immigrants or welfare recipients, irrational conspiracist theories about secret elites, the globalization of the economy and government, and intelligence agency misconduct.[8] The hard right has a significant presence in cyberspace.

In contrast to the hard right, the secular conservative and theocratic wings of the electoral right have pursued a two-pronged strategy of cultivating a productive relationship with existing corporate media while also building alternative media, often linked into networks. These alternative media are used as a testing ground before moving ideas into the mass corporate media. An example is the theocratic right's testing of various homophobic themes before focusing on the claim that gays and lesbians want "special rights."

Secular Conservatives and Media Framing

Secular conservatives have launched themselves into cyberspace, with a major clearinghouse being the Town Hall section on Compuserve or the Town Hall Web page on the Internet. Town Hall is the best starting point for exploring the secular right online.[9] Town Hall contains articles and press releases from secular conservative groups such as the Heritage Foundation, *National Review,* and Empower America but also from a few theocratic right groups such as the Family Research Council.

Secular conservatives, however, have long molded public opinion in major traditional corporate media and large-circulation publications such as *Reader's Digest,* conservative commentators on radio and TV, and even through TV dramas such as *I Led Three Lives,* and *The FBI.* There is an important dynamic relationship between right-wing alternative media and the corporate media. Many of the conceptual frameworks and arguments used to marginalize left and liberal ideas in the media are first developed at think tanks funded by right-wing foundations and corporations. After these ideas are sharpened through feedback at conferences and other meetings, they are cooperatively field-tested within right-wing alternative media such as small-circulation newsletters and journals; responses to rhetoric in direct mail appeals are also tracked. As popular themes that resonate with conservative audiences emerge, they are moved into more mainstream corporate media through columns by conservative luminaries, press releases picked up as articles in the print media, conversations on radio talk shows, and discussions on TV news roundtables.

As the increasingly refined arguments reach a broader audience, they help mobilize mass constituencies for rightist ideas. This in turn adds to the impression that all fresh ideas are coming from the right, as there is no comparable left infrastructure for the refinement and distribution of ideas.[10] For example, between 1990 and 1993 four influential conservative magazines (*National Interest, Public Interest, The New Criterion,* and *American Spectator*) received a total of $2.7 million in grants, while the four top left magazines (*The Nation, The Progressive, In These Times,* and *Mother Jones*) received less than 10 percent of that amount, under $270 thousand.[11]

A good example of this process was documented by the National Council for Research on Women in an analysis of the way the false idea that campuses were under siege by radical "PC police" was constructed.[12] Ellen Messer-Davidow explored the way foundation-funded conservative think tanks dominate political discourse with claims that are frequently open to challenge on a factual or logical basis.[13] The increased demand for packaged information by reporters with diminishing resources to conduct their own thorough research and investigations has amplified this dynamic. As Lawrence Soley concluded in his article on right-wing foundations and think tanks:

> While the research of conservative think tanks isn't serious, their lobbying efforts on behalf of corporate contributors are... Although information on the shallowness of [conservative] think tank research is available to the news media, reporters appear to have turned their backs on it in order to get easy access to a sound bite or quote. Rather than asking think tank representatives hard questions about their funding and their lobbying efforts, reporters turn to them for their ideologically prefabricated opinions on domestic and foreign affairs. And that's the way the news gets made.[14]

The right often uses media campaigns to construct a popular view of dissident liberals and radicals that reframes them as outlaws. An example of this reframing process involves the environmental movement.[15] In the early 1990s the two environmental groups that came under the heaviest fire from the right were Earth First! and Greenpeace.[16] Right-wing alternative publications had been reframing the environmental movement for several years, and articles in mainstream media began to reflect this paradigm shift.

For instance, *USA Today* in April 1992 ran two opposing views of Rachel Carson's book *Silent Spring* on the thirtieth anniversary of its first publication.[17] After claiming Carsons's warnings about DDT were unfounded, author Patrick Cox, "an associate policy analyst for the Competitive Enterprise Institute," went on to frame Carson and the antitoxics activists as hysterical ideologues. An analysis of Cox's polemic results in the following:

Frame established for antitoxics movement

Persons who oppose pesticides and believe DDT is unsafe

- Reject science
- Are afflicted with "environmental hypochondria"
- Circulate "apocalyptic, tabloid charges"
- Have "no evidence" to back their "hysterical predictions"
- Use "gross manipulation" to fool the media
- Are "unscrupulous, Luddite fundraisers"
- Suffer from "knee-jerk, chemophobic rejection of pesticides"
- Create "vast and needless costs" for consumers and farmers

Frame established for pro-pesticide industry

Persons who do not oppose pesticides or DDT

- Are pro-science and pro-logic
- Have support from the "real scientific community—the community of controlled studies, double blind experiments and peer review"
- Are on the side of U.S. consumers and farmers and save them money

The rhetoric in other articles attempting to frame the environmental movement is equally biased and vivid:

- "Willing to sacrifice people to save trees."[18]
- "We are in a war with fanatics ... they will go to any extreme."[19]
- "Behind the Sierra Club calendars ... lies a full-fledged ideology ... every bit as powerful as Marxism and every bit as dangerous to individual freedom and human happiness."[20]
- "Blinded by misinformation, fear tactics, or doomsday syndromes."[21]
- "The core of this environmental totalitarianism is anti-God."[22]
- "An ideology as pitiless and Messianic as Marxism."[23]
- "Since communism has been thoroughly discredited, it has been repackaged and relabeled and called environmentalism."[24]
- "The radical animal-rights wing of the environmental movement has a lot in common with Hitler's Nazis."[25]

This type of countersubversive rhetoric exposes environmental activists to threats and assaults by angry persons inflamed by the scapegoating. This rhetoric also has consequences in the policy-making arena. For instance, in 1994 a right-wing campaign to block U.S. Senate ratification of the International Convention on Biological Diversity succeeded in stopping ratification by the 104th Congress. According to the Environmental Working Group: "Sudden and unexpected opposition in early August 1994 from 'wise use' groups and farm organizations" was based on a widely circulated report containing alarmist and conspiracist claims authored primarily by an associate of the neofascist Lyndon LaRouche organization.[26]

Hard Right and Apocalyptic Millennialism

The armed militia movement formed as the militant wing of the broad patriot movement following the government's excessive use of force against the Weaver family in Idaho and the Branch Davidians in Texas. Patriots, especially militia members, have an antigovernment agenda laced with paranoid-sounding conspiracist theories, many of which echo the apocalyptic millennialism of some Christian fundamentalists.[27] Persons in the patriot movement fear impending attack by government or U.N. troops and the establishment of a dictatorship as part of a New World Order. They distrust all mainstream media. The patriot movement, which coalesced during the Gulf War, makes aggressive use of alternative electronic media such as fax networks, radio talk shows, shortwave radio, and online computer telecommunications.[28]

Much of the information circulated in this sector of the hard right is undocumented rumor and irrational conspiracist theory, some of it merely paranoid lunacy, some of it based on classic white supremacist and segregationist legal arguments or anti-Semitic allegations of secret plots by international Jewish bankers that can be traced to the hoax text *The Protocols of the Meetings of the Learned Elders of Zion.*[29] Print sources frequently cited as having "proof" of the conspiracy include the *New American* magazine from the reactionary John Birch Society, the *Spotlight* newspaper from the anti-Semitic Liberty Lobby, and *Executive Intelligence Review* (EIR) and *The New Federalist* from the neofascist Lyndon LaRouche movement. Most of the contemporary conspiracist allegations in the United States are variations on the themes propounded in the late 1700s by John Robison in his *Proofs of a Conspiracy* and by Abbé Augustin Barruel in his *Memoirs Illustrating the History of Jacobinism,* which claimed that the Illuminati had subverted the Freemasons into a conspiracy to undermine church and state and create one world government.[30]

One of the earliest examples of the use of online computer networks for mass organizing occurred during the 1992 presidential campaign of independent candidate Ross Perot. Libertarians and populist conservatives, who appear to have strongly influenced the politics of early cyberculture and the Internet, helped circulate organizing documents and position papers for the Perot campaign, quickly reaching a large audience.[31] Perot's antigovernment themes also attracted support from some persons in the hard right who later went on to promote the patriot and armed militia movements. These preexisting online relationships were a factor in the use of computer networks and other emerging technologies by the patriot and militia movements, which was apparently the first major U.S. social movement organized extensively via horizontal telecommunications networks.[32]

A voluminous amount of information and numerous discussions about tactics and strategy for the armed militia and patriot movements moved across the Internet, appearing in Usenet newsgroup conferences such as alt.conspiracy, talk.politics.guns, alt.sovereignty, misc.survivalism, and alt.politics.usa.constitution. Eventually a militia conference was established at misc.activism.militia. Information also appeared online at individual BBSs set up by patriot and militia technophiles, tossed to multiple BBSs through FidoNet and other messaging and echoing networks, and appeared in commercial online system discussion groups and chat rooms.[33]

Not all scapegoating conspiracist theories originate on the right. Alternative analysts who merge the rhetoric of the right and the left in their conspiracist diatribes include Linda Thompson, Mark Koernke (Mark of Michigan), Sherman Skolnick, Dan Brandt, David Emory, Bob Fletcher, John Judge, and Ace Hayes. In a lengthy article on snowballing conspiracism in *The New Yorker,* Michael Kelly called this "fusion paranoia."[34] With the rise of "infotainment" news programs and talk shows, hard right conspiracism, especially about alleged government misconduct, jumps into the corporate media with increasing regularity. As Kelly observes: "It is not remarkable that accusations of abuse of power should be levelled against Presidents—particularly in light of Vietnam, Watergate, and Iran-Contra. But now, in the age of fusion paranoia, there is no longer any distinction made between credible charges and utterly unfounded slanders."[35]

A-albionic Consulting and Research describes itself as "a private network of researchers dedicated to identifying the nature of the ruling class/Conspiracy(ies)." A-albionic and the New Paradigms Project Web page, *http://www.a-albionic.com,* are run by James H. Daugherty, a mail-order distributor of printed matter who believes the Vatican and the British Empire are locked in a mortal battle for world control.[36] Daugherty's anti-Catholic bigotry tracks back to earlier allegations that the pope was the Antichrist.[37]

Conspiracist information circulates in online newsletters such as *Conspiracy Nation* by Brian Francis Redman and *The People's Spellbreaker* by John DiNardo. Glenda Stocks runs a computer information network pushing even more exotic theories. DiNardo's *The People's Spellbreaker* carries the flag motto "News They Never Told You... News They'll Never Tell You." *The People's Spellbreaker* sometimes consists of transcripts of radio programs. In the following excerpt, the text is transcribed from *A World of Prophecy,* a conspiracist radio program hosted by apocalyptic preacher Texe Marrs. The title was "New Currency: The Banksters' Way to Rob Us of Our Life Earnings":[38]

> **TEXE MARRS:** You know, most investment advisors don't understand how the money system works. They don't know of the problems being concocted by the New World Order. They don't know the Illuminati conspiracies. And they simply cannot address these things. But I've got a gentleman on the line, and I'll bet he has got some exciting information to give you. And keep in mind God's prophetic word, and see how these things are working out. David Dennis, I'm so glad to have you on *A World of Prophecy.*
>
> **DAVID DENNIS:** Well, I'm certainly glad to be on your show, Texe, and I bring the greetings of Lawrence Paterson. He asked me to say hello.

> **TEXE MARRS:** Well, good. I'm glad to hear from Lawrence Paterson. I get *Criminal Politics* magazine every month. I love to open that envelope and read that magazine. It's one of the first things I grab ahold of when it comes in the mail. David, you're the resident editor there. One subject of interest is the new currency. You're sort of ahead of your time. You've been warning us about a "two-tier dollar." I'd like to get into that a little bit later. But what is this new money, this new currency?
>
> **DAVID DENNIS:** The new money actually was introduced not long ago. However, it might come as a surprise to all your listeners that the new money was NOT introduced here in the United States to our public. Rather, it was introduced in Moscow [Russia], by the United States Treasury Department. And the idea was to have it serve as sort of a trial run, if you will. And, also, to let the Russian People know that the United States currency, which they depend so much on for value, will continue to be of value, even after this new currency comes online. So, it's quite interesting that our new currency would not be discussed [or introduced] here in the U.S. first. Instead, it was introduced in Moscow to the Russian People.
>
> **TEXE MARRS:** That is just INCREDIBLE! [rest of text deleted]

The information in this posting certainly is "INCREDIBLE!," but it is typical of the genre. Note the plug for Paterson's conspiracist *Criminal Politics* newsletter and the mention of the Illuminati variation of the long-standing Freemason conspiracist theory. Marrs is the author of a book on the Illuminati titled *Dark Majesty: The Secret Brotherhood and the Magic of a Thousand Points of Light,* described in an ad in the John Birch Society magazine as revealing "a secret society of grotesque rituals . . . whose symbol is the death's head—the skull and bones . . . their plot has succeeded beyond their wildest dreams."[39]

This apocalyptic tone is typical even in secular contexts. Consider John DiNardo's tag line to *The People's Spellbreaker*:

> I urge you to post the episodes of this ongoing series to other newsgroups, networks, computer bulletin boards and mailing lists. It is also important to post hardcopies on the bulletin boards in campus halls, churches, supermarkets, laundromats, etc.—any place where concerned citizens can read this vital information. Our people's need for Paul Reveres and Ben Franklins is as urgent today as it was 220 years ago.

The most zealous sector of the hard right is the far right or ultraright, which mixes scapegoating conspiracism with open race hate, fascism, and neo-Nazism. Even in this sector there is a vigorous debate over policy.[40] Critics often join the fray. One online skinhead conference is dominated by neo-Nazi skinheads but attacked by antiracist skinheads.[41] The screed of

Holocaust revisionists can be found posted in alt.revisionism, where they are isolated by the majority of Internet "netizens" (citizens of cyberspace), who wish to preserve intellectual freedom but refuse to allow Holocaust deniers even the smallest space to spread their views on other conferences. In alt.revisionism one can find the rebuttals to the deniers posted by online human rights activists such as Ken McVay, Jamie McCarthy, Danny Keren, and others. Ted Frank posted scores of carefully researched rebuttals to hard right legal arguments on alt.conspiracy.[42]

A few ultraright participants manage to post messages in discussion groups on the commercial services such as America Online (AOL), sometimes suggesting the mail-order purchase of specific antigovernment books and pamphlets with innocuous-sounding titles. When the material arrives in the mail, it is often accompanied by a list of other materials with white supremacist or anti-Semitic themes. This attempt to hide or encode overt race hate and anti-Semitism is a common tactic of the ultraright. The following excerpt from the Pennsylvania-based Christian Posse Comitatus newsletter *The Watchman,* which promotes anti-Semitic Christian Identity, was found on the homepage of the neo-Nazi Stormfront:[43]

> *"Meet the torch with the torch; pillage with pillage; subjugation with extermination."*
> *—Colonel William C. Quantrill*

> As we enter the fall season, which is incidentally the best time of the year to recruit new people, I feel it necessary to comment briefly on new developments nationally. I received a phone call this morning from an acquaintance who asked me if I would like to receive an interesting fax. I did and it regarded a newspaper article about a "Klanwatch" report. Joe Roy of Klan Watch alleges that more than thirty right-wing extremist groups are gathering information about governmental agencies and so-called civil rights groups. He fears that this intelligence will be used in a future terrorist campaign against these same agencies. This is also evidently the fear of many law enforcement agencies as I have been contacted by such officials who expressed their concern. My answer to them was that public servants are supposed to be afraid of the people; do . . . us no further harm and all will be well.
>
> I regret that it does not appear that government learned this lesson in Oklahoma City. There is currently legislation pending that will effectively outlaw free speech and classify such organizations as Aryan Nations, militias and the Posse as terrorist organizations.
>
> Prepare for the men and boys to be separated! I personally believe the militia movement to be a bunch of well-intentioned persons who have a bit to learn. It is all well and good to prepare for another Ruby Ridge or Waco but the belief that hundreds or even thousands of conventional soldiers will be able to stand down the United States Army is ludicrous. It also stands to reason that the feds are infiltrating the mili-

> tias as they did the Klans in the 1960s. Use the militia movement as a place to spread the truth and to meet people but beware the agent provocateur. The militias are also filled with the ridiculous rhetoric about "black helicopters" and even "space aliens" controlling the government from a secret base in the desert and so on. The helicopters were green at Randy Weaver's and at Waco and they were sent and operated by White traitors.
>
> While there is yet a little time arm yourselves and prepare to face some very difficult decisions. Knowledge is power; go to the Gun shows and buy the how-to books and learn the art of war. Live free or die!
>
> FOURTEEN WORDS!

An average reader might miss the neo-Nazi subtext of this posting. The "Aryan Nations, militias and the Posse" are lumped together and portrayed only as victims of demonization whose free speech rights are threatened. The Aryan Nations and the Posse Comitatus promote a vicious anti-Semitic version of the religious philosophy Christian Identity that often overlaps with neo-Nazi beliefs. The phrase "fourteen words" is a coded reference to the phrase "to secure the existence of the white race and a future for our children."[44] Notice that the author derides the "ridiculous rhetoric" of conspiracism in the militias, but points out a real example of government infiltration.[45]

The networking through alternative media implied in this text is as interesting as the ideological assumptions. A phone call leads to the receipt of a fax containing a facsimile of a text article. This in turn leads to an article in a print newsletter that is then posted on the Internet and ends up on the Web homepage of a sympathetic group in another state.

The gun shows mentioned are a major meeting place for patriot and revolutionary right activists, and though most attendees and display tables focus on weapons, a handful provide books, magazines, pamphlets, audiotapes, and videotapes servicing the armed hard right.[46] At gun shows different tables have different selections based on ideological loyalty, with tables featuring *The New American* magazine from the John Birch Society, videotapes of militia stars Linda Thompson and Mark Koernke, copies of the *Spotlight* newspaper, and overt white supremacist and neo-Nazi books.[47]

Radio is another vehicle for education and recruitment into various sectors of the hard right. Generic right-wing scapegoating theories are broadcast daily on mainstream commercial AM and FM stations, with programs featuring Rush Limbaugh, Oliver North, G. Gordon Liddy, and scores of similar hosts. Much antigovernment rhetoric flows back and forth on right-wing radio, and it helped create the mind-set that led to the growth of the patriot and armed militia movements.[48] Sometimes there is crossover, such as Colorado Springs AM radio host Chuck Baker interviewing Linda Thompson in

August 1994 about her plans for an armed march on Washington, D.C. to remove the "traitors" in Congress. Thompson later canceled the march and lost much credibility in the militia movement, but one Baker listener, Francisco Martin Duran, drove to Washington, D.C., in October and shot up the White House.[49]

Major purveyors of right-wing conspiracist scapegoating in recent years have included radio personalities Tom Valentine, Chuck Harder, Craig Hulet, Mark Koernke, John Stadtmiller, Norm Resnick, William Cooper, Linda Thompson, Jack McLamb, Tom Donahue, and Bo Gritz. Sometimes right-wing populist radio shows introduce hard right ideologues as innocuous experts. On his *For the People* syndicated program, Chuck Harder used notorious anti-Semite Eustace Mullins as an expert on the Federal Reserve. Harder's newspaper, tied to the radio program, sold several of Mullins's books—including one claiming that there was a Rothschild family Jewish banking conspiracy—for over a year. Yet neither Harder nor Mullins sounded anti-Semitic on the air.[50]

Many programs are part of elaborate information networks. For example, Tom Valentine hosts a daily talk show called *Radio Free America* (*RFA*) that is originally broadcast from WBDN 760 AM in Tampa, Florida. *RFA* is also broadcast on the shortwave band operated by World Wide Christian Radio (WWCR).[51] The *RFA* program is also carried by satellite into homes with receiving dishes.[52] Most people are unaware that audio programs can arrive through a home satellite dish simply by turning off the video and tuning in a specific audio frequency. Audiotapes of *RFA* are sold through the quasi-Nazi Liberty Lobby's *Spotlight* newspaper, which carries capsule descriptions of recent *RFA* programs in every issue accompanied by an order blank. Valentine is affiliated with the southern regional bureau of the *Spotlight* newspaper, but his on-air demeanor avoids hateful rhetoric.

WWCR carries mainstream evangelical programs along with hard right programs broadcast on several shortwave frequencies. WWCR played a key role in networking and assisting the growth of the patriot and armed militia movements in 1994 and 1995, airing a program by Linda Thompson and the program *The Intelligence Report,* hosted by Mark Koernke and John Stadtmiller, which was pulled off the air after the Oklahoma City bombing. A number of conspiracist radio programs are sponsored by precious metals commodities dealers and by persons selling gold and silver coins. The pitch is that precious metal is a secure investment to hedge against possible financial chaos and economic collapse that might deflate paper currency or cause bank failures.[53] Shortwave listeners can also hear conspiracism and scapegoating from WRNO, based in Louisiana; WINB from Pennsylvania; and several other stations.[54] There are so many right-wing shortwave radio programs that a progressive shortwave radio station broadcasting out of Costa Rica, Radio for Peace International, has a radio program called *Far Right Radio Review* devoted exclusively to monitoring and discussing the right-wing broadcasts.

Another emerging alternative media, fax networks and fax trees, were used extensively by the armed militia movement in its formative stages and continue to be utilized by the hard right and the far right. *The Spotlight* featured a cover story on the distribution by right-wing populists in New Jersey of fliers and faxes opposing a proposed state environmental law. According to *The Spotlight*: "Virtually overnight hundreds of thousands of copies of the flier appeared as if by magic on bulletin boards, store windows and fax machines throughout the state." The flier was circulated in part through a fax hotline operated by northern New Jersey resident Franklin Reich.[55]

Theocratic Right and Media Campaigns

It is a common prejudice that the religiously devout are neither intellectually nor technologically sophisticated. Since Christians have a mandate to spread the gospel of Christ throughout the world, there is a powerful motive to be on the cutting edge of new information technologies. The first printing presses with movable type were used to print the Bible. Centuries later Christian publishers followed the trend to the more flexible and efficient offset printing technology, replacing the older metal-type letterpress. Both mainstream liberal denominations and individual conservative evangelical preachers and churches moved into radio and television to spread their messages.[56]

Christian activism online is a significant phenomenon. Christian-oriented bulletin board systems (BBSs) were among the first wave of nontechnical BBSs emerging in the mid-1980s, and there are now thousands of local Christian BBSs, mostly aimed at local audiences. Commercial computer services also have active Christian and theocratic sections, such as James Dobson's parachurch ministry, Focus on the Family, which has a forum on America Online.

To be sure, devout Evangelicals relate to new technology in a way consistent with their worldview. Consider the following text from a letter from Dr. T. B. Boyd III, of the National Baptist Publishing Board, explaining to supporters the installation of a new computerized system:

> God has shown us His miraculous powers and grace by allowing us to behold the manifold blessings He continuously bestows upon us. His power over nature has given the blessed opportunity to see the change of seasons, thus testifying to His sovereignty... [With] transition to state of the art computer systems... [the National Baptist] Publishing Board

> is now expanding the capabilities of our Customer Service by adding a new software package called Contact Management.

Christian broadcasting began as a form of outreach to spread the gospel and reflected the long-standing division between mainstream denominations and the more conservative evangelicals and their orthodox cousins, the fundamentalists. Theocratic right institutions moved beyond evangelism and now operate more overtly political outlets such as the Christian Broadcasting Network and National Empowerment Television.[57] Christian radio stations play a significant role in building a mass electoral movement out of previously uninvolved constituencies of Christian Evangelicals and fundamentalists. For instance, James C. Dobson's daily *Focus on the Family* radio program is aired on hundreds of stations blanketing the country.

In the last few years many politically active white Protestant Evangelicals have made an effort to reach out to African Americans, Hispanics, and Asians. Though the basic themes of the cultural supremacy of straight, white, northern European, Christian male norms is unchanged, the overall rejection of genetic racism is an important shift. At the same time, theocratic groups such as the Christian Coalition have sought to build bridges to conservative and orthodox Catholic and Jewish voters. One result is that Christian radio in general often appears more sensitive to racial and religious bigotry than some commercial radio stations, although casual sexism and homophobia are still commonplace. In contrast, on some commercial radio talk shows the barriers to overt racial and religious prejudice have dropped quite far, so that white supremacist and anti-Semitic comments are commonplace. Bob Grant's AM radio talk show from WABC in New York is a good example. Grant was finally removed after ABC was purchased by Disney but surfaced on WOR, also in New York.[58] Homophobia and sexism are hardly considered a prejudice on many commercial radio stations; consider the wide acceptance of Rush Limbaugh's references to "feminazis."

Case Study: Marketing Homophobia

Reframing is just one of a set of techniques used by the right in media campaigns to demonize scapegoats as part of a combined educational, organizational, and fund-raising strategy. These strategies are honed in the right-wing alternative media before they seep into the mainstream media. The theocratic right's opposition to abortion is still strong, but homophobia has emerged as the most galvanizing and lucrative theme since the mid-1980s.

The theocratic right used sophisticated media techniques to attack President Bill Clinton's plan to end the ban on gays in the military. Because of Clinton's support, the fight against open inclusion of gay men, lesbians, and bisexuals in the military was used as a major focus of both religious fervor and fund-raising opportunity. Former Ronald Reagan aide Gary Bauer at the Family Research Council sent out one ad with the headline "Every good soldier knows you don't march through a minefield!" The text warned that "Bill Clinton's decision to lift the military's homosexual ban will erode civilian authority and weaken the fitness of our forces... unless you act now."[59]

For the theocratic right, keeping U.S. troops in the field protecting the free market, keeping women at home and out of combat, and keeping gays in the closet and out of the military are all family values ordained by God. The Free Congress Foundation, Concerned Women for America (CWA), Focus on the Family, Family Research Council, and other Christian right groups have long maintained cordial ties with military and intelligence officials, a relationship that flourished during the Reagan and Bush administrations.[60] These and other theocratic groups supported high levels of military spending to keep our country safe from godless communism, terrorism, and secular humanism. Reagan and Bush paid these groups back for their electoral support by appointing group leaders to government policy posts.

In 1992, for instance, President George Bush appointed former CWA employee Sarah White, a master sergeant in the Air Force Reserves, to sit on the Presidential Commission on the Assignment of Women in the Armed Forces. In that position, she became "a key player in winning the pro-family victory of keeping women out of combat aircraft."[61] In 1988 White wrote an article for the CWA newsletter, "Soviet Influence: Active in Our Midst," which warned that "the American public must not be caught off guard by the seemingly virtuous intentions of groups or summits promoting peace" since they might be part of a Soviet intelligence "Active Measures" campaign to weaken and ultimately smash America.[62] This Red Menace conspiricism translated easily to post–Cold War fears of a Lavender Menace.

The right had been formulating an antigay media strategy for years prior to the controversy over gays in the military. Antigay "No Special Rights" themes were developed over almost a decade of field-testing various slogans before they were used in several state campaigns against equal rights for gays. In 1992 in Colorado, after an infusion of right-wing propaganda and cash, voters narrowly passed Amendment 2, framed as a bill that would legislate "No Special Rights for Homosexuals" but that actually would have prevented gays, lesbians, and bisexuals from fully exercising their constitutional rights. After a vigorous legal battle, the U.S. Supreme Court eventually ruled that the law should not be implemented. An even more draconian homophobic measure was narrowly defeated by voters in Oregon. While homophobia is widespread in U.S. culture, the politicization of homophobia was carefully constructed using marketing techniques in a series of media campaigns that began in right-wing alternative media.

Articles in the right-wing alternative press escalated hyperbolic rhetoric concerning homosexuals starting in the late 1970s as gay rights activists moved out of the closet. Anita Bryant's early antihomosexual campaign caused a media flurry but couldn't sustain momentum.[63] Attempts to find the right formula to inflame homophobia continued, nonetheless.

Dr. Ed Rowe, author of *Homosexual Politics: Road to Ruin for America,* provides an example of rhetoric used to outlaw a targeted movement. In his book he states: "Homosexual politics is a moral cancer eating at the fabric of America. It is an unholy, satanic crusade... this evil movement must be stopped!"[64] Senator Jesse Helms's introduction to Rowe's book also demonstrates nonrational zealousness: "Homosexual politics continues in fanatical pursuit of its goal of carving out a new 'civil right' based on the sexual appetite of its adherents."[65]

Neofascist hatemonger Lyndon LaRouche was among the first in the paranoid right to move the homophobic campaign into the political arena.[66] LaRouchians spawned restrictive propositions that were placed on the California ballot and that were successfully defeated only after broad-based organizing efforts reversed early polls showing passage of measures that essentially called for firings and quarantines for persons with signs of AIDS. LaRouche even obliquely suggested murder as a tactic, writing that history would not judge harshly those persons who took baseball bats and beat to death homosexuals to stop the spread of AIDS. One 1985 pamphlet published by LaRouche's National Democratic Policy Committee (NDPC) was titled *AIDS Is More Deadly Than Nuclear War,* which turned out to be a repackaged attack on the International Monetary Fund and the Federal Reserve.[67] There are hundreds of other right-wing books and pamphlets that marginalize the lesbian and gay men's movements and frame them as threats to the American way of life.[68]

The right's major strategic ideological counterattack against gay rights began in 1982 after Free Congress Foundation (FCF) president Paul Weyrich asked staff member Father Enrique Rueda "to research the social and political impact of the homosexual movement in America."[69] The result, *The Homosexual Network,* was "intended primarily for academics and legislators," according to one FCF memo.[70] Rueda concluded that "the homosexual movement is a subset of the spectrum of American liberal movements."[71] Rueda was alarmed by "the extent to which it has infiltrated many national institutions."[72] One jacket blurb writer gushed that Rueda had revealed "the widening homosexual power-grab in our society."[73] Rueda's book served as the FCF's first campaign against homosexuals and was widely quoted in political and religious right-wing publications. Still, just like Anita Bryant's earlier antihomosexual campaign, interest soon dwindled.

The FCF conducted a marketing survey at the American Bookseller's Association convention in 1987 and found a consensus that Rueda's book was not selling well because it was "too long and expensive" and it needed to be "updated and include information on AIDS." The FCF responded with a marketing plan for a revitalized homophobic campaign built around a new, shorter book suitable for mass distribution. It would promote the idea that a "Homosexual Network is benefiting from AIDS to the considerable detriment of family life and our culture." The book was titled *Gays, AIDS, and You.*[74]

Gays, AIDS, and You was commissioned after the FCF concluded it was "a hot topic" and obtained tentative commitments from the Reverend Jerry Falwell's Moral Majority to purchase 5,000–10,000 copies and from the Conservative Book Club for 6,000–7,000 copies. Both commitments were "subject to their approval of the manuscript," according to an FCF memo date 20 May 1987. *Gays, AIDS, and You* includes text drawn from Rueda's earlier, seminal effort, *The Homosexual Network,* and new material on AIDS by Michael Schwartz, director of FCF's Catholic Center.

Though Rueda and Schwartz are credited as authors, according to FCF memos the book was actually compiled and edited at Storm King Press, then based in Washington, D.C. The FCF signed a $10,000 editing contract with Storm King Press, owned by Herb Meyer, whose writing skills were honed while he was an associate editor at *Fortune* magazine. Meyer was a former executive assistant to late CIA director William Casey.[75]

Although the FCF coordinated the entire process of producing *Gays, AIDS, and You,* an FCF memo reveals "the new book will show Devin Adair as publisher (which will keep FCF out of the Gay's [*sic*] clutches)." Devin Adair negotiated with the FCF for royalties from the derivative *Gays, AIDS, and You,* since it had originally published Rueda's *The Homosexual Network.* Promotion plans—including an FCF search for endorsements—went into high gear in July 1987, even before *Gays, AIDS, and You* was completed. As one draft letter from Paul Weyrich explained:

> You will find enclosed a prospectus of the new book and I would particularly appreciate it if you would be good enough to send me an endorsement by return mail. I realize that it is a bit unusual to ask for an endorsement on the strength of a prospectus, but time is of the essence. I should add that Dr. Ben Armstrong, President of the National Religious Broadcasters (NRB), has already agreed to help us to the maximum extent with the promotion of this book.

Beverly LaHaye, president of CWA, sent in the following endorsement: "The efforts of the homosexual network to gain special legal rights, to undermine family and church, and to resist sensible public health measures against AIDS has put our families and society under severe strain. This valuable book reminds us of the necessity to reaffirm our civilization's Biblical heritage."

A November 1987 FCF memo reported that over 1,000 copies were shipped to the Christian Connection for use "as a premium for this organization's fund raising." Some 350 copies were shipped to Pastor John Bussey for his consortium of "500 pastors opposed to gay rights" in the greater Washington, D.C., area.

A January 1988 FCF memo discussed various media appearances and promotions, including placing an FCF-written article in CWA's magazine along with an order form for $18.75 "Action Kits" to "Fight the Gay Lobby." FCF considered the kits "central to our marketing strategy for *Gays, AIDS, and You*. We will clear about $8 to $9 per kit—CWA will simply give us the orders and we will have the names forever" for the FCF's direct mail fundraising list. "The National Federation for Decency is reprinting the article and the side bar promoting the kits will include an 800 number which will increase the returns," noted the memo. "Focus on the Family will re-print the article in the March issue of their magazine, *Citizen*. Also Dr. Dobson will use our book as a premium." Author Michael Schwartz was also scheduled for an appearance on Pat Robertson's *700 Club* television program "with viewership of 31 million." John L. Swan of the Archdiocese of New York was reported as wanting to "do all he can to help with distribution" and providing "good leads." Senator Orrin Hatch, noted as a bishop in the Mormon Church, was said to have provided information to the FCF on how to "contact the leadership of the church," and the November 1987 memo by FCF's Bruce Frazer indicated he would "jump on it!"

The introduction to *Gays, AIDS, and You* warns: "The homosexual political agenda represents a radical departure from what we as Americans believe . . . a terrible threat—to ourselves, our children, our communities, our country . . . a radical, anti-family agenda."[76] The authors suggest the movement for homosexual rights is different from movements involving "legitimate" minorities, and using rhetoric that suggests conspiracy, they write:

> This movement is stronger, more widespread, more skillfully structured than most Americans realize. It reaches into our media, our political institutions, our schools, even into our mainline churches . . . And now this movement is using the AIDS crisis to pursue its political agenda. This in turn, threatens not only our values but our lives.[77]

Back cover blurbs include snippets from Senator Bill Armstrong ("An urgent warning"), Beverly LaHaye ("reminds us of the necessity to reaffirm our civilization's Biblical heritage"), and Congressman William E. Dannemeyer ("failure to affirm our heterosexual values not only is unhealthy, but could result in the demise of our civilization").[78]

An order form for the book *Gays, AIDS, and You* circulated by the FCF included a picture of a man at a desk, his face in shadows, and the headline: "This Man Wants His 'Freedom' So Bad He's Ready to Let America Die for It." The text added: "Our civilization stands in the path of his fulfillment as a freely promiscuous homosexual."[79]

In 1987, when *Gays, AIDS, and You* was published, FCF's Board of Directors included Coloradans Jeffrey Coors and Senator William Armstrong (R.–Colo.). *Gays, AIDS, and You* popularized many of the myths and slogans later circulated in public homophobic campaigns such as that which accompanied the Colorado initiative. The 1990s saw a significant wave of physical attacks on and harassment of those trying to raise awareness about AIDS or seeking human rights for lesbians and gay men.[80] The concerted right-wing media campaigns to frame gays and lesbians as undeserving outlaws helped create an atmosphere conducive to these attacks.

Conclusions

Advances in electronic technologies have given dissident voices across the political spectrum an increased ability to reach larger audiences faster. This in turn accelerates the ability of organizers to mobilize people into issue-oriented campaigns and more durable movements. Increased access to mass media by people currently left out of the political system is a positive change for those who value the democratic process.

Lack of education regarding the use of false propaganda and the process of scapegoating, however, does create problems. Much of the material circulated by the hard right is undocumented assertion, rumor, and conspiracism, some of it based on classic white supremacist legal arguments or anti-Semitic allegations of secret plots by international Jewish bankers. When demagogues, conspiracists, hucksters, and lunatics compete on an equal intellectual footing with rational persons of all political stripes who value civil discourse and documented arguments, informed consent is eroded. One curriculum that teaches young people about the manipulative techniques used by the enemies of democracy is Facing History and Ourselves, which uses as examples the Nazi genocide of Jews and the Roma (Gypsies), U.S. slavery, and the genocide of Armenians by ethno-nationalist Turks.[81]

Conspiracist mania needs to be confronted as a form of scapegoating, and all campaigns to demonize and dehumanize need to be challenged by persons across the political spectrum. The practice of field-testing scapegoating and marginalizing rhetoric in right-wing alternative media before moving it into the corporate media deserves further study as one way the secular and theocratic right have been able to manipulate and dominate public discourse.

Limiting access and increasing surveillance are not valid solutions to the problems created by the use of new electronic media by dissidents, at least not for a country that aspires to be a democracy rather than a police state. We should be especially wary of attempts to create panic and thereby peddle an erosion of civil liberties through hyperventilated anecdotes about terrorists and bigots who use electronic media. Only a tiny portion of online traffic involves bigotry, and the far right presence is disproportional to their actual numbers and influence.[82]

Because there are no visual or audio cues in online posts, it is more difficult to evaluate sources of information in cyberspace. If someone on the right posts a message full of inaccurate information, then someone on the left needs to debunk it with accurate information. Eventually the persons who post cybergarbage will be ignored or banished to newsgroups like alt.dittoheads. Filters are already being established. Some conferences and e-mail lists are moderated by cybereditors who delete material they judge to be inaccurate or objectionable, just as do print editors. There should always be forums that are completely open, but the future will see more online versions of magazines and moderated discussion groups where the industrious crackpots and liars are filtered out. And there will be moderated discussions between persons of differing political outlooks who agree in advance to certain civilities. The *Utne Reader* hosts online discussions and debates that follow this model. Cyberdemocracy doesn't need to be feared; it needs to be engaged. The norms of the Internet will evolve so that the demagogues and bigots will always have their storefronts, but the auditoriums will be filled with people who value accurate information and who want the type of open and honest debate that nourishes democracy.

Secularists need to accept that there must be space in the public square for persons who wish to express views that are faith-based. People should not whine that the religious and secular right are not playing fair because they have been better at using the new online technologies. At the same time, we all must insist that when it comes to the passage of laws and regulations, compelling state interest needs to be demonstrated through facts based on documentation and arguments based on logic. What needs to be confronted is the faulty logic and febrile arguments of the religious and secular right and the antidemocratic ideas underlying many of their mean-spirited proposals. We need better rhetoric, not stronger regulations. We need more citizenship, not more censorship.

Notes

1. *Factsheet Five* chronicles the world of zines and other specialized alternative printed matter. P.O. Box 170099, San Francisco, Calif., 94117–0099.

2. Sara Diamond, *Roads to Dominion: Right-Wing Movements and Political Power in the United States* (New York: Guilford Press, 1995), 9. Diamond's definition seems the most useful in describing the variety of beliefs often characterized as rightist. The right, especially as seen historically by the left, includes conservatives, reac-

tionaries, business nationalists, anarcho-capitalists, racial nationalists, theocrats, fascists, and nazis, as well as most persons who oppose strong central state action for economic planning or redistribution, value orthodoxy in cultural and moral norms, and support authoritarian state measures to enforce order. The left, especially as seen by the right, includes liberals, business internationalists, progressives, radicals, socialists, Communists, and anarcho-socialists, as well as most persons who support strong central state action for economic planning or redistribution, value diversity in cultural and moral norms, and oppose authoritarian state measures to enforce order. Some persons, such as anarchists and libertarians, have divided loyalities, especially over the issue of valuing orthodoxy in cultural and moral norms.

3. Lucy A. Williams, "The Right's Attack on Aid to Families with Dependent Children," *The Public Eye* 10, nos. 3, 4 (Fall-Winter 1996): 18.

4. For the distinction between the Christian right and the subset that is the theocratic right, see Frederick Clarkson, *Eternal Hostility: The Struggle between Theocracy and Democracy* (Monroe, Maine: Common Courage Press, 1997). Not all Christian evangelicals or fundamentalists are theocrats.

5. Roland H. Bainton, *The Travail of Religious Liberty* (Philadelphia: Westminster Press, 1951), 208–28.

6. For general background on various sectors of the U.S. right, in addition to Diamond, *Roads to Dominion,* see also George Marsden, *Understanding Fundamentalism and Evangelicalism* (Grand Rapids, Mich.: Eerdmans, 1991); Jerome L. Himmelstein, *To the Right: The Transformation of American Conservatism* (Berkeley and Los Angeles: University of California Press, 1990); James Corcoran, *Bitter Harvest: The Birth of Paramilitary Terrorism in the Heartland* (New York: Viking Penguin, 1995 [1990]); Frank P. Mintz, *The Liberty Lobby and the American Right: Race, Conspiracy, and Culture* (Westport, Conn.: Greenwood Press, 1985); Leo P. Ribuffo, *The Old Christian Right: The Protestant Hard Right from the Great Depression to the Cold War* (Philadelphia: Temple University Press, 1983); James A. Aho, *The Politics of Righteousness: Idaho Christian Patriotism* (Seattle: University of Washington Press, 1990). A useful article on racial nationalism is by Leonard Zeskind, "White-Shoed Supremacy," *The Nation,* 10 June 1996, 21–24. For a short overview on various sectors of the contemporary right and the culture war, see Chip Berlet and Margaret Quigley, "Theocracy and White Supremacy," in *Eyes Right! Challenging the Right Wing Backlash* (Boston: South End Press, 1995), 15–43.

7. Detailed articles on the general theme of right-wing media can be found in *Afterimage* (Visual Studies Workshop, Rochester, N.Y.), special issue on "Fundamentalist Media," 22, nos. 7, 8 (February-March 1995); and *Extra!* (Fairness and Accuracy in Reporting), special issue on "The Right-Wing Media Machine," March-April 1995; and Jim Danky and John Cherney, "Beyond Limbaugh: The Hard Right's Publishing Spectrum," *Reference Services Review* (Spring 1996): 43–56.

8. Sensible debates can address power elites, sovereignty, globalization, and intelligence agency abuses. Here we refer only to conspiracist allegations based on myth, rumor, irrational conjecture, arguments that employ fallacies of debate, or outright hucksterism.

9. All citations of addresses in cyberspace and radio frequencies were accurate when the information was collected, but these are ephemeral locations and may have changed by the time you read this. A regularly updated list of links to Web pages of various groups on the right is posted by Political Research Associates at *http://www.publiceye.org/lnk_dem.html* and by Hatewatch at *http://hatewatch.org*. For radio programs, consult Far Right Radio Review online at *http://www.clark.net/pub/cwilkins/rfpi/frwr.html.*

10. David Callahan, "Liberal Policy's Weak Foundations: Fighting the 'Bull Curve,'" *The Nation,* 13 November 1995, 568–72.

11. Beth Schulman, "Foundations for a Movement: How the Right Wing Subsidizes Its Press," *Extra!,* special issue on "The Right-Wing Media Machine," March–April 1995, 11. Attempts to call *The New Republic* a left magazine will be met with laughter.

12. *To Reclaim a Legacy of Diversity: Analyzing the "Political Correctness" Debates in Higher Education* (Washington, D.C.: National Council for Research on Women, 1993).

13. Ellen Messer-Davidow, "Manufacturing the Attack on Liberalized Higher Education," *Social Text* (Fall 1993): 40–80, and "Who (Ac)Counts and How," *MMLA* (the Journal of the Midwest Modern Language Association) (Spring 1994).

14. Lawrence Soley, "Right-Think Inc.," *City Pages* (Minneapolis, Minn.), 31 October 1990, 10.

15. Portions of this section were originally published in *Covert Action Quarterly* and *The Humanist.*

16. Johan Carlisle, "Bombs, Lies, and Body Wires: Targetting the Environmental Movement," *Covert Action Information Bulletin* (now *Covert Action Quarterly*), no. 38 (Fall 1991). See also Chip Berlet, "Hunting the Green Menace," *The Humanist,* July-August 1991; Chip Berlet and William K. Burke, "Corporate Fronts: Inside the Anti-Environmental Movement," *Greenpeace,* January-March 1992; Sheila O'Donnell, "Targetting Environmentalists: Activists Charge Corporate Goon Squad in Florida," *Covert Action Information Bulletin* (now *CovertAction Quarterly*) (Summer 1992).

17. *USA Today,* 14 April 1992.

18. Cited in Margaret Knox, "Meet the Anti-Greens: The 'Wise Use' Movement Fronts for Industry," *The Progressive,* October 1991, 22.

19. Cited in Howard Goldenthal, "Polarizing the Public Debate to Subvert Ecology Activism," *NOW* (Toronto), 13–19 July 1989, 21.

20. Virginia I. Postrel, "The Green Road To Serfdom," *Reason,* April 1990, 22.

21. Merrill Sikorski, "Neo-Environmentalism: Balancing Protection and Development," *American Freedom Journal,* December 1988–January 1989, 8.

22. Edward C. Krug, "Save the Planet, Sacrifice the People: The Environmental Party's Bid for Power," *Imprimis* (Hillsdale College, Michigan), July 1991, 5.

23. Llewellyn H. Rockwell Jr., "An Anti-Environmentalist Manifesto," *From the Right* (newsletter of Patrick J. Buchanan), 1, no. 6 (2d quarter 1990): 1.

24. Walter E. Williams, column distributed for publication 4 June 1991, as reprinted in *Summit Journal,* July 1991, 3, citing Rockwell, "An Anti-Environmentalist Manifesto."

25. Ibid., 4.

26. Daniel J. Barry and Kenneth A. Cook, *How the Biodiversity Treaty Went Down: The Intersecting Worlds of 'Wise Use' and Lyndon LaRouche*" (Washington, D.C.: Environmental Working Group, 1994), 1.

27. Daniel Junas, "Rise of the Citizen Militias: Angry White Guys with Guns," *Covert Action Quarterly* (Spring 1995); Chip Berlet and Matthew N. Lyons, "Militia Nation," *The Progressive,* June 1995, 22–25; Kenneth S. Stern, *A Force upon the Plain: The American Militia Movement and the Politics of Hate* (New York: Simon and Schuster, 1996).

28. See Brian E. Albrecht, "Hate Speech," *The Plain Dealer* (Cleveland), 11 June 1995, 1, 16–17.

29. Eric Ward, ed., *Conspiracies: Real Grievances, Paranoia, and Mass Movements* (Seattle, Wash.: Northwest Coalition against Malicious Harassment [Peanut But-

ter Publishing], 1996). On *The Protocols,* see Norman Cohn, *Warrant for Genocide* (New York: Harper and Row, 1969).

30. On nativist roots, see Ray Allen Billington, *The Origins of Nativism in the United States, 1800–1844* (New York: Arno Press, 1974); John Higham, *Strangers in the Land: Patterns of American Nativism, 1860–1925* (New York: Atheneum, 1972); David H. Bennett, *The Party of Fear: The American Far Right from Nativism to the Militia Movement* (New York: Vintage Books, 1995 [1988]); Richard Hofstadter, "The Paranoid Style in American Politics," in *The Paranoid Style in American Politics and Other Essays* (New York: Knopf, 1965); David Brion Davis, "Some Themes of Counter-Subversion: An Analysis of Anti-Masonic, Anti-Catholic, and Anti-Mormon Literature," in David Brion Davis, ed., *The Fear of Conspiracy* (Ithaca, N.Y.: Cornell University Press, 1971), 9–22.

31. On Perot's online support, author's monitoring of political postings on the Internet and various bulletin board system (BBS) conferences. On the libertarian influence on cyberculture, November 1996 conversation with Paulina Borsook based on her forthcoming book.

32. Some of my research into the right wing online was carried out in preparation for an interview by Grant Kester that appeared as "Net Profits: Chip Berlet Tracks Computer Networks of the Religious Right," *Afterimage,* February-March 1995, 8–10.

33. A BBS in its simplest form is a single computer hooked to a phone line through a modem that allows off-site computer users with a modem to connect through a phone line to a menu-driven list of information and messages. More elaborate BBSs can handle multiple phone lines, and some are networked through systems such as FidoNet or linked into the Internet. For an excellent overview of the phenomenon, see Todd J. Schroer, "White Racialists, Computers, and the Internet." Paper presented at American Sociological Association annual meeting, Toronto, 1997.

34. Michael Kelly, "The Road to Paranoia," *The New Yorker,* 19 June 1995, 60–70.

35. Ibid., 66. Kelly, in his *New Yorker* article, writes of this phenomenon of seepage from alternative to mainstream in terms of conspiracist antigovernment allegations.

36. David McHugh, "Conspiracy Theories Grow," *Detroit Free Press,* 29 April 1995.

37. Davis, *The Fear of Conspiracy,* 9–22.

38. From *A World of Prophecy,* hosted by Texe Marrs, broadcast over WWCR, 5.065 megahertz shortwave, 23 December 1995, 8:00 P.M. eastern standard time. Downloaded in late 1995 from alt.conspiracy and posted to private e-mail list of persons studying the far right. Original posting by John DiNardo. Spelling corrected as a courtesy.

39. Ad for Texe Marrs, *Dark Majesty: The Secret Brotherhood and the Magic of a Thousand Points of Light* in *The New American,* 5 October 1992, 41.

40. Betty A. Dobratz and Stephanie Shanks-Meile, "Conflict in the White Supremacist/Racialist Movement in the United States," *International Journal of Group Tensions* 25, no. 1 (1995): 57–75.

41. In the United States many skinheads are culturally identified youth rebels who are not explicitly racist and who in some cases are actively antiracist.

42. Rebuttals to Holocaust deniers is collected globally at *http://www.nizkor.org.*

43. Newsletter from Fall 1995, located and downloaded in early 1996 and posted on private e-mail list for persons studying the far right. Stormfront homepage was at the time *http://www.stormfront.org/watchman/watch-on.html.* Spelling and punctuation corrected as a courtesy.

44. According to the Coalition for Human Dignity, the phrase "fourteen words" is a coded white supremacist greeting that originated with David Lane, a member of the Neo-Nazi terror cell the Order. Another coded phrase is "88," in which "8" represents the eighth letter in the alphabet; thus, "HH" for "Heil Hitler."

45. Although the FBI infiltrated some ultraright groups during the 1960s and 1970s, it also formed alliances with the paramilitary right to infiltrate left groups and people-of-color groups, which sometimes faced extralegal and sometimes lethal repression not experienced by the right until the 1980s. See, for example, Frank J. Donner, *The Age of Surveillance: The Aims and Methods of America's Political Intelligence System* (New York: Knopf, 1980); Ward Churchill and Jim Vander Wall, *Agents of Repression: The FBI's Secret Wars against the Black Panther Party and the American Indian Movement* (Boston: South End Press, 1988); Kenneth O'Reilly, *"Racial Matters": The FBI's Secret File on Black America, 1960–1972* (New York: Free Press, 1988); Ward Churchill and Jim Vander Wall, *COINTELPRO Papers: Documents from the FBI's Secret Wars against Dissent in the United States* (Boston: South End Press, 1989); Brian Glick, *War at Home: Covert Action against U.S. Activists and What We Can Do about It* (Boston: South End Press, 1989).

46. Kristen Rand, *Gun Shows in America: Tupperware® Parties for Criminals* (Washington, D.C.: Violence Policy Center, 1996).

47. Author's visit to gun shows in Ohio and Massachusetts.

48. Leslie Jorgensen, "AM Armies," *Extra*!, March-April 1995, 2022; Larry Smith, "Hate Talk," *Extra!,* March-April 1995, 23; Ed Vulliamy, "Clinton Tackles the Mighty Right," *The Observer* (London), 30 April 1995, 16; Steve Lipsher, "The Radical Right," *The Denver Post,* 22 January 1995.

49. Jorgensen, "AM Armies."

50. Marc Cooper, "The Paranoid Style," *The Nation,* 10 April 1995, 486–92; William H. Freivogel, "Talking Tough on 300 Radio Stations, Chuck Harder's Show Airs Conspiracy Theories," *St. Louis Post Dispatch,* 10 May 1995.

51. Through 1996, at shortwave band 5.065 kHz .

52. Satcom1, transponder 15, audio channel 7.56.

53. David McHugh and Nancy Costello, "Radio Host off the Air; Militia Chief May Be Out," *Detroit Free Press,* 29 April 1995.

54. The author monitors far right shortwave broadcasts on a Radio Shack DX-390. See also James Latham, "The Rise of Far-Right/Hate Programming on the Shortwave Bands,"*Vista* (Radio for Peace International, RFPI), October 1994, 24. Contact RFPI, P.O. Box 20728, Portland, Ore., 97220.

55. *The Spotlight,* November 12, 1995, 1.

56. Sara Diamond, *Spiritual Warfare: The Politics of the Christian Right* (Boston: South End Press, 1989), 1–4.

57. *Extra!,* March/April 1995.

58. *Extra!* Update, June 1996, 3.

59. Direct mail fund-raising letter on file at Political Research Associates.

60. See generally Diamond, *Roads to Dominion* and *Spiritual Warfare*; Tom Barry, Deb Preusch, and Beth Sims, *The New Right Humanitarians* (Albuquerque, N.M.: The Resource Center, 1986).

61. CWA, "*Family Voice,*" January 1993, 27.

62. CWA, *Concerned Women,* March 1988, back cover. For a Christian critique of this type of conspiracism, see Bruce Barron, "A Summary Critique," *Christian Research Journal,* Winter 1993: 44–45.

63. Jean Hardisty, "Constructing Homophobia," *The Public Eye,* March 1993, 1–10, collected in Chip Berlet, ed., *Eyes Right! Challenging the Right Wing Backlash* (Boston: South End Press, 1995), 86–104.

64. Ed Rowe, *Homosexual Politics: Road to Ruin for America* (Herndon, Va.: Growth Book and Tape Co., [Church League of America-Washington, D.C., office], 1984), back cover.

65. Ibid., 4.

66. Dennis King, *Lyndon LaRouche and the New American Fascism* (New York: Doubleday, 1989); Chip Berlet and Joel Bellman, *Lyndon LaRouche: Fascism Wrapped in an American Flag* (Boston: PRA, 1989).

67. National Democratic Policy Committee, *AIDS Is More Deadly than Nuclear War* (Washington, D.C.: NDPC, 1985).

68. See, for instance, Stanley Monteith, *AIDS: The Unnecessary Epidemic—America under Seige* (Sevierville, Tenn.: Covenant House Books, 1991); Tim LaHaye, *The Unhappy Gays* (Wheaton, Ill.: Tyndale House Publishers, 1978); David A. Noebel, *The Homosexual Revolution* (Tulsa, Okla.: American Christian College Press, 1977). See also various pamphlets and reprints from the John Birch Society, including "The Truth about AIDS," *The New American,* 31 August 1987, and *What They Are Not Telling You about AIDS,* a pamphlet reprinting articles from the 19 January 1987 issue of *The New American.*

69. Enrique T. Rueda, *The Homosexual Network: Private Lives and Public Policy* (Old Greenwich, Conn.: Adair, 1982), xv.

70. All FCF memos and letters to the FCF mentioned throughout this chapter were obtained from a source close to the FCF and are on file at PRA.

71. Rueda, *The Homosexual Network,* 18.

72. Ibid., 15.

73. Ibid., back cover.

74. Enrique T. Rueda and Michael Schwartz, *Gays, AIDS, and You* (Old Greenwich, Conn.: Adair, 1987).

75. The FCF claimed no knowledge of Meyer's role in the book and stated that Rueda and Schwartz were the authors.

76. Rueda and Schwartz, *Gays, AIDS, and You,* 7.

77. Ibid., 8.

78. Ibid., back cover.

79. Ad for *Gays, AIDS, and You,* from the FCF, circa 1988, as reproduced in Russ Bellant, *The Coors Connection* (Boston: South End Press, 1991), 65.

80. Esther Kaplan, "Act Up under Seige—Phone Harassment, Death Threats, Police Violence: Is the Government out to Destroy This Group?," *Village Voice,* 16 July 1991, 35–36.

81. The curriculum and process of Facing History and Ourselves is analyzed in Melinda Fine, *Habits of Mind: Struggling over Values in America's Classrooms* (San Francisco: Jossey-Bass, 1995).

82. Devin Burghardt, "Cyberhate: A Reappraisal," *The Dignity Report* (Coalition for Human Dignity) (Fall 1996): 12–16; Wayne Madsen, "The Battle for Cyberspace: Spooks v. Civil Liberties and Social Unrest," *Covert Action Quarterly* (Winter 1996–97).

11

Conservative Media Activism: The Free Congress Foundation and National Empowerment Television

Anna Williams

National Empowerment Television (NET), a satellite television station that since its beginning in 1991 has emerged as one of the most powerful forces in conservative media, started as a subscription satellite service. It was developed by the Free Congress Foundation to transmit activist programming organized around specific lobbying tasks. NET, which presents itself as television for political "outsiders," empowers its viewers by providing unmediated access to national government. Unlike C-SPAN, which broadcasts congressional proceedings, NET's programming consists largely of news shows in which "experts" report on a variety of legislative issues. These experts function to decode current political events, providing an insider's perspective for viewers who are assumed to be uninformed about the real nature of the political system. The programs thus perpetuate the idea that political power depends on access to restricted information. NET is just one of a set of new technological initiatives in the conservative "ideas industry": a vertically integrated system that produces and disseminates conservative ideas.[1]

In the early 1970s alignments of political power in the United States began to change dramatically; economic productivity was declining in the face of an increasingly competitive global economy, and the country was beginning to suffer from the new phenomenon of stagflation, that is, simultaneous unemployment and inflation, due in part to increased oil prices. Internationally, U.S. prestige was at a low ebb after two costly failed wars in Korea and Vietnam. The configuration of electoral politics was changing as the Democratic coalition began to disintegrate under the pressure of demands for racial, gender, and sexual equality.

The nomination of the conservative Arizona senator Barry Goldwater as the Republican presidential candidate for the 1964 election brought conservatives together around a common cause and initiated a nationwide conservative political organization. Although Goldwater lost the election, his nomination signaled the possibility of a triumphant conservatism in the Republican Party and the White House. However, during the Nixon administration conservative Republicans saw their influence in government diminish. They recognized the key role played by the orthodox Republican American Enterprise Institute (AEI) and by the more liberal Brookings Institute in giving mainstream Republicans access to government. These think tanks demonstrated the need for conservatives to consolidate their resources and form similar institutions.

This desire for an organized intellectual and administrative apparatus is demonstrated in a 1972 memo sent to President Richard Nixon by his then-speechwriter Patrick Buchanan. Buchanan called for the creation of a permanent "New Majority" and told the president that Republicans needed "a new 'cadre' of Republican governmental professionals who can survive this administration and be prepared to take over future ones."[2] Buchanan pointed out that since there was no ready supply of conservative experts to work in government, an organization was needed to train them, to act as a repository of conservative ideas, and to provide a "talent bank" for future governments.[3] This desire to organize was strengthened by Nixon's perceived slide to the center on welfare legislation, notably the passing of the Family Assistance Plan and the Child Development Act, and his perceived "softness" on communism as demonstrated by his 1972 visit to China.

Out of this climate of political frustration and opportunism, conservatives began to establish an "ideas industry"—in the form of various research institutes—and the mechanisms necessary to disseminate and implement those ideas (that is, a sophisticated distribution network made up of conservative books, journals, policy reports, college newspapers, and TV shows). Building on and working side by side with this information infrastructure, conservative political organizing began to capitalize on voter apathy by mobilizing demographically targeted segments of the electorate with campaigns that pivot on divisive social issues. It is within the context of this ideas industry that I will examine NET.

The increased organizational activity of conservatives from the 1970s onward is to a large degree due to corporate patronage.[4] The 1970s were marked by the political mobilization of business behind an aggressive agenda of tax cuts and deregulation that transcended the narrow interests of particular companies or industries. It was this mobilization that provided new financial resources for conservatives and allowed the movement's organizers to translate their plans into action, through an apparatus of interlocking organizations for the production, dissemination, and application of conservative ideas. The publicity that has been accorded to a small number of conservative patrons (for example, members of the Coors family and Richard Mellon Scaife) should not obscure the degree to which the last twenty years of conservative patronage is part of a wider structural change in corporate and foundation philanthropy that transcends the idiosyncrasies of individual benefactors.

Conservative discontent over the inadequate marketing of their ideas was complemented by a vigorous demand by U.S. business and industry to reeducate the public about the virtues of unrestricted capitalism. Referring to a study of business seminars from 1974–1975, Jerome Himmelstein describes a widespread perception that

> public approval and understanding of business was at a low ebb. The root cause they [executives] believed, was "failure of communication": the media, universities, and businessmen themselves had not communicated to the people the importance of capitalist enterprise and private profit to their lives and well-being.[5]

As one businessman put it: "We have been successful in selling products, but not ourselves."[6] The growth of the conservative ideas industry is in part a response to this corporate demand for better marketing.

The mobilization of business was evident in the organization in 1972 of the Business Roundtable, a corporate lobbying group that addressed a variety of legislative issues[7] and the growth in corporate-funded political action committees (PACs) to support pro-business candidates. In 1974 labor PACs outnumbered corporate PACs by 201 to 89, but by 1984 the picture was dramatically reversed, with corporate PACs outnumbering labor PACs by more than 4 to 1 and the spending of the former ($84.9 million) more than double that of the latter ($35 million).[8] Corporate philanthropy extended beyond the apparently narrow pragmatism of pro-business PACs and into the production and dissemination of pro-capitalist ideas through the funding of right-wing think tanks—a task that conservatives were ready and able to take on. The 1970s thus saw a rapid expansion in existing research institutions, such as the AEI and the Hoover Institution, and the development of a slew of new organizations, such as the Heritage Foundation.

The Heritage Foundation is the result of an early and auspicious meeting between alienated conservatives within the Republican Party and corporate largesse. One of its two founders, Paul Weyrich, is the man later responsible for NET. Weyrich, a former broadcast journalist, began his political career as press secretary to former Colorado Republican senator Gordon Allott in the late 1960s.[9] Weyrich's entry into politics coincided with Colorado brewer Joseph Coors's 1971 decision to bankroll right-wing organizations. In Coors, Weyrich found his first patron. Their meeting in 1971 initiated a funding pattern that continues to this day, with Joseph Coors's political commitment being continued by his son Jeffrey. After two failed bids to influence existing conservative research organizations with large financial contributions,[10] Weyrich and Coors struck out on their own and began the Heritage Foundation in 1973.

In 1971 Paul Weyrich and Edwin Feulner, a staffer to Illinois Republican congressman Philip R. Crane, organized a conservative House faction modeled on the Liberal Study Group: the Republican Study Committee (RSC).[11] The RSC allowed conservative representatives to pursue their goals by pooling their resources at a time when they had more resources at their command due to increased staff positions.[12] The RSC coalesced into the Heritage Foundation in 1973, with Feulner as its president. The seed money of $250,000 from Joseph Coors was quickly augmented by a grant of $900,000 from Richard Mellon Scaife and large donations from the Noble and Olin Foundations.[13] Heritage expanded rapidly with generous corporate backing. In the mid-1980s, for example, donors of over $10,000 to a fund-raising drive (which raised a total of $35 million) included Chase Manhattan Bank, Dow Chemical, Mobil Corporation, Pfizer, *Reader's Digest,* SmithKline Beckman, Coors Industries, Mesa Petroleum, Mr. and Mrs. Joseph Coors, Lewis E. Lehrman, the Carthage Foundation, J. M. Foundation, J. Howard Pew Freedom Trust, and the Sarah Scaife Foundations.[14] In 1985, twelve years after its inception, Heritage had a staff of 105, a budget of $10.5 million, and thirty-six of its people had been appointed to administrative positions in the federal government;[15] by 1989 its budget was close to $18 million and its staff in 1992 was 135.[16]

Following the earlier lead of the AEI, Heritage has become particularly adept at marketing its ideas to the people who are in a position to put them into action. The foundation describes itself as "feeding" into Congress through the careful cultivation of congressional staffers by its policy analysts. These analysts stay informed about the passage of current bills and other legislative issues, providing strategically timed papers to appropriate staffers when a hearing is imminent. Heritage also disseminates its ideas through its Academic Bank. This is a data base of conservative scholars that can be called upon to provide "experts" on current legislative issues.[17] Edwin Feulner told writer Sydney Blumenthal: "We don't just stress credibility, we stress timeliness. We stress an efficient, effective delivery system. Production is one side; marketing is equally important."[18] Heritage also keeps computer records of all congressional staffers and over 3,500 journalists. The foundation produces around two hundred publications a year, from short policy briefings to complete books[19] and runs a Features Syndicate that distributes op-ed versions of its studies to newspapers likely to print them.[20] Emphasizing marketing, the Heritage Foundation makes clear that its success depends on a practical knowledge of political procedure and of the communications industry.

The status of conservative information is somewhat ambivalent. On the one hand, its value depends on its content, as a conservative opinion is taken to be self-evidently correct and compelling. But at the same time, it is useful only to the extent that it can be strategically inserted into current debates through its delivery to the targeted demographic of congressional staffers and media personnel, hence the emphasis on timeliness. Furthermore, the Heritage Foundation also depends on a wider climate of corporately funded and pro-business opinion; Burton Pines of the Heritage Foundation illustrated this point when he told Sydney Blumenthal: "AEI is like the big gun on an offshore battleship. We are the landing party. If they hadn't softened it up, we wouldn't have landed."[21]

It is notable that although conservatives have continuously styled themselves as outsiders to the two-party system, the philanthropy from which they began to benefit in the 1970s is part of a larger pattern of increasing industrial sponsorship of the GOP. In 1976 corporations spent money equally between Democrats and Republicans, but by 1978 this funding had become significantly skewed toward the Republican Party. For example, in 1978 each corporation from the country's top ten donated an average of $70,000 to Republican PACs, whereas those at the bottom of the top five hundred gave $6,000 each. The pattern of corporate funding effectively led to the blocking in Congress of labor law reform, of the creation of a consumer protection agency, of the passage of common situs legislation, and of the enforcement of Federal Trade Commission (FTC) and Occupational Safety and Health Administration (OSHA) regulations. In addition to direct corporate financing, the Republican Party rapidly increased its contributions well beyond those of its Democratic rival: Between 1977 and 1978 the Republican National Committee, the Republican Senate Campaign Committee, and the Republican Congressional Campaign Committee received $84.5 million compared to Democratic committees' $25.4 million. This trend increased from 1979 to 1980, with a Republican annual revenue of $169.5 million compared to the Democrats' $37.2 million,[22] contributing in no small measure to Reagan's success in the 1980 presidential election.

Equipped with increased resources at a time when the Democratic coalition was beginning to unravel,[23] conservatives were able to create a loose electoral coalition of disenchanted Democrats and newly politicized right-wing evangelical Christians.[24] Appealing to these diverse populations, conservative candidates tended to run on a platform of aggressive foreign policy, deregulation and limited domestic government, antiunionism, and support for "traditional social values." The ideology that conservatives began to aggressively market in the 1970s was not a new product but, rather, was a modified form of "fusionism": a conservative ideology developed in the 1950s that combined libertarian economics with a concern for "traditional social values."[25] Although fusionism expressed a concern with cultural issues, as is evident in the John Birch Society's opposition to sex education, its primary focus was on the economy and the free market. For conservatives in the 1970s, the structure of fusionism remained the same, but its specific content was adapted to contemporary events. The important conservative campaigns during this period included opposition to the SALT II treaty (anticommunism), the return of the Panama Canal (rigid nationalism), and opposition to labor rights. In 1978 Paul Weyrich's organization, the Committee for the Survival of a Free Congress (CSFC), selected five House votes as a kind of litmus test with which to measure representatives' political credibility:

1. Roll Call No. 98, March 23, 1977. Common-site picketing. Passage of the bill to permit a labor union with a grievance with one contractor to picket all contractors on the same construction site and to establish a construction industry collective bargaining committee.
2. Roll Call No. 265, May 18, 1977. Hatch Act amendments. Ashbrook (R-OH) amendment to prohibit a federal employee organization from coercing, threatening, or intimidating its workers into participating in any form of political activity and to prohibit the organizations from using dues or fees for political purposes.
3. Roll Call No. 317, June 7, 1977. Hatch Act amendments. Kindness (R-OH) amendment to add language to define the term extortion as an attempt to obtain property from another person by the use of threatened force or fear with reference to labor.
4. Roll Call No. 365, June 22, 1977. Foreign assistance appropriations for Fiscal 1978. Young (R-FL) amendment to prohibit the use of any funds contained in the bill for direct or indirect assistance to Uganda, Cambodia, Laos, or Vietnam.
5. Roll Call No. 384, June 27, 1977. Legal Services Corporation Act. McDonald (D-GA) amendment to prohibit legal assistance in cases arising out of disputes or controversies on the issue of homosexuality or gay rights.[26]

The CSFC-approved voting record was a "no" to the first proposal and "yes" to the remaining four. This legislative selection demonstrates the close adherence of Republican conservatives to the fusionist structure of corporate interest/unrestricted capitalism (antilabor measures), anticommunism (rejecting U.S. aid to supposed Communist governments), and "traditional" values (withholding legal aid from gay rights cases). However, as the decade progressed conservatives began to appeal to voters more and more on the basis of social issues, a trend that began to reverse fusionism's previous privileging of economic issues and that allowed the Republican Party to attract alienated working- and lower-middle-class voters, who might otherwise have been put off by the party's pro-business image.

Conservatives began to elevate social issues over economic issues at a time when fusionism's cherished "traditional" values had been actively opposed by civil rights legislation, demands for equal rights for women and gays, and the legalization of abortion. This foregrounding of social policy was an attempt to win voters who resented legislative attempts to ensure social equality, as in Phyllis Schlafly's organization of opposition to the Equal Rights Amendment and the attack on affirmative action and multiculturalism.[27] This appeal to white racism (particularly on the part of southern conservatives) should be viewed in the context of a historic shift of white voters from the Democrats to the Republicans, caused in part by Lyndon Johnson's sponsorship of civil rights legislation in the 1960s.[28]

Conservatives provide voters with a narrative explanation for social and economic change, a narrative that appeals to nostalgia for a lost patriarchal, segregated past while simultaneously promising its return. Taking benign capitalism as one of its basic assumptions, this ideology must deny the harsh realities of the global marketplace and posit false causes for its many shortcomings (for example, unemployment among the white lower middle class is "caused" by affirmative action and not by the relocation of manufacturing to cheaper overseas labor markets).[29] It is striking that conservatives were able to reverse fusionism's previous privileging of economics, representing themselves as a political group primarily concerned with social issues, at a time when business was sponsoring a massive wave of unprecedented deregulatory legislation through its contributions to the Republican Party, contributions from which conservatives directly benefited. This revised fusionism was repackaged in the early 1980s as the ideology of "family values."[30] The family values agenda defines itself primarily by its opposition to reproductive rights, sex education, affirmative action, gay rights, the welfare system, gun control and "government expansion."[31] This position creates an ideological climate in which calls for limited government can coexist with insistent demands for legislative solutions to social problems.

To organize voting constituencies around this revised fusionism and to better coordinate conservative campaigns, Paul Weyrich founded the CSFC in 1974. Replicating exactly the pattern of the Heritage Foundation, the CSFC was modeled on a liberal organization, the National Committee for an Effective Congress, and financed by a seed grant from Joseph Coors.[32] The CSFC specialized in assisting conservative challengers who were trying to oust "liberal" incumbents. In its first year the CSFC worked closely with Richard Viguerie to raise $194,000 for thirty-seven congressional candidates. In 1978 the *National Journal* reported that the CSFC

> will contribute about $400,000 to candidates this year...The group has a $1.2 million budget and spends much of the rest on strategy sessions, lobbying, and direct mail. Most of the campaign money will go for ser-

> vices rather than for direct cash contributions because "we find this has a greater influence on the direction of the campaign," Weyrich said... About 80 percent of the $400,000 will go to Republicans and nearly all of that to challengers.[33]

In 1978 the CSFC became the Free Congress Research and Education Foundation (FCF), a 501(c)(3) organization, and widened its activities to include research on domestic and foreign policy issues. The campaign assistance provided by the CSFC was now undertaken by the Free Congress PAC. Besides the training of political candidates, a function which it continues today, this organization undertakes research on social and foreign policy issues. The FCF is an umbrella group and organizing center for the secular and religious right and functions as the ideological complement to the Heritage Foundation.[34] A former chief assistant to Joseph Coors told journalist Sara Diamond that the FCF, the Heritage Foundation, and the Moral Majority were ostensibly secular organizations "intended to mobilize conservative Christians and shift the political makeup of Congress."[35]

Supplementing the Heritage Foundation's economic focus, the FCF undertakes the training and support of conservative political candidates at all levels and the development and promotion of an ideology of "Cultural Conservatism."[36] The two work together to produce, disseminate, and implement a coherent conservative ideology. The FCF works to "educate" politicians and voters, describing its research interests as judicial reform, ballot initiatives, election practices and theory, and educational, social, and family policy matters,[37] and claims among its alumni Orrin Hatch, Dan Quayle, and members of activist groups like James Dobson's Focus on the Family.[38] The FCF is organized into "centers" that pursue different activities, for example, government and politics, law and democracy, cultural conservatism, state policy, conservative governance, child and family policy, foreign policy, transportation policy, and catholic policy.[39]

In the mid-1980s the FCF began to redefine and widen the appeal of the family values agenda. The resultant ideology of "Cultural Conservatism"[40] was then represented as the result of a national consensus. Cultural Conservatism retains the political positions of the previously marginalized far right but carefully avoids its explicitly racist and xenophobic language. It argues that traditional conservative values are not merely morally correct but ultimately utilitarian. Describing Cultural Conservatism, conservative William S. Lind writes that

> Cultural Conservatism is the belief that there is a necessary, unbreakable, and causal relationship between traditional Western, Judeo-Christian values, definitions of right and wrong, ways of thinking and ways of living—the parameters of Western culture—and the secular success of Western societies: their prosperity, their liberties, and the opportuni-

> ties they offer their citizens to lead fulfilling, rewarding lives. If the former are abandoned, the latter will be lost . . . traditional values are functional values.[41]

Cultural Conservatism therefore replaces fusionism's central utilitarian defense of unregulated capitalism with a utilitarian defense of "traditional values": "If the culture is not sound, neither a free market nor any other economic system will work well."[42] As education secretary during the Reagan administration, William Bennett became the principal mouthpiece of cultural conservatism, a mission in which he has since become overshadowed by House Speaker Newt Gingrich.

In an attempt to deny its ideological partiality and to suppress its historical relation to the more explicitly racist and xenophobic politics of the John Birch Society,[43] the Liberty Lobby, and people like George Wallace and pre–Equal Rights Amendment Phyllis Schlafly, Cultural Conservatism defines its goals in terms of a universal standard of verisimilitude. This ideology defines itself not in terms of a narrow right-wing constituency but as the expression of a national collective will, as the title of Rush Limbaugh's recent book *The Way Things Ought to Be* suggests. Cultural Conservatism expresses a desire to return to a lost (or rapidly disappearing) past and carefully avoids phrasing its goals in terms of cultural and political change. The collective experience of this illusory past is emphasized in order to construct future political goals as the result of prior consensual agreement; this is the strategy of the so-called culture war. Therefore Cultural Conservatism continually resorts to the vocabulary of communal experience, shared values, and common sense while at the same time focusing on a narrow group of issues clustered around education (school prayer and the multicultural curriculum, self-esteem, and sex education programs), affirmative action, gay rights, and reproductive rights. Claims that Cultural Conservatism is supported by a majority of Americans are then bolstered by the political success of various "family values" initiatives, such as Measure 9 in Oregon and Proposition 22 in Austin, Texas.[44] Demonstrating the continued importance of racial politics to Cultural Conservatism, Paul Weyrich supported former Louisiana gubernatorial candidate David Duke's attack on affirmative action, saying: "Conservatives should continue to repudiate David Duke and his background and lying. But we cannot back away from some of the issues he raises."[45]

National Empowerment Television

The FCF has been highly effective in organizing local groups of conservative voters. From the early 1980s onward, Paul Weyrich worked closely with Pat Robertson and Jerry Falwell to politicize conservative fundamentalist Christians, and he is widely credited with masterminding and naming the Moral Majority. This mobilization of conservative Christians was already underway in the early 1970s,[46] but it was intensified in the early 1980s with the widespread perception among conservatives that the Reagan administration had failed to implement suitably conservative policies on social issues. This failure was attributed to the administration's preoccupation with economics and to the absence of local political bases of potential conservative activists.[47] According to Paul Weyrich, it was entrenched liberals in state legislatures and city councils who "put the brakes on the so-called Reagan Revolution."[48] The political organizing of the FCF is part of a long-term strategy to correct this perceived liberal monopoly at the local level.

A memo that Weyrich sent to White House Chief of Staff James Baker in 1982 encouraging the cultivation of a local conservative constituency anticipated the issues and audience that NET would subsequently address, as well as the technology it would later employ. The memo suggested that for the 1982 congressional election the administration should focus on "prayer, busing, quotas, cultural and neighborhood issues and inflation." Reagan, Weyrich suggested, should use the U.S. Chamber of Commerce's Busnet closed circuit TV system to campaign on those issues with fundamentalists, small businessmen, and other interest groups.[49] The Reagan administration declined to take up Weyrich's suggestions, but the FCF committed itself to the cultivation and organization of a conservative power base around an ideology of Cultural Conservatism and to the portrayal of this limited constituency as a silent majority. Another precedent for conservative interest in regulating media content and in making use of new technologies came in the early 1970s, when Joseph Coors briefly funded a satellite news distribution service called Television News, Inc. (TVN).[50] The purpose of the news service was to provide an alternative to the "liberal bias" of network news—a structuring assumption behind all conservative media ventures. As Coors told the *Rocky Mountain News* in August 1974: "We got into it [TVN] because of our strong belief that the network news is slanted to the liberal left side of the spectrum and does not give an objective view to the American public."[51] TVN foundered over internal disagreements and ceased operation in October 1975, but its claim to provide an "objective view to the American public" would be exactly reiterated by NET fifteen years later—with funding from the same source.[52]

Thus, well before the actual advent of NET the groundwork had been laid for a conservative news delivery mechanism. NET began broadcasting via satellite in 1991 with an audience of subscribing groups of conservative activists across the country, relying again on a start-up grant from Coors. Although it was originally transmitted on the noncommercial Ku band,[53] in 1992 the FCF began to broadcast NET programming on C band, which carries commercial stations. The switch to C band gave the FCF access to a new demographic group, home viewers who could be reached through commercial satellite TV guides. NET began to solicit these new viewers by taking out selective ads in *OnSat,* the U.S. programming guide to satellite TV.[54]

It is important to note that NET has no provision for members of its dispersed audience to communicate with each other. These groups are only linked together inasmuch as they all receive the directives of the FCF. This is the paradox of local conservative activism: Apparently spontaneous conservative protests that take place beyond the capital depend for their efficacy on a hierarchical and extremely privileged access to government and legislative activity. The same people who insist on less government in the name of democracy attempt to maximally influence the legislative process by using their detailed knowledge of how the political system works, as the information distribution of the Heritage Foundation demonstrates.

NET began production with four monthly shows tailored to specific constituencies: *Family Forum Live* addresses white, middle-class pro-family activists, *A Second Look Live* is targeted at black conservatives, *Campus Connection* is aimed at college students, and *Empowerment Outreach Live* speaks to business people. These shows present "experts" who discuss specific legislative issues, usually pending legislation at both the state and federal levels, and direct viewers to lobbying action—usually writing letters and making telephone calls. NET has been used to organize conservative activists around such issues as gays in the military, school vouchers, the nomination of Judge Clarence Thomas[55] to the Supreme Court, and health care reform. In the second halves of these shows viewers may call in to the studio on a toll-free line with their questions. This solicitation of telephone calls provides the spectacle of a two-way communication, constructing the conservative movement as one that works through democratic consensus: "By interviewing and questioning America's leading policy experts, ordinary citizens can participate directly in the making of the nation's policy."[56] The FCF describes NET as a tool for nationwide organizing:

> Linked to all the other groups of NET activists meeting simultaneously across the country, [activists] participate in an interactive "national town meeting," centered in NET's studios in Washington D.C.... because their efforts are not local and isolated, but coordinated nationwide, they are powerful.[57]

Each NET affiliate is made up of a group of individual activists whose collective reception of NET's transmissions is understood to be crucial to the station's success. This collective reception is presumed to generate group cohesion and increased political activity. The FCF compared NET to direct mail as a means of facilitating political action:

> Unlike a piece of direct-mail which asks citizens to sign petitions or write letters, [NET] brings local activists together and sparks a group

> dynamic. When local activists (usually affiliates of up to 40 individuals) meet around [NET] programming on a regular basis, dramatic results can be attained... [NET] brings these individuals together on a regular basis and keeps their "batteries charged." [NET] is the ideal tool to sustain long-term grassroots activism.[58]

NET represents a long-term commitment to covert political activism pioneered by the FCF as part of a wider strategy to intervene in the U.S. electoral system in order to shift political representation further to the right. It provides a regular forum at which activists can meet, and it directs its viewers to constructive, nationally coordinated tasks. It addresses its audience as a grassroots community that is separate, and alienated, from Washington's "beltway" culture. *Family Forum Live,* hosted by Paul Weyrich and Michael Schwartz, on 15 June 1993 aired the following items:

1. South Carolina Governor Carrol Campbell discussed his free-market plan to reduce infant mortality. He said there is plenty of money to help teenage mothers, but they aren't using existing services. He has developed a "coupon book," which is used as an incentive for pregnant teenagers to visit doctors and health clinics. As Campbell stated: "There are people who said 'Why don't you just tell them to have an abortion?' We think this [the coupon book] is a better alternative."
   Action Item: Weyrich urged viewers to call their representatives and push for the institution of a coupon book system.

2. Dean Clancy, Legislative Assistant to Congressman Dick Armey, promoted his boss's plan that would allocate 25 percent of all education funds for school choice.
   Action Item: Schwartz, saying Armey's plan "defines the pro-family education agenda," urged viewers to call their congressional representatives in support of the measure.

3. Tim Hutchinson, freshman congressman for Arkansas, presented his "putting families first" tax plan, which would give families a $500 tax credit per child and would freeze spending at 2 percent.
   Action Item: Schwartz asked audience members to call the office of Congressman Rod Gramms, where signatures are being collected for this bill.

4. Thomas Jipping, director of the Judicial Selection Monitoring Project, attacked Clinton's nomination of Ruth Bader-Ginsburg to the Supreme Court. Bader-Ginsburg was described as "another liberal Clinton nominee" and likened to former attorney general candidate Lani Gunier.
   Action Item: Schwartz said viewers should call their political leaders, especially their senators, to make sure that the right questions are asked of Bader-Ginsburg.

The show closed with special guest Oliver North replying to questions from viewers on a number of issues, concentrating on the need for conservative Republicans to take over Virginian politics. He said that if they can win the races for governor, lieutenant governor, and attorney general and win ten seats in the legislature, they can change the state.[59]

Besides its four affiliate shows, NET periodically broadcasts "training conferences featuring the most effective conservative organizers."[60] This aspect of political training has been best developed in the FCF's activities in Eastern Europe. In 1992 Weyrich; John Fund, a member of the *Wall Street Journal* editorial board; and Representative Joseph DioGuardi (R.–N.Y.), president of the Albanian American Civic League and special adviser to the FCF, visited Albania to conduct campaign training sessions for anticommunists in the forthcoming election in Macedonia.[61] The FCF claims that its training sessions in Moscow helped to elect Boris Yeltsin in 1991. Weyrich claimed that three dozen training seminars had been held in Eastern Europe, half in Russia. Training staff included Mark Nuttel, an employee of the FCF who formerly worked as an adviser to the Reagan-Bush campaign and as campaign manager for Patrick Buchanan in his attempt to win the 1988 Republican presidential nomination.[62]

On 6 December 1993 the FCF introduced a new, twenty-four-hour interactive television channel that, it claimed, would provide Americans with long-denied access to government in Washington. This new service took over the name "NET," while the "old" NET service changed its name to C-NET, an acronym for Coalitions National Empowerment Television.[63] The new station is, as of this writing, transmitted via the Hughes Communications satellite Galaxy 7 and is available free and unscrambled throughout the continental United States, Canada, and Mexico. The FCF hopes that NET will eventually get picked up by local cable services when the transfer from coaxial to fiber optic cable increases available channel space.[64] Soliciting a similar audience to NET's, Pat Robertson's Christian Broadcasting Network also began as a satellite station in 1977 and subsequently made a successful transition to cable.[65]

While C-NET addresses a narrow, preselected audience and changes its broadcast coordinates regularly to prevent unauthorized reception by nonsubscribers, the FCF uses a public service rhetoric to characterize NET. Positioning NET as part of the interactive cable future, Weyrich described the station as a trailblazing venture on the information superhighway that uses new technology to empower the people (Weyrich has called NET a "megaphone in the hands of the people").[66] NET's use of live call-in shows is represented as an innovative means of making politicians accountable to the public while simultaneously allowing viewers to participate in policy decisions. Describing itself as "C-Span with an attitude,"[67] the station's programming presents contemporary political issues from the point of view of the secular and religious right. During the week the station runs five live daily shows. These include *Mitchells in the Morning,* a breakfast show hosted by an economist from the Heritage Foundation; *Direct Line with Paul Weyrich,* in which the founder of both the Free Congress and Heritage Foundations invites viewers to call in and chat with guests such as Jesse Helms and Oliver North; and *Capitol Watch,* a daily report on government by Newt Gingrich.[68] NET also broadcasts programming produced by outside organizations such as Concerned Women for America (*Putting Families First*); the American Life League (*Celebrate Life*); Accuracy in Media (*The Other Side*), and the National Rifle Association (*On Target with the NRA*).[69]

To understand the way the FCF is trying to construct a national consensus around Cultural Conservatism, it is necessary to analyze the complex strategic and ideological interrelationship between NET and C-NET. Both NET and C-NET depend on a set of three interdependent subject positions:

1. the disempowered citizen who belongs to the excluded conservative majority;
2. the politically empowered subject—a transformed version of the previously disempowered citizen—whose new access to government is provided by NET; and
3. the activist viewer of C-NET.

NET begins with the premise that there is a vast unrepresented conservative public that is excluded from national government and that is dominated by an out-of-touch liberal elite. It addresses potential viewers as members of this excluded group. Consider, for example, the advertisements for NET published in *Onsat* (the *TV Guide* of satellite TV). One asks: "What Did Congress Do to You Today? To Find Out, Tune In to Capitol Watch."[70] Constructing a helpless viewer made passive by liberals and the government, another asks: "Cut Off? From the People in Washington Who Make the Rules? From Anyone Who Counts? We Can Hook You Up. Give You a Voice. And Make Them Listen."[71] To the disempowered subject, NET offers itself as the only hope for political expression. The station will act as a conduit between the U.S. electorate and national government. At the time of its public launch as a satellite channel in December 1993, Weyrich described NET in the *Washington Times* as "an unfettered link between the American electorate and their representatives in Washington . . . we know that when the people have all the information, unfettered by intermediary filters, they will make the right decisions and send the right messages to Washington."[72]

These remarks construct NET as a public service (not as "the Conservative Channel") with a public that is solidly conservative. This public service rhetoric can then be repeated by cable companies when presenting the channel to their clients. Inquiring about demand for new channels, a 1995 survey sent to cable subscribers in Rochester, New York, described NET as providing "a non-partisan look at what Washington does and how Washington's actions affect Americans."[73]

Structured as an empowering conduit that will transform the viewer, NET borrows a language that Grant Kester has described as the "informational sublime."[74] This liberal model, now widely employed in descriptions of the Internet, constructs communications technologies as means through which all social hierarchies and inequalities are dissolved to usher in an egalitarian community based on unmediated dialogue between individuals. To conform to this model, NET repeatedly describes itself as "interactive television,"[75] even though its current claim to "interactivity" rests on the use of live telephone calls from viewers. Positioning the channel on the cutting edge of new technology, Paul Weyrich calls NET part of

> an explosion of modern technology [that] is about to provide our citizens with the same ability to voice concerns, hopes and fears directly to their elected officials in much the same manner as did the town meetings of 200 years ago. NET is one of the very few early forces to utilize this technology... Unencumbered by intermediaries, citizens throughout the United States can now express their concerns from a national platform directly to their political leaders.[76]

This description conflates the silent conservative majority with the egalitarian community promised by the informational sublime to imply that the political positions expressed on NET are the result of national dialogue. By articulating the long-suppressed "voice of the people," NET seems to look forward to an imminent conservative political revolution precipitated by "new technology" that will result in the liberation of democracy.[77]

The language of the informational sublime invokes an egalitarian community but defers the transformation of the disempowered subject into the future. This fantasy of egalitarian dialogue strengthens the need to correct the perceived deafness to conservative voices in federal government decision making. NET provides a remedy to the inaccessibility of government by providing a platform for these excluded citizens, but in so doing it must continually reinscribe the exclusion that it claims to redress. NET addresses its viewers as already marginalized and must continue to do so since it claims as its raison d'être the provision of a voice for the voiceless, while its parade of right-wing politicians and activists testify to the exclusion that conservatives face, an exclusion that compelled NET into existence. NET thus enacts the New Right's outsider claims, while the FCF offers the subscription service C-NET, an alternative solution to NET's disempowered subject. Prior to the launch of NET in 1993, a subscriber to C-NET inquired about the function of the new station in a letter to the C-NET newsletter. Replying in print, Weyrich described the anticipated relationship between these two services. He wrote: "As NET grows, it will fuel the growth and impact of C-NET. As more people watch NET, they will realize that the best way for them to influence public policy themselves is to join or start a new C-NET affiliate."[78]

NET alerts its viewers to the existence of C-NET by broadcasting the descriptive parts of the affiliate shows without the lobbying instructions. These instructions, NET viewers are told, are confined to a "closed session" that they can't see. But NET invites its viewers to call the FCF to find out how they can start an affiliate and become politically involved.

Instead of NET's promise of access to national government, C-NET offers viewers a pragmatic approach to politics and membership in a committed community of local activists. C-NET's political success depends on the failure of participatory democracy and not on the collective political involvement imagined by the informational sublime and NET. Weyrich demonstrated his awareness of this condition when he addressed the 1992 Christian Coalition Conference. Weyrich told his audience:

> In politics only ten percent of the people really know what's going on, ninety percent of the people never do, and only two percent of the people make things happen. This is the network for the two percent. It is a network specifically designed to tell people how to participate in the political process, what to do that's effective . . . It's not for ordinary people. It's for people like you who want to make a difference in the political process.[79]

Although this is the station of the 2 percent, the program of activism C-NET represents is invariably described as "grassroots." This misleading description overlooks the extent to which such activism is secretively organized from the top down by a centralized, hierarchical organization funded by a small group of wealthy conservative foundations. The populist politics the right claims to represent uses a narrow set of ideas generated by a network of right-wing think tanks. It is with a critique of this "grassroots" status and its illusory consensus that a progressive response to the right must begin.

Notes

1. Ellen Messer-Davidow, "Manufacturing the Attack on Liberalized Higher Education," *Social Text* 36 (1993): 40–80.

2. James A. Smith, *The Ideas Brokers: Think Tanks and the Rise of the New Policy Elite* (New York: Free Press, 1991), 197. Buchanan borrowed the concept of the new Republican majority from Kevin Phillips, *The Emerging Republican Majority* (New Rochelle, N.Y.: Arlington House, 1969).

3. Paul Weyrich took up this theme in a 1981 interview. He told Richard Neuhaus: "The problem is that for so long the liberals have claimed important issues as their own,

and we often made the mistake of believing them. So they end up using all the expertise for their own ideological purposes. We have to develop our own experts," Richard John Neuhaus, "The Right to Fight," *Commonweal,* 9 October 1981, 557. On the development of the conservative ideas industry, see also Scott Henson and Tom Philpott, "The Right Declares a Culture War," *The Humanist* 10, no. 16 (March–April 1992): 46, and Messer-Davidow, "Manufacturing the Attack on Liberalized Higher Education."

4. Jerome Himmelstein, *To the Right: The Transformation of American Conservativism* (Berkeley and Los Angeles: University of California Press, 1990), 129–65; Zina Klapper, "Do You Know These Godfathers?," *Mother Jones,* February-March 1981, 33–34; Karen Rothmeyer, "Citizen Scaife," *Columbia Journalism Review,* July-August 1981, 41–50; Anne Zore, "The Corporate Connection: Who Is Bankrolling the Right?," *Co-op America Quarterly* (Winter 1994): 21–22, 33. This last article includes an interesting analysis of the financial support of the Oregon Citizen's Alliance.

5. Himmelstein, *To the Right,* 137.

6. Ibid.

7. Ibid., 139–40.

8. Ibid., 141.

9. Alan Crawford, *Thunder on the Right* (New York: Pantheon Books, 1980), 10.

10. Ibid., 11. From 1971–1973 Joseph Coors contributed $200,000 to the Analysis Research Corporation, an organization that conducted research for conservative members of Congress. When internal conflicts diminished the group's effectiveness, Coors redirected his largesse to a similar group that focused on public interest law: the Robert M. Schuchman Foundation. Weyrich's and Coors's activist-oriented goals clashed with those of others in the foundation; Alan Crawford quotes an observer: "What Weyrich and Coors really wanted was a vehicle for their activities, which included a certain degree of lobbying and political action. It was less expensive, of course, if they could conduct this business under the tax exemption that the foundation enjoyed—but this could risk revocation of that exemption, or worse."

11. Smith, *The Ideas Brokers,* 198–99. Feulner's 1981 doctoral dissertation is about the RSC.

12. Sydney Blumenthal quotes former Heritage Foundation vice president Philip Truluck on the formation of the RSC: "There was a feeling among the younger ones of us in this town that the old conservative system wasn't working. Conservatives ended up losing most of the time. There was no strategy. We had a pretty clear idea of what we wanted to do. We felt we needed research groups that could address legislative issues. There was no lack of talent and manpower for the liberal perspective. They had Brookings and the majority of the committee staffs. The conservatives did not have the staffs. They didn't have too many places to turn to for research work" *The Rise of the Counter Establishment* (New York: Harper and Row, 1986), 47.

13. Smith, *The Ideas Brokers,* 200.

14. Himmelstein, *To the Right,* 148.

15. Blumenthal, *The Rise of the Counter Establishment,* 37.

16. Smith, *The Ideas Brokers,* 200.

17. Blumenthal, *The Rise of the Counter Establishment,* 48–49.

18. Ibid., 49.

19. Smith, *The Ideas Brokers,* 201.

20. Blumenthal, *The Rise of the Counter Establishment,* 49.

21. Ibid., 45.

22. William C. Berman, *America's Right Turn* (Baltimore, Md.: Johns Hopkins University Press, 1994), 71.

23. See Thomas Byrne Edsall and Mary D. Edsall, *Chain Reaction* (New York: Norton, 1991).

24. The history of the political organization of right-wing evangelical Christians is both contentious and complex. I found the following books particularly useful: Sara Diamond, *Spiritual Warfare* (Boston: South End Press, 1989); Robert C. Liebman and Robert Wuthnow, *The New Christian Right* (New York: Aldine, 1983); Matthew Moen, *The Transformation of the Christian Right* (Tuscaloosa: University of Alabama Press, 1992).

25. See Himmelstein, *To the Right,* on fusionism.

26. Thomas J. McIntyre, *The Fear Brokers* (Boston: Beacon Press, 1979), 70.

27. For a detailed description of the conservative attack on the multicultural curriculum, see Messer-Davidow, "Manufacturing the Attack on Liberalized Higher Education."

28. Berman, *America's Right Turn,* 61.

29. Fusionism continues to provide the architecture for contemporary conservative policy. See, for example, Dick Armey, "Freedom's Choir: Social and Economic Conservatives Sing the Same Song," *Policy Review* 67 (Winter 1994): 27–34. This article is a contemporary attempt to resolve the internal contradictions of fusionism.

30. For a concrete example of a family values policy initiative, see William Hixson's discussion of the Family Protection Act, a legislative proposal drafted by Conaught Marshner, an employee of the Free Congress Foundation. William B. Hixson, *Search for the American Right Wing* (Princeton, N.J.: Princeton University Press, 1992), 221–22.

31. Republicans are forced into a contradictory position when they insist on economic deregulation and increased moral surveillance by the state; an example of the latter is described in a recent *Nation* article: David Kirp, "Queer Education," *The Nation,* 1 January 1996, 5–6.

32. Flo Conway and Jim Seligman, *Holy Terror* (Garden City, N.Y.: Doubleday, 1982), 304.

33. McIntyre, *The Fear Brokers,* 69.

34. The Free Congress Foundation grew out of an earlier Weyrich political action committee, the Committee for the Survival of a Free Congress, which counted among its successes the 1977 election of Utah Republican senator Orrin Hatch. See Crawford, *Thunder on the Right,* 15–16, 269–73.

35. Diamond, *Spiritual Warfare,* p. 42, footnote 24.

36. Russ Bellant, *The Coors Connection* (Cambridge, Mass.: Political Research Associates/South End Press, 1991), 1–35.

37. *Research Centers Directory,* 18th ed. (Detroit, Mich.: Gale Publishers, 1994), 1240.

38. This reference is from an FCF letter addressed "Dear Citizen Leader" that accompanied a 1992 mailing about NET: *NET Today's Vision for Conservative American Philanthropists.*

39. Bellant, *The Coors Connection* 22.

40. See William S. Lind and William H. Marshner, eds., *Cultural Conservatism: Toward a New National Agenda* (Lanham, Md.: University Presses of America, 1987), and William S. Lind and William H. Marshner, eds., *Cultural Conservatism: Theory and Practise* (Washington D.C.: Free Congress Foundation Center for Cultural Conservatism, 1991).

41. Lind and Marshner, *Cultural Conservatism,* 1.

42. *Ibid.*, 2–3.

43. In the mid-1980s Paul Weyrich was deferentially interviewed in the John Birch Society publication *The Review of the News.* The introduction stated that "Paul Weyrich

is of course no stranger to readers of *The Review of the News* as his reports on politics appear here regularly," John Rees, "Paul M. Weyrich," *The Review of the News,* 6 June 1984, 31.

44. On Measure 9, see Robert Sullivan, "An Army of the Faithful," *New York Times Magazine* 25 April 1993, 32–35, 40, 42, 44. Proposition 22 was discussed on National Public Radio's *Morning Edition,* 9 May 1994; the transcript is available through the Nexus/Lexus database. News coverage of this issue also appeared in the *New York Times* on 9 May 1994.

45. Adam Meyerson, "Conscience of a Cultural Conservative: Paul M. Weyrich on the Politics of Character in Russia and America," *Policy Review* 59 (Winter 1992): 15. The following anthology is a useful resource for material on Duke's political career: Douglas Rose, ed., *The Emergence of David Duke and the Politics of Race* (Chapel Hill: University of North Carolina Press, 1992); of particular interest from a media studies perspective is Gary Esolen's essay "More Than a Pretty Face: David Duke's Use of Television as a Political Tool," 136–55.

46. Diamond, *Spiritual Warfare,* 45–81.

47. Paul Weyrich, "Ideas and Strategies to Unite the Conservative Majority," *Heritage Foundation Reports* 24 November 1992, 2.

48. Ibid.

49. Quoted in Morton Kondracke, "Hard Times for the Hard Right," *New Republic,* 20 December 1982, 20–23.

50. Stanhope Gould, "Coors Brews the News," *Columbia Journalism Review* 13, no. 6 (March-April 1975): 17–30.

51. Ibid., 19.

52. "TVN News Service, Losing Coors Support, Will Cease Operations," *Wall Street Journal,* 1 October 1975, 24.

53. This satellite band is used for data transmission and teleconferencing. It does not run commercial consumer services.

54. *Onsat,* 26 July-1 August 1993, 4–6.

55. Clarence Thomas has been a frequent guest on NET.

56. This quotation is taken from a 1992 FCF fund-raising letter, *NET Today's Vision for Conservative American Philanthropists.*

57. Ibid.

58. This quote taken from a 1993 FCF mailing providing updated material on NET.

59. The transcript of this broadcast of *Family Forum Live,* 15 June 1993, was provided by People for the American Way, Washington, D.C.

60. This quotation is taken from a 1992 FCF fund-raising letter, *NET Today's Vision for Conservative American Philanthropists.*

61. *Business Wire,* 6 January 1992.

62. United Press International, "Americans Teach Democracy to Soviets," 3 November 1991.

63. Peter J. Brown, "National Empowerment Television," *Onsat,* 26 July–1 August 1993, 6–8. My description of C-NET is also based on undated materials printed by the Free Congress Foundation provided by People for the American Way in Washington D.C. These documents include a description of C-NET entitled "NET: Today's Vision for Conservative American Philanthropists" and the "C-NET Coalition Building Manual."

64. Brent Stinar, "The People's Network," *NET on Screen* (Summer 1993): 1–2.

65. Diamond, *Spiritual Warfare,* 19.

66. Paul Weyrich, "Welcome to the Birth of the New Media Age," *Washington Times,* 15 December 1993.

67. *NET on Screen* (Spring 1994): 2.

68. The other two shows are *American Family* and *Home Business, NET on Screen* (Spring 1994): 4–5.

69. Ibid.

70. *Onsat,* 27 June–3 July 1994, 102.

71. *Onsat,* 16–22 May 1994, 55.

72. Paul Weyrich, "Welcome to the Birth of the New Media Age," *Washington Times,* 15 December 1993.

73. This description of NET is taken from a *Greater Rochester Cablevision Programming Survey* (Spring 1994) sent to the author. NET appeared as one of twenty-six potentially available channels, including "The Food Channel," "The Sci-Fi Channel," and "Nostalgia." At the time of this writing, Greater Rochester Cable does not carry NET.

74. Grant Kester, "Access Denied: Informational Policy and the Limits of Liberalism," *Afterimage,* January 1994, 5–10.

75. NET's description of itself as interactive currently refers to its use of live call-in shows, but at the end of June 1994 NET became a licensee of Zing Systems LP, allowing the TV station to use Zing Writer software to create and encode interactive software into its programming. See *Onsat,* 27 June–3 July 1994, 4.

76. *Onsat,* 27 July–3 August 1994, 3.

77. A similar use of the informational sublime model is employed in the plot of a book called *The Telecom Revolution* that was recently advertised on the Internet.

78. *NET on Screen* (Summer 1993): 7.

79. Paul Weyrich's address to the Christian Coalition Conference in Washington D.C., 1992. A transcript of this speech is available in *Paul Weyrich: Key Strategist for the Secular and Religious Right (A Collection of Primary and Secondary Material)* (Boston: Political Research Associates, 1993), 7–8.

12

Christian Coalition Leadership Training

Julia Lesage

I became interested in studying the Christian right, especially its more moderate electoral sector as represented by the Christian Coalition, because this style of organizing and the attitudes it builds on remind me of the people I knew in the small midwestern town, Dixon, Illinois, where I grew up. In that environment, the professional class of doctors, lawyers, bankers, and teachers mingled every day with farmers and tradespeople, and we shared a general sense of mutual decorum and respect in our relations with each other. The state of Illinois, like many other states, has long had an urban/rural, Democrat/Republican split. In Dixon, which was generally a Republican town, many people, mostly men, felt free to comment liberally on national "politics." However, they displaced overt expressions of homophobia, sexism, and racism onto the realm of humor, what Freud would call "tendentious" jokes, rather than raise these as specific social issues. My mother was a Democrat, a Jew from New York. She and her small group of Jewish friends always provided for me a refracted optic on this small-town world that I both loved and found constricting. In my adulthood, I also began to see the ways in which Dixon residents would set aside the generally accepted decorum that prohibited raising controversial topics. In particular, in the 1970s and 1980s, I heard women openly, albeit still politely, disagree with each other about abortion.

In the academic towns or urban environments where I have spent most of my adult life, this world of small town mores remains mostly unacknowledged, even though many of my friends and associates have their origins there. And in the university where I teach, my peers also cling to a now self-destructive ignorance about the Christian right, ignoring the way it strategically defunds their workplace, that is, public education, and having little understanding of the conservative right's cultural agenda or its social base. For me, looking at the Christian right is often like looking in a mirror because its participants choose to live within a politically resistant counterculture. Similarly, in my adult life, I have participated in forming a left and feminist counterculture, one that has much in common with the dreams of the utopian socialists of the nineteenth and early twentieth centuries in both the United States and Europe. Like those in right-wing, single-issue pressure groups, I know the appeal of an intellectual and social community that places itself apart from mainstream values. To find this kind of social fulfillment, I too have participated in running an underground newspaper, helped found a university women's studies program, founded and coedited for twenty years *Jump Cut: A Review of Contemporary Media,* an independent "alternative" publication in media studies and media activism, and made low-budget social activist videos as part of the independent film and video community. These experiences have made me sympathetic to the notion of an "alternative" or "parallel culture," which offers its participants another, perhaps saner cultural experience than that offered by the dominant culture.

Ironically, this utopian mentality has much in common with the countercultural strategies of what Ralph Reed calls "the 'leave-us-alone' coalition of pro-lifers, anti-tax groups, conservative Christians, home schoolers, small businessmen, and gun advocates" (Reed 1996, 71), although those people often see my subcultural world as the enemy. Furthermore, whereas that conservative coalition studies my world in terms of what it sees as a dominant liberal, "secular humanist" ideology and whereas it organizes politically to engage liberalism in battle, my academic and media colleagues usually eschew knowledge of or intellectual contact with this diverse, widespread, often very popular, and increasingly powerful conservative cultural force. Instead, they conveniently demonize the Christian right—in much the same way that right-wing legislators' attacks on the National Endowment for the Arts or the National Endowment for the Humanities demonize liberal academics and artists (Schapiro 1994).

The people whom the Christian right is grooming to enter political office and to lobby legislators are not the "crazies" that many people associate with the militia movement, with Timothy McVeigh and the Oklahoma City bombing—although Christian Coalition members may know and associate with those like McVeigh. Rather, in the ranks of these activists are women who speak courteously and dress tastefully when they go out in public and educated men who would never throw pig's blood on the staff of an abortion clinic or shout obscenities at the women going in. For the most part, these people become involved in politics out of their evangelist conviction that it is necessary to spread the Word, to be a beacon on a hill. Furthermore, the skills that Christian Coalition activists learn through studying political organizing tactics and refine through fieldwork pull them into the social process of the community at large. In addition, political experience often helps make them more upwardly mobile economically or more secure professionally. The conservative political leadership training offered by the Christian Coalition also has a special appeal to women who had children young or who have worked mainly in the pink-collar ghetto, to retirees who need to find ways to earn a supplemental income or are isolated socially and have free time on their hands, or to working-class or lower-middle-class men in transition from one kind of work to another, as happens so often in their careers. It also appeals to professionals and small business persons, who would gravitate toward the Republican Party for its pro-business and antiregulation stance and who would benefit from learning how to solidify contacts with the state political apparatus.

Ralph Reed, founding executive director of the Christian Coalition, says that a 1993 survey found that the average "committed" Christian in their ranks is a forty-year-old woman who went to college, is married with children, with a household income of about $40,000 (Reed 1996, 193). She often works outside the home and lives in the suburbs or exurbs of a major metropolitan area. In other words, the demographics of conservative Christians are often those of baby boomers struggling to maintain a middle-class lifestyle, which requires that both adults in the family work. The focus of such a group as the Christian Coalition on "family values" is a rhetorical device that unifies people around their desire for a folkloric traditionalism, their fears about economic insecurity and their ability to maintain a "home," and their wish that child rearing, especially when both parents have to work, might somehow be more predictable. Both demographics and rhetoric unite the Christian right into a loosely defined subculture that finds its unity around the expression of moral values.

As a subculture, the Christian right must coexist with the many other subcultures in the United States, some of them antagonistic to each other. In general, subcultures are both constraining and enabling for their participants; although everyone participates in various subcultures, some individuals are more self-consciously "border crossers" than others. When a subculture that was previously isolated, such as the religious right, chooses to enter electoral politics, as does the Christian Coalition, then it becomes important to analyze certain aspects of the subculture—in this case, the degree to which religious conservatives cling to their shared worldview, the degree to which their relation to other subcultures shifts or stays the same, and the ways in which they relate to the dominant culture (which is white, middle class, male, politically conservative in some key institutions like the military, and politically liberal in other important institutions like the press). Some subcultures with which I am familiar include ethnic and religious ones (Jewish, Catholic, Italian, black, Latino), political ones (left/feminist, gay male, cultural lesbian, black nationalist, ecology activist, New Age), vocationally or demographically based ones (teens, children, retired people, college students, college teachers in the arts and sciences, independent media makers), and the major economically determined ones (working, middle, and upper middle classes).

Subcultures govern style, both lifestyle and language style. Semantically they perpetuate discourse communities that legislate the range of what can or cannot be said, should or should not be imagined, and is or is not valorized or vilified. Conservative rhetoric indicates the shared values of the religious right subculture. Conservative discourse praises manliness and femininity, the family with a father and mother, parental control over children, private property, the deserving poor, the individual's right to try and to fail economically, the free market, private property, lower taxes, less government, military duty, and U.S. patriotism. Similarly, words that indicate consensus about the malevolent forces in society are used to refer to the media, immigrants, public schools, illegitimacy, welfare, "redistributionist" economics, the counterculture (mine, that is), multiculturalism, homosexuality, feminism, government spending (except on the military), and any indication that gender roles might be socially constructed. Not only does the religious right articulate such a moral consensus, it has also developed a media-savvy, politically active, interconnected subculture. This large, diverse network receives little analytic attention from either progressive activists or mainstream media, which the conservative right's political activity always seems to take by surprise. Ralph Reed glowingly describes his own subcultural world in the following terms:

> Few in Washington understand what Bill Kristol has called "the parallel universe" in which religious conservatives live, where the radio and television programs reach more people every day than network newscasts and where pro-family organizations can mobilize the grassroots as effectively as the labor unions and civil rights movements did at their peak. Home-school parents and students, for instance, use personal computers to access lessons and communicate with hundreds of other home schoolers, constituting a ready-made network of hundreds of thousands of cybercitizens. (Reed 1996, 177)

The research material that has stimulated this chapter is a set of leadership training tapes prepared in 1993 by the Christian Coalition for its political action leadership schools. My analysis of the tapes will describe the specific political advice they contain as well as explore their wider implications, including the psychology upon which the tapes' speakers rely and the place filled by this kind of organizing within the panorama of contemporary U.S.

social life. The tapes provide an insight into how the Christian Coalition functions as a religious organization oriented to electoral politics; my analysis will look specifically at the Christian Coalition's self-definition as a "grassroots" organization, its understanding of routine electoral politics in the United States, its economic aspects, and its development of a specific kind of rhetorical strategy. In examining the way this organization functions, I also want to assess how participating in the coalition might affect its members.

Christian Coalition

In 1986, a year before Pat Robertson decided to run for the 1988 presidential election, he announced to viewers of *The 700 Club* nationwide: "If, by September 17, 1987, one year from today, three million registered voters have signed petitions telling me that they will pray, that they will work, that they will give toward my election, then I will run" (Boston 1996, 35–36).

Such a plea did not make him the Republican candidate, but it did result in a very successful fund-raising campaign. Robertson raised $10 million by the time he actually entered the race, and in 1988 when he dropped out, he had spent almost all the $27 million that U.S. Campaign Law allows (Rosenbaum 1988). Robertson failed politically in 1988 because he campaigned on the basis of evangelical rhetoric and had a seriously faulty understanding of the U.S. political process (Boston 1996, 35–62). Afterward, he returned to his teleministry, which had lost much of its viewership in his absence, and once again managed his Christian Broadcasting Network (CBN), pulling it out of serious financial straits; he now defines his social role mainly as a family broadcasting entrepreneur. However, Robertson did not want to give up his large financial investment in electoral politics, his base of political support, or his newly gathered political mailing list. At a George Bush inaugural dinner in 1988 in Washington, D.C., Robertson met his future protégé, Ralph Reed, former executive director of College Republicans; he asked Reed to send him a memo on how to organize a grassroots organization. In 1989, Reed worked to establish this new political vehicle, the Christian Coalition.

On the basis of the mailing lists of CBN and Robertson's political campaign, Reed began recruiting activists from the Robertson political organization. His goal was to build a grassroots organization that would conduct voter surveys and recruit and train local candidates for office and for precinct work in the Republican Party. In establishing the Christian Coalition, Reed refined the strategy of a direct mail campaign developed by Washington, D.C., fund-raiser Richard Viguerie in the 1970s and subsequently exploited by Moral Majority leader Jerry Falwell. Reed and other conservative strategists had long understood how valuable a political tool direct mail could be for raising money and building a political base, but earlier direct mail campaigns had primarily focused on raising money for national candidates and hot-button conservative causes since the 1970s. These included such esoteric fund-raising efforts as Spiro Agnew's defense fund. However, Robertson's summary defeat in the 1988 primaries and before that the Moral Majority's failure to establish a serious electoral presence indicated that direct mail and television alone could not develop the political activism and mass base required for a permanent religious conservative presence in U.S. politics. Furthermore, as Reed puts it: "One of the first things we learned was that the red-hot rhetoric that sizzled in direct mail and on cable television may drive core supporters to their checkbooks but ultimately limits one's effectiveness in the broader society" (Reed 1996, 119).

In the unofficial Reed-Robertson partnership, lasting until 1997, when Reed resigned as Christian Coalition executive director, the two men's rhetorical differences have consistently revealed their division of labor in the Christian Coalition. Operating with a new, politically sensitive style, Reed characteristically describes political issues in terms of social problems and desirable social policy outcomes. He avoids religious reasoning, especially references to verses of Scripture. In contrast, Robertson continues a line of millenarian thinking long familiar to his evangelical viewers and readers.

Politically such a rhetorical shift is extremely important. Today, as the Christian Coalition has moved into the mainstream, it has taken control of many state Republican Party organizations. Now local Christian Coalition chapters generate their own mailing lists, annotated with a variety of information about potentially sympathetic voters, and these mailing lists are used for electoral and lobbying campaigns, even more than for fund-raising for specific causes. With 1,700 chapters established in 1995 in voting districts scattered throughout the United States, the Christian Coalition targets and identifies its constituencies in far more subtle ways than the earlier direct mail solicitations did. Currently, the philosophy behind generating and using the mailing list is to locate those voters who in some ways agree with conservative Christian social philosophy; follow-up surveys refine these points of agreement, to which letters sent out to supporters then refer.

Chapter members often talk face-to-face with prospective conservative voters and maintain personalized, regular contact. And Christian Coalition members' active participation in local churches turns church voter-education groups, church mailing lists, and even the support of local clergy into very powerful tools at the coalition's disposal, for they function like mailing lists to help set up an initial contact with the desired voting bloc and they make the follow-up face-to-face contact even more effective. The payoff comes when the voters receive and act on items such as candidate "report cards" that they can take into the voting booth, fax alerts about upcoming statewide or national legislative struggles, or a letter or phone call about a local controversy, such as the need for a conservative group to build support to remove a text from a school curriculum.

The Training Tapes

In the original 1989 memo that Reed sent Robertson about how to form a grassroots organization, he laid down a basic principle that has made the Christian Coalition a dynamic institution able to respond to the exigencies of electoral politics and to energize and educate its core members. He insisted that the organization launch and maintain "an ambitious training program modeled after the leadership schools of Morton Blackwell" (Reed 1996, 13). Like Reed, Blackwell had served as the executive director of the College Republican National Committee and later had set up his own conservative Leadership Institute in Virginia. Reed used this connection to develop the Christian Coalition's training program, now carried out in two-day workshops throughout the United States. As the Christian Coalition has grown, these training schools have proven vital to the organization's ongoing practice, educating coalition members as socially effective activists, especially its 550 county chapter organizers and its even-more-numerous precinct leaders. In particular, the training schools teach a detailed understanding of political process and develop sophisticated public relations skills. Conducted over a period of a weekend, leadership, citizen action, or schoolboard seminars are held frequently in many moderate-sized cities; in spring 1995, for example, the coalition's Internet posting listed upcoming seminars in Anchorage, Alaska; Topeka, Kansas; Fargo, North Dakota; Albany, New York; Baton Rouge, Louisiana; Aurora, Illinois; Alexandria, Virginia; Charleston, North Carolina; and Queens, New York (Christian Coalition World Wide Web site, 16 January 1996).

In the videotapes made for the Christian Coalition Leadership Schools, one of the speakers is, in fact, Morton Blackwell, and some tapes bear introductory remarks from Pat Robertson. These tapes were filmed in 1992 or 1993, although the leadership manual accompanying them has an earlier 1990 copyright date, indicating that this particular set of tapes comes out of several years' experience on the part of the coalition's national organizers (Fisher, Reed, and Weinhold 1990). At the seminar where most of these tapes were shot, attendees indicate that many are running for local or state office or are working on the staff of an avowedly Christian candidate, suggesting that many are already active politically in the electoral sector. Although the speakers and the audience members do not *contrast* themselves to other Christian conservatives involved primarily in single-issue organizing campaigns, such as right-to-life picketing at clinics, most of the tape's presenters insist that electoral politics has to focus on winning votes from the undecided center—a crucial 15 percent. Although the tapes' speakers occasionally use religious rhetoric for motivational purposes, the political advice they offer is general enough to be of use to anyone entering electoral politics. And clearly some of the presenters have worked for both Republican and Democratic candidates since they speak from the perspective of high-powered professionals who run public relations or public-opinion survey firms. They offer advice that is more secular than religious.

Christian Coalition members have used this leadership training to great advantage, with particular success in local elections to county commissions, city councils, and school boards. After their initial organizing experiences, coalition members seek even more ways to share and gain political acumen. As a follow-up to the initial leadership training in a group setting and their subsequent political experience, many Christian Coalition organizers or local political office holders look forward to attending the yearly Christian Coalition National Conventions, where they go to more how-to workshops and, equally important, swap political wisdom among themselves, often about tactical victories achieved at the grassroots level by people new to politics.

The Christian Coalition Leadership School training tapes are part of a kind of video production broadly known as "industrial video." Within that broad category, they belong to the genre of "training tapes." In the media industry, such production takes place outside the entertainment industry in the industrial video sector, and it makes up the bulk of what professional media makers do. In the United States, for example, the social service and business sectors constantly generate how-to videotapes for specialized training. In terms of distribution, such tapes are often promoted within a "training package." This means that the tapes will be presented by a live facilitator, perhaps an expert, who introduces the tapes and leads a discussion. The package also includes a training manual to be given to each participant; the attendees annotate the manual with notes from lectures and discussions, perhaps fill out some of the pages as part of the workshop, and refer to it later to refresh their memories. Sometimes participants can check the training tapes out again from a local office; the tapes then reinforce what they learned. Or they may use the tapes themselves to do new training sessions, creating a chain effect. The training workshops' group setting allows attendees to learn strategies and techniques from the videotaped experts and also from the more experienced presenter. An equally important result of the training session is that participants meet and share experiences with like-minded people in the same line of work with whom they may maintain professional contact for years.

To prepare for this chapter, I watched and took careful notes on the verbal content of the thirteen 1993 training tapes, each from thirty to forty-five minutes long. The tapes show mainly talking heads lecturing, with some projected overhead transparencies, and there are almost no cutaways to show audience members' responses. Cumulatively, the tapes are so full of political savoir faire that I took over eighty-five pages of notes on them, and they taught me much about electoral processes, grassroots organizing, and rhetorical strategies for public self-presentation, especially for dealing with the press. In a broader sense, the tapes also fascinate me not only for their Realpolitik but for the questions they raise and the contradictions they reveal.

Grassroots Organizing

In one tape, *How to Organize a Christian County Chapter,* Guy Rodgers, then-director of Christian Coalition chapter organizing, discusses the process of chapter development. "By 1996," he declares, "we want to have identified ten million pro-family voters." To identify those voters and get them to the polls, each Christian Coalition chapter conducts and maintains an up-to-date, precise constituency analysis, household by household in its district. Sometimes such a canvass will help political candidates' fund-raising; other times it will facilitate mobilizing people to lobby for a specific issue. Of course, it is used most directly to get conservative voters to the polls. Rodgers says chapters should redo their survey every six months because issues and voters' feelings about them change.

Rodgers advises coalition canvassers who phone households in their voting district initially to ask one or two rather liberal-sounding questions as well as a few questions oriented toward conservative issues. All the caller has to do is get a yes or no answer to discover the coalition's potential supporters. Then the canvassers phone those potential conservative voters for a more detailed follow-up interview. Finally, those interviewed get a written response tailored to the phone survey; each letter includes literature targeted specifically to the issues they support—and not mailings that would anger them (for example, a pro-life letter). In this way, contact with the conservative constituency remains nuanced and does not assume that people agree on the same issues. The Christian Coalition has learned more and more to use an appeal to common sense and a broad definition of traditional values to build its base.

Rodgers explains further how to build a local Christian Coalition chapter, speaking with grassroots savvy and citing details and tactics familiar to anyone who has done this kind of work. He presents a time line for increasing a chapter's numbers from three to eighty committed members over eight weeks. In organizing a chapter, the final step comes when the core group of activists invite 400–500 people to a countywide organizing meeting, out of which group of contacts Rodgers expects eighty interested people to attend. To locate the potential attendees, Rodgers suggests contacting people from preexisting antipornography lists and church directories. At the organizing meeting, people sign up for positions such as running a finance committee, acting as public-affairs liaisons to churches to set up social action "mission" committees in each parish (for voter registration, for example), or serving as precinct captains who conduct the strategically important voter-identification surveys. Rodgers adds as an aside that since the canvass director should be attentive to detail and good at follow-up, that task is usually taken by a woman. Very little strategy is improvised in this kind of activism, and even novices can have the confidence to execute their tasks well since the process of doing the survey and the questions to ask are all carefully laid out in the Christian Coalition's "leadership packet."

This strategy for political activism has two immediate effects: First, it provides a "grassroots" network of like-minded religious conservatives. For the coalition members involved in canvassing or making local phone calls, the activity creates a sense of being enveloped in a conservative community as the caller becomes acquainted with names and addresses of sympathetic voters who live nearby. Not only does doing the voter survey institutionally reinforce the activists' shared structure of feelings, but those moral convictions now gain the force of a public voice, if not yet public policy. And the simplicity and certainty that comes with political action give the symbolic structure of "like-mindedness" or "commonsense morality" even more coherence. For the local political organizer is usually motivated by moral issues that have long been of personal concern. When he or she persuades others to *act* on these concerns, both the grassroots organizer and those recruited to action are energized by a sense that change is possible and that they can act collectively as effective agents of change.

Evangelism charges its adherents to go out into the world to make converts. When evangelists enter social action movements, they demonstrate their commitment to a widely socially acceptable cause, social reform, which they join to their religious motivation. For many committed Christians, it is probably easier and less embarrassing to collect petitions to place an initiative on the state ballot than it is to hand out religious pamphlets or to preach the Bible in a public place. Particularly for women, Christian political activity means that they can move out of the domestic sphere into a movement with social impact. Sometimes such women's zeal also reflects their need to escape the conservative mores imposed by their extended family or by the small community in which they live, mores that have limited the women's social options. From their participation in a national organization and in local organizing across class lines, Christian Coalition activists move into a satisfyingly larger "community."

In this light, Christian Coalition activism can be seen as creating new "conditions of possibility" for its members. That is, it gives people a historical sense that they are participating in a new kind of politically significant, empowering, religious-conservative community. The term "conditions of possibility" comes from Lawrence Grossberg's *We Gotta Get out of This Place* (1992), an analysis of the increasing cultural conservatism in the United States over the last two decades. Grossberg's thesis is that any culture at a given historical moment offers its participants possibilities for emotional investment and thus for "making meaning." Grossberg describes contemporary social life, what some have called "the postmodern condition," in terms of a struggle to care about something, to organize moments of stable identity, and to find the passion needed to enact one's own projects and possibilities (Grossberg 1992, 83). For grassroots political activists, the ritual of participating indeed "organizes moments of stable identity"; when an activist arouses in another the passion to act politically, that social act creates its own gratification and thus ensures the activists' further involvement.

This sense of involvement extends to those who are not political activists. Religious conservatives throughout the United States find that political life is being made available to them in new ways, empowering them with a newfound sense of participating in national issues. Because of the Christian Coalition's success in gaining control of local Republican Parties and in wielding a large influence nationally, it has given a new kind of self-esteem to the larger body of religious conservatives. For example, Ralph Reed's oft-repeated statement "We just want our place at the table" plays on fundamentalist Christians' perception of themselves as perpetual outsiders, indeed martyrs. Their grassroots political success, however, means that the fundamentalist community that had formerly seen itself as an oppressed minority finds pleasure in its sustained local and national political successes. Because of the communal reinforcement that many people gain from identifying with these victories, more and more conservatives can then be politically organized into effective locally or nationally targeted single-issue campaigns, in which large, well-organized groups always exert a powerful influence.

At this point, it seems important to address the question of the relation between electoral organizing, grassroots politics, and a popular movement. To energize a large group of people, to instill in them a conviction that change is possible, and to get them to act collectively is to form a popular movement. Such movements depend on effecting both subjective and objective changes, changes that potentiate each other. That is, to act, people have to believe that change is possible, and it may be the success or martyrdom of an early few that galvanize the many to take action in a broad-based movement for social change. Action shapes the imagination, and a renewed sense of possibility in turn shapes future action. Organizing that originates at the base is *grassroots* organizing, and popular struggles may reinforce or contradict the struggle for official political power, particularly state power.

In this specific instance, although political organization on the precinct level may guarantee its success in local elections, the degree to which the Christian Coalition represents or intends to become a broader, *popular* movement is not clear. First of all, there are limits to the assertion that the Christian Coalition is a grassroots political organization. It has much in common with traditional party organizations, especially at the precinct level, since all electoral campaigns face the same two tasks. Electoral campaigns have to convince the undecided to get out and vote, and they must influence people to vote for their candidate. To do that, in their campaign propaganda they must use a rhetoric that appeals to the swing vote, usually the centrist middle. When the Christian Coalition does this kind of electoral work on the precinct level, it does not seem to function much differently from the way I observed party politics functioning in Chicago, especially in immigrant and working-class neighborhoods. Additionally, the Christian Coalition has to increase religious conservatives' turnout from the usual 40 percent to a very high 70 to 80 percent. And to do that, the organizing drive has to turn about and use a rhetoric that supports the issues most favored by the religious right.

Earlier I spoke of the empowerment experienced by the like-minded when they have political success. There are also drawbacks to this heady sense of common cause. Not just fundamentalist Christians but any committed, cohesive social group—subcultural, ethnic, minority, trade union, or religious denominational—has a certain inward-looking aspect. When members of a subcultural group become politically active, their like-mindedness often acts to their detriment, particularly in blinding them to the political realities of the coalition building upon which electoral politics rely. In the mid-1990s, religious conservative groups in action often fell into the trap of what presenter Mike Murphy labels in these tapes "listening to the echo chamber." By that Murphy means that any group of political activists who take their view of social reality mainly from those who agree with them may fail to grasp the political realities of the campaign, especially what's on voters' minds.

Ralph Reed and the Christian Coalition leadership understand that in casting a wider electoral net, the organization has to persuade fundamentalists to embrace members of groups toward whom they otherwise might feel antipathy. In particular, because of its pro-family, antidrug, self-help stance, the Christian Coalition can tailor a special pitch to conservative blacks, and it has already found many allies among anti-abortion Catholic activists and clergy as well as orthodox and conservative Jews. The question that remains is whether "casting a wider net" will liberalize the religiously oriented political movement. If it has 40 percent of the vote and needs 51 percent, it must develop a language style to communicate with secular voters. In particular, because the mainstream press may eagerly jump in a sensationalistic way from citing the platforms of conservative candidates to making references to militia violence and that movement's role in events like the Oklahoma City bombing, the electorally active Christian right needs to control its public rhetoric to capture the high ground rather than giving the press an occasion to describe it as driven by violence-prone crazies.

On another level, if we analyze the Christian Coalition structurally, other factors belie the notion that it is a grassroots organization. There is built-in tension between its top-down organizational style and local members' needs and desires. The nationally organized Christian right funds and organizes Christian Coalition chapters because it has a need for large numbers of activists, whom it trains to make more effective. However, in the process, the national leadership may ignore the fact that local issues on a grassroots level are often what coalition members most urgently want to deal with. For example, the Christian Coalition has a national television show on the satellite feed from National Empowerment Television. Coalition chapters frequently meet to watch and discuss a show, and members are asked to organize to support issues raised at the national level. Obviously national mobilization has a powerful political effect. Yet it is in organizing around local issues closer to home that the coalition has had most of its political victories, so much so that at the 1995 National Convention, Ralph Reed declared that the coalition would not try to pick a presidential candidate, saying that it would concentrate its efforts at the grassroots level, where it is the most effective.

A permanent tension exists between the exigencies of electoral politics and the need to recruit followers who otherwise strive to promote a much narrower conservative cause. For example, coalition members are now running for local or state office—on school boards, city councils, state legislatures, planning and zoning commissions, or county commissions; they campaign openly as conservatives, knowing they have an organized base and a national organization, the Christian Coalition, to support them. However, there are many other fundamentalist leaders who do not want to compromise and adopt the broadly popular rhetoric needed to win elections. These people eschew the secular basis of electoral campaigns. Instead, they prefer to work on single-issue struggles in which they can openly state the problem in terms of their religious and moral beliefs. Currently such activists come into conflict with longtime members of the Republican Party. For example, many conservative religious voters adamantly demand that the Christian Coalition and ultimately the Republican Party require a strong anti-abortion stand from any candidate whom it supports, even though that insistence may cost the Republican Party electoral victory. Influential fundamentalist leaders such as James "Dr." Dobson, head of the large family-oriented publications and media group Focus on the Family, reinforce such a demand by insisting that any backing down on the abortion issue would betray all the Christians recruited into mainstream political life.

In general, in contrast to working in precinct party politics, when people struggle for a single-issue cause, they experience a particular kind of emotional gratification: that of socially aroused and discharged passion. For example, in the campaigns for and against gay rights, communities experience all the emotions of social polarization. People who attend rallies not only use the occasion to release their own anger but see that anger socially reinforced. Socially shared anger creates meaning; for the religious right, anger against homosexuality itself becomes its own just cause. However, emotional meaning may not coincide with a rationally effective political strategy. In this case, conservative politicians' very common tactic of using antihomosexual rhetoric to unite and energize their subculture has also often resulted in a failed, overtly anti-homosexual electoral campaign. Furthermore, extending Grossberg's analysis about historical conditions creating new "conditions of possibility . . . discursive mediations and strategic deployments" (Grossberg 1992, 13), it is clear that when the religious conservative leadership strategically deploys antihomosexual discourse in a subculture already antagonistic to gays, that leadership irresponsibly creates "conditions of possibility" for violence against homosexuals, even though many people in that subculture would not participate in such violence directly. Looked at from the perspective of its shared, almost-universal condemnation of homosexuality, the conservative Christian community perpetuates its common ground and promotes a sense of cohesion in contradictory ways, sometimes around retrograde goals.

Sara Diamond has argued that such contradictions are common within the democratic process of struggling for political power. She asserts that the differences between the goals of the Christian right single-issue causes and the Christian Coalition's electoral strategy affirm the vigor of the Christian right political movement as a whole. This may be true even though religious conservatives variously support many issues that remain a political liability in the larger electoral sphere. Diamond describes one group, Christian Action Network (CAN), which focuses on single-issue campaigns, and CAN's relation to the Christian Coalition:

> CAN was front and center in last year's [1993's] lobbying to maintain the bans on gay military personnel and on federal funding for poor women's abortions. CAN also took credit for persuading Congress to cut the budget of the National Endowment for the Arts by $8.6 million. Though CAN opposes subordinating Christian right activism to the interests of the Republican Party per se, there is nothing particularly "extreme" about its tactics. CAN uses direct mailing to mobilize phone calls

> and letters to Congress members. That CAN pursues a narrow-issue focus and the Christian Coalition hopes to make itself indispensable to the Republican Party is, if anything, a sign of the Christian right's maturity. Social movements are successful to the extent that activists and leaders with divergent strategies can each find a niche... Both types of groups [single issue and electoral] are successful because they exploit elements of routine electoral politics: Congress members' response to constituent lobbying and persistent low voter turnout, both of which are advantageous to the highly mobilized evangelical minority. (Diamond 1996, 91–92)

Although I generally support Diamond's thesis, I am worried about the degree to which right rhetoric and single-issue campaigns, waged with so much passion, create a climate of opinion that facilitates acts of extreme violence. Although most conservative religious people would denounce the Oklahoma City bombing as a horrific act of terrorism, the religious conservative political umbrella is offered to groups like the militia movement, the National Rifle Association, and the "wise-use" land movement. Such groups belong well within what Ralph Reed calls "the leave-us-alone coalition." Conservative political discourse has currently opened up a social space to groups that once had general social opprobrium. In this vein, the trials of Timothy McVeigh and the Montana Freemen may reveal the groups' self-justification through dominion theology and thus expose a seamier side of the fringe groups that share much of the ideology of Christian right (Diamond 1996, 47–56). In this tension between the Christian conservative mainstream and its margins, the violence that comes from right-wing fringe groups may yet irrevocably taint mainstream religious-conservative activism and, especially, public opinion about it.

Routine Electoral Politics

It is in the area of "routine electoral politics" that the Christian Coalition leadership training tapes are so brilliant. The speakers include successful politicians and highly paid consultants who do liability analyses for candidates, fund-raising, polling, publicity, and public relations. In half-hour sessions, they each summarize lessons from their areas of expertise with the kind of succinctness that only comes from years of experience in the field. For example, political consultant Bill Fisher speaks fascinatingly about what might ordinarily be a dry subject, the legislative process of a bill at the federal, state, and local levels. He indicates all the structural points in the formal process where lobbyists can exert pressure, from the drafting of new legislation (get to the bill's congressional sponsor) to influencing which committee will get the bill. Legislators, he tells his audience, often vote on bills they have not read, and especially at the higher levels, they depend on staff advice. Lobbyists can also influence which legislators get on the bill's conference committee, again at the state level. Fisher recommends that those trying to influence the legislature look for some unrelated bill to which they might get their phrasing added or their positions inserted as amendments, especially if their own issue would go down if presented in a bill of its own.

He and many of the other speakers understand what activism in electoral politics demands: negotiation, compromise, and broadening one's base of support. He describes the kinds of face-to-face interaction a conservative lobbyist, staff person, or legislator must become skilled at: being always available to constituents, having good relations with the press, and getting the friendship and respect, if not necessarily agreement, of key legislative figures. Roger Byrd, a young southern businessman who is the youngest state representative elected in Georgia, concurs when he talks about what he's learned in office: "Become allies with your former opponents and cultivate your friends, even making friends of enemies . . . Bring them into your tent." Byrd and Fisher's advice has the kind of acumen that might attract small business owners and professionals to coalition activism.

Most of the tapes in this series contain information on conducting an electoral campaign. In particular, they emphasize the importance of advance planning, of studying all aspects of each issue and candidate. Every campaign organization must know how to target its resources. It must spend money wisely and approach the right voters with the right issues. Advance planning indicates when and where to fight and also how to lead the opponent into shadowboxing around issues that no one ultimately cares about. An example in this vein is conservative congressional Republicans' success with the Whitewater investigation: Even though it was inconclusive, the investigation consumed an enormous amount of the Clintons' economic resources and probably wore down their morale. At the same time, it has remained an issue generally unimportant to the public.

Political research includes the systematic study and follow-up that must accompany any phase of shaping public policy. Campaigns, for example, investigate every detail about the people running and gather other background data. This information allows speechwriters and publicists to create effective campaign literature since only by sifting through previously gathered information can writers finally put all relevant details into glaring relief and in a way that voters will grasp at once and sympathize with.

To understand the current political situation in a candidate's district, the campaign may use professional canvassing and polling and do a follow-up at regular intervals, but such polling is very expensive. A less expensive way to find out about voters' concerns is to conduct in-depth conversations with people in the district from all walks of life. Such conversations must avoid indulging in the ego gratification that comes from listening to those with concurring views. The interviewers or the candidate him- or herself should especially try to find out what people like about the other side's candidate and positions and listen with a subtle ear, sensitive to the conversation's shadings and nuances. If a campaign can map voters' feelings, it can identify its target constituencies and effectively make a pitch to them; only gradually does a campaign learn what kind of pitches will work with each of the targeted groups. Finally, if the campaign still needs professional public opinion research, at least the organizers have identified the conceptual areas around which pollsters should frame questions.

Christian Coalition researcher on legislators, Terry Cooper, describes how to do opposition research. In some ways Cooper gives a lesson in negative campaigning, and in some ways he eschews that. Following the research, Cooper advises that campaign strategists make a detailed list of contrasts between their candidate and the opponent, and from that set of contrasts, some spoken and some not spoken publicly, the strategists can elaborate a campaign's themes and rationale. Opposition research teaches the key tactical lessons about where one's openings are and will be. Much of the research is done by studying the public record. If the opponent is an incumbent, a lot can be learned from his or her voting history and also from a literature analysis of his or her public persona. Much is written about legislators, for example, in profiles in the *Congressional Quarterly,* Sunday magazine supplements, city magazines, the liberal press, financial disclosure statements, and speeches—both political speeches delivered by the opposition candidate and those he or she delivered in the legislature.

Unearthing dirty laundry about the other side comes from doing vulnerability analyses, which the researcher must conduct as rigorously about one's own candidate as about the opposition. Cooper says that as a consultant, he has to interrogate his own candidate in a ruthlessly frank way since if he knows his candidate's potential weaknesses well in advance, then the campaign strategists can take the initiative in framing the discussion when these weaknesses come up publicly. "There are no secrets in a campaign," Cooper emphasizes. Most important, personal attacks do not provide the most effective or demoralizing attack strategy. Cooper points out that a far more powerful strategy is to undermine the opposing candidate's strengths rather than emphasizing his or her weaknesses. It is better to explain how the opposition's strong points are not so good after all and how the coalition candidate's strengths are more significant and his or her platform covers more issues. Cooper indicates the great effectiveness of a very simple strategy: Demolish the opponent's strength. When this strategy is used, the opponent easily loses while the victor avoids the stigma of negative campaigning. This is the kind of strategy that results in conservatives' denouncing Democrats' social welfare legislation as one more wasteful proposal from "tax-and-spend liberals" or noting that an opposition candidate had a 100 percent perfect voting record on most issues—as evaluated by the Sierra Club or the AFL-CIO.

Cooper and other presenters emphasize the results that come from detailed research. The more knowledge a campaign has, the more its organizers can act with strategic accuracy. They gain a capacity to predict and a certain amount of control. As they learn their candidate's strengths, they know where to target the campaign's resources. Because they have analyzed the opponent and their own candidate so well, they can predict what the opponent might do or say, where their candidate might be attacked, and how voters might react in each case.

Embourgeoisement

The Christian Coalition may foster in its activists a kind of embourgeoisement that often accompanies political work. "Embourgeoisement" refers to the fact that doing political organizing means becoming an administrator and usually moving up in class (it is a phenomenon that often has been studied in terms of trade unions or European labor parties). Especially at the local level, coalition members will find a close fit between business, politics, and Christian right philosophy and organizing. Working in the Christian Coalition clearly gives members a hand up the ladder in their own local business community. To study one's own socioeconomic environment, in this case, the local precinct or district, in such great detail makes a coalition member quickly divest him- or herself of many class prejudices in order to develop strategies based on fact and not myth. Vulnerability studies and voter canvassing use procedures similar to market research. Just studying these Christian Coalition Leadership School tapes and putting them into practice is like getting an M.B.A. in public relations and marketing.

One of the main gratifications from going through a Leadership School, for example, is to discover the systematic nature of the U.S. political process and investigate its mode of operation—to learn how it works. Understanding that society functions in a systematic way may be a new insight for these activists; indeed, few people would have access to understanding the systematic nature of U.S. politics as laid out in the Christian Coalition's Leadership School tapes. Analyzing the origins of differential understandings of U.S. society, social theorist Robert Coles has published a number of books, the "Children of Crisis" series, which investigate the very different kinds of education that children from different social classes and ethnic groups receive. One of his main conclusions is that children from poor and working-class families receive an education that at best just fits them *into* the system, often at a low-wage job, such as a secretary or electronics repair technician, whereas children from families with higher incomes, often in elite suburban or private schools, receive an education that teaches that there *is* a system. Affluent children learn the systematic nature of social processes, including psychology, sociology, and economics. In this way, the Christian Coalition, as well as conservative think tanks, attempts to bring to its constituency an education about social processes. Most of these people were previously denied an understanding of the systematic nature of society since they lived largely removed from active participation in the electoral sphere.

In contrast, Christian conservative women now often enter right-wing politics by working from within the domestic sphere, in what Concerned Women for America calls "kitchen table politics." Many of the same housewives who have heeded the call to serve God as angel of the hearth are entering the world again through the Christian Coalition, which provides them with a sense of agency in a protected way. That is, it supports (keeps them locked within) fundamentalism's normative view of the family, its fear of public education, and its rejection of state-sponsored social services as intrusions in family life. Such organizing also can be a sublimation for sexual repression or dissatisfaction with domestic boredom. Once housewives become involved in the organization, the Christian Coalition provides field experience that teaches them a wide range of skills. Within a lobbying or electoral campaign, women can learn, for example, to speak publicly about "uncomfortable" issues through practice with friends or by writing fact sheets and position papers. Furthermore, building relations, being responsive, or making follow-up calls and writing notes are things women are already trained in and things a political organization needs.

For other interested organizers who have the time and interest to do this kind of detail work, Christian Coalition work may also provide the kind of training and professionalization that would make them more employable. Many of the women involved in activism are returning to the workforce or upgrading from low-level to white-collar jobs. Other activists are often underemployed youth in their twenties. Their work in the Christian Coalition gives them skills that may qualify them for jobs in the state legislature, civil service, or business.

In particular, they learn about face-to-face organizing and selling and about the kind of interpersonal relations cultivated in the business world. For example, engaging in the specific task of fund-raising brings a Christian Coalition member into contact with both the bourgeoisie and those of modest means. According to one of the tapes' speakers, David Miner, contact with business people should typically go like this: If I were to phone a business person, I'd say: "I'm Julia Lesage. I am running for school board and have a conservative political philosophy. I'd like to come and speak with you for about a half hour about your ideas on the future of the school board." Miner points out that businesspersons expect, with amour propre, the fund-raiser to ask for enough money to flatter their ego. They also expect their coalition visitor to have an accurate or even elevated perception of the businessperson's status, success, reputation, and worth. And they will remember the person they gave money to, even giving a second time to protect their original investment. When organizers try to raise money from poorer givers, the philosophy behind the fund-raising is that such a donation has merit as a profound moral gesture, since working-class people can put their money where their heart and their beliefs lie, and they may become energized by this act of political commitment. In this way, the business-aspirant organizer learns to do sales and pitch a line effectively to both the affluent and the poor.

Many aspects of Christian Coalition organizing would also be attractive to a professional such as a lawyer or schoolteacher or to a small business owner, who could establish face-to-face contact with the elites and the politically influential people in their community or state. These middle-class professionals and business people would learn the skills to be effective lobbyists. Business and political acumen enhance each other. As Fisher says in the tapes, not only is building a relation with legislators crucial for anyone wanting to shape public policy, but the process of doing so closely resembles that of building a business or establishing a professional reputation. The chapter's committed workers need to build long-term interpersonal relations—with political figures, reporters, clergy, potential donors—which is accomplished only through consistency, promptness, and reliability. In speaking with the committed on the coalition's mailing list, a good organizer makes them feel that they are a part of the action. And the chapter's pro-business stance will make the organizer familiar to many individual businesspersons.

In fact, one might wonder whether in targeting districts that pick probusiness candidates, such as the suburbs, coalition activists might adopt more of a philosophy of corporate liberalism than of libertarianism or Christian political correctness. The role of the martyr and perpetual outsider takes a toll, and the lure to throw it all overboard might come not from secular humanism but from entrepreneurship and the lure of an even better life in the suburbs.

Interestingly, even in a grassroots movement, the candidate must act as the main fund-raiser and either be rich or cultivate ties with the rich. Wealthy people are the main givers to political campaigns, with donations of over $500 forming the bulk of the funds raised. As Miner says, only in September before a November election can the candidate start delivering speeches. Until then he or she has to be locked in a room with only a telephone and made to do full time fund-raising for a half a day every day, with no distractions. Campaigning means begging, no matter how embarrassing it is. For example, all the people working on the campaign have to accept their role in demanding that their families and friends make large contributions. Especially those on the finance committee must expect that they, their families, and their friends will work full-time on fund-raising and will also put a lot of their own money into the campaign.

The relation of the Christian Coalition to mainstream U.S. corporate capitalism remains as yet untried. The conservative coalition in U.S. politics consists of both social and economic conservatives, whom political leaders like Newt Gingrich and Ralph Reed know must be brought together as a unified force within the Republican Party. For that reason, conservative social legislation is regularly paired with legislation that the U.S. bourgeoisie has long fought for, in particular, a reduction in the capital gains tax, which primarily affects those who make a living from buying and selling property or securities. Furthermore, ruling-class culture is often conservative culture, with high culture already tightly tied to money and corporations. However, the Christian right does not necessarily support contemporary marketing principles, such as "sex sells." And on a broader scale, we have yet to see worked out the relation of the Christian right to international and multinational capital, especially in terms of the international policies that protect the stability of multinational corporations and transnational financial markets. Is Christian conservatism compatible with corporate liberalism or with Japanese corporate paternalism? I suspect that capitalism is flexible enough to adopt to a renewed puritanism in the United States, but the contradictions between the agendas of the religious right and international capital have not even begun to be explored. Right now, a big distance still separates a Rockefeller Republican from a fundamentalist one.

Rhetoric

Public relations means trying to control the agenda of every political discussion, to define the issues for both one's own and the opponent's sides as these come into the public forum. In the most astute tape in the Christian Coalition's Leadership School series, Rebecca Hagelin, media director for some key right organizations, teaches political organizers how to frame public discussions. Hagelin insists that each chapter develop a public relations and media plan that articulates a strategy as detailed as the chapter's political organizing plan. The public relations plan has to evaluate personnel, financial resources, and time lines with the same probity as does the chapter's electoral strategy. For example, Hagelin insists that each group pick a public relations director and a press spokesperson. The press automatically turns to the State Director of an organization such as the Christian Coalition, but that person may not be sufficiently verbally adept, well rehearsed, or available to meet with the press on demand. Decisions about media representation, Hagelin insists, should be made by the group, not just by the chairperson since the person who meets the press has special responsibilities to prepare him- or herself for those events.

Hagelin's advice to those selected to be spokespersons for the Christian Coalition matches the organization's overall strategy vis-à-vis public discourse, so it is worth noting her advice in detail. This strategy is partially based on advertising principles—including the use of catchy phrases loaded with emotional connotations, an avoidance of analysis, and an assumption of "moral unity" among the listeners. In fact, the strategy calculatedly shapes the issues around which morality should or will be discussed publicly. First of all, as Hagelin instructs, a coalition chapter or lobbying group must plan ahead what issues they wish to discuss publicly. Then, still working well in advance of a political move, they should write press releases and rehearse spokespersons in the best phrasing of these issues.

Hagelin teaches a tactic that I pass on regularly to media production students, that is, how to be savvy in front of the camera if they themselves are interviewed. Any press or newspaper interviewee should make only three to five major points—Hagelin calls these the coalition's "nuggets of truth." The reason for doing so is to guarantee that the edited story will indeed show the interviewee making one of his or her main points; the interviewee also knows never to offer a recorded aside that the reporter or news editor might use instead. For that reason, people experienced in speaking to the press or doing talk shows learn to make a few points, and only those points, over and over, no matter what other arguments reporters or opponents raise.

Though this advice presents the interview as performance and offers tips on how to avoid stage fright or politically disadvantageous statements, Hagelin also knows the value of *research* for speech making, even when that speech making seems to be spontaneous. Like other speakers in the series, she insists that coalition organizers, especially the chapter or campaign's public relations committee, know in advance the issues that will come up; they should research these, especially the ones they need to refute. Not only should the group gather facts to back up their points, but, even more important, says Hagelin, they should brainstorm to learn how to phrase the issues in a catchy and quotable way.

In terms of propaganda, the apt phrase, cultivated so carefully through extensive preplanning, has proven to be the Christian Coalition's genius; it turns a moral conviction into a well-turned phrase that seems to sum up rational social-policy agenda. When Hagelin gives an example of this process, she points to what must be a common occurrence on the right: A spokesperson often feels uncomfortable refuting the argument that a woman or girl needs access to abortion in a case of incest. To surmount this discomfort, Hagelin suggests that the spokesperson meet with friends to plan answers that make him or her feel comfortable; as a result of practicing, the spokesperson will learn not to shy away from difficult questions but will become eager to take them on in defending the legitimacy of the group's political agenda. This is assertiveness training taken to a new level. It represents the kind of empowerment that allows people active in the Christian Coalition to make a strong impression in the business world and potentially to rise in social position, as I discussed previously. Hagelin's way of training public spokespersons makes them feel like experts, confident to take on most issues, since they have studied the controversial points and have prepared responses in advance.

Because verbal phrasing shapes voters'—and reporters'—attitudes, Hagelin indicates that the organization's public relations wing must do the following:

> Write catchy phrases that are well thought-out and designed to leave an image in people's minds. Learn to make a direct and concise statement about any issue so that you can come up with language that reflects what *you* want to say. Refuse to use the opposition's buzz- or keywords and try always to place them on defensive. For example, say *pro-life* not *anti-abortion,* since you believe in an intrinsic value to human life, from the unborn to the elderly and sick. Also say *homosexual special privileges,* not *gay rights,* since more than equal rights, homosexuals are after a new set of privileges designed to further their lifestyle. Say *traditional,* not *old-fashioned values*; you believe in the timeless values of family, life, and liberty, but not necessarily in conventional actions in the home. Do exercises to sharpen your language: Write down opposition's buzzwords and then brainstorm collectively with others to find replacements. Write down difficult statements on any given issue and again brainstorm with someone to figure out your response. (Paraphrased from the tape)

Beyond its efficacy for grooming spokespersons to talk to the press, such advice reveals two aspects of Christian Coalition strategy: its relation to voters and its struggle to shape public discourse at large in the United States. The kind of language used in these "catchy phrases" assumes that people vote out of emotion and the campaign's resonance with their beliefs, and that support for a given political move can be marshaled more from appealing to sentiments of dissatisfaction than from presenting the details and consequences of a specific piece of legislation or political issue. In particular, the Christian Coalition, which seems to have studied both market research and left organizing tactics, differs from the left social movements of the 1960s and 1970s in that it consistently eschews educating the public about social structures.

Market research perceives its targets as sheeplike, responding predictably to certain stimuli. The Christian right sees the public at large in somewhat the same way and seeks to make it react predictably to certain well-thought-out verbal stimuli. Thus the Christian Coalition develops press strategies like those outlined above. In addition, it makes huge financial and logistical investments in its major electoral strategy—printing and distributing millions of voter "report cards." These state in one or two highly selective, connotatively slanted sentences a "summary" of the candidates' positions and records. It does likewise for the initiatives and referenda on the ballot, noting in a terse conclusion which issues the Christian Coalition supports and which it opposes. Information is parceled out to voters in small doses, and any position that was supported previously can always reverse itself (which, for example, we can expect in regards to term limits now that more Christian right candidates are ascending to local, state, and national office).

On a larger scale, part of the Christian right's fierce need to control discourse comes from the fact that it has long seen itself as an outsider, a pariah within dominant liberal discourse communities in the United States. In the society at large and within the conservative religious community, institutional discourse is normative, establishing parameters of what can and cannot be said within a given framework; furthermore, these parameters tend to become internalized so that a discourse community establishes what can and cannot be thought. One way of looking at political conflict in the United States today is in terms of a clash between two discourse communities, which is what religious conservatives refer to as a "culture war." From the perspective of Christian fundamentalists, for example, the law denies them religious freedom, social services would intervene in parental control over the child, medicine legitimizes abortion, public education secularizes youth, and the press demonizes the right. In this sense, Christian teleministries and secular conservative talk shows like Rush Limbaugh's offer the satisfaction of providing the Christian right a mediated "home," an alternative public discourse community. In addition, for those who concur, the tidy catchphrases that sum up areas of moral or political agreement now affirm one's membership in a newly established, aspiring power bloc. Furthermore, the older vision of oneself as martyr and the newer vision of oneself as socially empowered become melded when a person keeps these catchphrases alive by publicly uttering them, easily assuming that they bear analytic weight.

In its discursive concerns, the Christian right seems especially obsessed with sexuality. Sexual issues that concern the right include AIDS education and research funding, teen pregnancy, social and personal aspects of birth control, "illegitimacy," pornography, and abortion. Mostly the right seeks to control discourses around sexuality by placing a moral premium on the social fantasy of a healthy family: one with a father, mother, and children living together under the same roof and never fragmenting in divorce.

However, the historical circumstances shaping the family and sexuality have shifted in the last twenty-five years, and they continue to change. To earn enough to support a family or, if middle class, to maintain that lifestyle, women, especially mothers, have had to enter the workforce; with many areas of work opening up to women, the structure of the U.S. family has also shifted. In terms of sexuality, with the advent of AIDS the social circumstances shaping sexual practices have also changed, showing desire ever more visibly as historically shifting in its expression. Is conservative discourse only catching up to social change? And can it offer very many people a social alternative?

Consider an example of the kind of contradictions the Christian Coalition does not address when it promotes family values: Working couples nationwide face difficult issues related to day care. This problem has become a structural feature of contemporary life. Day care is often called by the Christian right "social parenting," and, as part of the right's larger social agenda of keeping the social welfare system out of the family, fundamentalists often condemn it. However, day care is not condemned or even mentioned in these activist training tapes, most probably because most of the women in the Christian Coalition will need day care. To fulfill its fantasy of "Mom at home," the Christian Coalition has instead proposed congressional legislation to enact a substantial tax credit for each child, originally to apply to families with a joint annual income of up to $200,000, so that families in which one parent wants to stay home as a full-time homemaker would not be penalized.

The right also uses sexuality to proffer an easy condemnation of groups deemed to be Other, which the right wants to make disappear. In the Leadership School tapes, the speakers often make in passing easy condemnations of abortion, as well as sometimes scurrilous references to homosexuality. For example, Terry Cooper, in discussing opposition research, notes that one national legislator was effectively denounced for joining the Health and Education Subcommittee, which the opposition within the legislator's constituency had relabeled the Fairy Committee because it was responsible for AIDS funding. Yet even in the ranks of activists there are many women who have had abortions, as well as people who have helped a family member or friend get an abortion, or who have a homosexual in their family. As those of us on the other side develop a way to oppose this targeting of the sexually "sinful"—the accused including people as diverse as teens, welfare mothers, homosexuals, artists, media makers in the entertainment industry, or women seeking abortion—we have to find more points of personal contact, to get ordinary people on the right to admit the many ways that they have an intimate tie to that which they oppose.

It is equally important to denounce at every turn the racism that lies behind the right rhetoric defining sexuality and the family. When conservative legislators seek to deny rights to children born in the United States to undocumented immigrants, the lawmakers implicitly act out of fear, and perhaps also jealousy, that the poor have babies at a faster rate than does the middle class, that people of color in the United States have a higher reproductive rate than whites. Terms like "illegitimacy," "teenage pregnancy," and "welfare" refer in a coded way to the presumed illicit sexuality of urban African Americans (Hacker 1995). Conservative political discourse's reliance on racially inflected social condemnations of poor, single-parent families indicates that veiled racist discourse is one of the traits that makes the religious conservative movement so effective. In a voice seemingly opposed to racist practices and attitudes, Ralph Reed frequently denounces conservative Christianity's historical support of slavery and its ongoing role in perpetuating slavery's legacy (Reed 1994, 235). However, many other Christian conservative leaders demonstrate their capacity to contain and use both voices at once, a tactic that proves useful at both the national policy-making level and the "grassroots" level.

On another level, in its ongoing attacks against the arts and public education, one of the right's easiest victories came when it took a phrase wittily used on the left to criticize overzealous ideologues, "political correctness," and turned it into a catchword to criticize all liberal efforts at social change or even efforts to analyze or publicly discuss issues of injustice. The arts and humanities, especially in the educational sphere, elicit the right's special rage. Again, feeling itself the outsider, the right fears the left's cultural capital in the arts and humanities and targets it. But it also studies the left, especially left phraseology, and then it turns that phraseology around 180 degrees. It is not a new strategy; the 1979 Supreme Court case *Regents of the University of California v. Bakke* brought the phrase "reverse discrimination" into common parlance. But this verbal strategy has now become greatly potentiated when so effectively used by a political organization aiming at electoral control.

In the electoral sphere, one of the more recent versions of taking liberal phrasing and turning it to right purposes is the California Civil Rights Initiative, which appeared on the state ballot in 1996 and was enacted into law in November of that year. With different phrasing, this initiative had a trial run as Colorado's Amendment 2 to the state constitution, which the electorate voted into law in 1992 and which was judged unconstitutional by the United States Supreme Court in 1996. Proponents of the California initiative, learning from the Colorado trial how to phrase an anti–civil rights law, proposed the following wording for ballot Proposition 209, which became an amendment to the California Constitution:

> The stage shall not discriminate against, or grant preferential treatment to, any individual or group on the basis of race, sex, color, ethnicity, or national origin in the operation of public employment, public education, or public contracting. (Jones 1996)

Christian American, the Christian Coalition's magazine, also available online on the Internet, introduced this issue for the first time to its readers in April 1995, when it noted: "Already clones of CCRI [California Civil Rights Initiative] are being readied in other states. And there will be an effort to put a national version in the Republican platform of 1996, if not to pass another into federal law even before then" (Peyton 1996).

The California Civil Rights Initiative makes a useful case study of how the Christian Coalition "introduces" a new issue and then builds it into a legislative platform. The move from clever phrasing to lobbying campaigns to writing new laws based on that phrasing reveals the Christian Coalition's innovativeness on the political scene. Time and time again we can see how the coalition leadership has studied left vocabulary and very deliberately, almost ironically, recast it. The phrasing of the original Equal Rights Amendment is: "Equality of rights under the law shall not be denied or abridged by the United States or any State on the basis of sex." The California Equal Rights Initiative was also phrased in a way that would restrict the state from acting on the basis of certain characteristics. Because of its phrasing, it seemed to echo the Equal Rights Amendment's progressive goals when, in fact, the initiative's supporters wished to reverse the effect of equal rights and affirmative action legislation that had been widely enacted in national, state, and local law.

The Christian Coalition leadership is very aware of the relation of discourse's key role in political organizing—in particular, the relation of discursive struggles to the kind of political processes that religious conservatives have set in motion. Here, well before the 1996 vote, the *Christian American* in its April 1995 issue mentions the question of the California Civil Rights Initiative. It indicates hopefully that this initiative may become a major part of the Christian right's national platform, even the Republican Party's national platform. In a top-down way, the coalition news magazine times how the organization will build support for a national anti–civil rights law, now labeled in Orwellian fashion a civil rights law. This planting of the idea reveals a characteristic Christian right discursive strategy, and it indicates how far the chapters are from being grassroots organizations, since the timing with which they take up national issues is so well paced-out for them in advance.

The Christian Coalition reaps many benefits from the time and money it spends on "framing the issues." Its discursive intervention in shaping what can and cannot be said has already had an impact in the U.S. social sphere.

Because the Christian Coalition has created a mechanism, the voter survey, to constantly assess its constituency's emotional and social needs, it can tailor its propaganda to common prejudices. It formulates ways of stating issues that imply a consensus, that imply that these issues are directly related to values everyone shares, especially the need to promote the family. For these reasons, any effective opposition to right-wing political moves must analyze the discursive history of a given political issue and trace the way the right's vocabulary and propositions are uniquely tied to a larger political agenda. As we analyze the larger context behind any right-wing discursive move, we also resist our constantly being "framed" by them, too.

In Conclusion, Some Personal Reflections

At this point, I would like to consider some of the contradictions I see in the political organizing of the Christian right. I have found it useful to examine the relation of this kind of organizing to other movements with which I am more familiar. Not only has the right studied the progressive social movements of the last three decades, its tendencies also echo my experiences in the left and in the women's movement. Conservative activists like Ralph Reed study my world and I study theirs. The goals and tactics of the Christian Coalition's organizing seem eerily familiar, as do the positions of the single-issue groups that do not want to compromise in order to appeal to the broader electorate. As repugnant as their discourse and goals are, the unwillingness of the 1994 House of Representatives freshmen to compromise on issues such as the budget, because of their sense of moral and political urgency, mirrors my own desire for the purity of an alternative culture and disdain for legislative bargaining, which so often seems to be a process in which the poor, women, and ethnic minorities lose out.

However, a big gap separates Christian right organizing from that in which I have participated. Perhaps the biggest difference lies in our goals in educating the public. On the left and in the women's movement, intellectuals and artists have taken as their main task the attempt to teach others how to analyze social structures and how to gain knowledge whose efficacy will persist over time. The Christian right also has a faith in learning about and teaching underlying structures, but its analysis always assumes the "naturalness" of capitalism and gender roles, so that the systematic nature of capitalism and the cultural shaping of gender go uninvestigated. In this way, for example, it exposes the failure of the liberal compromise, that is, the failure of welfare programs to move the underclass out of poverty, but it posits private charity as the alternative to welfare. It cannot tackle an analysis of capitalism as an institution that needs and perpetuates an underclass. In contrast, left and feminist intellectual work also reflects a conviction that people need to dig below the surface in order to interpret the world around them more accurately, but to us this means understanding and teaching the mechanisms of capitalism, imperialism, racism, and patriarchy. I and my coworkers have put in many hours doing research so as to educate our readership, viewership, and students about the processes of mystification operating in the world. In 1971, for example, when I was working on a college underground paper, the editorial staff read *Le Monde,* airmailed to a university library, to inform our readers about the events surrounding the invasion of Cambodia even though a U.S. news blackout existed there. And in the last thirty years in the world of left and feminist media production and criticism, film and video makers and scholars have seen as their major roles analyzing the ideology of image production and using media production and criticism to make visible the social realities and perspectives of communities ignored by the dominant media. The depth of analysis found in progressive publications is what conservatives cannot provide their constituencies since their goals are limited to taking over the Republican Party and U.S. political power.

There is a purpose to seeking the most in-depth, broadly explanatory, and accurate analysis. In order to change society in a just way, we have to know where it has been and where it might go. As Sara Diamond summarizes the difference between the two cultures, "To be 'radical' means to seize the roots of social problems, to advocate and work for profound change. The Christian Right, on the contrary, supports existing conditions that effectively maintain inequality between rich and poor, white and black, men and women" (Diamond 1996, 89).

The right's goal is currently to effect moral legislation by electoral means. Yet for them as for us, electoral politics may have a limit. As Christian Coalition activists make the compromises necessary to win and stay in office, they will probably find that their political victories do not cause a right agenda to percolate down throughout the system. As feminists we have seen some aspects of our agenda widely picked up by society; but more of our goals are never discussed seriously, just discarded. To cite a small example, though women and people of color have progressed in terms of media representation so that they now see their faces on the TV screen as news announcers, that is a very minor victory. Such token inclusions have hardly defused institutional racism and sexism, of which too many people constantly still feel the effects.

In this vein, as I do this research, I ask myself with pressing urgency: "Why is the Christian right so comfortable merging with local and state politics when many of us were never and perhaps still are not willing to define this as our principal social role?" I think it is because of the easy fit between pro-business and pro-family politics, the Christian right's phrasing of political issues, and capitalism itself. For women on the right, tied to the ideology of motherhood, schools and peer groups seem dangerous for their children, as do sexual knowledge and sexual activity. Libertarian philosophies of minimal government "interference" and especially minimal taxation seem to be attractive across religious lines. And a tough-on-crime and tough-on-welfare (coded phrases signifying tough-on-urban-blacks) approach has been a tactic exploited by both parties. Even though we can see through these political "lines" to their ideological underpinnings and their social consequences, few of the people I work with politically have had enough faith in the "system" to want to devote all their time to taking it over, especially not to working full-time within the Democratic Party to give it a more progressive cast.

In contrast, in the case of the Christian right, the call to political participation is heavily coded with the rhetoric of Christian duty and the establishing of God's kingdom on earth. For this reason, to give them their founder's imprimatur, a number of these Christian Coalition Leadership School tapes have an introduction by Pat Robertson providing a ultimately theological justification for Christian right activism:

> God has endowed us with the authority to govern the world, and with that comes the duty to exercise it. If we are going to be good stewards, we will learn to exercise the precious gift of freedom that God has given to each one of us. Without a well-founded strategy, even the most powerful vision may fail.

In this exhortation, the code phrases "endowed us with the authority to govern" and "be good stewards" remind fundamentalists that Pat Robertson adheres to the doctrine of postmillenarianism. This tenet of faith holds that the elect shall rule on earth for a thousand years after the coming of Christ. More sophisticated religious right strategists base their social policy arguments less on the tenet of millenarianism and more on arguments from natural law or widespread moral consensus around certain issues. As a political organizer, Ralph Reed has consistently advised conservative religious activists speaking in public to rephrase their religious concerns into language dealing only with social issues. However, the gap that separates Pat Robertson's millenarian frame of reference from Ralph Reed's frame of reference as a political organizer is not large at all. Reed, Robertson's former alter ego in the Christian Coalition, may explicitly reject theocracy, the use of political power to enact God's will on earth, and may offer instead a pluralist argument: that conservative Christians, just like any other group in this culture, have the right to participate actively in the political sphere. Yet for many on the religious right, the theocratic argument *is* the reason for their political commitment. Disclaimers aside, it is still conservative religious thinking that informs the public policy goals of the religious right.

Works Cited

Boston, Robert. 1996. *The Most Dangerous Man in America?—Pat Robertson and the Rise of the Christian Coalition*. Amherst, Mass.: Prometheus Books.

Christian Coalition Leadership School Videotape Series. 1993. Chesapeake, Va.: Christian Coalition.

Christian Coalition World Wide Web site. 1996. *http://www.cc.org/cc/*.

Diamond, Sara. 1996. *Facing the Wrath: Confronting the Right in Dangerous Times*. Monroe, ME: Common Courage Press.

Fisher, William, Ralph Reed, and Richard Weinhold. 1990. *Christian Coalition Leadership School Training Manual*. Chesapeake, Va.: Christian Coalition.

Grossberg, Lawrence. 1992. *We Gotta Get out of This Place: Popular Conservatism and Postmodern Culture*. New York: Routledge.

Hacker, Andrew. 1995. "The Crackdown on African-Americans." *The Nation* 261, no. 2 (10 July): 45–49.

Jones, Bill. 1996. Proposition 209: Text of Proposed Law. Proposed Amendment to Article 1, Sec. 31.(a), from the California Secretary of State Web site, *http://www.ss.ca.gov/Vote 96/html/BP/209text.htm*.

Peyton, Jeffrey M. 1996. "High Court to Hear Colorado Case." *Christian American*, April 1995. Taken from Christian Coalition World Wide Web site, 17 January. *http://cc.org/cc/ca/ca04index.html*.

Reed, Ralph. 1994. *Politically Incorrect: The Emerging Faith Factor in American Politics*. Dallas, Tex.: Word Publishing.

———. 1996. *Active Faith: How Christians Are Changing the Soul of American Politics*. New York: Simon and Schuster.

Rosenbaum, David E. 1988. "Robertson Ends Active Campaigning." *New York Times*, 7 April.

Schapiro, Mark. 1994. *Who's Behind the Culture War? Contemporary Assaults on Freedom of Expression*. Boston: The Nathan Cummings Foundation.

13

"Facts Don't Hate; They Just Are"

Laurie Schulze and Frances Guilfoyle

In the 1992 elections, the voters of Colorado passed a controversial amendment to the state constitution limiting the civil rights of lesbians, male homosexuals, and bisexuals. This chapter examines how it is that the religious right was able to call upon and legitimate a "commonsense" hate discourse against gays during this compaign.

John Fiske provides a useful summary of how discourse functions socially:

> Discourse is a language or system of representation that has developed socially in order to make and circulate a coherent set of meanings about an important topic area. These meanings serve the interests of that section of society within which the discourse originates and which works ideologically to naturalize those meanings into common sense. "Discourses are power relations."[1]

Fiske draws on the work of Michel Foucault, who has analyzed certain institutions to discuss the relations among power, discourse, and knowledge. According to Foucault, there are anxieties and uncertainties associated with the production of discourse for us because "we suspect the conflicts, triumphs, injuries, dominations and enslavements" that result from the power behind it. Discourse is dangerous, and for this reason, "in every society the production of discourse is at once controlled, selected, organized and redistributed according to a certain number of procedures, whose role is to avert its powers and its dangers, to cope with chance events, to evade its ponderous awesome materiality."[2]

Policing the boundaries of discourse are what Foucault calls "rules of exclusion." These systems, "active on the exterior," "concern that part of discourse which deals with power and desire" (220). Within discourse, some things can and some things cannot be spoken. "We know perfectly well that we are not free to say anything, that we cannot simply speak of anything when we like or where we like; not just anyone, finally, may speak of just anything" (216).

Different areas of discursive prohibition work to reinforce each other and form a "complex web" of regulation. Foucault tells us that "the areas where this web is most tightly woven today, where the danger spots are most numerous, are those dealing with politics and sexuality" (216).

In November 1992, Colorado's electorate voted in favor of the following amendment to the Colorado Constitution, "Amendment 2":

> NO PROTECTED STATUS BASED ON HOMOSEXUAL, LESBIAN, OR BISEXUAL ORIENTATION. Neither the State of Colorado through any of its branches or departments nor any of its agencies, political subdivisions, municipalities, or school districts shall enact, adopt, or enforce any statute, regulation, ordinance, or policy whereby homosexual, lesbian, or bisexual orientation, conduct, practices, or relationships shall constitute or otherwise be the basis of or entitle any person or class of persons to have or claim any minority status, quota preferences, protected status, or claim of discrimination. This section of the constitution shall be in all respects self-executing.

Foucault's critical framework helps analyze what this amendment is about and why it was passed. The Amendment 2 campaigns provide a compelling example of the way in which power and desire come together in the discursive arena. The phrasing of the amendment and the language used in the struggle around it are at the very heart of the nexus of politics and sexuality that, as Foucault reminds us, is full of "danger spots."

This amendment legislates silence, silencing the dangerous discourse of gay civil rights. Terms like "minority status" and "quota preferences" are its alibis. The amendment's supporters used such phrases deliberately to justify legalized discrimination against gay people. Since this amendment proscribes any claim of discrimination on the basis of homosexuality, it literally rules out of legal discourse the speech of the homosexual. Its primary function seems to be to exclude, through prohibition, the voice of the homosexual in the Colorado courts.

In the United States many attempts have been made to pass legislation designed to enact, through the manipulation of discourse, the symbolic annihilation of homosexuality. Amendment 2 will not be the last. In this chapter, we analyze the discursive strategies used by the amendment's supporters in this particular political struggle. We examine the ideological work of words and images circulated by the right and try to understand the reasons for the effectiveness of this material. We hope that this analysis will aid those trying to make sense of the strategies used in similar attempts to further legalize discrimination against gay people and that it will contribute to the development of tactics that can be used to fight the very real violence these discourses engender.

By 1991, the Colorado cities of Boulder, Aspen, and Denver had all extended their antidiscrimination ordinances to include sexual orientation, thereby protecting heterosexual people, lesbians, gay men, and bisexual people against discrimination in employment, housing, and public accommodations. In February 1991, Colorado for Family Values (CFV), a nonprofit coalition based in Colorado Springs, was established in order to oppose the inclusion of sexual orientation in antidiscrimination legislation throughout the state. Its first direct political action was to oppose just such a revision to the state Ethnic Harassment Bill so that the revision was defeated in committee in February 1991. In April 1991, the Human Rights Commission in Colorado Springs recommended that the city council include sexual orientation in its antidiscrimination ordinance. The city council of Colorado Springs rejected this recommendation, due in large part to CFV's intervention. CFV's first forays into Colorado politics were essentially reactive. However, in July 1991, CFV submitted a ballot initiative to the Colorado secretary of state that proposed an amendment to Article 2 of the state constitution, the state's Bill of Rights. This became Amendment 2 on the November 1992 ballot. In the elections, Amendment 2 was passed by the voters of Colorado 53.6 percent to 46.3 percent, despite the efforts of a broad coalition of organizations to defeat it. Declared unconstitutional by the Colorado Supreme Court, the amendment went to the U.S. Supreme Court in October 1995. On 20 May 1996, the U.S. Supreme Court ruled Amendment 2 unconstitutional. For the moment, Amendment 2 is dead. However, the forces behind it are very much alive, and we must be prepared for similar legislative attacks in the future.

A news release sent out by CFV on 31 July 1991 includes a description of its mission and a brief history of the organization. Its mission summary reads as follows:

> CFV will through the statewide initiative process facilitate the expression of the will of the people of Colorado on granting special rights or protected status to homosexual, bisexual, and lesbian behavior.
>
> CFV's organizers feel that the voters of this state will not allow homosexual/bisexual/lesbian orientation of any kind to be given a protected class status or special rights. We have chosen the ballot initiative process as the most effective and only true direct method of letting the people themselves decide.

At the conclusion of the "brief history" segment, CFV states that it is

> now networking with thousands of Colorado citizens statewide to educate the public on all the facts about the homosexual lifestyle to assist the public in making an informed, responsible decision about whether to give this lifestyle protected status and this state's legal sanction.[3]

A close analysis of CFV's "educational" material reveals a complex set of discourses. These discourses function to define people who are other than heterosexual within a specific framework, one designed to maintain and amplify antigay fear, hostility, and prejudice.

It is important to realize, as Fiske says, that "discourses are not produced by the individual speaker or author, they are socially produced; the meanings that they bear preexist their use in any one discursive practice," and "discourse is thus a social act which may promote or oppose the dominant ideology."[4] CFV's discourse of (homo)sexuality already enjoyed a hegemonic advantage before this particular campaign began. CFV's task, therefore, was to promote rather than oppose the dominant ideology. The dominance of what Monique Wittig calls "the straight mind" provided the context within which CFV's claims amounted to common sense. As Wittig points out: "The discourses which particularly oppress all of us, lesbians, women and homosexual men, are those discourses which take for granted that what founds society, any society, is heterosexuality."[5]

Since heterosexuality is privileged, thought of as one of the very foundations of social order itself, CFV does not have very far to go in its attempt to position homosexuality as a threat to the state and all "traditional" institutions, political and civil. Late in the campaign, CFV published and distributed approximately 800,000 copies of a tabloid-style newspaper entitled *Equal Rights—Not Special Rights! STOP Special Class Status for Homosexuality. Vote Yes! on Amendment 2*. Readers are invited to "Turn inside for the shocking truth" about such topics as "Gay Propaganda in Schools," "Target: Children," "Attack on the Family," "Ethnic 'Civil Rights' Destroyed!," "Churches Attacked Nationwide," and "Free Speech—An Endangered Right!"[6]

The tabloid accuses homosexuals of attempting to undermine key social institutions, those thought to be foundational to social order. It should not surprise anyone, however, that the focal point of these institutions' strategic array is "the family." All these institutions circulate discourses in which heterosexuality functions as the foundation of social order; for all of them, the family is symbolically central. Analyzing "the new moralism and the New Right," historian Jeffrey Weeks argues that the family and sexuality are extremely useful social issues for the New Right's political agenda. They constitute an "ideological framework through which to construct and organize a potentially powerful mass base to articulate genuine social anxiety through a referential system in which sexual anarchy [becomes] the explanation for social ill."[7] The family functions as a signifier around which people can

> condense a number of hopes and fears, anxieties and possibilities around the social and the sexual. In the United States . . . this combination [taps] a huge reservoir of moral belief and dissatisfaction . . . [and makes] for a potent political force. (34)

In much of its literature, CFV promotes the notion that sexual otherness, especially homosexuality, is to blame for *all* social ills. As its name suggests, CFV uses the family as a site upon which to condense all its fears and anxieties about sexuality. Bill Armstrong, former Colorado senator and a CFV supporter, wrote a fund-raising letter circulated before the election on behalf of CFV. In it he says that "gays have made it clear in their writings that they have no use for the traditional family, [or] for traditional moral standards."[8]

A section in the CFV tabloid, "Objective: Destroy the Family," tells readers that gays are "an angry, alienated minority" for whom the family is "the symbol of everything they attack." As evidence, the tabloid presents a brief quotation from Michael Swift's "Gay Revolutionary": "The family unit is a spawning ground of lies, betrayal, mediocrity, hypocrisy and violence—and will be abolished." The tabloid also cites gay "manifestos" that call for children to be raised communally under the direction of lesbian women and for legislation to extend marriage laws to same-sex and multiple-person marriages.[9]

The rhetoric of family values carries a huge amount of ideological weight. It crosses many lines of social difference, thus appealing to a wide constituency. And the term "family" is implicitly governed by "natural" patriarchal values and compulsory heterosexuality in the service of procreation. "Family" *means* the patriarchal family, *means* a heterosexual man plus a heterosexual woman plus children. In turn, the family defines sexuality. Foucault traces this relation historically between the family and sex. He notes that in the late eighteenth century (at least in Western societies) "sexuality was carefully confined; it moved into the home. The conjugal family took custody of it, and absorbed it into the serious function of reproduction."[10] Sexuality that escaped the confines of this economy has consequently been labeled deviant and perverse.

The semiotic history of the very words "family" and "sexuality" rules homosexuality out of bounds. Within the dominant discourse about the family, it "makes no sense" that lesbians or gay men could stand in for a heterosexual couple. In one of its TV campaign ads, CFV promotes this notion. The ad asserts that homosexuality should have nothing to do with families and children. A voice-over narration says: "Where gays have special rights, school kids are taught *this* lifestyle is healthy and normal by law. Do we want to protect our children? Yes we do. Vote yes on 2." The ad uses images of "gay excess." We see home-video footage shot at a gay pride parade. The images show a transvestite mistress and a male slave, a close-up of two men kissing, and leather lesbians repeating the mistress/slave motif.

The last three shots show a small child, probably about five years old, holding the hand of an adult. The adult stands mostly out of the frame but we can see that he or she is carrying a rainbow flag. The child's mouth is open; she is visibly crying and appears to be trying to pull away from the adult. The ad ends with freeze-frame blowups of the child that move progressively closer until her screaming face fills the screen. This image together with the voice-over narration encourage the viewer to infer that the child does not want to be a part of this parade or this "lifestyle" and that the homosexual parent is an unfit parent. Such an inference fits the dominant discourse's assumption about "what makes sense" for family life.

The dominance of "Christian values" in shaping concepts of the family and sexuality also contributes to CFV's hegemonic advantage. Christianity has, in fact, been shaping Western thought for many centuries, and a mainstream understanding of sexuality is steeped in Christian theology. The church has traditionally concerned itself with regulating sexuality; in the United States dominant notions of sexuality are heavily inflected with Christian concepts of morality and normality. CFV can count on most people's believing that sexuality has to be carefully controlled and regulated by particular moral values such as monogamy, fidelity, discretion, chastity before marriage (although the latter is not strictly observed, it remains the ideal), romantic love, and, as the ultimate validation of sex, procreation. CFV insists that, in contrast, for gay men and lesbians, sex is a desperate, uncontrolled addiction, serving no higher value than itself. In the CFV tabloid, homosexuals are depicted by definition as promiscuous, unable to procreate and unable to sustain long-term relationships. For homosexuals, sex seemingly does not take place in the context of an intimate, loving relationship. Citing a Kinsey survey, the CFV tabloid asserts that "typical homosexuals" have five hundred partners in their lifetime and that 79 percent of white male homosexuals "said that over half their partners were strangers." One of the few footnotes about lesbians in CFV's printed material refers to a survey that reports 38 percent of lesbians as having between eleven and three hundred lifetime partners. According to CFV, monogamy is "virtually unknown in the gay lifestyle."[11]

A second CFV television ad, again using home-video footage from a gay pride parade, provides a visual summary of homosexual sexual degeneracy and promiscuity. The ad's voice-over says: "Special rights for gays forces the law to protect this behavior." We see a series of images that have had "censored" signs superimposed on them. In one shot, for example, two men are lying in the street. The middle third of the frame is blocked out by a censored bar. What the men are actually doing is difficult to discern, but the positioning of the censored bar could lead the viewer to believe that both men are naked and actually having sex. Homosexual sexuality is presumably exhibitionist, licentious, and completely out of control. These censored images serve to reinforce CFV's insistence that homosexuality consists of a set of virtually unrepresentable behaviors.

CFV is able to tap into naturalized moral values without even directly invoking religion. It smuggles its moral and religious imperatives into the political debate under the guise of numbers and facts. Although it is common knowledge that CFV is closely affiliated with religious institutions and doctrines, fundamentalist Christianity in particular, its promotional and campaign materials place religion firmly to one side. While accusing gays of being antireligious, CFV studiously avoids using religious doctrine in support of its anti-gay position. It carefully disarticulates its politics from its religion—on the surface: "Amendment 2 doesn't hinge on religion or morality" (6). CFV does not use a single biblical quotation in its entire eight-page tabloid. This reticence, along with its extensive use of statistics and the language of the social sciences, maintains the illusion of a nonideological position.

CFV repeatedly protests that it is simply presenting the facts. On the tabloid's front page, readers are told: "Arm yourself with the facts about Amendment 2." CFV is infatuated with statistics, published reports, studies, and expert opinions. It consistently takes aim with statistical ammunition. Under its empiricist guise, CFV maintains a logical, reasonable, even detached tone. Science seemingly does not take a position. It simply states the facts, tells the truth. And statistics make great press. As Liliane Jaddou and Jon Williams quote from *Policing the Crisis*:

> Statistics . . . have an ideological function: they appear to ground free-floating and controversial impressions in the hard and incontrovertible soil of numbers. Both the media and the public have enormous respect for the "facts"—hard facts. And there is no fact so "hard" as a number—unless it is the percentage difference between two numbers.[12]

Statistics and numbers are scattered liberally throughout the CFV tabloid. The paper asserts that gay men with AIDS "average 1,100 partners" in their lifetime. With envy it says that gays are "three times as likely to hold professional or managerial positions" compared with the "average" American. And the average life expectancy of lesbians is held to be "45 years." Similarly, a twenty-minute video called *The Gay Agenda,* distributed in Colorado during the Amendment 2 campaign, consists predominantly of talking heads who cite statistics and render expert opinions.[13] In the video, Dr. Stanley Monteith, author of *AIDS: The Unnecessary Epidemic,* rattles off number after number. For example, Monteith claims that 92 percent of homosexuals practice rimming which, he adds, could not be done without some ingestion of feces, and he says that 17 percent of homosexuals "actively eat human feces." CFV has a number to attach to practically everything it says.

In the CFV television campaign ads, these statistical truth claims are accompanied by documentary images. Three of CFV's ads depend upon home-video footage of a gay pride parade taken from *The Gay Agenda*. The ads give the impression of an almost accidental capturing of images by an objective camera that is simply observing the real. The camera work connotes live, on-the-spot reporting of presumably unstaged events. This footage draws upon images of a public spectacle produced by homosexuals; it is ostensibly a record of the way in which homosexuals present themselves to the world and a record that CFV can say it did not have a hand in engineering. The documentary video camera simply "reflects the reality" of homosexuality on parade. Of course, through the careful selection of particular images and deliberate editing, music, and voice-over narration, CFV has a great deal to do with the construction of homosexuality displayed in these ads, but it is able to hide behind the "truth" of video documentation.

Statistics, documentary images, and science allow CFV to disavow the hatred of its speech and the violence of its discourse. In answer to opponents' charges that "Amendment 2 stands for hatred of gays," CFV says that it has "spoken out against hatred all along. Facts don't hate; they just are."[14] During the campaign, a letter to Amendment 2's opponents pledges that CFV will conduct itself "peaceably and responsibly" and will do everything within its power to "ensure that no unpleasantness takes place." CFV claims "we would be greatly distressed to see Colorado's 'gay' citizens victimized by any sort of abuse. (Note: we do not regard the citing of authentic documented medical information about homosexual behavior as 'abuse.')"[15] However, CFV's endless citations of "facts"—produced by experts, laced with statistics, and filtered through scientific discourse—are profoundly abusive. We must not think that because we call this language "discourse" it is somehow less abusive than the kind of violence CFV disingenuously deplores. CFV's "abstract and scientific discourses" both provide support for the kind of violence it pretends to disavow and form instruments of violence in and of themselves. Monique Wittig phrases in precise terms just how this violence works:

> When we use the overgeneralizing term "ideology" to designate all the discourses of the dominating group, we relegate these discourses to the domain of Irreal Ideas, we forget the material (physical) violence that they directly do to the oppressed people, a violence produced by the abstract and "scientific" discourses as well as by the discourses of the mass media. I would like to insist upon the material oppression of individuals by discourses.[16]

The violence of CFV's discourse lies primarily in its ability to make homosexuality stand for something grotesque, lurid, excessive, and completely undisciplined. It seems to be a violation of multiple taboos, a crossing of boundaries of all kinds, a crude carnivalesque sacrilegious disrespect for all the things that hold the social-sexual order together. CFV plays upon and perpetuates a stereotype of homosexuality that makes it monstrous. The homosexual becomes the Other, the utterly abject. Hatred thus becomes legitimized and perhaps even mandated. And hatred translates into action. In his powerful work on stereotypes, *Difference and Pathology: Stereotypes of Sexuality, Race, and Madness,* Sander Gilman says,

> Our fantasies about difference, our anxieties about our status, can result in medical theories about the Other which relegate human beings to the status of laboratory animals . . . in racial theories that reduce the Other to the status of exotic, either dangerous . . . or benign . . . in social codes that ostracize specific groups as inherently, unpleasantly different . . . the structure of our universe is the basis for our actions in this universe. We view our own images, our own mirages, our own stereotypes as embodying qualities that exist in the world. And we act upon them.[17]

In *Powers of Horror,* Julia Kristeva defines the abject: "What disturbs identity, system, order. What does not respect borders, positions, rules. The in-between, the ambiguous, the composite. The traitor, the liar, the criminal with a good conscience, the shameless rapist, the killer who claims he is a savior."[18] Kristeva points out that abjection "accompanies all religious structurings" to such an extent that "the various means of purifying the abject . . . make up the history of religions" (4). In the Judeo-Christian religion sexuality is a central site for the formation of abjection, prohibitions, and taboos. Both the Old Testament and the New Testament are replete with examples of sexual abomination, sins of the flesh and the unclean body. In the twentieth century in Colorado, however, CFV can translate its religious discourse into a medical one, where medical pathology and psychiatric illness can stand in for immorality, sin, and abomination.

At the end of the eighteenth century, there was an appropriation of sexuality by the medical institution as medicine established a norm of sexual development. From that time on, Foucault says, "the technology of sex was ordered in relation to the medical institution, the exigency of normality, and—instead of the question of death and everlasting punishment—the problem of life and illness." This did not mean, however, that sexuality became "truly independent of the thematics of sin."[19] Rather, sexuality also became a discourse, "subordinated in the main to the imperatives of a morality whose division it reiterated under the guise of the medical norm" (53). Gilman agrees that eighteenth-century interest in degenerate sexuality had a "clearly theological" motivation.[20] Furthermore, Gilman says: "No realm of human experience is as closely tied to the concept of degeneration as that of sexuality. The two are inseparable in nineteenth-century thought. They evolved together and provided complementary paradigms for understanding human development" (191). So ideologically loaded is the notion of sexuality that stereotypes often include sexuality in order to give them more weight: "Sexually different is tantamount to pathological" (24–25).

The Gay Agenda constructs the homosexual body as a site of perversion and disease. Monteith defines homosexual sex of any kind as unnatural and unhealthy. For example, according to Monteith, 93 percent of homosexuals engage in rectal sex; "of course the rectum was not built for intercourse so when you carry out rectal intercourse you manage to tear the rectal mucosa... it's not a healthy activity." *The Gay Agenda's* voice-over narration also refers to studies claiming that 37 percent of homosexuals practice sadomasochism. And "compared to heterosexuals," homosexuals are eight times more likely to contract hepatitis.

Not only does the gay *body* bear disease but, as CFV would have it, homosexuals are psychologically and spiritually sick. They are seen to be emotionally immature, addicted to pleasure, desperate, lonely, godless. *The Gay Agenda* uses "reformed" homosexuals to provide empirical evidence. In the video, witness John Smid refers to the gay men he knew as "desperate men... there was a lot of desperation in the bars." Smid provides personal testimony to "prove" that homosexuality is a symptom of arrested psychological development: "I was stuck in that little boy stage of hungering for relationships with other little boys... an adult, twenty years old, in a grade-school mind." CFV defines homosexuality as a psychological disease that can be cured, offering a "hand of hope" to people "struggling with homosexuality." Gay people, "with each other's help and the help of God," can leave "the lifestyle" and recover mental and spiritual health.

CFV admonishes that homosexuality is a willful behavioral choice, not an identity. In *The History of Sexuality,* Foucault tracks the history of the "homosexual." Prior to the nineteenth century, the homosexual did not exist. What existed were perpetrators of sodomy and other "forbidden acts." Foucault notes that in the nineteenth century, there was an "incorporation of perversions and a new specification of individuals." The medical and social sciences turned the juridical subject of certain legal perversions into "a personage, a past, a case history... a life form."[21] The appearance of the homosexual was accompanied by a battery of discourses designed to control it. But this acknowledgment and legislation "also made possible the formation of a 'reverse' discourse. Homosexuality began to speak in its own behalf, to demand that its legitimacy or 'naturality' be acknowledged" (101).

In its insistence that homosexuality is simply a behavior, CFV returns to a pre–nineteenth century episteme in which the homosexual as a person does not exist. CFV's discourse claims that "homosexuality isn't something you 'are', it's something you 'do.'" Thus the CFV tabloid admonishes that any attempt by "militant gays" to "manufacture evidence that homosexuality is a genetic condition" is simply a desperate attempt to strengthen their argument in favor of special class status.[22] This functions in a number of ways for CFV. It may operate to mute the reverse discourse that Foucault speaks of by dismantling one of the conditions of the resistant discourse's existence. It certainly allows CFV to insist that Amendment 2 would not deprive homosexuals of their civil rights. Homosexuals already have equal rights; any kind of legislated protection, according to CFV, would be a "special right." If there are no homosexuals, only homosexual behavior, then no group exists to qualify for minority status.

CFV further pathologizes homosexuality by conflating it with pedophilia. The tabloid features a whole section entitled "Target: Children." Referring to the "terrible epidemic" of child sexual abuse, CFV alleges that "what militant homosexuals don't want you to know is the large role they play in this epidemic." The tabloid cites an article in a journal called *Psychological Reports*: "Homosexuals, who represent perhaps 2% of the population, perpetrate more than one-third of all reported child molestations." If not all homosexuals are child molesters, according to CFV, nonetheless pedophilia is "an accepted part of the homosexual community" (4). In the video *The Gay Agenda,* Monteith tells us that young boys are "being actively recruited out of our homes, out of our schools, today," by homosexual pedophiles.

AIDS, or more precisely, the dominant representation of AIDS, provides CFV with the ultimate example of homosexuality's degeneracy. According to CFV, AIDS is still the gay epidemic. "The wages of sin is death" hangs like smoke in the air above CFV's descriptions of homosexuality. Homosexuality causes its own contagion. Moral pollution becomes translated into the physical degeneration of AIDS. In *Disease and Representation,* Sander Gilman claims:

> The infected individual is never value-neutral, that is, solely a person exhibiting specific pathological signs or symptoms. Like any complex text, the signs of illness are read within the conventions of an interpretive community that comprehends them in the light of earlier, powerful readings of what are understood to be similar or parallel texts.[23]

According to Gilman, the major context for the representation of the person with AIDS is "the five-hundred-year-old iconography of the syphilitic." Throughout that history, the syphilitic has been represented as "isolated, visually recognizable by his signs and symptoms, and sexually deviant." This notion of sexual deviancy also becomes linked, most blatantly in religious discourse, to the argument that those who have sexually transmitted diseases are really afflicted with "a punishment for sexual irresponsibility" (248–50). Gilman argues that "the association of the image of the AIDS patient with the iconography of syphilis is not random. It is clear that the initial association rests on that population of AIDS patients, homosexuals, and society's perception of them as having suffered a sexually transmitted disease." Additionally, the HIV+ homosexual "is not only the sufferer but also the source of his own pollution," which neatly collapses the way in which men and women have been depicted differently in the history of the representation of syphilis: the woman as the source of infection, the man as the sufferer of the disease (258). In the representation of the homosexual AIDS patient, sufferer and source become one, facilitating an argument that blames the sufferer for his suffering.

According to CFV's tabloid, even the threat of death as the final punishment for sexual degeneracy cannot deter homosexuals, so compulsive is homosexual behavior: "Gays have been unwilling (or unable) to curb their voracious, unsafe sex practices in the face of AIDS." The tabloid also reports that "45% of gay men remain [*sic*] sexually active after learning that they were HIV+, and incredibly, 52% of them *did not inform their partners*! . . . No wonder 83% of Colorado AIDS cases have occurred in gay males—it's a tragedy but it's true."[24] Homosexuals do not merely endanger each other, however: CFV points out that " 'gay-rights' threaten . . . health care providers and workers, vulnerable to disease because of 'privacy' given AIDS as a disease with 'civil rights' " (7). The bottom line is that homosexuality itself is a terminal disease: If gay men do not die of HIV-related illnesses, CFV claims that the homosexual lifestyle is so unhealthy, the median age of death for a gay man who is HIV− is forty-two (4).

Following the recent resignation of its director, Kevin Tebedo, who wanted to branch out into a wider political arena, CFV says that it is committed to continuing its specific focus on blocking "special rights" for homosexuals. Why is CFV so fixated on homosexuality? Why, three years after the beginning of the Amendment 2 campaigns, does CFV still insist on repeating over and over its litany of homosexuality's perversions and dangers? In the July 1995 edition of *CFV Report,* Linda Tebedo writes: "In the continuing campaign to expose the truth . . . this month we discuss the myth that homosexuality is 'just like' heterosexuality."[25] For four years at regular intervals, CFV has disseminated lavishly detailed descriptions of homosexual practices. The "truth" to which Linda Tebedo refers has been exposed *already.* Why would it need to be exposed repeatedly unless homosexuality were functioning as CFV's Other, the Other necessary for CFV to maintain its very existence? In his discussion of Orientalism, Edward Said says that Orientalism—the position of the missionary, for one—needs an Oriental reality.[26] Homosexual orientation is CFV's Orient. The perpetrator of homosexual acts is CFV's heathen. Without them, CFV's members would cease to exist as missionaries.

Kristeva argues that the abject must be endured, even desired, because excluding that which is opposed to the self serves a necessary function in the very formation of subjectivity. It is necessary for taking up one's place in the symbolic, for maintaining the borders of the symbolic system. As Georges Bataille puts it, the "imperative act of excluding abject things establishes the very foundations of collective existence."[27] More specifically, as Gilman says, "the fear of collapse, the sense of dissolution," lies behind representations of the Other as diseased. We turn "the fear we have of our own collapse" outward "onto the world in order to localize it and, indeed, to domesticate it . . . then it is not we who totter on the brink of collapse, but rather the Other. And it is an Other who has already shown his or her vulnerability by having collapsed."[28] Thus, what CFV is doing with homosexuality involves absolutely foundational psychological and social processes, which, as Gilman describes, are "constructed on the basis of specific ideological needs" (2).

Further evidence of how far CFV is willing to go in its bid to position the homosexual as Other can be found in its "special rights" rhetoric. Robert C. Allen argues that rather than there being some essential and inevitable alliance of the cultural practices of people occupying more or less subordinate social positions, we frequently discover that " 'resistant' [cultural] practices might well be polyvalent, not only directed against those conceived as 'above,' but constructing yet another object of subordination."[29] In its insistence that gay rights constitutes a civil rights fraud, CFV encourages, as Allen puts it, this "slide from one register of social power to another," this displacement of abjection and attempt to block any form of coalition between homosexuals and other subordinate groups. CFV's tabloid makes the argument that to grant gays special rights would undermine the civil rights movement itself and deprive "real" minorities of the protection and help they deserve. The tabloid claims that the antidiscrimination laws "were made to protect disadvantaged, politically powerless people, not because of how they behave or what kind of kinky desires they have."[30] In one of its news releases, CFV says: "We are attempting to maintain the integrity of our civil rights laws to protect citizens from discrimination for characteristics of true ethnicity, not for questionable behavioral aspects such as sexual preference."[31]

The tabloid features brief interviews with "civil rights leaders" who are asked how "special class status for gays threaten [*sic*] the hard-won gains of disadvantaged minorities." Ignacio Rodriguez, former chair of the Colorado Civil Rights Commission, replies to the query:

> If we include a group of people who are generally identified as a deviant group sexually it would erode and seriously damage the legitimate civil rights protections that have been gained by ethnic minorities.

John Franklin, another member of the Colorado Civil Rights Commission, adds:

> Making sexual preference a protected class does a disservice to all those people presently being discriminated against or mistreated, by diluting the significance of civil rights protection. I hate to see resources taken away from those who are truly in need.[32]

Homosexuals are set up as the Other of racial and ethnic minorities, who are encouraged to see homosexuals as a "deviant group" and not deserving of legalized protection against discrimination. In fact, CFV claims, since gays are already privileged, rich, well educated, and politically powerful, any suffering they experience is entirely their own fault. In his fund-raising letter, Bill Armstrong writes:

> To equate the self-created personal miseries of pleasure-addicted gays—who sport average incomes of nearly $55,500 a year—with the innocent sufferings and crippling poverty of legitimate minority groups is an insult to those who've struggled to achieve true civil rights in America.[33]

In its campaign material, CFV never once acknowledges the gay people who belong to racial and ethnic minorities or working-class gay people, further encouraging subordinated or marginalized groups to think of homosexuals as the Other. On the other hand, CFV's insistence that gays belong to the privileged classes also plays on existing racism and dissatisfaction among those members of the white lower and middle classes who believe that affirmative action and civil rights have taken jobs and opportunities away from them and given those opportunities to racial and ethnic minorities. To allow gays "special rights" would effectively put one more group ahead of them in line, and an already affluent group at that.

CFV's "no special rights" argument allows it to occupy contradictory positions. On the one hand, that argument seems to align itself with a progressive civil rights philosophy, arguing that gays' efforts to enter the civil rights arena amount to a reactionary attack upon civil rights itself. Indeed, CFV implies that the gay civil rights movement is un-American, undemocratic. The tabloid says that "militant gays want to create a whole new category of anti-discrimination protections. Now they want rich, 'horny' political power brokers to enjoy special protection from discrimination. They're counting on Americans to not know what 'discrimination' really means."[34] On the other hand, CFV also easily wins the support of people who are politically and socially conservative. It champions "traditional values" and criticizes the gay rights movement for its radical politics. CFV's rhetorical strategies are, in fact, rife with contradictions and reversals; these do not undermine its position but, rather, seem to strengthen it. CFV maintains that gay people are miserable and diseased; yet at the same time, gays are affluent, well educated, and powerful. Gays enjoy the same rights as everyone else, and yet if they are oppressed and disadvantaged it is their own fault. Gays are disgusting and immoral and do not deserve protection from discrimination, but Amendment 2 "*certainly* isn't about hatred. It's about fairness" (6, emphasis in original).

The ability to absorb contradictions is one of CFV's main strengths and is precisely what gains it a hegemonic advantage. Hegemony occurs only through accommodation, that is, making a place within itself for oppositional and conflicting values. Hegemonic ideology is never pure or univocal. It achieves hegemony because it is a mobile embodiment of multiple ideological elements that speak to different social interests and identities. Because CFV is willing to contradict itself in order to occupy a range of ideological positions that are not necessarily coherent, it has an argument for any occasion and an incredible flexibility. Combined with the dominance of the discourses that it draws upon, CFV's ideological mobility makes it a formidable political opponent.

In conclusion, we would like to return to Monique Wittig's insistence on the real, material violence done by discourses built on domination, prejudice, and hatred. Wittig points out that "Others" are not created equal. Despite CFV's protestations that it supports equal rights for gays—just not special rights—it does not consider the homosexual Other that it constructs as equal at all. Wittig quotes Claude Faugeron and Phillipe Robert: "Everybody tries to show the other as different, but not everybody succeeds in doing so. One has to be socially dominant to succeed in it."[35] Unfortunately, CFV can align itself with socially dominant discourses and purchase the power to define the different, to name the Other. And as Wittig asks: "What is the different/other if not the dominated?" CFV clearly means to dominate the homosexual, to demonstrate its mastery over anyone "less" than strictly heterosexual.[36] This domination is destructive, hurtful, and violent, whether CFV wants to admit it or not.

Pat Romero, a heterosexual woman who actively campaigned against Amendment 2, was involved in an incident that clearly demonstrates the hatred sanctioned by CFV's rhetoric. In the television documentary *Inner Journeys, Public Stands,* Romero recalls what happened to her on the night of the election as she stood on a street corner in Denver with a "No on 2" sign:

> There was a man in a pickup truck in the center lane who changed lanes and started right at me and it was snowing and it was slick and I really thought he was going to run me over. I really did. And my reaction... I was just frozen to the spot with my sign. He slammed into the curb and he rolled his window down and he spit at me and he said "Fuck you dyke." And he drove off. And in that moment, for the first time in my life, I had just a little inkling of what it's like to be gay. That

> man hated me. I mean, his spit didn't touch me, but his hate just washed over me.[37]

That CFV actively denies the violence it commits is perhaps the most vicious strategy in its arsenal.

The Anti-Violence Project of the Gay, Lesbian, and Bisexual Community Services Center of Colorado issued a press release in March 1994. The project found that antigay violence increased 13 percent from 1992 to 1993. The most compelling statistics indicated that in November 1992—following the passage of Amendment 2—violence reports to the project were 283 percent above the monthly average (from January 1992 to October 1992), and up over 100 percent for December 1992 through February 1993. Unlike CFV, we do not have a number for every argument (whether we should or not is debatable). It is a matter of fact, however, that prior to November 1992, neither of us had ever personally known a lesbian who was refused service in a Colorado place of business *because and only because* she was perceived to be CFV's homosexual Other. Now we do. The annihilation of the homosexual legislated in Amendment 2 is not and never was only symbolic.

In "The Spectacle of AIDS," Simon Watney discusses the ways in which "the powerful emergent forms of a secularized fundamentalism" put homosexuality and AIDS in the frame of medical discourse, conservative politics, and family values to produce a rhetoric bound up with particular "ideological configurations" that also provoke "deep psychic anxieties."[38] The links that have been and continue to be forged between homosexuality and AIDS, he argues, are

> increasingly being used to underwrite a widespread ambition to erase the distinction between "the public" and "the private," and to establish in their place a monolithic and legally binding category—"the family"—understood as the central term through which the world and the self are henceforth to be rendered intelligible. Consent to this strategy is sought by tapping into lay perceptions of health, sickness and disease, unevenly accreted down the centuries, and sharing only the common human fear and disavowal of death. Health education thus emerges as the central site of hegemonic struggle in the coming decades . . . a new and essentially talismanic model of power is emerging, offering to protect subjectivities carefully nurtured in folklore and superstition, now rearticulated in a discourse of ostensibly medical authority. We are witness to the precipitation of a moralized bio-politics of potentially awesome power—a cunning combination of leechcraft and radiotherapy, eugenics and a master narrative of "family health"—with social policies that aspire with sober fanaticism to the creation of a modernity in which *we* will no longer exist. The spectacle of AIDS thus promises a stainless world in which *we* will only be recalled, in textbooks and carefully edited documentary "evidence," as signs of plagues and conta-

> gions averted—intolerable interruptions of the familial, subjects "cured" and disinfected of desire, and "therapeutically" denied the right to life itself. (86)

Watney is worth quoting at length because he so neatly summarizes the discursive landscape constructed by groups like CFV and because he clearly states the deadly implications of CFV's ideological project. We have tried to show, through our analysis of the discourses brought together in CFV's Amendment 2 campaign, that it is precisely the species of "moralized bio-politics" that Watney describes that reared its head in Colorado in 1992. Through its hegemonic advantages, this moralized bio-politics won consent for itself in this instance, and it continues to extend its reach, mobilizing familial, moral/theological, and political discourses under the protection of seemingly authoritative and "objective" medical justification. If Watney is right, health education may well be one of the arenas in which the struggle must be joined, in which attempts must be made to deconstruct the centuries-old conflation of disease and homosexuality and to challenge the alliances among "common sense," fundamentalist Christian theology, and a popularized pseudo-science. That ideological nexus is perhaps the most powerful card CFV has to play. If it carried a bit less weight, if the threads were loosened so that the web were less tightly woven, the hegemonic balance might shift enough to prevent future legislation of propositions like Amendment 2.

Notes

1. John Fiske, *Television Culture* (New York: Methuen, 1987), 14.
2. Michel Foucault, *The Archaeology of Knowledge and the Discourse on Language* (New York: Pantheon Books, 1972), 216.
3. CFV, "News Release: Colorado for Family Values Submits Initiative Banning Sexual Orientation from Special Status under Civil Rights Laws," 31 July 1991.
4. Fiske, *Television Culture,* 15.
5. Monique Wittig, "The Straight Mind," *Feminist Issues* (Summer 1980): 105.
6. CFV, *STOP Special Class Status for Homosexuality* (Colorado Springs, Colo.: Colorado for Family Values, 1992), 1.
7. Jeffrey Weeks, *Sexuality and Its Discontents: Meanings, Myths, and Modern Sexualities* (London: Routledge, 1985), 34.
8. Bill Armstrong, "Letter," 27 August 1991, 2. Unpublished.
9. CFV, *STOP Special Class Status,* 4.
10. Michel Foucault, *The History of Sexuality: An Introduction,* volume 1 (New York: Vintage Books, 1990), 3, 36.
11. CFV, *STOP Special Class Status,* 4.
12. Stuart Hall et al., eds., *Policing the Crisis: Mugging, the State, and Law and Order* (London: Macmillan, 1978). Quoted in Liliane Jaddou and Jon Williams, "A Theoretical Contribution to the Struggle against the Dominant Representations of Women," *Media, Culture, and Society* 3 (1981): 105.
13. *The Gay Agenda,* Antelope Valley Springs of Life Ministries, Lancaster, California, 1992, videocassette.

14. CFV, STOP *Special Class Status,* 3.

15. Tony Marco, "Letter to Tony Ogden," 29 July 1991, 2. Unpublished.

16. Wittig, "The Straight Mind," 105–6.

17. Sander L. Gilman, *Difference and Pathology: Stereotypes of Sexuality, Race, and Madness* (Ithaca, N.Y.: Cornell University Press, 1985), 241–42.

18. Julia Kristeva, *Powers of Horror: An Essay on Abjection* (New York: Columbia University Press, 1982), 4.

19. Foucault, *The History of Sexuality,* 116–17.

20. Gilman, *Difference and Pathology,* 191.

21. Foucault, *The History of Sexuality,* 43.

22. CFV, STOP *Special Class Status,* 4.

23. Sander Gilman, *Disease and Representation: Images of Illness from Madness to AIDS* (Ithaca, N.Y.: Cornell University Press, 1988), 7.

24. CFV, STOP *Special Class Status,* 4.

25. Linda Tebedo, "'Normal' Perversions," *CFV Report* 30 (July 1995): 1.

26. Edward Said, *Orientalism* (New York: Random House, 1978), 7.

27. Quoted in Kristeva, *Powers of Horror,* 56.

28. Gilman, *Disease and Representation,* 1.

29. Robert C. Allen, *Horrible Prettiness: Burlesque and American Culture* (Chapel Hill: University of North Carolina Press, 1991), 33.

30. CFV, STOP *Special Class Status,* 6.

31. CFV, "News Release," 31 July 1991.

32. CFV, STOP *Special Class Status,* 6.

33. Bill Armstrong, "Letter," 27 August 1991, 2. Unpublished.

34. CFV, STOP *Special Class Status,* 6.

35. Claude Faugeron and Phillipe Robert, *La Justice et les représentations sociales du systèm penal* (Paris: Masson, 1978). Quoted in Wittig, "The Straight Mind," 108.

36. Actually, the terms are narrower than that. Linda Tebedo defines the "healthy heterosexual ideal" as "monogamous love between a grown man and a grown woman whose sexual intercourse is vaginal and private," Tebedo, "'Normal' Perversions," 1.

37. *Inner Journeys, Public Stands,* Barbara Jabaily, producer/director, 1995.

38. Simon Watney, "The Spectacle of AIDS," in Douglas Crimp, ed., *AIDS: Cultural Analysis, Cultural Activism* (Cambridge: MIT Press, 1988), 86, 74.

14

Faultlines: Homophobic Innovation in Gay Rights/Special Rights

Ioannis Mookas

> *Civil rights may be thought of in a broad sense as all those rights necessary to participate fully in society— the rights that make citizenship operative. Civil rights are the birthright of democracy, not an added enhancement to citizenship.*
>
> —*Renee DeLapp*

Any lingering doubts one may have had about the conservative revolution underway in this country ought to have been erased by the seismic rearrangement of our political landscape that resulted from the 1994 midterm congressional and gubernatorial elections. Republicans are the party standing tall, but the sound and the fury of their triumph is supplied by the religious right, a growing countercultural movement to which over 15 million U.S. citizens who identify themselves as born-again Christians pledge allegiance. The religious right's leaders, increasingly influenced by the militant theocratic ideology of Christian reconstructionism,[1] have embarked on a quest to subdue our secular government at every level and to subordinate it to biblical law in order to establish a Christian nation as the kingdom of God on earth, in preparation for the second coming of Christ. Sounds preposterous, doesn't it? But the religious right has made giant strides toward this goal. Having chosen the previously moribund Republican Party as their earthly vessel out of practical necessity, religious conservatives now dominate the GOP committees in eighteen states; these religious conservatives are aligned closely with the Christian Coalition, a political juggernaut backed by the extreme rightist Pat Robertson.[2] The November 1994 elections were thus a chilling testament to the religious right's extraordinary effectiveness in mobilizing disciplined Christian voters to elect Christian candidates; more than 60 percent of the 600 candidates fielded by the religious right won their races, with Christian conservatives reported as casting fully one-third of the vote nationwide.[3]

Although these developments have received widespread attention only since the apocalyptic televised spectacle of the 1992 Republican National Convention in Houston, at which Robertson and other religious right potentates held center stage, their foundations have been painstakingly laid, with little fanfare, since the late 1970s.[4] To properly contextualize this chapter, it is necessary to bear in mind the history of this period, with its convergence of three discrete social trajectories: the ascendancy of the religious right and its alter ego, the New Right; the deindustrialization and globalization of the U.S. economy; and the steadily worsening economic disenfranchisement of enormous sectors of the populace and a concomitant social polarization. Without this context, we cannot begin to make sense of how lesbians and gay men, as a distinct social category, have come to be the object of a concerted political assault of epic proportions. In the past several years, the religious right has renewed efforts first undertaken in the late 1970s to repeal or rescind the existing protections against discrimination toward lesbians and gay men and to put in their stead constitutional or statutory provisions aimed at keeping such protections permanently in abeyance and, more generally, at criminalizing homosexuality.[5] In the absence of any federal civil rights law including lesbians and gay men among its protected groups, the only legal protections lesbians and gay men have from homophobic discrimination is a patchwork of local and state laws and judicial rulings; it is this patchwork that the religious right is intent upon dismantling. Their vehicle is the initiative, a process of citizen petitioning for the placement of a question (or referendum) onto a ballot, which has also, and not incidentally, been historically abused by majorities of voters to the detriment of people of color and the poor.[6]

By now, many people are familiar with the statewide initiative campaigns waged in 1992 for the failed Ballot Measure 9, sponsored by the Oregon Citizens Alliance, and its successful counterpart, Amendment 2, sponsored by Colorado for Family Values. Although Amendment 2 was found unconstitutional by the Colorado Supreme Court and then by the U.S. Supreme Court,[7] its passage by a majority of Colorado voters confirmed the homophobic initiative as a viable national strategy for the religious right. In 1994, Amendment 2 spawned proposed statewide antigay initiatives in eight other states, all virtually identical in design, two of which qualified for the November 1994 ballot, in Idaho and again in Oregon.[8] While both of these were defeated (by the narrowest of margins), a pair of initiatives were passed in Alachua County, Florida, the newest of several smaller initiatives to be passed in municipalities and counties across the United States. Each antigay initiative has thrust lesbian and gay communities and others alarmed at the erosion of democratic principles into the typically arduous work of mounting electoral campaigns, leaving even seasoned organizers emotionally and physically exhausted and straining community resources to the limit, as already-scarce funds are diverted from other pressing needs, such as health services or antiviolence work, to finance campaigns. Conversely, the religious right's base expands, as each initiative boosts organizational fund-raising and hones their get-out-the-vote mechanism. This sweeping political program of action is the context for the production of *Gay Rights/Special Rights,* the video to which we now turn.

Gay Rights/Special Rights was produced by Jeremiah Films, a southern California–based fundamentalist production company, principally for use by the Traditional Values Coalition and its adherents. The Traditional Values Coalition is widely identified as one of the foremost political institutions of the religious right, with an annual operating budget of approximately half a million dollars; staffed offices in California, Colorado, Nebraska, and Washington, D.C.; and active chapters in twenty states.[9] The Traditional Values Coalition's founder and chairman, Reverend Lou Sheldon, occupies the highest echelon of far right leadership. An inveterate homophobe, Sheldon has made opposition to lesbian and gay enfranchisement the stock-in-trade of his political career and seems almost pathologically obsessed with homosexuality. Significantly, he represents a concrete link between the anti-homosexual crusade of the late 1970s and its most recent manifestation. In 1978, Sheldon served as executive director of California Defend Our Children, the organized support behind then–state senator John V. Briggs for the so-called Briggs Initiative, an initiative overtly modeled on born-again entertainer Anita Bryant's successful repeal of a Dade County, Florida, gay rights ordinance the preceding year. The conservative avalanche of the November 1994 elections has, among other things, brought extreme rightists like Reverend Sheldon into closer proximity to governance than ever before. As the *New York Times* duly noted after the elections: "Sheldon counts as a friend the new assistant majority leader of the Senate, Trent Lott of Mississippi. The Republican Senator was featured in the coalition's 1993 videotape, *Gay Rights/ Special Rights.*"[10]

Like *The Gay Agenda,* its notorious precursor, *Gay Rights/Special Rights* is vivid propaganda, a titillating peepshow that conceals a battering ram designed to soften the viewer's judgment and pave the way for the right's ideological cut-and-thrust. Whereas *The Gay Agenda* tied together almost every strand of previously heard homophobic rhetoric, *Gay Rights/Special Rights* represents a genuine, if dreadful, innovation. Brilliantly extending the twin notions of "special rights" and "minority status" coined in *The Gay Agenda, Gay Rights/Special Rights* cynically seeks to cash in on the moral capital accumulated by the civil rights establishment by having African American fundamentalists, who are presented as the ultimate arbiters of "legitimate" and "illegitimate" minorities, inveigh against the lesbian and gay movement—and by extension, lesbians and gay men as a whole—as a fraudulent trespasser upon the hallowed ground of civil rights struggle. At the same time, the Traditional Values Coalition and its cohorts are portrayed as stalwart defenders of African Americans, eager to expose the malevolent nature of the "militant homosexuals." The argument set forth in *Gay Rights/Special Rights* is poised between two emblematic historical events: the 1963 March on Washington and the 1993 March on Washington for Lesbian, Gay, and Bisexual Equal Rights and Liberation. Even as *Gay Rights/Special Rights* actively molds the image of lesbians and gay men in relation to race, it recycles the familiar stereotype of homosexuals as predatory pedophiles and offers AIDS as "proof" of the essential unworthiness (or *unfitness*) of lesbians and gay men to participate in what it constructs as a closed system of rights and as an implicit justification for violence against us. Furthermore, *Gay Rights/Special Rights* exacerbates the self-hatred experienced by many lesbians and gay men in ways that are profoundly damaging. With *Gay Rights/Special Rights,* the Traditional Values Coalition ushers in the latest phase of the religious right's cruel culture war.

Many observers in queer activist circles have surmised, upon seeing *Gay Rights/Special Rights* for the first time, that the religious right has a new audience in mind: conservative people of color.[11] As a largely unknown quantity, conservative people of color may barely be a blip on the radar screen of many white queers, or of whites in general. But as black gay journalist Eric K. Washington has observed, if conservative African American opinion appears implausible, it is because popular demography has not been geared to reflect it.[12] The far right's overtures to people of color are actually not all that new; *Gay Rights/Special Rights* may have been just a glimmer in Lou Sheldon's eye when he was mobilizing African American pastors in 1991 to lobby senators in favor of then-Supreme Court nominee Clarence Thomas.[13] Yet though the cooperation of fundamentalist African American ministers in using *Gay Rights/Special Rights*[14] could bring the religious right a step closer to its sought-after goal of incorporating the congregations of conservative African American churches into its already-formidable voting bloc,[15] contradictions within the video's own structure suggest that it is born-again whites—the right's historic political constituency—who constitute the video's master subject position and who remain its most important audience.

To simulate a broad consensus among people of color on the question of lesbian and gay rights, *Gay Rights/Special Rights* fetishistically includes Lou Lopez and Raymond Kwong, individuals claiming to speak for the Hispanic American and Asian American communities, respectively, denouncing homosexuals' demands for civil rights. It is bitterly ironic, then, that *Gay Rights/Special Rights* should be the tool used to call the lesbian and gay movement so incisively on its "diversity bluff."[16] For though lesbians and gay men belong to every race and ethnicity, the institutional leadership of the lesbian and gay political movement has been disproportionately white and, intentionally or not, has put a decidedly white face on its public countenance. This dilemma is compounded, on the one hand, by the tendency of many individual white lesbian and gay activists to unproblematically conflate homophobia with racism, overlooking the historic specificities of these and other oppressions,[17] and, on the other hand, by a chronic lack of commitment on the part of lesbian and gay political institutions to a broad antiracist agenda.[18] We can immediately observe, as many queer activists have, that *Gay Rights/Special Rights* includes virtually no lesbians or gay men of color in its inventory of homosexual "types." Yet this is no more an absence structured by the video than it is a measure of the place of lesbians and gay men of color within the leadership of the gay movement at large. After all, it's not as if there were a surfeit of African Americans, Asians, Pacific Islanders, Arabs, Latinos, or Native Americans at the forefront of the 1993 March on Washington for Lesbian, Gay, and Bisexual Equal Rights and Liberation for the religious right's—or anyone's—cameras to record. Mainstream news coverage of the March on Washington was also marked by the same absence, yet white lesbian and gay spokespersons were almost unanimously approving of it.[19] To the Traditional Values Coalition, lesbians and gay men of color may be the great unimaginable, and though their presence would certainly disequilibrate the neat binary opposition between African Americans and lesbians and gay men, their invisibility in *Gay Rights/Special Rights* is a painfully accurate index of their status in the gay movement's public life as well.

Gay Rights/Special Rights offers an indelible image of polarization in the split-screen device, which places on the left a color image of white gay men and on the right a black-and-white image of African Americans while a black male voice-over asks the viewer to compare the advantages enjoyed by homosexuals with the hardship suffered by African Americans, measured in alleged percentages of each group's participation in such activities as graduating from college, working in management-level jobs, and taking vacations abroad. On the one side, two youthful white gay men clad only in shorts and sneakers are seen at close range, dancing energetically, with other white gay men visible in the background behind them. On the other side, African Americans are clustered together in a large, undifferentiated mass, seen from a distance at a high angle, in grainy, black-and-white archival footage. Whereas the close-up image of the topless gay men emphasizes their corporeality and the brightness of their shorts underscores the pinkness of their skin, the image of African Americans presents a disembodied wall of heads and shoulders. The carefree homosexuals dance festively while the African Americans are composed in motionless order, solemnity incarnate. First by literalizing a dividing line, then by attempting to quantify discrimination, the split-screen device renders a near-perfect representation of mutual exclusivity, thereby cementing the premise that these are two groups in competition with each other and distilling the video's signifying systems into a stark binarism that literally leaves no room for lesbians and gay men of color.

Gay Rights/Special Rights retreads a well-worn conservative discourse of scarcity and deservedness, which says that rights are advantages and in mean times there are not enough advantages to go around. Developing the thematic of scarcity in relation to people of color, *Gay Rights/Special Rights* says that the attainment of civil rights by lesbians and gay men will rob people of color of theirs and diminish the achievements of the African American–led civil rights movement of the 1950s and 1960s. It's a propagandistic reversal worthy of Orwell: The religious right tells us that lesbians and gay men are opportunistically trying to hitch their wagon to African Americans' political gains, when it is the religious right itself that, by this very argument, is making this bid. Emmanuel McLittle, the first African American conservative to appear in *Gay Rights/Special Rights,* tells us: "Homosexuals are using not only the language, but they are beginning to insist that the statutes, the laws, all of the *advantages* gained by civil rights leaders such as Martin Luther King be now applied to homosexuals" (emphasis added). Such a statement immediately suggests competition and implies that civil rights confer an edge over others. Civil rights, of course, are not advantages but highly partial, constantly evolving remedies for historic disadvantages. Fortunately for the religious right, most people's lack of understanding of civil rights law and its history permits such claims to sound credible. Appropriately, Lou Sheldon utters the statement that encapsulates the video's core argument, hitting all of the irrational chords that make it resonate with African American and white conservatives alike: "Homosexuals have equal rights under the First Amendment, the Fourteenth Amendment, and the state constitution of every state in which they reside. But the issue here today is *special rights,* a special category of protection. They want to be *elevated*... to a true *minority status* that would give them *special rights*" (emphasis added).

In order to fix what is in fact a continually evolving cultural and legal process of interpreting the meaning and scope of civil rights, *Gay Rights/Special Rights* tries to stabilize the picture of the civil rights struggle, to enshrine in the rearview mirror of history, as it were, a static, totalizing, and mythic representation of the Civil Rights Era. The authenticating aura that surrounds the black-and-white footage of the 1963 March on Washington, coupled with the almost-sacred[20] presence of Dr. Martin Luther King Jr., locates the civil rights narrative as belonging to a safely remote past. King's magisterial voice—the first sound to be heard in *Gay Rights/Special Rights*—is shrewdly calculated to induce a visceral surge of identification, not only in African American viewers, for whom King signifies moral authority itself, but, significantly, in whites also. Impossible as this would have been thirty years ago, the religious right's white constituents, sufficiently acquainted with the heroic narrative popularized in *Eyes on the Prize,* can today accept King as the personification of moral authority with which he invests the African American fundamentalists who appear in *Gay Rights/Special Rights* and which in turn certifies them, in the white spectators' minds, to pronounce lesbians and gay men as pretenders to the civil rights struggle. How cunning, then, that the emotional swelling cued by King sets the stage for a potent *dis*identification as the black-and-white footage of King at the 1963 March abruptly gives way to the rather less-than-charismatic figure of Larry Kramer, dyspeptic diva of contemporary gay politics, who paraphrases King in front of a scattered-looking assembly of folks at the 1993 March on Washington for Lesbian, Gay, and Bisexual Equal Rights and Liberation.

Any discourse on rights is also necessarily a discourse on democracy. The far right's vision of U.S. democracy flows from a warped interpretation of the Constitution as the final word on rights. As conservatives never tire of repeating, the founding documents of the United States government hold that "all men [*sic*] are created equal." Civil rights laws and social service entitlements created to repair the imbalances wrought by discrimination are therefore seen as special. By this illogic, the far right can claim that "homosexuals have equal rights . . . but the issue here today is *special rights,* a special category of protection" (emphasis added). In a moment of surreal comedy, Edwin Meese, the porcine former attorney general who appears in *Gay Rights/Special Rights,* states: "As a white male, I have no rights whatsoever, other than what is shared with everybody else." Over archival black-and-white shots of storefronts displaying Jim Crow signs, he continues: "We have granted certain rights to take care of past discrimination . . . based on such things as race." Meese soothingly speaks of racism as a thing of the past, a thing "taken care of" (partly to efface contemporary racism, of which Meese himself is a pillar).[21] But just how was this accomplished? Depending on the viewer, the reading of this statement can cut two ways. Conservative people of color—the target audience of *Gay Rights/Special Rights*—might indeed agree that de jure racial discrimination was vanquished by the African American civil rights movement, mythologized in the video, with the enactment of the 1964 Civil Rights Act and subsequent civil rights legislation; they might also agree that, as white supremacist Charles Murray would have it, any vestigial inequities experienced by African Americans or other people of color are a matter of their own individual personal deficiencies. The "we" that Meese speaks for and counts himself among, however, will implicitly understand that the conferral of such rights (or, for that matter, their withdrawal) is the sovereign function of those properly ordained to regulate them: namely, heterosexual white males.

Further elaboration of this notion is provided by Michael P. Farris, a favorite son of the Religious Right, in his 1992 book, *Where Do I Draw the Line?*:

> We have decided as a nation that some things are so important that we are willing to give up a little of our freedom to achieve other goals. We have decided, for instance, that racial equality is so important we've given up our "freedom" to discriminate against another person on the basis of race. That decision is a good one and widely supported by the American people. We have similar laws banning discrimination on the basis of gender, national origin, or religion...
>
> For a gay rights law, we have to ask ourselves: Is homosexuality so important that we are willing to sacrifice our freedom to grant special protection to homosexuality? I don't think so. Why should we lose our freedom to advance their choice of sexual practices? Racial harmony is good for the nation and worthy of some sacrifices. Homosexuality cannot be construed to be good for our nation.[22]

In the scheme of things as delineated by Farris, he and the other guardians of white supremacist, patriarchal order benevolently restrain their freedom—their "right"—to discriminate. The threat of exercising this prerogative, which remains only thinly veiled with regard to people of color, is simply made explicit against lesbians and gay men.

Gradually, *Gay Rights/Special Rights* shifts in emphasis, leaving behind its African American spokespersons and giving way to an almost uninterrupted succession of white male authorities that drive the video's latter half. Although the same black male voice-over continues to narrate during interstitial transitions, a virtual hit parade of far right savants—Ralph Reed of the Christian Coalition, David Noebel of Summit Ministries, former secretary of education William Bennett—assumes the task of telling us what's what. This shift signals a repositioning in subjectivity, returning our attention to the white, born-again, middle-class viewers of *Gay Rights/Special Rights,* for whom the thematics of scarcity and deservedness are crucial.

By reexamining the genealogy of "special rights" as a discourse of white reaction, spawned in the 1970s in opposition to busing, affirmative action, and equal opportunity programs, the racist underpinnings of "special rights" and the *transference* that this discourse effects when applied to lesbians and gay men becomes clear. In the right's self-styled attempt at mainstreaming, overt racism, which was once part and parcel of rightist idiom, was jettisoned from its public rhetoric in favor of submerged messages on race that a broad-based constituency would not find objectionable. In their classic study of race and reaction, Michael Omi and Howard Winant detail how overt racism was rearticulated in numerous ways by neoconservatives and the New Right:

> As the right understood them, racial problems from the 1970s consisted of new forms of racial injustice which... conferred group rights on racial minority groups, thus granting a new form of privilege—that of "preferential treatment."
>
> The culprit behind this new form of "racism" was the state itself. In attempting to eliminate racial discrimination, the state went too far. It legitimated group rights, established affirmative action mandates, and spent money on a range of social programs which, according to the right, debilitated rather than uplifted, its target populations. In this scenario, the victims of racial discrimination had dramatically shifted from racial minorities to whites, particularly white males.[23]

The discourse of "reverse discrimination" identified by Omi and Winant reached its apex with the now-infamous 1990 electoral campaign advertisement for Senator Jesse Helms, which depicted a white male hand crumpling a job rejection slip while a male voice-over ominously intoned: "They had to give it to a minority because of a racial quota." This spot struck the nerve of a majority of the electorate in North Carolina, who voted against Harvey Gantt, Helms's African American opponent.

Gay Rights/Special Rights tells us that homosexuals "want to be *elevated*... to a true *minority status* that would give them *special rights*" (emphasis added). A term without any legal definition, "minority status" is actually a clever mutation of "protected classes," the legal term for discrete groups historically prevented from sharing fully and equally in civic realms such as employment, housing, and public accommodations because of bias, discrimination, or prejudice. Since we are still accustomed to thinking of minorities as primarily racial, "minority status" is employed to inflame the deeply rooted anxieties in white subjectivity over economic displacement. The pairing of homosexuals and "minority status" within the thematic of scarcity articulated by *Gay Rights/Special Rights* instigates a transference of racial associations whereby lesbians and gay men, rather than people of color, are encoded as encroaching upon the employment opportunities of economically threatened whites. *Gay Rights/Special Rights* is a spectacular example of this subterranean approach because it enlists people of color to enunciate its thematic of racial deservedness and, through them, aligns white viewers with this argument.

To better understand how the meanings produced by *Gay Rights/Special Rights* are assimilated by the conservative audience it addresses, we can selectively adapt Jacques Ellul's helpful distinction between agitational and integrational propaganda.[24] To do so, however, we must yet again distinguish between the religious right's leaders and their born-again followers. *Gay Rights/Special Rights* is designed to promote the strategic interests and advance the political platform of the religious right's leadership, the political professionals who run such national institutions as the Christian Coalition, Focus on the Family, or Concerned Women for America, and the scores of local organizations affiliated with them that both direct the course of a homophobic political program and incorporate audiovisual resources such as these in its execution. Theirs is the concentrated ideological base to which *Gay Rights/Special Rights* seeks to align the rank-and-file viewer and voter. This is not to say that garden-variety evangelicals do not maintain or even cherish homophobic perspectives of their own. On the contrary: It is exactly the prosaic homophobia felt by most heterosexuals, regardless of race or religion, that brings coherence and cohesion to *Gay Rights/Special Rights*. The video is a sorting mechanism for the surplus homophobia that no one in a heterosexist culture can be free of. But by situating lesbians and gay men specifically as the group against which the average evangelical's identity is defined and sharpened, it crystallizes an otherwise random structure of feelings into purposeful expression. *Gay Rights/Special Rights* is thus simultaneously integrational *and* agitational. I have already tried to suggest ways in which the video's integrational strategies seek to fuse conservative African American sentiment with white fundamentalist subjectivity; additionally, *Gay Rights/Special Rights* serves the integrational function of consolidating the raw material of ordinary prejudice into orchestrated public opinion. It is agitational by forming a spur to action, whether intentional, in the case of securing votes for initiatives such as Ballot Measure 9 or Amendment 2, or putatively unintentional, in the case of encouraging those who use knives, fire, or just their fists instead of the ballot.

Violence is always already present in the everyday lives of lesbians and gay men; it is part of the air we breathe. To comprehend the extent to which violence permeates our lives, we may think of a *continuum* of violence on which it is possible to situate the manifold registers of violent expression. At one end is liminal or latent violence, expressed through looks or gestures of hostility; following this are all the violent speech acts—the slurs, catcalls, taunts, epithets—that any visibly out lesbian or gay man is so accustomed to that they almost become ambient; these fall just short of intimidation and harassment, which then can spill with terrifying ease into vandalism and, finally, bodily harm. When added to the daily circulation of homophobic messages in popular culture, *Gay Rights/Special Rights* becomes a powerful incitement to violence, too powerful for some to resist. It would, of course, be absurd to suggest that merely watching a video could in and of itself transform the viewer into a bloodthirsty queer-basher. However, *Gay*

Rights/Special Rights grants the homophobic viewer who has a propensity for violence an unequivocal permission to obey violent impulses, a permission preceded by and stamped with the authority that the video borrows from African American civil rights struggle, enabling the homophobe to feel not only sanctioned but righteous in the administration of violence. Needless to say, the religious right's refusal to acknowledge the brutality inflicted on lesbians and gay men as one by-product of their campaigns, let alone to accept any responsibility for it, is a tactical absolute of the culture war as basic as the very practice of scapegoating.

Ironically, queer viewers may find themselves just as agitated by the distortions these videos traffic in and consequently disposed to take action toward countering them. Much of the organized lesbian and gay response to the religious right's homophobic campaign has been propelled by what Ella Habib Shohat and Robert Stam identify as the "corrective" urge; they observe that "an obsession with 'realism' casts the question as simply one of 'errors' and 'distortions,' as if the 'truth' of a community were unproblematic, transparent, and easily accessible, and 'lies' about that community easily unmasked."[25] Yet while the necessity—indeed, the urgency—of vehemently contradicting the falsity of *Gay Rights/Special Rights* is indisputable, to anchor one's criticism of it in truth claims is in some sense to miss the point that, to a large extent, the video operates best in the cognitive realms outside of logic. Consider, for example, the trope of child molestation common to all homophobic discourse. When publicly conducting analyses of *Gay Rights/Special Rights* and similar videos, lesbian and gay organizers routinely point out the exhaustively documented fact that child abuse is a crime overwhelmingly committed by heterosexual males, as a means of refuting the religious right's patently distorted construction of lesbians and gay men as menacing pedophiles out to "recruit" unsuspecting minors to the "homosexual lifestyle." This matter-of-fact approach can hardly be faulted, but it still proves inadequate in addressing the attendant question of the persistence of this trope. Its resonance, I suspect, has to do with a projection of the real anxieties felt by parents about child abuse onto the representational figure of the child—a figure that is itself an externalization of the parent. *Gay Rights/Special Rights* raises many such questions that, although beyond the scope of the present chapter, clearly warrant further analysis.

I have had the opportunity to be present in a number of different lesbian and gay audiences where *Gay Rights/Special Rights* has been screened. These audiences have been variously small and large, composed of people who identify themselves as activists or just interested viewers, and alternately multiracial and predominantly white. Yet there is an audience response common to every one of these screenings: laughter. At specific moments, the video invariably elicits a peculiar laughter that cannot solely be ascribed to the camp sensibilities and readings-against-the-grain that queers bring to a text. This laughter may be interpreted as expressing at least two corresponding anxieties. On its surface, it seems to say: "You can't be serious, this is too outrageous, how over the top can you be?" The cursory knowledge of where *Gay Rights/Special Rights* originates activates a facile and commonplace condescension toward born-again Christians, prompting the more worldly, urban queers to scoff—after all, aren't those fundamentalists just kooks, crackpots? This very condescension, however, also allowed many a cloistered urban queer to avoid treating the Oregon Citizens Alliance and Colorado for Family Values as serious political entities capable of manipulating the democratic mechanism of the initiative for their own antidemocratic purposes until the fruit of their efforts could no longer be ignored. But the queer laughter at *Gay Rights/Special Rights* may also be understood as nervous, or should I say embarrassed, laughter,[26] an embarrassment rooted in the element of self-recognition in viewing a caricature of oneself. *Gay Rights/Special Rights* visually isolates members of the lesbian and gay community's own marginalized sexual subcultures—S/M leatherfolk, drag queens and drag kings, homocore punks—and combines them with the spectacle, unique to homophobic propaganda, of the "reformed" or "recovered" homosexual to puncture the respectable veneer of straight-acting lesbians and gay men and underwrite their construction of the essential pathology of lesbians and gay men. The laughter heard during screenings of *Gay Rights/Special Rights* is the sound of sparks thrown up by the scraping of the right's wedge against the shell of queer identity.

Durham, North Carolina, was the site of the 1993 Creating Change conference, an annual gathering sponsored by the National Gay and Lesbian Task Force. During a three-day intensive workshop on fighting the religious right, *Gay Rights/Special Rights* was screened before an audience of nearly 400 organizers and activists from around the United States, many of whom had not seen the video previously. As usual, some people laughed out loud while watching it, but for the most part, emotions were brought to a rolling boil. The discussion that followed was punctuated by several impassioned comments about the more outrageously flamboyant leatherfolk and drag queens depicted in that video's gay pride parade footage. Prior to the screening, one of the facilitators had rather sternly cautioned participants against making statements that marginalized leatherfolk or other sexual subcultures, thereby replicating the same marginalization practiced by heterosexuals against lesbians and gay men as a whole. Despite this injunction, one anguished participant, who had evidently summoned all her courage to stand up in front of the roomful of people and speak, tearfully demanded to know: "Why do they have to go out there and do that when we know that these people will be there with their cameras? Don't they know it only hurts us?" In this woman's cri de coeur there was a distant echo of gay liberationist Martha Shelley's observation, made after the North American Conference of Homophile Organizations exactly twenty-five years earlier: "I have seen the respectable homosexual wincing in agony at the presence of a swish queen, or an obvious bull dyke—not out of dislike for [him or her] as a person, but out of fear of being associated with 'that queer,' even in an all-gay crowd."[27]

A staple of queer activist discussions such as the one at the Creating Change conference is the ritual invocation of "internalized homophobia." As activist shorthand that serves to denote a queer-specific mode of "false consciousness," internalized homophobia is at once taken to stand for a complex edifice of meaning and presumed to be transparent to every lesbian or gay man; much like a parking garage, internalized homophobia is a massive structure that one can see right through. Self-hatred, however, refuses to be banished quite so easily. Gay clinical psychologist Walt Odets even submits that self-hatred is constitutive of contemporary gay identity, noting that "homophobia ... instills in the developing [lesbian or gay] adolescent a self-hatred and self-doubt that are, to varying degrees, lifelong problems."[28] Thus, the repetition of the mantra of internalized homophobia not only diverts us from the actual operation of self-hatred within lesbian and gay experience but also elides a more nuanced inquiry into how homophobic representations, such as those issued by *Gay Rights/Special Rights,* generate contradictions within objects of homophobia and how anti-gay propaganda, of which *Gay Rights/Special Rights* is emblematic, functions directly as psychological warfare against lesbians and gay men.

The psychic toll taken by homophobic propaganda upon lesbians and gay men goes far deeper than activist discourse admits. The incendiary rhetoric and images of *Gay Rights/Special Rights* have traumatized many lesbians and gay men who have viewed it. Bombarded with the concentrated pressure of its images, our ever-fragile self-esteem begins to bifurcate. We shudder at the "spoiled" images of our collective selves. I do not mean to suggest that *Gay Rights/Special Rights* by itself causes this bifurcation or fragmentation in the lesbian or gay viewer; rather, it is the cumulative force of having virtually every awful thing straight society has ever said about us—"sick," "guilty," "worthless," "doomed"—amalgamated into one terrific wallop. Apart from the obvious feelings of anger that videos like *Gay Rights/Special Rights* and *The Gay Agenda* provoke, many viewers I have spoken with described feelings of overwhelming disconsolation or despair after seeing it. The video blends half-truths with gross distortions and outright lies so seamlessly that, even for the viewer equipped with critical viewing skills and vocabulary, the cumulative effect is one of inundation or helplessness.

One scarcely knows where to begin to refute the claims made in the video. The toxic nuggets lodge tenaciously, like shrapnel, in the unconscious of the queer viewer, where they continue to seethe long afterward.

Although the power of the religious right can no longer be underestimated, there are also ample reasons why it should not be exaggerated, either. Demagogues such as Pat Robertson and Lou Sheldon are enjoying a moment of legitimation, yet the far right's hold on the actual levers of government is not as hegemonic as their spokespersons would have us believe. To some extent, this is because the extreme views of the religious right's leaders on a spectrum of issues engender internecine ambivalence, if not outright scorn, within many of the secular and comparatively more moderate precincts of the Republican Party. What is more, the November 1994 elections have had the incontrovertible effect of putting the far right's ascendance, and strategies for reversing it, firmly on the agenda of progressive activists and intellectuals virtually everywhere, occasioning a flood of public discussion and debate that is long overdue. Cultural producers, in particular, have been quick to recognize the phenomenon of the far right as both a challenge and an incentive. Even among the media interventions produced by queers to specifically address the right's homophobic agenda, we can already look to examples as formally varied as electoral campaign commercials, feature-length documentaries (Deborah Fort and Ann Skinner-Jones's *The Great Divide,* 1994; Heather MacDonald's *Ballot Measure 9,* 1995), portions of public television series ("Culture Wars," the second installment of Testing the Limits' *The Question of Equality,* 1995), first-person video diaries (Pam Walton's *Family Values,* 1996), and experimental shorts (Tom Kalin's *Confirmed Bachelor,* 1994). There is a tendency, evident in many of these works, to refute or replace the claims made by such videos as *Gay Rights/Special Rights* or *The Gay Agenda* with truth claims of our own. Yet even when this tendency takes the form of satire or inversion, as in the lesbian and gay film festival favorite, *The Straight Agenda* (John Binninger and Jacqueline Turnure, 1994), it seems to bind these works in an ultimately circular relationship in which the work ends up chasing the tail of its referent.[29] A more efficacious strategy for progressive media producers might be to examine any number of the larger social, cultural, or economic issues raised by the religious right's propaganda, instead of trying to dismantle this propaganda itself.

At the end of the day, even the smartest piece of media is no replacement for the exacting work of political organization. In conclusion, I want to mention just one example of community-based "fight the right" organizing that holds unique potential for mining the contradictions in the current situation, a few of which I have attempted to outline in this chapter. Early in 1994, several longtime African American lesbian and gay movement professionals, including Mandy Carter, of the Washington, D.C.–based Human Rights Campaign (HRC), and Donald Suggs, formerly of the New York branch of the Gay and Lesbian Alliance against Defamation, initiated a peer-oriented dialogue about the religious right's nascent alliance with conservative people of color, the reactions of white lesbian and gay leaders to this alliance, and the larger cultural confrontation over the rhetoric of special rights. The result of this dialogue was the National Call to Resist, a joint project of the HRC and the Black Gay and Lesbian Leadership Forum. Carter took the Call to Resist on the road and spent much of 1994 traveling to St. Louis, Detroit, Cleveland, and other cities targeted by the religious right for antigay initiatives, where she worked with African American lesbians and gay men on formulating local strategies for counteracting the incursions made by the religious right into communities of color. At every step, Carter screened and facilitated analyses of *Gay Rights/Special Rights* with local organizers. Her "traveling dialogue" then culminated in a September 1994 summit of lesbian and gay people of color that convened in Washington, D.C. on the same weekend as the Christian Coalition's annual Road to Victory conference, where once again *Gay Rights/Special Rights* was screened, and the community-wide analysis of the video and the issues it raises evolved even further.[30] I do not cite the efforts of Carter or other lesbian and gay people of color activists simply because their efforts are exemplary or because they systematically combine media education with organizing but because such activists are, as they themselves have pointed out, ideally situated to cultivate and exploit the contradictions involved in the courtship of people of color by the historically racist religious right. For it is these irreconcilable contradictions that will short-circuit the religious right's ability to use *Gay Rights/Special Rights* to pit queers and people of color against each other by falsely constructing us as rivals over our inalienable rights.

Notes

1. See Bruce Barron, *Heaven on Earth? The Social and Political Agendas of Dominion Theology* (Grand Rapids, Mich.: Zondervan, 1992), 9–18; Frederick Clarkson, "Christian Reconstructionism: Theocratic Dominionism Gains Influence," *The Public Eye* 8, nos. 1, 2 (March, June 1994); and Clarkson, *Eternal Hostility: The Struggle between Theocracy and Democracy* (Monroe, Maine: Common Courage Press, 1996).

2. See Joe Conason, "The Religious Right's Quiet Revival," *The Nation,* 27 April 1992; Kate Cornell, "The Covert Tactics and Overt Agenda of the New Christian Right," *Covert Action Quarterly,* no. 43 (Winter 1992–1993): 46; and John F. Persinos, "Has the Christian Right Taken over the Republican Party?" *Campaigns and Elections,* September 1994, 21.

3. Marc Cooper, "Salvation City," *The Nation,* 2 January 1995, 9.

4. Jerome L. Himmelstein, *To the Right: The Transformation of American Conservatism* (Berkeley and Los Angeles: University of California Press, 1990). See also Sara Diamond, *Roads to Dominion: Right-Wing Movements and Political Power in the United States* (New York: Guilford, 1995), especially chapters 7–9.

5. Jean Hardisty, "Constructing Homophobia," *The Public Eye,* March 1993, 1.

6. Derrick A. Bell Jr., "The Referendum: Democracy's Barrier to Racial Equality," *Washington Law Review* 54, no. 1 (1978).

7. Dirk Johnson, "Colorado Justices Strike Down a Law against Gay Rights," *New York Times,* 12 October 1994. Justice Kennedy's opinion for the Supreme Court decision on Amendment 2 startled many in the lesbian and gay movement with its forceful eloquence: "Amendment 2 goes well beyond merely depriving [gay men and lesbians] of special rights. It imposes a broad disability upon those persons alone, forbidding them, but no others, to seek specific legal protection from injuries caused by discrimination.... [I]ts sheer breadth is so discontinuous with the reasons offered for it that the amendment seems inexplicable by anything but animus toward the class that it effects; it lacks a rational relationship to legitimate state interests.... Amendment 2, in making a general announcement that gays and lesbians shall not have any particular protections from the law, inflicts on them immediate, continuing, and real injuries that outrun and belie any justifications that may be claimed for it.... We must conclude that Amendment 2 classifies homosexuals not to further a proper legislative end but to make them unequal to everyone else. This Colorado cannot do. A State cannot so deem a class of persons a stranger to its laws" (*Romer v. Evans,* No. 94-1039, 20 May 1996).

8. Elise Harris, "Seizing the Initiative," *Out,* no. 17 (November 1994): 102.

9. Frederick Clarkson and Skipp Porteous, *Challenging the Christian Right: The Activist's Handbook* (Great Barrington, Mass.: Institute for First Amendment Studies, 1993), 183; and Hardisty, "Constructing Homophobia."

10. David W. Dunlap, "Minister Brings Anti-Gay Message to the Spotlight," *New York Times,* 19 December 1994.

11. Renee DeLapp, Summary of Discussion Points, Traditional Values Coalition Video, *Gay Rights/Special Rights*. Report prepared by the Western States Center, P.O. Box 40305, Portland, OR 97240 (Portland, Ore., 1993), 7.

12. Eric K. Washington, "Freedom Rings: The Alliance between Blacks and Gays Is Threatened by Mutual Inscrutability," *The Village Voice,* 29 June 1993, 25. See also, Deborah Toler, "Black Conservatives," *The Public Eye* 7, nos. 3, 4 (September, December 1993).

13. Sara Diamond, "The Right's Grass Roots," *Z Magazine,* March 1992, 19. It is worth noting that as a Supreme Court Justice, Clarence Thomas joined Justices Scalia and Rehnquist in dissenting to the court's decision on Amendment 2 in *Romer V. Evans*.

14. Donald Suggs and Mandy Carter, "Cincinnati's Odd Couple," *New York Times,* 13 December 1993.

15. James M. Perry, "Soul Mates: The Christian Coalition Crusades to Broaden Rightist Political Base," *Wall Street Journal,* 19 July 1994.

16. Mab Segrest, *Memoir of a Race Traitor* (Boston: South End Press, 1994), 231.

17. For two divergent but mutually enriching perspectives on the differences and similarities between racism and homophobia, see Henry Louis Gates Jr., "Backlash?" *The New Yorker,* 17 May 1993, 42; and Phillip Brian Harper, "Racism and Homophobia as Reflections on Their Perpetrators," in Warren J. Blumenfeld, ed., *Homophobia: How We All Pay the Price* (Boston: Beacon Press, 1992), 57. See also Barbara Smith, "Blacks and Gays: Healing the Great Divide," *Gay Community News* (fall 1993).

18. I refer here to the lesbian and gay movement's "official" political institutions such as the Human Rights Campaign, the Gay and Lesbian Victory Fund, and the Gay and Lesbian Alliance against Defamation. Only one national political organization, the National Gay and Lesbian Task Force, has made a consistent, good-faith attempt at fostering a critical dialogue on race.

19. I am grateful to Donald Suggs, former public affairs director at the Gay and Lesbian Alliance against Defamation (GLAAD), for this observation.

20. Washington, "Freedom Rings."

21. Liz Galst, "Voting with the Enemy," *The Village Voice,* 8 December 8 1993.

22. Michael P. Farris, *Where Do I Draw the Line?* (Minneapolis, Minn.: Bethany House, 1992), 142.

23. Michael Omi and Howard Winant, *Racial Formation in the United States from the 1960s to the 1990s* (New York: Routledge, 1986), 117.

24. Jacques Ellul, *Propaganda: The Formation of Men's Attitudes* (New York: Vintage, 1973), 70.

25. Ella Habib Shohat and Robert Stam, *Unthinking Eurocentrism: Multiculturalism and the Media* (New York: Routledge, 1994), 178.

26. I am indebted to David Deitcher for suggesting this to me.

27. Martha Shelley, "Respectability," *The Ladder* 14, nos. 1, 2 (October, November 1969): 24.

28. Walt Odets, "Psychological and Educational Challenges for the Gay and Bisexual Male Communities" (Paper presented to the AIDS Prevention Summit sponsored by the American Association of Physicians for Human Rights, Dallas, Texas, (July 1994).

29. These videos are available from the following distributors:

Ballot Measure 9 (1995), produced by Heather MacDonald, distributed by Zeitgeist Films, 247 Centre Street, 2d Floor, New York, N.Y., 10012; *Confirmed Bachelor* (1994), produced by Tom Kalin, distributed by Electronic Arts Intermix, 536 Broadway, 9th Floor, New York, N.Y., 10012; *The Great Divide* (1994), produced by Deborah Fort and Ann Skinner-Jones, distributed by DNA Productions, P.O. Box 22216, Santa Fe, N.M., 87505; *The Question of Equality* (1995), produced by Testing the Limits, distributed by KQED Books and Tapes, 2601 Mariposa Street, San Francisco, Calif., 94110–1400; *The Straight Agenda* (1994), produced by John Binninger and Jacqueline Turnure, distributed by John Binninger, Fair Is Fair Productions, 784 Dolores Street, San Francisco, Calif., 94110; *Family Values* (1996), produced by Pam Walton, distributed by Filmmaker's Library, 124 East 40th Street, New York, N.Y., 10016.

30. Lisa Keen, "Leadership Forum to March into the Fray," *The Washington Blade,* 29 April 1994; Darice Clark, "People of Color Decry 'Racist and Anti-gay Agenda,'" *The Washington Blade,* 23 September 1994; and Michelle Garcia, "Religious Conservatives and Communities of Color," a roundtable discussion with Mandy Carter, Carmen Chavez, Scot Nakagawa, et al, *Third Force,* September/October 1994.

Contributors

Nancy T. Ammerman is professor of sociology of religion at the Center for Social and Religious Research at Hartford Seminary. She has written extensively on fundamentalism, including *Bible Believers: Fundamentalists in the Modern World* and *Baptist Battles: Social Change and Religious Conflict in the Southern Baptist Convention.*

Chip Berlet is a senior analyst at Political Research Associates in Somerville, Massachusetts. He has edited *Eyes Right! Challenging the Right Wing Backlash* and has coauthored, with Matthew N. Lyons, *Too Close for Comfort: Right Wing Populism, Scapegoating, and Fascist Potentials in U.S. Political Traditions.*

Meryem Ersoz has recently completed a dissertation at the University of Oregon about literary and visual representations of spectral technologies at the turn of the century.

Razelle Frankl is professor of management at Rowan College, where she has been teaching since 1977. She is best known for her 1987 book *Televangelism.*

Steven Gardiner is a graduate student holding a Sage fellowship in the Department of Anthropology at Cornell University. He is the former research director for the Coalition for Human Dignity, a nonprofit civil rights group based in Portland, Oregon, and he is the author of *Rolling Back Civil Rights: The Oregon Citizens Alliance at Religious War.*

Frances Guilfoyle has an M.A. in mass communications from the University of Denver and is a doctoral student in the Radio-Television-Film Department at the University of Texas, Austin.

Eithne Johnson is a Ph.D. candidate in the Department of Radio-Television-Film at the University of Texas. In addition to Christian media, she has studied cable programming and pornography for women. She has taught film and media studies at Emerson College and Wellesley College.

Linda Kintz is an associate professor of English at the University of Oregon. She is the author of *The Subject's Tragedy: Political Poetics, Feminist Theory, and Drama* and *Between Jesus and the Market: The Emotions That Matter in Right-Wing America*.

Jeff Land teaches in the Sociology Department at the University of Oregon. He is currently writing about the anti-Semitic stereotypes and the role of emotions in the teaching of the Holocaust. His history of Pacifica Radio is forthcoming from the University of Minnesota Press.

Julia Lesage is an associate professor of English at the University of Oregon, where she teaches film studies. She is cofounder and coeditor of *Jump Cut: A Review of Contemporary Media*.

Ioannis Mookas is an independent producer, writer, and media activist. His videos include *Peer Education, Not Fear Education* (1995) and *Only Human: HIV-Negative Gay Men in the AIDS Epidemic* (1998). He was assistant editor of *The Question of Equality* (Scribner, 1995), published to accompany the public television series of the same name produced for the Independent Television Service (ITVS). He is editor of the *AIVF Self-Distribution Toolkit*, a comprehensive resource guide published by the Foundation for Independent Video and Film.

Laurie Schulze has taught at the University of North Carolina–Chapel Hill and the University of Denver. She has published articles about female bodybuilding, made-for-television movies, and Madonna.

Anna Williams lives in Moscow, Idaho, and is completing her Ph.D. in visual and cultural studies at the University of Rochester. Her research interests include conservative media and rhetoric, the representation and treatment of animals in contemporary society, and the politics of diet.

Index